GOOD HOUSEKEEPING'S

BOOK OF

Today's Etiquette

GOOD HOUSEKEEPING'S

BOOK OF

Today's Etiquette

By

LOUISE RAYMOND

With Good Housekeeping Institute

Illustrations by Burmah Burris

Harper & Row, Publishers

New York

Contents

YOUR MANNERS ARE PART OF YOU

1. Today's Manners   3
2. Be a Woman with Charm   6
3. Manners and Dress for Men   20
4. The Woman Alone   28
5. Married Manners   38
6. Your Children's Manners   45
7. Your Teen-Ager's Manners   54
8. To You the Teen-Ager   59

YOU AND YOUR FRIENDS

9. Introductions   71
10. Telephone Manners   77
11. Table Manners   81
12. Dining at a Restaurant   89
13. Entertaining Away from Home   96
14. When You Entertain at Home   102
15. How to Be a Guest   135
16. Having House Guests   140
17. How to Be a House Guest   148

YOUR WELCOMING HOUSE

18. Your Linen and Silver, China, and Glass   159
19. Table Settings   174
20. How To Serve   194
21. When You Have a Servant   200

WRITE IT RIGHT

22. Your Stationery   213
23. Your Social Letters   220
24. Your Business Letters   239
25. Greetings by Card   249
26. Invitations and Replies   257

YOUR MANNERS IN SPECIAL SITUATIONS

27. Some of Those Special Situations   281
28. Manners for the Clubwoman   300
29. Traveling   308

OCCASIONS OF CEREMONY

30. The Debut   329
31. The Engagement   334
32. Planning for the Wedding   341
33. Wedding Invitations and Announcements   358
34. The Wedding Day   370
35. The Reception   382
36. Anniversary and Shower Parties   388
37. Christening and Brit Milah   394
38. Confirmation and Bar Mitzvah   399
39. Funerals and Mourning   403

BUSINESS ETIQUETTE

40. Manners for Women in Business   415

41. Manners for Men in Business   422

HELPFUL HOW-TO'S

Some Common French Menu Terms   427

How to Eat Difficult Foods   431

Tipping   440

Forms of Address   449

YOUR MANNERS

ARE PART OF YOU

1

Today's Manners

THERE ALWAYS WAS AND ALWAYS WILL BE A BIT MORE TO BEING A TRULY well-mannered person than remembering to consider others. That is a good rule of thumb and a necessary foundation for good manners, but it can't be the whole answer. Knowledge of the basic rules always makes things run more smoothly. If a man and a woman both know what is expected of them, all sorts of awkwardness is avoided in many special situations. And then there are some things which acceptedly go by rote. Affairs of religious significance such as weddings and christenings are very special occasions whether elaborate or simple, and are always governed by a certain form. The writing of a letter to a high government official must have a particular address, salutation, and closing. There is one and only one correct way to address the President of the United States. These occasions may not arise frequently in your life or mine; but when they do, no amount of sensibility to the feelings of others can guide us very far. Unless we are walking encyclopedias of etiquette we have to look up the form —and we are much more comfortable when we do.

Day-by-day manners are not nearly so ritualistic. In these it is indeed well to be guided in general by the idea of thinking of other people rather than yourself, to be warm, outgoing, interested. And if you know the rather few and simple rules of making introductions, writing letters, tipping, and entertaining, what to expect of your escort and what he should expect of you, you *will* be outgoing because you can relax and be yourself. Because you're at ease, others will be—or if they aren't, you'll know how to make them feel so.

Fortunately, it's much easier to learn the rules these days than it used to be. The mobility of our society, the economic leveling that has taken place over the past decades, the large number of women who work and the still larger number who stay home but hold down the jobs of parent, cook, maid, chauffeur, hostess, and community worker—all of this has led to the abandonment of much of the fussy etiquette of our grandmothers. The elaborate ritual of "leaving cards" has gone by the board. Children wear simple clothes that are easy to clean, entertaining has been deformalized to a great degree. Our lives have become busier, and we have had to make them simpler by taking short cuts when we can.

On the other hand, we are less insulated than earlier generations. We are active in community work and as a rule we get acquainted quickly with new neighbors. We travel more. We know more and more kinds of people, many of them from foreign lands. Often the demands of our husbands' careers uproot us suddenly and plump us into a new and possibly quite different kind of community. Many of us are clubwomen. Most are active in the PTA. For all these reasons our public relations are important; our manners show more than they used to. We need to know which rules fit *our* lives and how to be flexible about them without straying from the bounds of good taste.

So rules are still needed—and here again, just "consideration for others" won't answer all questions. In the community where you have lived all your life, an invitation to a barbecue supper would mean a daytime cotton for the wives, slacks and sport shirts for the husbands. But in the new community, it may be a dressier affair.

In the city you came from, an invitation to a luncheon would mean your blue sheer wool, a hat, gloves, maybe a fur. In your new surroundings, you'll want to find out whether or not local custom calls for hatlessness with a plain suit or even a sweater and skirt.

Like most books about etiquette, this one will address itself often directly to the woman, because a woman's daily role is so frequently that of social secretary and entertainment planner as well as that of competent and charming wife. Men will find sensible guidance for their roles as escort, host, and husband in many of the general chapters as well as in those containing specific information on men's clothes and men's manners.

Just as we, in these changing situations, need guidance, so do our children and our teen-agers. In fact, the teen-agers need a little more, not only because they have had less experience, but also because most of them are so busy trying to find out what kind of people they are that they are hardly in the habit of considering others before themselves. Not being certain just what is the right thing to do, they often show their lack of confidence in brusqueness, brashness, insolence, or worse. They don't want to be thought of by their contemporaries as "square" or stuffy, but most of them would like the comfort of knowing at least a few of the proprieties for occasions when they are not just a foursome in blue jeans going out for Cokes—and when they know these, they'll have more fun.

Everybody likes to be liked—men, women, and children. If you know the rules, know them well enough so that they are almost second nature to you; you will find you're forgetting yourself. Then you become genuinely interested in others and warm and responsive toward them—one of the best recipes for popularity that has ever been concocted!

2

Be a Woman with Charm

WHAT *is* CHARM? "AN IRRESISTIBLE POWER TO PLEASE AND ATTRACT" is a dictionary definition. James Barrie called it "a sort of bloom on a woman." Whatever it is, we know it when we see it, and there isn't one of us who wouldn't choose to be charming. There have been many recipes for charm over the ages, but an ingredient common to all of them is poise—that lovely composure and quiet assurance that makes a charming woman. Possibly there are people who are born with this—if so, they are few—but it is not too hard for any of us to acquire.

Three particular elements of poise characterize the kind of woman to whom people are inevitably drawn. One is an attractive speaking voice, another is the quality of repose, and the third is the habit of attentive listening.

Some fortunate individuals are blessed by nature with a voice that is low, musical, and resonant, but most women must devote some conscious effort to developing good speaking habits. Remember to speak distinctly and in a tone low enough to block any tendency to be shrill. Many of us ought to lower our voices at least one tone and practice this until it becomes second nature.

How much appreciated is the woman who's restful to be with! Not apathetic or wooden—that's something else again—but a woman who can be animated when animation suits the occasion, yet relaxed when repose is the appropriate keynote. No matter how hard it may be on days when the clock seems to be racing you, when you feel pushed and harried, make the effort to slow down both mentally and physically, especially when you are—however briefly—with other people. It's salutary for you and good for your friendships too, because people are nearly always uncomfortably conscious of a divided mind and may be hurt by it. Take care too to avoid forming the twitchy mannerisms of tension, which can so quickly become ugly (and aging) habits—pulling at your hair, pursing your mouth, wrinkling your brow.

The charming woman is almost invariably a good listener. She pays attention to the person who is talking to her and that attention is real. The quality of it is flattering to the speaker. Her replies and her questions show she's registered every syllable. She looks at the one who's speaking rather than letting her eyes rove around the room. Even though the topic be the speaker's recent appendectomy, not a subject that a charming woman would introduce, and she a veteran of many such scalpel skirmishes, she firmly resolves not to tell the story of *her* operation at the first pause in the conversation.

When a woman finds herself with a talker who is not only non-stop, but boring in the bargain, she may have to tear loose, but this she always tries to do with some graceful excuse that leaves the other person's vanity intact.

A woman with charm and poise is born with or has acquired the attributes we have just been speaking of. Beyond this she wants to forget herself and enjoy other people. This she can do if she is so familiar with the rules of behavior that she can put them out of her mind and be outgoing to others instead of centering most of her attention on herself. Another source of assurance is the knowledge that she is appropriately groomed and dressed.

DRESS FOR THE OCCASION

Suitability is the touchstone for your costume. Your clothes should be suitable for you, too. They should enhance your good points and minimize your bad ones. Above all, they must be appropriate to the occasion and each part appropriate to the other. Pointed needle-heel pumps don't go either with your tweed suit or the country week-end at which you are wearing it. You will feel out of place in your aqua faille, no matter what it does for your skin, at a luncheon where the other women are wearing suits or wool dresses.

BE COMFORTABLE

No matter how stylish your clothes, you cannot look or be poised if you are uncomfortable. If your shoes pinch or your skirt is too tight, even though you may look enchanting when you leave home, you won't stay that way. Strain just has to betray itself in your expression, in your manner, in your conversation. So by all means look smart, express yourself in your clothes, and dress as becomingly as you can, but by all means make sure you can sit and stand comfortably in what you're wearing.

DON'T BE AFRAID TO BE YOURSELF

A woman of charm is not a slavish follower of fad and fashion. One of her greatest assets can be the ability to select from the current styles in color and cut the ones that do the most for her. Don't let your clothes be so striking and stunning that they obscure the real you. Choose the kind of clothes you enjoy and that go with the life you lead and they will enhance your personality and bring out all your charm.

GROOMING

Of course you, and everything you have from foundation garment to gloves should be fresh and clean. An even faintly soiled glove can spoil the whole effect, and so can a rumpled handkerchief streaked with lipstick. Be positive your shoulder straps don't show and won't, that your stockings seams are straight, your skirt centered, your shoes freshly shined or brushed with no runover heels.

MAKE-UP

Suit your make-up to your personality, your age, and the occasion, as well as to your skin and hair tones. Many well-dressed women feel that elaborate eye make-up ought to be confined to evening; many others use it in the daytime. This is a matter of personal preference, but if you do use eye-shadow and eye-liner during the day keep your eyes from looking *too* theatrical. Always be sure your brows are brushed into line and free of powder. See to it that your lipstick is on your mouth where it belongs and not on your teeth. If your nail polish is chipped and you haven't time to put on a fresh coat, take it all off and polish with a buffer.

PERFUME

This is always an added attraction if the scent is one that suits your personality and is subtly applied. Select from the dozens and dozens on the market that you feel at home with and that does not belie your type. Though there are always exceptions, as a rule the heavy Oriental or musky perfumes are most becoming to exotic, sophisticated women, the woodsy and floral scents to those whose charm is of a quieter sort.

Your perfume should be like a part of you, not like a heavy fog that precedes and follows you. If it's so overpowering that it's the first thing people notice about you, then you've overdone it, the scent is wrong for you—or both. Never put perfume directly on your clothing—it will go stale and may stain. Put it behind your ears and on pulse points such as temples and wrists; dab or spray a bit on your handkerchief, if you like. The perfumes that come in spray bottles are ideal, particularly the purse size. With these you can renew your scent if it is inclined to fade away altogether after an hour or two as it does with many women. And don't overlook the uses of cologne and spray cologne, especially valuable on those occasions when you very much want your perfume to be a private affair, such as in an office or on the golf course.

MAKING UP IN PUBLIC

The ladies' room is the only place for anything involving your hair-do, except for a bit of inconspicuous smoothing with your hand if you absolutely must. No combing at the table ever—and no use of cosmetics, though you may peek discreetly into your compact mirror to see whether you need to go and put on a new face. Few spectacles are less attractive to watch than a woman who publicly makes up with the same single-mindedness as if she were alone in her bedroom: elbows on the table, compact held aloft, mouth wide open while the coloring is rubbed into the corners. And all the while this very uncharming lady is deaf, dumb, and blind (though unfortunately not invisible) to her escort or dinner companions.

For use in the ladies' room or in your hostess' powder room, always carry in your handbag the minimum of grooming aids: comb, powder, small lash brush, lipstick, tiny emery board, and a mirror, plus whatever eye make-up you use. (Always make sure that you have some money with you, too—not only change for the ladies' room, but also folding money for emergencies.)

And while we're on the subject of the ladies' room, do, when you wish to go there just rise, murmur, "Excuse me, please," and *go*. No need to refer to your destination (especially not as the "little girls' room"), and no need to round up a contingent of the other women to accompany you.

HATS

The hatless mode is fine for the country and nowadays allowable even in the city. Nevertheless, every woman should have at least one hat—many suits, for example, look unappreciated or at least incomplete without one, especially in town. You may need one for church, too—practically all Protestant, Roman Catholic, and Orthodox Jewish places of worship require some kind of head covering. You would also wear a hat at any religious ceremony performed elsewhere than in church, such as a home wedding or christening or a burial service. Hats are often worn at cocktail parties and luncheons, although never by the hostess. At a theater or movie, always remember that unless you are wearing a little nothing of a piece of veiling or flowers or a close-fitting turban that couldn't possibly obstruct anyone's view, a courteous woman removes her hat when the performance begins.

GLOVES

The dictum that you should always wear gloves when you wear a hat is hardly applicable any more. Today's compromise is to wear them, hatless or not, in the streets of a large town or city. They should be worn on formal occasions such as luncheons, dinners, receptions, the theater, and so on, as well as at church and at any ceremony such as a wedding or a funeral.

These days gloves for all occasions may be of either leather or fabric. Even long evening gloves (above the elbow) may be of fabric, although if you have or want to buy supple white kid instead, these are still the most elegant.

Because country dwellers wear gloves to keep their hands warm as well as for convention, theirs are usually fabric for dressy occasions and wool for everyday. Women who drive usually buy wool or string with leather palms, or a long-wearing leather such as pigskin.

When you wear a long sleeveless evening dress, you wear long gloves with it—either opera length (to the middle of the upper arm) or shoulder length. Lengths for other occasions do not go so strictly by rule. If your arms are not your best point, match glove to sleeve length: three-quarter sleeve with mid-arm glove, elbow sleeve with elbow-length glove. If you have pretty arms, by all means wear a shortie or a bracelet-length glove. But if you do plan to match glove to sleeve, be sure to have the glove long enough; if there's an awkward gap between midarm sleeve and bracelet-length glove, it looks as if your sleeve had shrunk.

Glove lengths used to be designated as "two-button," "eight-button," "twelve-button," and so on. Now that buttons are seldom used except for ornament, the terms are pretty meaningless although you still see them advertised. When you do, the shorties are one-button, which means that they measure an inch from the base of the thumb, or two-button (two inches from the thumb). The bracelet is four, the mid-arm is eight, and the others range from a crush length of ten buttons all the way up to shoulder length of twenty buttons.

Never wear rings over gloves. It is allowable, though, to wear bracelets over them.

REMOVING YOUR GLOVES

Once you're inside wherever you're going, you may take off your gloves when you want to, as a rule. At receptions and formal dances and dinners, they are kept on more often than not, unless you wish to eat. Then you should either remove them entirely or, if you have the long ones with a slit at the wrist, slip off the hand part and tuck it into the rest of the glove. If you are sitting at a table to eat, the gloves should come off altogether, no matter what kind.

Any white gloves must be spanking clean or stay at home. If you are wearing white or light gloves into the city for the day and plan to stay on for dinner, it is well to carry a clean pair in your handbag.

SHOES

Here suitability and comfort are the two essentials. Especially for everyday, select shoes that give some support to your feet and have a comfortable heel height. Very pointed toes and needle heels are not for country wear nor do they in any way complement the tailored tweed suit. Sandals do not look right with a suit, either, city or country. The best shoe for a suit is a plain or very nearly plain pump, a low-heeled walking shoe, or loafers, depending on the occasion. Above all, don't wear high heels with tailored slacks—it looks and is all wrong.

With dinner and evening clothes, you may be as dressy as you like, with pointed toes, high heels, cut-out sandals. Remember that if you elect open sandals, your stockings should have sheer heels and toes, even though one night's dancing will probably finish off the hose.

Summer shoes, like summer clothes, are often gay and light-hearted. White shoes are appropriate nearly always, but they are so hard to keep clean, especially in cities, that more and more women turn to the beige or tan or multicolored styles, in straw and related materials as well as leather and patent.

Needless to say, shoes should be kept clean and polished. Be sure to get new lifts before you need them—it is amazing what a single morning's shopping along city pavements can do to those heels!

SPORTS CLOTHES

In general, sweater and slacks or sweater and skirt are appropriate for many occasions, as are shorts with blouse or sweater—if shorts are becoming to you. But some sports require very special clothes, and it might be wise to try the sport that interests you before buying the whole outfit for it. You can play your first tennis in an easy-fitting blouse, full skirt, and sneakers, and you can take your first horseback rides in flannel shirt and blue jeans. But when you become seriously interested in a sport, then is the time to invest carefully in the basic clothes for it. The wisest thing to do is to consult a knowledgeable friend or an outfitter to find out what is worn for riding, sailing, golfing, tennis, skiing, or whatever you have elected to pursue. The rules of dress are very rigid, particularly for riding, and you shouldn't mix-and-match haphazardly.

In general, the clothes for any sport must be cut very simply, with enough fullness to allow for freedom of action, and must be without distracting frippery. The footgear is often the most important single item and the most expensive. Sneakers or rubber-soled shoes with broad heels are absolutely essential for tennis or boating, not only for your own safety but to protect a carefully rolled tennis court or the polished surface of a boat deck. Whether or not you like wearing slacks, you will find them almost indispensable for sailing. You won't want to be bothered with skirts as you duck to avoid the boom or scramble to the other side of the cockpit as the skipper comes about.

WHAT TO WEAR WHEN

If you are in doubt what to wear for a particular occasion, it is always safe, and never rude, to ask the hostess. If she turns out to be not much help, as sometimes happens, choose the less dressy of the two outfits you may have been considering. Always check your costume as a whole for the appropriateness of its parts.

EVENING DRESS

There are two kinds of evening dress for women—informal or dinner dress and an evening gown which is worn at formal dances and on other formal evening occasions. A dinner dress is usually short and covers the shoulders; some may even have cap sleeves. But it is made of a dressier fabric than an afternoon dress; and its detail is designed for gala evenings. This is appropriate for dinner and the theater. It can be worn without a hat or with one of those delightful apologies for hats made of flowers or ribbon plus veiling. However, unless you are part of a group that is dressing for the evening, it is quite correct to wear an afternoon dress or a suit to the theater.

If an invitation specifies "black tie," your husband will wear a dinner jacket and you will wear a dinner dress or an evening dress, long or waltz length. On a quite formal occasion, with long dress and long gloves, you can wear more jewelry than you ordinarily would —necklace and bracelets *and* earrings, if you want to. With both evening and dinner dress, a small evening bag and dressy shoes are of course appropriate.

When a "white tie" invitation is received, evening dress for the woman and tails for the man are indicated. However, this convention for the man is no longer strictly observed. It is not unusual to see a number of men in dinner jackets at formal functions.

FOR THE WOMAN WHO WORKS

Clothes for office wear should be neat and inconspicuous, but they needn't be dull and they needn't always be dark-colored as long as they are fresh and clean. Suits are always good; so are wool dresses or sweaters and skirts in the winter. In the summer, cottons are fine. They may be sleeveless but not cut too low. Shoes should be comfortable as well as stylish, plain rather than ornate.

CLOTHES FOR TRAVEL

The happiest traveler is she who travels light and yet always has the right thing to wear. This means careful planning, especially for air travel, because you are limited as to the total weight you can take along. It is a good idea to make a list in two parts: the first a complete itemizing of what you will wear and carry en route; the second, notes of all the outfits you want to take, including the proper accessories for each—shoes, gloves, jewelry, handbag, blouse, or belt if any. Add your toiletries and underthings, night clothes, robe, and slippers.

Then sit down with your two lists to cut and co-ordinate. When you visualize yourself in each outfit in its entirety, you can see at once that certain ones would be impractical to take because each needs its special shoes and bag. So you substitute costumes that your travel coat, shoes, and handbag will complement. If you're taking evening clothes, try to select the ones that will go with just one evening bag and one pair of evening shoes. If you don't expect much evening gaiety, two additional daytime costumes and possibly a dinner dress should see you through. Try to take things that don't crush easily; getting things pressed on arrival can be expensive and bothersome, if not impossible.

If you use drip-drys you can cut down considerably on the amount of underthings you have to pack.

What you wear en route will vary with your means of travel and the season. Train, plane, ship, or car, a coat is essential—a warm one in winter, a light one (or a jacket or sweater) even in summer, for cool evenings and rainy or windy days.

Most people are inclined to take too many dressy shoes. Remember that if you are to do much sightseeing, at least one comfortable pair of walking shoes is a necessity.

The travel planning we have been discussing is appropriate for plane, train, or car. For a cruise or Atlantic crossing, you can take along more clothes since you are not confined to limits of weight or space and you'll probably want to add more dressy clothes. Your travel agent will tell you whether your ship is one that "dresses" in the evening; the first and last nights out no one dresses in any event, and tourist or third-class passengers don't dress.

MATTERS OF POSTURE

The poise of a charming woman has much to do with the way she moves and carries herself. An erect carriage and a graceful walk not only make you look poised but also make you feel it. Carry your head up, not out and leading you as a turtle's neck leads him, nor drawn back like a turkey-gobbler's. Step out as if you know just where you're going and are happy to be going there, with a free-flowing step as if you were hearing music as you walk.

CLIMBING OUT OF CARS AND TAXIS

This is often a very difficult stunt to perform gracefully these days, especially in the compact cars. Getting in is not too hard; getting out is another matter. If you're laden with bundles, umbrellas, and handbag, it's a real challenge. Practice a bit in the privacy of your own garage until you have the knack of doing it with the least possible awkwardness. Models recommend turning on the seat to face the door, putting the right foot out first and following with the left as, keeping your head low, you swivel out. If your legs are short or the door narrow, this isn't so easy—but find some way, comfortable for you and as graceful as possible, that avoids the ugliness of crawling out backwards with the derrière leading the rest of you.

SITTING

Crossed knees are hardly the scandal they used to be, but this position is not good for your circulation and seldom is graceful, especially if your skirt is narrow. It looks better to cross you ankles only. To rise gracefully, put your weight firmly on the leading foot and push up from the hips. Always try to pick a chair you *can* rise from gracefully. Especially if you are short, don't get trapped into one so low you need help to get out of it.

SMOKING AND CHEWING GUM

It really doesn't add to a woman's charm to be seen smoking on the street, although she may possibly do so while waiting for someone outside the meeting place, or at intermission time in those theaters where the audience has to go out in the street because there isn't enough room in the lobby. It is not impossible that women's smoking on the street may some day meet with general acceptance or at least tolerance, simply because there are so many restrictions put upon smoking elsewhere. But there's no denying it seems out of place for a woman.

It should not need saying that a smoker should be considerate. When with a nonsmoker or a much older woman, she should say, "Do you mind if I smoke?" before lighting up. The same rule applies when she is in another's office or in a home to which she is a new-comer—unless ashtrays are set out in such strategic spots that they are clearly intended for use rather than decoration. The smoker should be tidy with the ashes, being careful, especially in a car with the windows open, that they don't blow over everybody. In a crowd, such as during a theater intermission, she should handle her cigarette with extreme care so as not to char someone's floating gown (as we all know, just a warm ash can instantly melt a hole in some fabrics) or singe the guard hairs on her fur. When she extinguishes her cigarette, she should be sure it's *out*—this means special care with the stubborn filter tip.

Chewing gum isn't really a charming habit. But there's no denying it's enjoyable, soothing, good for the chinline, one hears, and sometimes essential, as on airplanes. But do remember, when you chew gum, to be selective about the occasion—make it an informal one, please. And remember to chew with your mouth shut and to dispose of the gum as quickly and inconspicuously as you can, wrapped in its own little silver paper in the nearest ashtray or wastebasket. Don't ever throw it unwrapped on the street, or "park" it under a seat, table, or railing.

COURTESY

Every charming woman is aware of the opportunities for small courtesies that present themselves throughout her day. She notices the little old lady who is apprehensive about tackling the revolving door against the out-coming flood of door spinners and helps her get through. She opens the heavy door for the woman behind her who has her arms and hands full. She gives her seat on the subway to a pregnant woman or an old lady. When she realizes that a group of three just hasn't room to sit together unless she moves over, she does so with a smile.

Naturally she doesn't block people's passage in aisles and elevators or at the top of the escalator.

A woman of charm remembers always, of course, to say "please" and "thank you." She is always courteous to those who serve her, at home or in public.

WHAT WOMEN DO THAT MEN DON'T LIKE

Of course women do lots of things that men don't like and vice versa, which is what makes the world go round. But there are a few small things in particular that a woman who wishes to be charming and popular should be careful not to do. A man doesn't mind carrying a suitcase or briefcase or a large package for a woman—if he does, manners forbid him to show it!—but he does resent being asked to stuff his pockets out of shape with cigarette packs, heavy compacts, and such. He dislikes being clutched by the arm.

One of the small things that annoy a man—and many women in these days of independence and self-reliance offend in this quite unconsciously—is seeming to brush off his attentions. It's very rude, for example, when he has leaned over toward you and is clicking his lighter to light your cigarette, to beat him to it and say brusquely, "I've got it," sometimes without even a "thank you." Rude, too, to open the heavy door before he has a chance to reach around and do it for you. Or to hang back in situations where you should precede him, as for instance following the head waiter to the table or following the usher down the aisle.

On the other hand, though he likes to do the things that men are expected to do, he often finds irritating the completely helpless type, who expects him to cross the room to light her cigarette. She is often the sort who never, never carries her own smokes but continually interrupts him with a plaintive "Cigarette, please?" And he seldom takes out twice (unless he has the bad luck to be married to her) the woman whom nothing ever suits—the service, the food, the play, and his choice in ties.

CONVERSATION

Although all of us know the don'ts about conversation, we sometimes forget and slide into bad habits without realizing it. It is a good idea occasionally to review a social evening to see whether you have been guilty of some of the cardinal sins, and if so, make resolutions for the future.

Don't monopolize the conversation. Don't interrupt (unless, of course, you have drawn a monologist, in which case you may have to, as tactfully as you can!). Beware of the constant capital *I*. Remember to be a good listener and to look into the face of the one you're addressing when you are doing the talking. Don't talk to the collarbone or midriff. At a large gathering like a cocktail party, don't break up a group that is obviously absorbed; wait for a pause or seek out another group that is just chatting casually. Try hard not to limit your conversation to the purely domestic, and don't trap another woman into the sofa corner and make her hold still for the latest stupidity on the part of your cleaning woman.

Learn to think before you speak, especially before broadcasting personal dislikes. It's fine to have convictions and to express them on matters of general interest. But unfortunately the floor will not swallow you, however much you wish it would, when you've volunteered that the one thing you can't stand is such-and-such and immediately realize that your hostess is wearing it or that it's a prominent part of the décor.

GREETINGS

A woman may offer to shake hands with a man to whom she is introduced or when meeting a man she knows. If this is awkward for any reason, she may simply bow her head as she says "How do you do?" If, however, the man offers his hand, it would be ungracious to ignore it.

Women don't seem to shake hands with other women much, or at least contemporaries don't. Many of the older generation do. So if you are greeting or being introduced to an older woman, take the cue if it is offered, or you may extend your hand without waiting for one.

A woman does not remove her gloves when shaking hands, nor should she apologize for not doing so. And don't give either a limp handshake or an over-hearty one.

Greet people as if you are truly glad to see them and really interested in how they are. If, at a casual meeting on the street, you see your friend is pressed for time, don't prolong the conversation. If you're the one in a rush, explain quickly that you must be off and briefly why, then exchange a few words and go. This is far more polite than letting the friend ramble on while your roving eye and shifting feet make it plain you aren't really listening.

WOMEN AND OLDER WOMEN

If you are a young girl or in your early twenties, you rise for an older woman and offer her your chair if there is no empty one nearby. You remember, if walking with her on the street, to accommodate your step to hers, hold the umbrella over her, carry her

package if it's heavy or large, show her other small courtesies without putting on such a to-do that she is made to feel both feeble and feeble-minded.

The only real problem that is likely to arise in relation to this convention is the definition of an "older woman." Thirty or forty may seem such to the teen-ager, but the average middle-aged woman would resent very much being treated like a grandmother even though she may happen to be one. With a picture-book grandmother, white hair and all, one knows. Often you can take your cue from the lady herself—you can tell by the way in which she is introduced or by her expression and bearing as she enters the room whether she expects deference or might resent it. When in doubt, it is a good rule to treat her as you would a contemporary, once you are out of your teens.

3

Manners and Dress for Men

PRESCRIBED MANNERS FOR MEN HAVE CHANGED TO A GREAT DEGREE during recent years. A much more casual relationship in general exists between men and women, and behavior that was subject to censure thirty years ago is now scarcely recognized as an infringement on courtesy.

However, the laws of common courtesy still persist. Cleanliness, neatness, punctuality, and thoughtfulness in all things are necessities of good manners for both sexes and always have been, although they may vary somewhat in their degree of importance.

HYGIENE

Cleanliness we may take as equally desirable in either sex. Neatness is perhaps not quite as imperative in a man as in a woman, but a sense of it is certainly greatly appreciated in a husband and an appearance of it is a must in all things formal. Personal neatness in a man involves clean nails, well-trimmed hair, and a closely shaved face, unless it is your fancy to sport an intended beard—a growing practice. Some men with heavy beards must shave twice a day to avoid evening shadows. A spare razor in the office isn't a bad idea for these unfortunates, especially in summertime. Well-tended shoes and clean and pressed suits and topcoats are essentials, needless to say, and, if one has all these, one shouldn't spoil everything by pulling a grimy ball of a handerchief out of one's hip pocket. Speaking of handkerchiefs, ones that match the tie or show initials are all right but should be worn casually, not as though they were sewn in the pocket by a mechanical engineer.

Punctuality is a highly desirable habit for all, although it has come to be expected rather more from men than from women, who seem to be given some leeway in this respect. Perhaps it is because it is more embarrassing for a woman to be kept waiting by a man than vice versa. A man should always be on time when keeping an engagement with a woman, especially if they are to meet in a public place; in fact, to that end, he should generally be a few minutes early, in case she happens to be on time. After all, a person who is late without a good excuse is simply indicating in effect that he thinks his time is more important than that of his appointee. It's a poor way to begin or to foster either a business relationship or a friendship.

For social engagements, particularly dinner parties, a peculiar tradition has developed in recent years that says it is almost impolite to be on time. How often one hears: "What time is dinner?" "I *asked* them for seven-thirty"—the implication being that there's not a chance of anyone appearing before a quarter to eight at the earliest. This is, perhaps, related to the lady's privilege of being a little late and the apparent feminine abhorrence of being the first one to arrive. Even at dinner parties, however, a man cannot be faulted for being punctual. If he is going to be really late, he should call up and explain the delay.

"Thoughtfulness in all things" is a virtue to be prized in all, but one that men perhaps have even more opportunity to display than women. This goes far beyond the struck match, the retrieved glove, the proffered arm, and the drawn chair. It includes crossing the room to converse with that under-developed lady in the bronze velvet dress rather than joining the group surrounding the latest debutante, listening to the problems of the head of the Ladies' Auxiliary on your left rather than recounting your prowess at squash racquets to the young charmer on your right; and in such elementals as admiring children and dogs of high or low degree, regardless possibly of personal prejudice.

Table manners for men are precisely the same as those for women. Although the practice of smoking at meals is pretty much taken for granted *in this country,* a man should still ask permission before lighting his cigarette at table if no one else is smoking.

WHO GOES FIRST

As a rule, women precede men in entering or leaving any public place. The major exception has been in getting in and out of conveyances where the man was expected to precede the lady in order to help her to the curb. Today, however, conditions in some circumstances have changed the rules. Take the question of taxicabs, for example. Their space is generally so limited that it is practically impossible for the gentleman to hand his lady into the near seat and then clamber over her feet and seat himself in the far corner as was the dubious procedure of the past. And landing operations when

they reach their destination are always complicated at best. If the cab draws up at the right-hand curb, either the lady must step out first or the gentleman must risk his life by getting out into the traffic to rush around the rear of the cab and present himself at the door. Head space—or lack of it—simply precludes his maneuvering past his companion inside the cab and squeezing himself precariously to the sidewalk to act as receptionist.

Under the circumstances, the convenient and practical procedure, both for getting in and getting out, becomes the correct one. The lady gets in first and moves to the farther side of the cab, leaving her escort in a position to be the first out in most cases. Of course, if the cab is on a one-way street and pulls over to the left curb, another problem presents itself, but this, too can be sensibly solved.

The gentleman allows the lady to get out first; then he simply follows her and escorts her to her door.

There are other instances in which the man permissibly takes the lead. In a crowded theater aisle he must step forward to present the ticket stubs to an usher. When the usher has indicated the row, the man naturally stands aside to allow the lady to enter and be seated first, but it is as unnecessary as it is inconvenient for him to delay proceedings by insisting on a formality of precedence in walking down the aisle.

In present-day life, there are other circumstances in which practicality takes precedence over established customs. In a crowded elevator, it is frequently more considerate for the man nearest the door to step out ahead of women passengers than to stand partially blocking the exit through which they must brush past him. If he simply gets out of the elevator and stands aside, it is both more sensible and, in its effect, more courteous.

To take off his hat when ladies are in the elevator with him is the natural reaction of the average male, if he is riding in a private, hotel, or apartment house elevator. But in an office building or railroad station, particularly in close quarters where the removal of his hat would be hard to negotiate, it is unnecessary.

When passing a feminine acquaintance in the street or a lady accompanied by someone he knows, a man naturally lifts his hat. If he stops to talk, he will normally hold it in his hand, perhaps, if the weather is cold or rainy, hoping the lady will suggest that he replace it. As he says good-by at the end of the conversation, he will tip his hat again before he goes on his way. Occasionally a younger man will tip his hat to an older one out of respect, but nowadays it is perfectly acceptable for two men acquaintances to exchange merely verbal greetings.

It seems hardly necessary to say that a man's hat is always removed during introductions, the playing of the national anthem, and if he is watching a parade, when the national flag passes. On entering a place of worship the average man would instinctively remove his hat, but it must be borne in mind that in synagogues of both the Orthodox and Conservative Jewish faith the men's heads must be covered.

SHAKING HANDS

In theory, a man shakes hands with a woman only if she offers her hand first, but there is nothing to apologize for if a genuine impulse causes the man to extend his own immediately. In being introduced, a man will normally simply bow unless the lady extends her hand. The question of the gloved hand is again regulated to some degree by expediency. If a man is wearing gloves and can quickly and easily bare his right hand, he does so. However, if he is carrying something in his left hand, it is understandable and forgivable for him to extend the gloved right hand. In shaking hands with a woman, the man should give a firm grip but he should remember his superior strength and be sure not to use a crushing one. Even when shaking hands with another man, a cordial, firm grasp is preferable to a demonstration of strength.

When two men are introduced by a third acquaintance, it is always courteous to acknowledge the introduction by repeating the name, and from a young man to an older one, the word "sir" is sometimes used. Use "sir" with discretion, however, as some older men do not like it.

In England new masculine acquaintances address each other by their surnames until they achieve a more friendly relationship. In America, however, it is generally thought better to stick to the "Mr." relationship until one or the other suggests a first-name basis. Although there are exceptions, the average American rather resents being addressed as "Robinson" or "Dinwoodie."

GETTING TO YOUR FEET

Except in a very crowded room, a man always rises to his feet when a woman enters. He always does so when she approaches him. In a restaurant, if a woman, accompanied or not, comes to his table, he rises and remains standing until she leaves or asks him to sit down. At a very small table in a crowded restaurant where rising involves real difficulty, he may half-rise and apologize for resuming his seat. Here again, it is simply a matter of expediency and cannot be misunderstood.

If a woman is constantly moving in and out of a room, there is no real reason why a man should rise on each entrance. Normally, it is up to her to relieve the man of his obligation by calling attention to her activities and asking him not to bother. If she fails to do so, the man may be forgiven for discarding the role of jumping jack after a couple of gestures of good faith.

WALKING WITH A WOMAN

A man customarily walks on the curb side of the street. In the daytime, a man does not offer his arm to a woman or take hers unless the streets are icy, there is some obstruction, or she is very old. In any case, he does not grab her elbow and try to steer her by it—he offers his arm as a support.

A man holds an umbrella over both the woman and himself. If the umbrella is hers and very small, he is supposed to hold it over her.

A man carries a woman's packages or suitcase. A man in uniform is, strictly speaking, forbidden to be so burdened, but the rule is often ignored.

CIGARETTES

When a man lights a cigarette, he should always offer one to his woman companion unless he knows she never smokes. If she accepts it, he should light it for her, as he will also do if she smokes her own. There is no need for him to leap up and cross the room to do this, but he would naturally do so if he were seated near her or at a table.

When he is with an older woman, it is always courteous for him to ask her whether she minds if he smokes. He should also ask permission of his hostess if he finds himself in a home where he sees no ashtrays or only one.

CLOTHES

Happily for both men and women, men's clothes seem each year to become more colorful and interesting and men feel more inclined to break away now and again from the most rigid of yesterday's standards. Our tastes are still on the conservative side and extremes of cut and color are frowned upon. But while suit styles and formal wear are still conventional and probably will stay so, in all kinds of leisure wear and even in business, men have far more leeway than they used to have.

Most banks and legal offices as well as service organizations stress conservatism almost to the point of regulation, but there is far greater freedom in the matter of business dress than in the past. Although anything extreme is to be avoided, there is no reason why all suits should be dark and all shirts white. A tweed coat is more appropriate to an editor than an optician, but unless a certain sort of garb is an earmark of the trade, neatness and cleanliness are the prime essentials to proper dress.

During recent years, there has been a more liberal attitude toward the use of color in men's clothes. During vacation hours, a man may indulge in a fairly broad range of color and design, and, if he avoids illustrative art or exaggerated monograms, he may give his sense of design fairly free rein.

HATS

The practice of dispensing with hats altogether appears to be a growing one, but it is still certainly correct to wear a hat, and, under certain formal conditions, necessary. The silk hat is still essential to white tie and tails in the evening and to public functions requiring cutaways in the afternoon, although the latter in these days appear to be pretty well limited to weddings and political parades. The collapsible opera hat is a rarity, but certainly may still be worn with evening clothes, especially to the opera, if the wearer does not mind being something of an individualist.

In summertime a panama or hard straw hat is proper headgear with a dinner jacket. In winter a derby or black homburg is equally proper. Even a soft gray hat is permissible, although black is preferable.

FORMAL DRESS

Very formal dress, white tie and tails, is so rarely demanded today in the life of the average man that those seen at true "functions" are frequently rented. The forked tail coat requires a white tie, a

white waistcoat, a *starched* white shirt with pearl studs and a bat-wing collar, and black—preferably patent leather—shoes or "pumps." There is no deviation.

The dinner jacket offers far more latitude. The old-fashioned black cloth or silk waistcoat has largely given way to the cummerbund or a waistcoat of fancy brocade. The cummerbund itself need no longer be black, but may be maroon, plaid, or blue. If a color other than black is used, the tie may match the cummerbund. The shirt may be soft and may have wide or narrow pleats. The cuffs are usually French and cuff links may be gold, pearl, or black. Sometimes cuff links match studs, if that is the sort of shirt being worn, but many evening shirts today have a sort of plain stud button used both as stud and button. The practice of wearing a plain white shirt with regular buttons is fairly common today, but it is not good form, and, particularly if the shirt has a pocket, don't do it!

Dinner jackets themselves vary in style and color. In summer, white, maroon, or even plaid coats are common and midnight blue may be worn the year round. Shawl or notched collar are equally proper.

SOME GENERAL OBSERVATIONS

There are a few important general rules to remember about dress, and most of them are *don'ts*:

Avoid extremes—don't be *too* different!
Don't be seen in a hand-painted tie or one of explosive design.
Bright colors are all right, but it's safer if they are solid.
Brown shoes don't go with blue suits.
Suede shoes are rarely in good taste.
Monograms preferably should be inconspicuous, although on sport shirts a little display is generally acceptable.
Belted coats (except for overcoats for sports wear—polo and trench coats) are out of fashion.
Bermuda shorts are a question of courage, rather than taste!

4

The Woman Alone

ALTHOUGH WE OFTEN ASSUME SO, THE "WOMAN ALONE" IS BY NO MEANS
invariably the young marriageable girl who has come to the big city
to pursue her career. There are also widows and divorcées of various
ages as well as women young and old who are single and intend for
reasons of their own to remain so. To each of these the problems
posed by living alone present a different face.

If you are a young marriageable girl away from home, you can live
in a woman's hotel, residence club, or the YWCA; all of these, con-
ventionally speaking, satisfy the grundiest Mrs. Grundy. The last
named is the least expensive as a rule. Certainly one of these will
provide a good temporary roosting place while you see how you and
your job are going to get along and while you are beginning to
make friends. When you start having dates, however, you will find
that since you cannot entertain a man except in the public rooms,
your beau usually feels he has to take you out, which is hard on his
pocketbook. Consequently, most girls soon consider some other arrangement.

Sometimes a young girl can live with a family she knows. If the
people are congenial, will allow you to entertain your friends, and
are not too rigid in their attitudes, this often works out very well.
It behooves the girl, however, even though she may be a paying guest,
to be courteous in *her* attitudes, to be considerate about noise, and to
keep her room and the bathroom she uses neat and tidy.

Having your own apartment, if you can afford it, sounds wonderful. But you are likely to find that the rent ties up all the funds

you might otherwise spend on a gay new handbag or a matinee, that you have many lonely evenings, and that cooking for one is a bore. And even though you are now able to get up a delicious steak dinner for your young man and give him an enjoyable evening of music and talk and a drink or two, you may in many communities risk your reputation by entertaining a man alone at night.

Most girls find the best solution is to share an apartment with one or two other girls. The rent is divided among you and so is the house-keeping; the reputation is safeguarded; and you have company on dateless nights. Here are a few pointers about entering into this kind of arrangement:

You should of course know your roommate or roommates fairly well and have seen them at their worst as well as best. Once you—and they—feel sure you can get along together, definite agreements should be made about certain things. Each girl should be quite clear not only about her financial responsibility in rent and utilities, but also about her share in the jobs of community living—the house-work, the meal planning, shopping, cooking, dishwashing. There should also be some sort of workable arrangement agreed upon so that each girl can have the sole use of the living room a couple of times a month or more.

It is just as well that all the sharers of an apartment have roughly equal incomes. If one is much better off than the others, over-spend-ing or guilt feelings, or maybe both, may result.

HOW TO MEET PEOPLE

Young women who take a job in a new community often find that their women coworkers are not only good to know in themselves, but lead to friendships with others and in many cases to dates. In many offices there are some unattached male coworkers too! In any event, it is never a good idea to get in the rut of going to the movies or stay-ing home to redo your nails or wash your undies while you wait for life to come to you. For the sake of your own development, as well as to meet interesting men and women, invest at least *one* night a week in some special activity that interests you. Take a course in modern art and go to the galleries; start reading about the faraway places you want to go to some day; or learn a foreign language. An inex-pensive camera and photography handbook will take you outdoors and perhaps guide you to a special hobby. You can swim, or dance, or paint, or learn to sew. Inexpensive YWCA courses and evening courses in adult education are two of the many ways to learn. And there are others. Your public library is a good place to go for information and may open some surprising doors to you.

You may find that it satisfies you most to work with people. The sisterhoods in your church, temple, or synagogue will undoubtedly

have groups and projects that will interest you. You may be good at volunteer work with Girl Scouts, mental health groups, in hospitals—if so you will be eagerly welcomed. And any effort you exert regularly to help yourself grow out instead of in makes you a more interesting and charming person, besides making life more fun.

DATING

While in this matter as in many others, etiquette is not nearly so strict as it used to be, it is still true that women cannot take as much initiative as men in pursuing an acquaintance. However, if you meet a man who interests you, you needn't completely conceal it. If you feel that he is also attracted to you, you might say, "I'm having some people for cocktails Sunday—do come if you're free," or "My roommate and I are having a party Saturday night—could you join us?" You can even say, "Do call me some time—I'd like to hear from you."

The only tactic you must beware of is stampeding him, so to speak, at first meeting. That is, you would not ask him to come to your apartment and let you cook him a steak, or tell him you've got two tickets to a new hit and won't he take you. Let your first move be general and casual. Should the acquaintance develop and he take you out of his own accord, then on occasion you may with perfect propriety dish up your special shrimp curry for him or ask him if he wants to take you to that show.

When you are going out with him, be ready and be appropriately dressed. It is to be hoped you know what to dress for, either because your escort has considerately told you or because you have known him long enough to have an idea. If, however, he turns up in sport clothes and you couldn't wait to wear your new organza, make him at home with a magazine and ashtray, excuse yourself, and change quickly. Be sure you have small change in your handbag for the ladies' room or for any phone call you might want to make. Unless it is understood you are going Dutch treat, these are the only expenses you should have to meet during the evening. It is, however, always wise to carry some bills for "mad money" in case of need.

Do be considerate of his pocketbook if you are his guest, especially if you are dining out. If he wants to celebrate and has the funds, he will undoubtedly give you a cue as you read the menu. If he doesn't, pick something in the lower or middle price range rather than the shrimp cocktail (fifty cents extra) with the five-dollar lamb chops and the cherries jubilee. Order one of the special dinners rather than à la carte, or at least suggest it.

When you have decided what you want, you tell your escort and he tells the waiter. If you have cocktails first, know your capacity and don't exceed it.

Be a dateworthy companion—be charming and warm and interested in him and in his work. But be yourself, too. And, above all, don't act blasé and bored in an elegant restaurant, or sulky and barely civil just because he took you to a roadside diner. This entertainment is his present to you. If you don't like it, you needn't go out with him again, but courtesy demands that when you are accepting his hospitality you act as though you are enjoying it.

It should always be the woman who suggests going home. If it is a weeknight and your escort has a hard day ahead of him, be considerate and make it early, or at least indicate that you are willing to. When he does take you home, don't forget to thank him for a wonderful evening. Should the hour be very late, it is up to you whether or not to ask him in for scrambled eggs or a nightcap. If you know him and yourself well enough to trust you both, whether your roommate is home or not, well and good. If not—well, remember that he just *may* consider your asking him in as an "anything goes" signal.

When you want to refuse a date, all you need to say is that you're so sorry, you're busy that night, but thanks a lot anyway, with some encouragement to call again if you want him to. Of course you never accept a date and cancel it when a better deal comes along. Not only is this very bad manners indeed, but if you make a practice of it you won't be bothered with many calls. If some emergency comes up so that you can't keep the date, let the man know just as soon as you can, with a truthful explanation of the reason.

A girl or woman living alone observes what is and is not done in her community about entertaining a man in her apartment or going to his. In many small communities, both are frowned upon and you will undoubtedly not want to flout this convention. In large cities, much more freedom is allowed. The kind of job you hold is also a consideration in just what is expected of you. School teachers, for example, have far more latitude than they used to in the days when they dared not smoke, drink, or fail to go to church regularly; but in many communities, the school board still expects them to behave quite conservatively.

The following are the conventions about chaperonage. You alone can be the judge of how explicitly you want to follow them.

A woman alone should not go to a single man's apartment after dinner unless others are there. She should not visit him in his hotel room alone; even if he has a sitting room, she should not visit him in his hotel alone after dark. If a woman is entertaining guests in her apartment, she should not allow a man to stay on after the others go; and if she is being entertained in his apartment, she should not stay after the others have left.

A single woman is, of course, not supposed to go out with a married man. In big cities especially, this convention has broken down somewhat. However, there is no doubt that no matter how innocent, such a date leaves a woman vulnerable to gossip.

For an unmarried couple to go away on an overnight trip is still frowned upon, unless it is a business trip. Of course, a number of couples can go away together, as to a beach or skiing resort, if at least one couple is married.

WHO PAYS FOR WHAT?

To repeat: on a date, unless it is understood you are going Dutch treat, it is assumed that the man pays for transportation, food, tips, and so on. But if you are having a lone lunch and a man you know and have gone out with turns up in the same restaurant and asks if he may join you, this does not mean he is under any obligation to pay your check, although he may offer to.

The woman always pays for the tickets to any event to which she has asked a man. It is a good idea to buy the tickets ahead of time so you won't embarrass him.

When a girl is asked for a college weekend, she must pay for her transportation and for her hotel or rooming house bill, even though the man will probably have arranged for her accommodations.

ACCEPTING GIFTS

A good rule is never to accept any gift from a man that is either very personal or very expensive. Handkerchiefs, books, gloves, a scarf, for example, are all right—a slip or nightie wouldn't be. Flowers and perfume, yes, or an amusing bit of costume jewelry that is

frankly just that, but not a jeweler's piece. Never furs. If a man gives you something you feel you can't accept, you should give it back to him as tactfully as possible, saying, "It is simply lovely, and you're very kind, but I'm afraid I couldn't possibly accept it." (Say "couldn't" rather than "shouldn't"; the latter implies that you might be persuaded.)

THE DIVORCÉE

The conventions we have been speaking of naturally apply to the divorced woman living alone. Although in many ways she might have more freedom than an unmarried girl, she is supposed to have better judgment than to flout the rules. Then too a divorcée is perhaps more subject to gossip and vulnerable to it than a single woman or a widow. If she is attractive and outgoing, it is sometimes taken for granted that she is out to snare a new husband, and instinctively the wives unite against her, while the husbands, however faithful they are at heart, cannot help playing up to her. A divorced woman doesn't have to act like a Griselda, but she should make it a point always to behave with dignity and propriety for her own sake as well as to keep intact her relationships with her women friends.

She should also try to behave with dignity about the reasons for the divorce and about her feelings for her former husband. It is unfortunate that so often the friends of a divorced couple seem automatically to split into factions, some on his side, some on hers. It's at least possible that he and she will keep most of their friends if both will discuss the matter as little as possible and simply say, "It's too bad, but John and I have had to decide to go our different ways, and we're getting a divorce. We do hope you'll be friends with both of us." Even though you do this, there will be speculation and discussion in your absence, of course, and your social relationships can't stay as before. Nor would you want your friends to ask you both to little dinner parties together. But, particularly in a small community, you may meet at some of the big affairs. You will find it much easier to be comfortable and matter-of-fact in such situations if you have been direct and unemotional with your friends from the beginning.

If a divorcée really wants to remake her life, she must realize that she needs to be more charming and more selfless than she ever was before. She must, above all, try not to be bitter and burden friends with rehashes of all the circumstances leading up to the divorce. She must sincerely and patiently reorient herself by degrees, and give of herself so that she will be a wanted companion. It is not always easy for a hostess to fit in an extra woman, but she will be much more likely to try if the extra woman can be depended upon to help the party go.

Hostesses do like to ask an escort for their lone women friends, but often they just don't know anyone who is free, attractive, and eligible. So if you meet and occasionally dine out with some man you know your friends would like, there is no reason not to ask the hostess whether you may bring him.

If you have children, then of course you have responsibilities for lives and happiness other than your own. Raising children without a father or with a part-time father isn't easy, but the children do keep you from being as lonely as you otherwise might be.

If you haven't children, you're free to look for a job or undertake some form of volunteer work in your community. As for evenings, don't just sit home and wait for invitations. Have a hobby or activity planned for at least one night of every week, and entertain frequently. Have friends in for a late breakfast on Sundays; give small cocktail parties; buffet suppers.

THE CHANGE OF NAME

A divorcée always changes her name. If she was Marian Green before she married Frank Watson, after her divorce she should call herself Mrs. Green Watson. This is the name that will appear on her visiting card and to which her mail should properly be addressed.

An exception to this form occurs when the divorced husband's first name is the same as the wife's maiden surname. In such a case, the former Mary Hawkins divorced from Hawkins Forrester would add her initial and call herself Mrs. M. Hawkins Forrester.

The signature to be used on checks and letters would be in the first case Marian Green Watson and, logically, Mary Hawkins Forrester in the second.

No public announcement is made of the divorce. A divorcée should, however, write to department stores and other places where she has carried charge accounts and notify them of the change of name—and of the change of address if there is one. No explanation whatever is needed; simply brief instructions to change the records from the former name to the new one.

A DIVORCÉE'S RINGS

A divorced woman may wear her wedding and engagement rings or not, just as she pleases. Some women, particularly if they have children, continue to wear the wedding ring. They may, if they want to indicate that they have been married but are no longer, wear it on the right hand. (Now and then a divorcée to whom her wedding ring is a daily reminder of a bitterly unhappy experience, buys a new one to wear.) Some have the engagement ring reset and wear it on the right hand. Others choose to wear no rings at all.

THE WIDOW

Much, but not all, of what has been said about the divorcée also applies to the situation of the widow. She also must begin a new life alone with her children. She too has suddenly become an extra woman. To all this is added the burden of a grief which is especially devastating if her marriage was a long and happy one. And she has no hurt pride to help stiffen her spine.

On the other hand, there is no question of any divided allegiance among her friends. They all rally round to do anything they can to help. Their sympathy and support do much to alleviate the intensity of the first sorrow. At this stage nothing much is expected of the widow. She is supposed to lean—and as a rule she does, especially when numbness supersedes active grief and lassitude overcomes her just when she needs to make important decisions.

Every widow must beware, all the same, of over-extending the period of her dependence. She has to rediscover her initiative and begin to remake her life on her own. She must learn to be outgoing again, to be considerate of her friends as they have been considerate of her. Although they love her still, they must go about their business. And so must she. No matter how sincere the sympathy, it just isn't possible for any human being to be a wailing wall forever. People will sympathize the more deeply and admire her grit as well, if in public she tries to be as cheerful as she can no matter how close, on occasion, the tears may be. As soon as she feels able to— and this may be before she really wants to—she should try to see people and to accept invitations. Perhaps, at first, just luncheon at a quiet restaurant with another woman and family dinners with old friends will be all she can manage. Soon, however, she should make efforts to entertain on her own, with a Sunday brunch or two, a cocktail party, a small dinner party.

The widow who has a job and who continues at it will find her work a blessing. It gives her days a structure that is invaluable. Having to get up early, dress, breakfast, and travel to the job is a comforting and strengthening discipline.

If she has no job and can't look for one because of her children, she will find that it is the children who supply the impetus to recovery. The daily responsibility for their care gives form to her days, their need of her love and courage warms and enlivens her.

The conventions of living alone apply of course to the widow in the same degree as they do to the divorcée. As a mature woman once married, the widow has more freedom than a young single woman, but naturally still does not want to make herself the subject of gossip.

A very young widow is in a somewhat different category than a middle-aged one. It is not assumed that her sorrow is any the less, but because she is so young and has so many years of living ahead, no one is critical if after a few months she resumes a young girl's way of life, with dances, parties, and dates.

MOURNING

The heavy black veil worn with black dress, hat, shoes, and stockings, is a costume that has largely passed from the American scene. There is no reason whatever why you should not wear it for some months if it comforts you to do so. But you will not be criticized for returning to everyday clothing almost immediately. Many, many women do. It doesn't shock people because they know it doesn't mean that your grief is any less deep. If it suits you better, you may go gradually from black dresses and accessories (you can wear beige or gun-metal hose rather than black) to subdued colors. The prolonged wearing of even half-mourning is a custom that is rarely adhered to nowadays. It should be said too that if you work in an office, out of consideration for your fellow employees you should avoid wearing all black.

At the funeral itself you would of course wear black. (For details see Chapter 39).

Like deep mourning, notepaper with a wide black border is seldom seen now, though it is available for those who want it. Most widows use plain white stationery, or paper with a very narrow black border.

A WIDOW'S NAME

A widow keeps and uses her husband's name socially in every way. If she has used her maiden name professionally, she continues to do so, of course. Otherwise, she is known as Mrs. Philips Stokes—never Mrs. Laura Stokes. Business letters, legal documents and checks she would sign (supposing her maiden name to have been Smith) Laura Smith Stokes.

A WIDOW'S RINGS

Every widow commonly keeps and wears her wedding and engagement rings. If she remarries, she of course ceases to wear them and removes them well before the wedding. In fact, she would probably, out of consideration for the feelings of her new mate, put both rings away as soon as she becomes engaged.

5

Married Manners

GOOD MARRIED MANNERS INDICATE TO THE WORLD NOT ONLY THAT EACH
partner in the marriage is a well-mannered person but also that each
is aware that he *is* a partner, the two presenting a united front before
children, friends, and servants. On the husband-wife team, each does
his job, each respects and supports the other. Ideally, their behavior
when they are with other people reflects this solidarity.

At home manners are another matter. Home is a refuge from pressures, a place to be comfortable and relaxed, and so in the bosom
of the family most of us choose to dispense with many of the formalities. This is as it should be. And yet manners are not just for party
wear, to be taken off and hung up with your hat and coat in the hall
closet. Consideration for others has a very definite place in your
home and simple manners should be practiced there, for your sake
as well as for the children. One of the strongest supports in the structure of a good marriage is the respect of wife and husband for each
other. And one of the best preservatives of this respect is ordinary
day in and day out courtesy—please and thank you; thoughtfulness
and consideration; tact and attention.

This does not mean "save the surface and you save all." A thick
veneer of politeness, covering up mutual hostility, is not protective
but destructive. A husband and wife and their children are only
people. They have to be real. They get irritable sometimes, or feel
hurt, or trample one another's feelings without meaning to. Home
is one place where one can be oneself and have things out if need be.
When occasions for disagreement arise, it's much better to clear the

air by saying what is on one's mind than to withdraw into chill civility while resentment smolders underneath.

The point is to make sure that all the steam is blown off at home— never in public. A married couple's impolite, hostile, or inconsiderate behavior to one another, even though their captive audience may not take it as a sign of an approaching break-up, is a mark of very bad taste and bad manners. Certain destructive attitudes, just as much as open quarreling, betray a most unmannerly lack of consideration for the feelings of other people.

HABITS TO BEWARE OF

Certain patterns of behavior couples sometimes acquire without intending to can make a social evening very uncomfortable for their friends. Bickering is one of the worst of these. Few people can remain unembarrassed, for example, when a tardy couple spends their first ten minutes at a party berating each other for their lateness like squabbling ten-year-olds. (And the hostess who has just congratulated herself on how well her party was going could throttle them both!) So no matter what the argument or how heated you both feel when you leave home, close the subject for the evening when you shut your front door—never mind now who's to blame.

Some breaches of good taste are not quite so painful to witness as bickering but nevertheless should be avoided. One of them is interrupting constantly, particularly to correct the totally unimportant details of a story. And the man or woman who steals the punch line from his mate's joke commits a marital felony!

Many a wife or husband falls unwittingly into the rude habit of ceasing to pay attention when the other is speaking and selecting that moment to initiate a conversation of his own with someone near him. *Sotto voce* or not, this gambit can only lead onlookers to suppose that, in John's opinion, he's already heard anything Sandra might have to say and it's dull.

Well-mannered wives and husbands put loyalty before etiquette. Better to let your mate be boisterous, use the wrong fork, or speak ungrammatically, than to criticize or correct in public.

Some husbands and wives tear each other down with gibes or "funny stories" in which the would-be humor is supposed to hide the barb. It never does. Sandra should think twice, no matter how good a story it makes, before she tells how John wrecked the kitchen making six pancakes. And John should take thought, too, before he recounts Sandra's latest excuse for running out of gas. No amount of cleverness keeps the listeners from realizing that, momentarily at least, John's idea is to make a butt of Sandra—or vice versa.

Aside from the conventional and communal moans and groans at tax time, all references to money matters should be left for private discussion between husband and wife. Both partners, of course, know better than to ask or hint at the cost of anything in their host's home. It's just as rude to discuss your own expenses, whether to complain about the high cost of food, help, or furnishings, or to describe, unasked and at length, projects and purchases that you know are well beyond your friends' pocketbooks.

Another pitfall to be wary of is criticism by either partner of the way the other handles the children. If John thinks that Sandra coddles Bobby when he's positive that what the boy needs is a firm hand, a social occasion is not the time to bring this matter up. Nor should Sandra carp at John because she thinks that in his eyes it's Janie who can do no wrong.

Avoid discussing the foibles of your mate's relatives in company. No matter how bossy John's mother is or how tedious Sandra's aunt may be on her lengthy, if infrequent, visits, they shouldn't be made the subject of public discussion. Even in the privacy of home, in fact, this is an area in which it is wisest to tread with discretion and most delicately. Family loyalty is such that it just doesn't permit us to welcome criticism of our relatives even though we may secretly agree. John may himself resent his mother's dominating ways, but this only makes it harder for him to hear her criticized. Nor will Sandra feel forced to leap angrily to her aunt's defense if John doesn't nag her about Auntie's nonstop conversation.

The bossy wife is seldom appreciated by friends of the couple, particularly by men friends. Most wives know better than to order their husbands around in public, even if they are foolish enough to make a habit of it in private. But many thoughtless women get in the habit of referring to *my* curtains, *my* new sofa, *my* dishwasher, with an ugly disregard for the fact that the sofa and curtains and everything else are the property of both. A wise and honest wife refers to *our* dishwasher and *our* sofa. By the same token, she never bruises her husband's ego by sounding as if she—and not he—were the head of the household. Although they may be thoughtlessly spoken rather than intentional, such comments as "I've decided we'll take a cruise this year" or "I've made up my mind military school is the place for Bobby," are humiliating to any husband. Remember, the two of you are a "we." Even if you make many such decisions because your husband prefers it that way, don't call attention to the fact in public.

It's rude for either husband or wife to stand up abruptly and inform the other it's time to go home now. Fortunately, most couples learn over the years a "time to go" code that needs only an exchange of glances. Very occasionally, the meaningful looks fail to register; in this case, the well-mannered spouse resorts to time and tact rather than nagging insistence. A wife who knows her husband has a particularly trying day ahead of him and will regret it if he stays on, will lean forward in her chair and say, "Tom, you have such a busy day tomorrow—don't you think we should be starting home?" There will be times too when this ploy is ineffective. If so, it's better not to make a scene about it.

It is in the worst possible taste, as well as cruel and dangerous, for either partner to behave seductively toward members of the opposite sex.

With all but newly married couples (and strictly speaking, even with them) public caressing makes others uncomfortable and is in bad taste.

A SPECIAL NOTE ON HOME MANNERS

As we said earlier, the at-home manners of a married couple are no doubt easy and casual—to what degree is their own business. However, there is one room in the house where married partners can't be too casual without payment of a considerable price. Small though

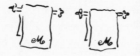

it is, the bathroom can make more trouble than any other room in the house. Very seldom are two people who marry accustomed to the same degree of neatness in the matters of toothpaste caps on or off, towels hung straight, crooked, or tossed on the floor, and so on. Women don't like shaving lather spattered about, men detest nylons hung on the shower rod. Each partner should *try* to be neat in consideration of the other. Most important of all, each should resolve never to let the bathroom become a battle scene. Changing another person's habits, if it must be done, is best accomplished by degrees, with gentleness and humor.

HOW WIVES AND HUSBANDS REFER
TO EACH OTHER

When a man is introducing his wife, he uses her first name. He may also refer to her as "my wife." He may use both together—"my wife, Sandra." The same principle applies when a wife is introducing her husband. In no case does one say "This is Mr. So-and-so" or "This is Mrs. So-and-so" when introducing one's husband or wife. In speaking of a wife or husband to a friend, it is proper to say "my wife" or "my husband"; the first name may be used if the listener is familiar with it.

Such expressions as "the missus," "the better half," or "my ball and chain" are not only in poor taste but also unfunny.

ESPECIALLY FOR WIVES

The average wife today is actually a combination of housekeeper, nurse, cleaning woman, and chauffeur, and it is almost impossible for her to carry out each of these tasks to perfection, especially when there are babies and small children to care for. She should, however, try to get in the habit of helping her husband begin and end his working day in peace by looking neat and attractive and by keeping the hall and living room at least picked up and tidy.

THE WIFE AS SOCIAL SECRETARY

The delight or burden, as the case may be (and it varies) of functioning as social secretary falls upon the wife. It is she who must write to thank Aunt Susan not only for the verbena bath salts that were her own gift but also, enthusiastically, for Herbert's tie whether or not it will ever be seen around Herbert's neck. It is she who makes up the Christmas card list, selects the card (most men would rather not be bothered), and sends them all out. It is she who issues invitations and accepts or refuses them, writes bread-and-butter letters, and remembers the relatives' birthdays and anniversaries.

A considerate husband who receives an invitation for himself and his wife while he is at his place of business, leaves the final decision up to his wife by saying either, "Won't you call Sandra—I'm not sure about our plans and she keeps the datebook" or "Let me call Sandra first, and she'll call Mary—I don't know what our plans are for Saturday." Similarly, a considerate wife will consult her husband before she accepts an invitation by making it clear that her own acceptance is tentative until she has a chance to see if he has made any plans she doesn't know about. And she always calls the hostess back *promptly*.

FOR MEN ESPECIALLY

It is the rare husband who leaps to his feet when his wife comes into the room or seats her every night at the dining room table or lights her every cigarette. However, it makes her feel very out of things and an ugly duckling indeed when, on a social evening, he rises for all the other women, lights *their* cigarettes, is alert for *their* empty glasses—and seems to forget her existence.

And don't, please don't, bring guests home for dinner without warning. Call from the office before giving the invitation. If you must do this on such short notice that there won't be time to thaw a roast, and your wife tells you that tonight's menu consists of four lamb chops, be prepared to say, "let's take them out to dinner" or to ask your people to come another time.

YOUR IN-LAWS

Whether or not you like your in-laws, you are obliged to be polite to them. You are lucky if, as is often the case, they mix well with your friends, don't criticize your way of life, and are agreeable to have around. If not, it is best, nonetheless, to maintain a polite relationship with them.

What to call your in-laws is initially something of a problem that usually straightens itself out in a little while. Mr. and Mrs. does seem too formal and cold; Mother and Father are not commonly used any more, nor the old-fashioned Mother Jones and Father Jones. First names are used a great deal nowadays, but of course you would not take the initiative in this but wait until you are asked When the grandchildren come along, they usually settle the matter for good and all with Nana and Grampy or similar nicknames.

6

Your Children's Manners

THE EXAMPLE THAT HIS ELDERS SET IS, PERHAPS, THE MOST IMPORTANT single factor in a child's acquisition of good manners. Training plays a very important role, of course. But if the parents are discourteous to each other and to their offspring and demand mannerly behavior only when guests are present, children will understandably equate good manners with hypocrisy and the veneer of formal training will be brittle indeed.

A good example can be set from toddling days on. By saying please and thank you when you get your child to hand you something he shouldn't be playing with, by letting him "help" you even when he's more hindrance than help and thanking him for his effort, by being patient in answering his questions, you help lay a solid foundation for *his* good manners. As he grows older, you extend these areas of respect and appreciation of him as a person, at the same time exacting more responsibility and initiative in the field of manners as in other fields.

A book such as this one is not the place for a discussion of the relative merits of permissiveness versus strictness in the matter of child upbringing. Sensible parents strive for a happy medium. Today, extreme strictness is pretty much outmoded. Certainly as far as manners are concerned, we have to feel that it is worse than useless to demand that the child be a miniature grownup.

On the other hand, over-permissive handling is hard on the child. He actually feels more comfortable with certain rules to guide him, and certainly he senses the unspoken disapproval of his parents' friends when he constantly interrupts, kicks the furniture, snatches canapés, and generally spoils the party.

The things you can and should teach your child as he grows are these: to respect other people's property and other people's privacy; to behave well at the table; to answer the telephone properly; to greet people politely; to handle simple introductions and invitations; to write thank-you notes; to be a hospitable host or hostess; not to interrupt or contradict; and not to be rowdy in public.

This may seem a lot to ask of a child. It *is* too much if you ask it all at once or expect perfection with never a lapse. There will be ages and stages when you can expect to make little if any progress —or so it will appear. But with patience and consistency and the daily setting of a good example, by the time your children reach their teens they not only will have a good foundation in manners but also will be eager and willing to absorb further refinements of etiquette because they appreciate etiquette's function.

PRIVACY

It is very important training for the child as well as a real strength in the parent-child relationship to respect his privacy as you want him to respect yours. Knock on his door if it is closed. Teach him to do likewise. Hand him his mail unopened even if he is so young you have to say, "Here's a letter for you from Grandma. Open it and I'll read it to you." Repeated example will make it clear to him that nobody opens or reads another person's letters.

It is well to maintain for your children—and allow them to maintain for themselves—a personal privacy in bathing and dressing, without acting prudish or self-conscious.

PROPERTY

Teach your child to have respect for his own belongings and for the belongings of others. Don't throw away toys that look broken or bedraggled to you; they may have a real meaning for him. Let him bang when he needs to, in his own room or in the kitchen, but don't let him think the living room and everything in it is his, too. Always have something of his available to trade for the Leeds ashtray that he wants to bang on the floor. It is important also to teach him to respect books. If you are yourself careful of the books you read to him, he will eventually get the idea that in this house we do not tear or scribble in or otherwise mishandle books.

TABLE MANNERS

The old-fashioned way with children and their table manners was to stress polite ways of eating as soon as the child was able to put food into his mouth by himself. Nowadays most of us believe that, for the sake of good nutrition, it is more important to lay the groundwork of good eating habits first. We feel that it is best, in the very early years, for the child to enjoy and appreciate his mealtime without demands that he "eat nicely." Today we know, too, what our grandmothers did not—that a very young child is physically unable to handle his eating utensils in the way we do. So in babyhood let the child enjoy his food. By presenting a variety of foods—in tiny amounts the first few times—and by not insisting that he eat when he isn't hungry or that he earn his dessert by finishing everything on

his plate first, we pave the way for the pleasant and pleasing diner-out of the future. Through the baby years, we may consider we are doing very well to produce a relaxed, nonfussy eater.

Training in table manners as such may begin slowly when the child can handle a glass of milk with some confidence and plays with his food infrequently if at all. Probably he has already been using his own table silver: small knife, fork, spoon, and pusher. As time goes by you may remind him gently to use his pusher instead of his fingers, to put his used silver on his plate and not on the table, not to put too much into his mouth at one time, and not to talk with his mouth full.

Expect to make progress only slowly along this line. Show him and help him. Don't nag at him, and be prepared to overlook many slips. It is important only to you, not to him, that he put his used knife and fork on the plate. He has so much to do and so many things to learn in this fascinating world that it is natural for him to want to go on right away to the next activity.

For the same reasons, when the child eats with the family (and it is important that he do this frequently if not daily), don't expect too much of him. Don't forget his limitations; he simply isn't able to sit through a leisurely dinner of even two courses. Let him ask to be excused when he has finished his main course, allow him to come back to the table for dessert, and if need be to drink his milk on the installment plan. Or if he is a very slow eater, let him go at his own pace while you eat your dessert when you're ready for it. As they grow older, children like to help clear the table and bring on another course; this not only relieves the tedium of sitting still but is good training in manners if you gently guide them from the beginning.

Above all, make your children feel welcome at your table. Your conversation need not be limited to their doings and they need not keep silence through an entire mealtime of politics and business talk. Draw them into the conversation now and then, let them talk about *their* day, too. Let them get used early to the give-and-take of dinner table conversation.

DINING OUT WITH CHILDREN

Taking your children out to dinner with you, even when they are quite young, is a welcome change for them and good training too. Select a family restaurant rather than one with perfect cuisine and elaborate service designed for gourmets. The children will not appreciate such a place and the place is not likely to appreciate the children. If you enjoy Chinese food, a Chinese restaurant is ideal— such restaurants are used to children and the waiters, for the most part, like and understand them. Make sure the children are comfortable at the table, with high chairs or seat raisers if necessary. Remove all unnecessary silver and stemmed glasses that tip easily.

Many restaurants have special plates for children. If not, impress on the waiter that you would like the children's helpings small even though you expect to pay the full price. Try to order for all of you in such a way that long waits are at a minimum—as few courses as possible. If you have cocktails, order something partyfied for the children to drink; most restaurants will fix up ginger ale with a piece of fruit or two in an old-fashioned glass.

Until your children are accustomed to enjoying many foods and somewhat used to dining out, it is best to order only things you know they like. This is not the time to urge some special delicacy on them. Let them taste yours if the name or look of something on your plate attracts them. As they grow older, they will gradually become adventurous eaters on their own.

Don't show concern if in spite of careful ordering and the smallest portions your waiter can persuade the kitchen to serve, the children leave much of it uneaten. They are excited, distracted, and restless, too much so to eat the way they do at home. But once in a while such a small meal won't hurt them.

Do not let them run around the restaurant between courses. If you have more than one child, letting them change places for dessert will help relieve the tedium. With older children a word game can while away the waiting times. Take care of the check promptly and when you are through, leave.

The hardest trial of parental self-control in the area of table manners occurs when the youngsters are in the early and middle teens. This is the age, especially among boys, when they seem to have to sprawl over the table, lower the mouth to the food, and tip back their chairs, feet hooked in the rungs. This tends to make parents particularly furious because, like as not, only last year the table manners of these same children may have been more than passable.

The trouble is that in a sense teen-agers *do* have to go through this phase even though they used to know better. Not only are they growing fast, but they're growing at different rates in different parts of their bodies and undergoing glandular changes, too, so they feel —and are—clumsy. And they're self-conscious and nervous as well; the constant moving about helps relieve their tension. The best thing for the parents to do is to be firm, to be insistent about some stand-·ards without being angry, and meanwhile to possess their souls in patience.

INTRODUCTIONS

The best plan with introductions, as with table manners, is to help the child feel at ease rather than to trot him through the social paces from the beginning. Small children go through some very acute stages of shyness and negativism. At these times it does little good to force them. Particularly if the negativism is an attention-getting device, as it often is, your insistence on the proprieties may even set up a lasting resistance to good manners. If Johnny won't look up from his blocks to say hello to Mrs. Thompson, it's safest not to make an issue of it at that moment. Oftentimes, though, a mother can quietly help her child along by preparing him—saying, for example, "Here comes Mrs. Waters. Let's say hello when we get close," or "Let's tell Aunt Jane we had a nice time at her house." He may want to go along with this and do his part or he may not; in any case, the force of example is not wasted.

By school age the child should remember to greet any visitor with a simple "hello," preferably with the visitor's name attached. He should be expected to say "how do you do" and smile and—if not too grimy—shake hands when he is introduced to friends of the

family. And he should become accustomed to introducing his friends to his parents. He need only say, "Mother, this is Mike," or "Mother, this is Mike Darrell." The important thing is that he make an introduction.

YOUR CHILD AS HOST AND GUEST

Just about nothing should be expected from a very small child at his own birthday party—or anybody else's, for that matter. If the group is small enough and the party simple and short enough for him to stay serene, that is the most you can expect. By three or four he can manage "hello" and "goodbye" and, on being reminded, "thank you" for the present. By school age these things should come more naturally to him and he will probably not blackmail the incoming guests for his presents or comment unfavorably on those he doesn't like or already has.

Frequent visits with friends who have children, at your house and theirs, help a child to learn how to be both host and guest. But make the visits short, and when your child is host, be watchful lest you fall into the habit of expecting him to make all the sacrifices and his guests none. This may teach him to be a spectacular host but a demanding guest!

It isn't easy to get a child always to ask you first when he wants his friends to stay for dinner. Certainly, you want to encourage his hospitable instincts, and yet if you are a small family you may not always be able to manage at the last minute. Try to help your child understand that you haven't always enough dinner on hand to satisfy *two* hungry third-graders and, to save embarrassment, will he ask you (privately) before extending a dinner invitation.

Teach him, too, that in general mothers are the clearinghouse for mealtime and overnight invitations; he may, with your consent, invite his friend by telephone and hand the phone over to you to second the invitation and clear it with the other mother.

When your child is to have a meal at someone else's house, remind him, before he goes, that at other people's houses we eat whatever is set before us whether we like it or not and that we always say "thank you for a nice time."

INVITATIONS AND THANK-YOU NOTES

It is a good idea to have your child help as much as he is able with filling in and addressing written invitations to birthday and Halloween parties and so on. When dealing with these, as well as

with invitations that come to him, impress on him the importance of answering such invitations promptly. Let him answer invitations himself as soon as he is able to, first with your assistance, later without.

Most children enjoy writing brief thank-you notes for their Christmas and birthday presents, at least up to a point. If the givers are very many, mother can incorporate the children's thank-you's with her own; but close relatives, especially grandparents, are delighted with the very shortest of notes in the most wobbly of capital letters. If the child hasn't been given his own notepaper, get him some. By ten a child should be handling some correspondence of this kind, and by the early teens be quite reliable about it, even though slow if not prodded.

A CHILD'S MANNERS IN PUBLIC

Try to teach your child not to be noisy on the street or in a bus or streetcar or place of business. Screaming children belong in the playground or at home, not in the supermarket or beauty parlor or library. You can help by making these outings brief while your young child is learning. If he must go with you on longer trips, be sure to take some quiet-time toys or books which will help to keep him quiet and pass the time.

YOUR CHILD AND SERVANTS

Never allow your child to be rude to any servant. Children have a pretty strong sense of what's fair and what isn't; they can understand when it is explained to them that it is especially unjust to be rude to a servant or to tease her, because she can't retaliate without risking the loss of her job.

CHILDREN AND THE TELEPHONE

Some mothers let their children answer the telephone at an age when they can't be expected to do it properly. It is discourteous to the caller to make him go through an exchange of baby talk before getting Mother—if indeed he can before baby hangs up! On the other hand, a child must learn sometime, and how else than by doing it? So when—but only when—he is able to speak quite well, Mother lets him first talk briefly on the phone to Grandma or Aunt Nell. She stays on hand, of course, to introduce him into the conversation and to tell him when to let her talk again. Then she teaches him what to say when receiving a call and lets him answer the telephone for her when she is right there. Dialing, especially now that it has become so complex, had better be strictly forbidden until the child is reading easily; then teach him how and let him make his first few calls in your presence.

When he is old enough for you to let him call his contemporaries, impress upon him the importance of politeness in asking for his friend when the friend's mother answers. Teach him to say, "This is Billy—may I speak to Johnny, please?" Somewhere between nine and twelve (it depends on his poise, and you should let it wait if he's quite shy), encourage him to say also, "How are you?" to the parent who answers, especially in cases where he knows that parent well and often visits in that home.

CHILDREN AND MANNERS OF SPEECH

Quite early your child becomes used to saying "please" and "thank you." It will be much harder to teach him not to interrupt, but with patience it can be done. Be sure he understands that if it is something that won't wait, like a phone call or the rice starting to boil over, he of course may interrupt you—with an "excuse me" first.

A bad habit that children fall into rather readily is that of contradicting. A child should be taught that it is rude to contradict, although it is perfectly proper for him to express a difference of opinion. He should learn, too, that it is bad manners for him not to answer when he is called or spoken to.

Parents ought always to bear in mind, however, that many times when children interrupt, contradict, or fail to answer when called, they honestly don't realize they are being rude. Even-tempered reminders will accomplish more for their training in manners in every field than will criticism and scoldings, particularly in front of other people.

CHILDREN'S MANNERS IN SPECIAL SITUATIONS

Even older children whose manners are thoroughly creditable may feel shy and unsure when confronted with their first experience with some of our ceremonies, such as christenings, weddings, funerals, or condolence calls. Even though nothing beyond, "How do you do" may be required of them, they need and deserve some special guidance—not so much drilling or coaching as an explanation of the structure of the occasion. They want to know what happens and what people do. When they know what to expect, they will be comfortable with their own roles, especially if what they need to say is kept simple, as it should be: "I hope you'll be very happy," or, "I'm so sorry about Tommy," and they know when to say it.

7

Your Teen-Ager's Manners

MOST PARENTS OF TEEN-AGERS FIND THEMSELVES BEWILDERED AT THE seemingly overnight changes in their children. Even those children who have been sunny and well-behaved up to now start having their moments of being withdrawn, surly, lazy, and downright rebellious. Often, manners are the first things these changelings seem to toss overboard. Rudeness, conscious or unconscious, appears to be the order of the day.

At this time parents are likely to put the pressures on harder than ever. "It's time that boy learned..." and "You're too young for lipstick and that's that!" the parents cry. Commands to leave the table may be more frequent than they have been in years. The most loving of parents can, out of sheer exasperation, let this sort of thing become a habit. But instead of nagging and constant correction, we need to listen and try to understand.

It is not that adolescents don't need guidance and rules of conduct. They do, and secretly they want them. But all too often we don't realize how suddenly growing up has come upon our children, and unconsciously we have continued to treat them as children. It is hard to remember that boys and girls of junior high school age are physically almost mature and that this maturing brings with it rapid changes, especially glandular ones, that are conducive to fatigue and tension. Furthermore, the adolescent's horizon at this time begins to widen rapidly. He suddenly has to try to take care of himself in the outside world, to be more responsible for his actions. He is not home-centered any more. Often the influences of the home come into conflict with ideas from outside, some good, some bad.

The bad ideas often seem to be the ones most invested with glamour just because they are contrary to home teachings and example. The group, the class, the team, become paramount for the teen-ager. Whatever his friends do is right, and your child feels he must do likewise—in dress, in dating, in curfews, in everything. Compromise is not in him.

It is important that parents not relax all their standards now, although there may be times when they feel they might as well— and there's no doubt it would make life easier. But they should first recognize that now more than ever it is essential to present a united front. Together they should decide just what standards they both feel they must insist upon—what is of real importance and what is not—and in what ways they can start releasing their children from close supervision. For instance, they may feel that although twelve-year-old Johnny should come into the living room and greet the long-time friends of the family, he need not join the group as he used to do unless he wants to. They may feel that at junior high school age Betsy should not wear mascara and eye-liner, but allow her a rose-colored lipstick.

Talking things over with other parents helps to draw some of the lines. What teen-agers are allowed to do varies greatly in different communities, but nearly everywhere alert parents can and do work out together certain standards, especially about curfews, supervision of dances, standards of dress for various occasions, and so on.

The most constructive single thing parents can do for adolescent children is to keep the lines of communication open between themselves and their offspring. Teen-agers are more likely to go along with their parents' ideas if they know that their side of the story will be at least listened to and considered, and if they know, too, that their occasional feelings of resentment are understood and tolerated. In fact, both parents and children ought to be free to express how they feel. As parents we cannot expect ourselves to remain invariably sweet and patient throughout the struggles of our children to establish their independence. Nor is it realistic to expect our children to submit happily to each and every restraint we put upon them. But adolescent rebellion will be more likely to express itself in talk rather than unacceptable actions if the teen-ager knows that parents can not only admit to their own occasional anger, but also can say, "I know how you feel"—and mean it.

While customs vary from family to family and community to

community, here are some generally accepted formulas for areas in which there is often conflict.

ALLOWANCES

Most authorities feel that a child's allowance, at whatever age and however small, should be quite distinctly something that he is entitled to and should not be payment for ordinary household chores or for achievement at school. Johnny and Betsy should understand that emptying the wastebaskets and helping with the dishes are their share of the family's total effort. Their allowances are their share of the family's income to spend as they wish. It should be said, however, that in many cases a job in the home that some outsider might be paid to do, such as washing the windows or mowing the lawn, provides an opportunity for a teen-ager to earn extra money.

It is impossible to say how much an allowance should be; this depends on the family's finances and the child's needs. A young child should have enough for what ought to be considered his "luxury" spending: ice cream now and then, a movie a week, an inexpensive toy or book. By the time he is eleven or twelve this allowance will have increased considerably and probably have been put on a monthly basis. Many parents of children in the middle and late teens increase their allowances enough to permit them to buy some of their clothes.

THE TELEPHONE

The telephone causes daily tidal waves of exasperation in every home with a teen-ager in it. Adolescents seem to consider the telephone as much a part of them as their hands or mouths, and they tie up the phone for hours talking to a friend last seen twenty minutes before the call. Setting a time limit on calls (incoming, too) sometimes helps. So does restricting outgoing calls to certain times of the day. If you (and they) can afford it, the most workable idea is to give them as a Christmas or birthday present the installation of a separate phone, with the proviso that they pay the monthly bills from their allowances or earnings. Note that in the beginning this will require firmness on your part with their friends who call *your* number to get Betsy when Betsy's line is busy!

Now is the time also to re-emphasize the lessons in telephone etiquette learned earlier and to see that at the very least your child identified himself civilly, and asks courteously to speak to his friend. Few things are more exasperating to any parent than hurrying to pick up the phone, only to be greeted with the belligerent (male) or delicately imperious (female) question, "Bill there?" Tell your teen-ager plainly that you don't like it when this happens to you

and you don't want it done to the parents of his *and* your friends and acquaintances.

USE OF THE CAR

When your teen-ager gets his driving license, particularly if some of his friends have their own cars, the sharing of the family car can become occasion for a real battle. Most parents allow their teen-ager to use it one night a week and perhaps one afternoon, and for special events by prearrangement. The evening, of course, is practically always Saturday, leaving the parents to stay home or beg

a lift. Some parents try to let their child have the car every other Saturday, some try to work out plans with him in advance. No one method works best for every family. It is usual, however, for the teen-ager to pay for the gas he uses, and both boys and girls ought willingly to wash the car once in a while. It should be clearly understood, of course, that no youngster takes the car without specific permission.

If a boy is earning money to any extent, he may save up to buy a second-hand car for himself. If he is at all handy with engines, he often gets a pretty useful vehicle by the time he is through. In many localities, however, the insurance rate for young drivers has gone up so steeply that he cannot possibly pay for it all himself. The family will have to decide whether they want to and can afford to pay for all or a large part of it in order to have their own car available when they need it.

A special note. The chapter immediately following this one is written to and for your teen-ager. Please let *him* read it first!

8

To You the Teen-Ager

To you in your teens, subjected to all the pressures of school and dating and clashes with parents, it must often seem that manners are something *not* to worry about. You have them, you assume— you were brought up to say "please" and "thank you," to eat nicely, and so on. Now you are busy finding out what kind of person you are, in relation to people your own age with your own interests. Remembering to use your manners every day in every situation may seem to fall in the last-straw department. In some sets and at some ages the very idea of manners may assume the direful shape of "square."

Not so. Because their foundation is consideration for others, good manners are the mark of maturity. The manners of a baby don't exist, for a baby is completely self-centered. Nor does anyone expect him to be otherwise. He has to do a lot of growing before he can realize that he isn't the only one on the planet, that other people have their rights, their wants, and their needs just as he does. There are some people who never learn this—they may have decent table manners and may occasionally mutter a "please," but they blithely trample other people's feelings every day. And some of these grownup babies may be thirty and forty and fifty years old. Everybody knows one or two of them. And nobody would choose to be like them.

Such people must in their hearts feel unappreciated. They may be treated civilly by the truly polite ones among those they meet, but they're surely conscious of the lack of warmth. They must *feel* their unpopularity. And this brings us to another reason for polishing your manners—a selfish one, perhaps, but perfectly valid. You want to be popular—who doesn't? To show consideration for others in the way you act, to prove that you acknowledge their rights and needs and not just your own, makes them appreciate *you*. They recognize you as a person instead of dismissing you as a big, fat ego. They thaw in the warmth of your courtesy.

It is often much easier for young people to use their manners away from home than when they are with their families. It seems to require very little effort or forethought to be polite to your best friend's mother, but your own parents bring out the worst in you. You occasionally break out in rudeness like a rash. Nor do *their* manners hold up consistently. "Consideration for others—ha!" That's what you feel like saying when you're nagged at about table manners, loud radio, losing things, answering back.

This tug of war is very common between adolescents and their parents. It comes about because both parents and children are changing. Your parents are having to learn to let go of some of their responsibility; you are having to learn how to be responsible for yourself. Neither your parents nor you is able to make the transition quickly and smoothly; it's not possible or even logical that they should. No young person can become an adult overnight. Your parents know this and they care about you. Because they care, they worry about your well-being, whether it's a matter of wearing a sweater or of going steady, just as you, deep down, care about them and wish you didn't have to fight them so often and so hard. But your ideas of what's best are bound often to conflict with theirs—and nobody's right all the time.

The "baby" treatment irritates you to the bottom of your soul, and justifiably so. Yet often you ask for it. You expect a hundred percent adult treatment while at the same time, in acts if not in words, you demand many of the privileges of childhood. Often you want to make all your own decisions, yet you won't assume the responsibilities that go with being a reliable family member. You don't want to pick up your room, keep your clothes in order, help regularly with a chore or two—you seem to want to be taken care of. Intentionally or not, you sometimes act as if your wants and needs come first.

Even those rare parents who are secure people with extra-sound nervous systems and no major worries can't help being irritated by this attitude. "She thinks we're running a hotel!" "Does he think we're *made* of money?" and similar comments express their frustration. And the honest teen-ager will admit that while they exaggerate, they sometimes have a point.

Parents can be offenders also. They, too, sometimes ask for the kind of treatment they get. They nag. They don't listen. They treat their teen-ager like a child. They interfere in unimportant areas as well as important ones. They may be inclined to invade every corner of your privacy, not only those areas in which they admittedly have a right to be informed and interested. They sometimes act as if you didn't have enough sense to come in out of the rain, let alone make some of your own decisions. Actually, they *want* you to grow up—in the interests of their future freedom as well as concern for your welfare—but they can't be comfortable about this until they're sure you're ready. *You* may feel you're practically there, but because you're not quite, you sometimes act like a child, especially in small things.

There's no doubt about it—adolescence is a battle. Your struggle to grow up is every bit as intense as your parents' struggle to learn to let you go. It hurts you just as much as it does them, and your feelings are just as real as theirs. If there is any difference at all, it is that you have the advantage of pushing *ahead*. Life demands that you climb fast up the mountain, bound for the top. Meanwhile your parents, who made the same journey once, are being left behind. They need to hold onto you, slow you down, try to pull you back. But no matter how much you love them and they love you, you have to grow up. You don't mean to hurt them, but you are bound to, because your drive to reach maturity has to be tremendously strong. Trying to understand that there are good reasons for the strains and stresses on both sides of the parent-child relationship makes the struggle easier to get through.

IN THE INTERESTS OF HARMONY

When it comes to day by day living, an excellent promoter of at least partial harmony is to remember to use your manners at home as well as abroad. A cheerful "good morning" at breakfast rather than sullen silence, a "thanks, Mom, for ironing my skirt (or shirt) . . ." or an *offer* to pick up bread or coffee at the market when you're headed for the candy store next door to it is not so difficult. Nor is a compliment for an especially good dinner or a warm greeting to your father when he comes home tired from work. It takes only a little thoughtfulness and a minute of your time to make your parents feel appreciated instead of merely endured. If you persist (don't expect one or two casual samples to work a miracle!), this outgoing attitude will go far indeed toward relaxing tensions all around. What's more, *you* will feel more appreciated than you have in the past, even though there will still be arguments over some issues.

You can also show that you are growing up by remembering to be considerate of the real needs of the other members of your family. Don't tie up the telephone in the late afternoon—your father may be trying to phone to say he'll be late for dinner. Try to ration yourself somewhat on those long chatty calls so the telephone bill doesn't seem like the cost of a jet plane. Make a point of introducing your friends to your family. Bear in mind that sometimes, when your parents want to know where you're going and when you'll be back, there's at least an even chance that they're truly interested. They enjoy hearing about your activities. They feel hurt and left out when you take the attitude that your comings and goings concern you and you alone. Then again, they may *need* to know—their plans may depend on yours. Top secret: If you volunteer the information now and then, they won't feel such an urge to cross-examine you!

If the volume of your radio exasperates the rest of the family, see if maybe they aren't right. Set it the way you like it. Then go elsewhere in the house and listen. You may find that you are forcing the whole family to listen to your programs. Most young people honestly do like their music loud—but having it *that* loud is usually just a habit. In only a few evenings you can train yourself to enjoy a volume that's no whisper and yet doesn't shout through the whole house.

Sometimes television is a source of conflict. Perhaps you are one of the rare few who can study while it's on. If you're not, face up to that fact. At times when the family turns the set on and you simply must finish reviewing for the French test tomorrow, take your books and papers to your room or the dining room or kitchen. There's no reason why they should forego their program just because you started studying in the room where the set is.

THE CAR

Use of the family car can be the source of bitter conflict between you and your parents. Much of this can be avoided with a little effort on your part. Naturally, you will ask for the favor politely. Be prepared to be as cheerful as humanly possible about a refusal if your parents need the car themselves, and be ready to work out a compromise, if this is possible. When you do get the car, make a point of being mannerly in your use of it. Treat it with respect by driving and parking carefully, by not taking off in a shower of gravel to the tune of squealing tires. Be sure to remove the Coke bottles, gum wrappers, and schoolbooks, which have a way of accumulating. It's fair in most cases for you to pay for the gas you use. (And never, never be so inconsiderate as to return the car with the gas tank empty.) It is very nice to show your gratitude for the privilege of using the car by washing it once in a while too.

Teen-agers have no monopoly on bad driving manners, as mentioned earlier. Many adults also offend by splashing people with dirty slush or rain water; by intimidating pedestrians at crossings; by cutting other drivers off. Ordinary courtesy should lead you to give other drivers a break when they need it. Common sense and intelligent regard for safety, as well as courtesy, dictate slowing down and maybe turning out when you approach roadside walkers, small children, stray animals, and bicycle riders. And the best drivers don't use the horn just to indicate they're in a hurry. They save it for warning and emergency. When another driver has shown you a courtesy, thank him with a smile or a wave of the hand. The gesture makes both him and you feel good and it is such an easy thing to do.

MANNERS IN PUBLIC PLACES

Make an effort when you're in public places to be aware of other people and their rights. For instance, when you're choosing a magazine at the newsstand of a crowded candy store, don't block the stand from other customers. Remind yourself not to get so deeply absorbed that you fail to notice the poor soul who can't get by and can't get the message through to you. Try not to talk or laugh too loudly in buses and on the streets. At the movies, don't annoy the people around you with whispers and semimuffled hysterics, or the rattling of candy wrappers. Don't indulge in shoving and horseplay on a public walk.

If circumstances force you to ride your bicycle on the sidewalk, slow down when you pass pedestrians instead of whizzing past with an inch to spare. *You* know it's a generous inch, but taken by surprise as they are, they feel practically scalped!

Hard though it is for you to do, when you're on the beach everyone around you will appreciate your remembering to walk, not run, to the nearest water or beachball game. You know how *you* would feel if some thoughtless kid sprinkled your well-oiled back with sand, to say nothing of seasoning your hamburger with it!

WHEN YOU'RE BABY SITTING

The do's and don'ts of baby sitting conduct hardly belong in a book about etiquette—except for a reminder not to forget your manners when you take on this employment. It's bad manners to have friends come in for the evening. This house isn't yours and you shouldn't ask people to come over any more than you would invite a gang to your friend Susie's house all on your own. And, aside from whatever washing up you may have agreed to do, you'll naturally clean up and put away after yourself when you've had the allowed late snack from the icebox.

A FEW CONVENTIONS

Just as adults do, you will want guidance from time to time on etiquette in special situations—how to eat difficult foods, forms of invitations and their answers, introductions, and so forth. You may feel more comfortable if you bone up occasionally on what is expected of a man and what of a woman, the proper behavior in a restaurant or theater, what to tip. We refer you to the chapters in this book dealing with all those matters, but here are some special reminders.

Make it a habit to answer all invitations promptly and to go if you said you would. The girl or boy who accepts and then doesn't turn up because something better has come along soon will get few, if any, more invitations.

Boys should be prompt in calling for their girls, especially when time really matters, as for a certain show at the movies or a dinner dance. Girls needn't hover expectantly behind the front door, as if afraid their date might get away; but they ought to make it a point not to keep him waiting more than a very few minutes. This means starting to dress in plenty of time to allow for runs in stockings, or hair that suddenly won't do what you want it to.

A courtesy that boys sometimes unintentionally overlook is opening doors for girls and grownups and letting them go through first. Another small point that boys may forget out of sheer friendliness (and a nice trait that is, too) is that in introductions and casual encounters with a girl or woman, she is supposed to offer to shake hands first. If you remember to watch for this, you will never be

in the somewhat foolish position of waiting with your hand out. Of
course, if she is a mannerly person she will quickly do a double take
and shake hands at once. But it's her privilege to decide on shake or
not shake, and often, for no special reason, she decides not to.

The question has been asked by many girls, "Joe never opens the
car door for me. Shouldn't he?" Well, Joe will never do himself
any harm by this thoughtful act—it gets high marks in every
woman's book. Certainly, he should do it when he is your escort to a
party or a movie. But it isn't any real reflection on Joe's manners
if he fails to do it when a group of you in blue jeans is bound for
hot dogs on the beach.

A reminder to Joe: when you're calling in a car for a girl, dressed
up or not, don't sit at the curb and honk. This is really rude and
indicates you don't know your way around. Always go to the door
and announce yourself.

Now and then boys are inclined to give up some of the courtesies
we have mentioned because the girls, consciously or not, brush them
off. (The courtesies, not the boys.) So it behooves the girl, if she
appreciates these special attentions, as she should, to give the boy a
chance to show them, and when he does, to accept them gracefully.

YOUR PERSONAL APPEARANCE

The way teen-agers want to dress often makes parents see red. The more understanding among grownups realize that an adolescent has a real need to dress the way his or her friends do, and to be if not the first, never the very last to take up a current fad. But even the most sympathetic adults are disturbed when a way of dress is in very bad taste, extremely unbecoming, or carries disagreeable social connotations. Exaggerated hair-do's, very short skirts, tight clothes, heavy eye make-up may be some of the questionable fads you take up in your natural desire to conform and to be more grownup.

The young adolescent looks best without any make-up other than a rose or coral lipstick. As you reach fifteen and sixteen, some of the more vivid lipsticks are fine, as long as you don't crayon it on too thickly or enlarge your natural mouth. When you look pale, use a little rouge, but make sure it is a good color for you, harmonizes with or matches your lipstick, and is put on subtly rather than in hard little circles. You don't want to look like a clown. Be certain, too, that you're the type for rouge; some brunettes with that enviable magnolia-petal skin, for instance, look much lovelier without it.

If your hair is soft and thin and fly-away, get a good permanent. Much better a permanent to give it some body than to tease your hair constantly, which is very bad for it.

As for eye make-up—best leave that for your very late teens. Any model will tell you that eye liner and mascara are very hard to use with any subtlety; in fact, they usually save conspicuous eye make-up for the camera. It's all right behind the footlights or in a fashion parade, but most boys don't like to gaze into stagey eyes. If your eyebrows and lashes are somewhat pale, it's perfectly all right, though, to define them (upper lashes only) with a little brown pencil and mascara.

When it comes to perfume, the height of sophistication at any age is to use it discreetly instead of sloshing it on. You want it to be elusive and teasing, not overpowering. You may find a cologne spray is more fun than perfume (and easier on the budget!) because since it is less concentrated you can use quite a lot of it. Flowery and woodsy scents are not only more suitable for adolescents than heavy Oriental types, but also are usually much preferred by boys.

"WHAT SHALL I WEAR?"

It's good sense as well as good taste to make your costume fit the occasion. Your date will usually give you a clue to what you'll be doing—bowling, movies, dancing, the beach. Then you can judge whether sweater and skirt are called for, or slacks, a casual dress, or a dressy dress. When in doubt, it's more comfortable and more stylish to be too little dressed-up rather than too much. If it should ever happen that your signals get crossed and Joe turns up in slacks and sweater to find you dressed in your party taffeta, don't go to pieces. Just ask him to excuse you for a minute, give him a magazine to read, and hop upstairs and change into something more suitable.

Boys as well as girls should give some thought to the matter of dress, for fads both harmless and otherwise come both ways. There may be a vogue for bulky sweaters, cords instead of chinos or vice versa. Who could or would object to this kind of thing? But a boy who goes in for long sideburns, or black leather jackets, tight low-slung pants and heavy boots puts a JD label on himself whether he deserves it or not. If you go in for these, you may be the best adjusted and brightest boy in the community, and one of the politest too. But people have to know you well before they're sure. The parents of a new girl won't think so. Nor the traffic cop. When there's any trouble, you are almost automatically suspect. Can you dream up a better way to be unfair to yourself? So think twice before you take to this way of dressing, just because some of your friends do.

For boys and girls both, cleanliness plays a big part in being attractive. Be sure you're spick and span where it doesn't show as well as where it does. All-over cleanliness and fresh underwear are just as important as scrubbed nails, clean neck, and shining hair. And don't forget the toothbrush and the deodorant.

SMOKING AND DRINKING

The question of whether to smoke or drink is only to a small extent a question of manners. It is more a matter of taste and common sense. There may be nothing wrong with an occasional cigarette if you're old enough and big enough not to look like a baby playing grownup. But it gets to be a habit so easily—and an expensive one which does you no good physically. It's more than possible that, like so many grownups, you will come to wish you'd never begun. Of course smoking does provide something to do with your hands. It may make you think that waving a cigarette around and blowing smoke covers up the uncertainty you feel deep down inside, but actually the cigarette is a dead giveaway. When young teen-agers smoke, they're pinning on a big label that says "immature."

Drinking is of course illegal for minors. For young teen-agers it is even more inappropriate than smoking, and looks even more show-offy and immature. Drinking, too, is an expensive habit. And you don't need it; you already have the zest and sparkle that some adults believe liquor gives them. If you decide that you really don't want to drink, though some in your crowd do, there's no need to worry that you'll look unsophisticated or holier-than-thou so long as you don't make a big deal out of refusing. Just say, "I think I'll have a Coke"—or ginger ale, or whatever.

MANNERS AND PERSONALITY

When you're young and seem to have to rebel against things as they are so much of the time, you naturally don't want to let go, ever, of your personality. It's been hard to find it—you don't want to lose it. Sometimes it may seem to you that being always courtesy-conscious may do just that. On the contrary, as you mature you'll find that easy, friendly manners improve your personality, add depth to it. You'd be right to avoid the artificial sort, the social manner*isms* that make you feel the real person is afraid to come out from behind them. Over-refinement—the mincing speech, the stuck-out little finger are horrid evidence of a false front. But ordinary good manners, with real warmth and friendliness will draw everyone to you. The more you use them, the more they will become second nature to you. And when that happens, you will have incorporated *into* your personality that valuable, mature and very comfortable quality that spells "poise."

YOU AND YOUR FRIENDS

9

Introductions

EVEN THE OUTGOING PERSON WHO SEEMS AT EASE IN MOST SITUATIONS may be inwardly flustered—and sometimes outwardly—when it comes to introducing one friend to another. We seem to have acquired a sort of complex about this; we're so afraid we'll forget the "rules" that sometimes we forget the people. And it's the people, not the rules, that are important.

Actually, introductions are not nearly so difficult as we imagine them to be. For very formal occasions, in which ceremony is involved, such as a receiving line or a tea in honor of some personage, there are a few special rules; those we shall come to later on. For most occasions, however, all you want to accomplish by an introduction is to make sure that your friends know each other's names.

Say first the name of the person who deserves the greater courtesy. If you are introducing a man and a woman, the woman's name would come first, unless he is much older or distinguished for some reason. "Mrs. Cotton, Mr. Gordon" constitutes the simplest form of introduction, and means that you are presenting Mr. Gordon to Mrs. Cotton. It may seem less stiff if instead of just the two names you say, "Marjorie, this is Jim Gordon—Mrs. Cotton." Or if you like, you may bridge the two names with a phrase such as "May I present" or "May I introduce." Here too the woman's name would be spoken first. Note, however, that when you use the phrase "I'd like you to meet" you say the man's name first because you are presenting him to the woman.

It's important to pronounce each name clearly and distinctly—don't mumble.

Sometimes when you're making an introduction it is friendly and helpful to give a clue about who the people are and what they do. Of course such hints would seem unsuitable and even gauche at a brief meeting on the street. But at a cocktail party, for example, where the two being introduced are expected to chat together at least briefly, it is the most tactful of hostesses who says, "Jim has just come back from Moscow" or "Marjorie's having her first gallery show next week." Note that you don't have to give a thumbnail biography of anyone, nor should you pin labels on both people—unless each is prominent in his own field and might not know about the other. And you don't have to say *why* Jim went to Moscow or whether Marjorie paints, sculpts, or makes mobiles. They'll find out when they gratefully follow the conversational lead you've given them.

If you are introducing older people, it is usually best to use last names and keep first names for the younger ones even if your group uses first names habitually. It is just as well to use "Mr." or "Mrs." and then give the first names: "Mrs. Cotton, this is Mrs. Gordon— Marjorie, Ellen." Your teen-agers will probably use only first names when they are introducing their friends to each other.

Remember that you introduce your husband or your wife by first name only, or as "my husband" or "my wife," never as "Mr." or "Mrs."

GROUP INTRODUCTIONS

When you are giving a party and are introducing a newly arrived couple to a group, don't try to introduce them to each of your other guests in turn unless the group is very small. The easiest and most comfortable way is to present the newcomers to the group as a whole, then identify each member of the group separately for the benefit of the new couple. Like this: "This is Ellen and John Gordon—Judy Palmer, Marjorie Cotton, Jack Palmer, Mary Wilkins, George Cotton, Tom Wilkins."

If you are giving a very large party such as a tea or cocktail party, then you can't and needn't introduce each new guest to all the others. Lead the person to a nearby small group, make the introductions, and go off about your duties as hostess. The newcomer will know that you can't escort him on a tour of the party and that your initial introduction at a gathering of this sort is intended to cover the whole situation.

If you bring a friend to a party, you introduce him to the host and hostess and they will handle the other introductions. Many authorities believe that one should not make introductions other than this in another person's house. If this rule is too strictly observed, it can lead to awkwardness, as when you are talking with a close friend and a woman known only to you joins the tête à tête.

According to the rule, she should introduce herself to your companion or your friend should introduce herself. But many people fail to do this. Instead, they look inquiringly at you in obvious expectation of being introduced. When that happens, naturally you don't stand on ceremony but make the introduction.

INTRODUCING YOUR CHILDREN

Always present your children *to* your friends, even when they've grown up or when you're introducing your daughter to a man. "Marjorie, this is my son Jim," and then, "Jim, this is Mrs. Cotton." If your daughter is married you would of course give her last name: "Mrs. Jenkins, this is my daughter, Betsy Corbin."

INTRODUCING YOUR FRIENDS TO YOUR PARENTS

You present your friends *to* your parents. "Mother, this is Tom Wilkins." You need not indicate your parents' last name unless it is different from your own, in which case you would add for Tom's benefit, "This is my mother, Mrs. Freeman."

INTRODUCING IN-LAWS

It is always best when introducing in-laws to make the relationship clear, rather than to say, "This is my mother" when she's really your mother-in-law or "my sister Judy Palmer" when she's really your husband's sister. Many warm-hearted people do this because they want the in-laws to feel less in-lawish, more a part of the family circle. Actually, it only confuses people. It's better to say, "This is my mother-in-law, Mrs. Stern" or "This is Bob's mother, Mrs. Stern." Do remember to introduce your friends *to* your in-laws.

INTRODUCING WOMEN TO MEN

The necessity of introducing a woman to a man doesn't arise often in the lives of most of us. But we should know that you do introduce a woman to a man if the man is: the President of the United States, a governor, a mayor, a foreign head of state, a church dignitary, or a royal personage.

INTRODUCING ONESELF

There are a number of occasions when one should not hesitate to introduce oneself. Sometimes it is clear that an acquaintance doesn't recall you, remembers your face but can't for the life of her think of your name, although she may in a minute. If you have ever been in such a predicament yourself—and who among us has not?—you will be the last to torture the poor soul with, "I remember you but I bet you don't remember me." That's not a greeting, it's a taunt. You will come to her rescue with, "I'm Lee Martin. We met at the Freemans' around Christmastime."

It is pleasant to go over and speak to someone older whom you may recognize as a friend of your family's, saying, "Mrs. Sidney? I'm John Gordon—Ruth Gordon's son. I remember you as a friend of my mother's when we lived in Merion."

At a large cocktail or dinner party it is part of your duty as well as your pleasure to introduce yourself to your party neighbor or dinner partner if you don't already know him. You say, "I'm Betsy Girard." Then he offers his name, you each acknowledge with a how-do-you-do—and there you are!

INTRODUCING SERVANTS

People with large houses and a staff of servants rarely introduce their servants except indirectly, such as: "Marie will unpack for you." In the style in which most of us live, it is never necessary to introduce a servant. It is, however, often done, especially when the servant is practically part of the household or has seen long service with the family. In such cases, the hostess may say to her guests, "I'm sure you remember Eileen" or "Aunt Evelyn, this is Lucille."

ACKNOWLEDGING INTRODUCTIONS

Most of us simply say "How do you do," and so does the person who is being introduced. (Needless to say, it is not a personal question about the state of your health and shouldn't be answered as such.) A plain "Hello" is often used. And the younger set is fond of "Hi!" After the how-do-you-do, if you really want to you may say, "I'm so glad to meet you" or "I've heard so much about you." But it isn't really necessary.

Never acknowledge an introduction with "Pleased to meet you," "Charmed, I'm sure," "Delighted to make your acquaintance," or similar phrases. These sound stilted.

A man, of course, rises to be introduced. He should shake hands with another man and bow to a woman, shaking hands if she offers to do so.

A woman does not rise to be introduced unless she is meeting an older woman or a really elderly man. She may offer her hand to a man if she likes, but she doesn't usually shake hands with another woman, although she would, and promptly, if the other woman offered her hand.

A hostess always rises to welcome and shake hands with each of her guests.

If you have been introduced to someone and the two or three of you are forming an island in the theater lobby or at a cocktail party, it is nice to say something after your how-do-you-do. If you're at the theater, you can say something about the play; if you're at a cocktail party, you may have to make do with the weather. Don't ever feel, however, that it is up to you alone to carry the conversational ball right down the field. And if the people you are introduced to have been talking, wait after your how-do-you-do's for them to resume their conversation. Listening is not only more polite, but will clue you for something to say at the next break.

GOODBYS

When you're leaving friends, you simply say "Goodby." It's warm and courteous to add, if you really want to, "It's been so nice to see you again" or "I do hope we'll see you soon." If you're on the receiving end of a warm farewell like any of these, you can say simply "Thank you," or you can respond in kind with, "I'm so glad to have met *you!*"

To one's hostess, of course, one says, "Goodby—it's been a wonderful evening—thanks so much," or perhaps, "We always have such a good time at your house." And the host and hostess with their goodbys indicate that they are glad the guests could come.

At parties, goodbys are sometimes awkwardly handled. It's a mistake to interrupt people's conversations by making a tour of the room shaking hands and saying goodby to each person. Although it is nice to say a special goodby to the couple you were last talking with, all you need do is say a general goodnight to the others, goodby and thank you to your host and hostess, and go. If the party is lively at this point and everybody is talking, it is perfectly proper to omit the general goodby and ask your hostess to tell them all goodnight for you.

Remember that goodby is a short word and it doesn't take all night to say it. It is rude to keep your host and hostess standing at the open door, neglecting their other guests and chilling the hall while you suddenly remember a long-winded joke or burden your hostess with your most recent servant problem.

10

Telephone Manners

So much of our communicating takes place over the telephone that it behooves us all to review our telephone manners from time to time. It's so easy to reach for the phone on an impulse to chat with a friend at length or persuade her to take some tickets for the benefit we're working on. Sometimes we forget that the person at the other end is a captive audience. We wouldn't think of bursting into her dining room at breakfast time to make her listen then and there to our woes or needs—but this is the sort of thing we do all too often when we telephone. Similarly, when we ourselves are interrupted at an awkward moment by the phone's ring, we forget that the caller can't *see* we're feeding the baby and that is why we sound irritable.

Always remember that no matter whether you're calling or being called, the telephone is an invader of privacy, often welcome, sometimes not. So whenever you use it, intuition, tact, and sensitivity to another's mood should guide you even more than in face-to-face conversation.

ANSWERING THE TELEPHONE

A simple "hello" is all that's needed when you answer the telephone. But do be sure you say it politely. No matter how frustrating your morning has been, it is unforgivable to snarl an ugly *"yes!"* or an aggressive *"hell-o!"*

Speak clearly and distinctly.

If someone has had the misfortune to dial incorrectly and gets you by mistake, be gracious about it. No need to bite his head off and hang up. Just say, "I think you have the wrong number—what number are you calling?"

If you are interrupted by the doorbell when you are on the phone, it is best, unless you are talking to a close friend who you know is not busy, to explain that someone is at the door and you will call back. The time it takes to give the cleaner the clothes and your instructions may seem only seconds to you but ages to the person tied to the other end of the line. Or if someone telephones while you have a visitor, it is considerate of both the visitor and the one who phones to say, "I'm sorry, Mary—I have a visitor just now. May I call you back?" (And *do* call back as soon as you're free!)

If you have a full-time or daily servant in the house, such as a butler or a housekeeper, he or she should answer the phone with "Mrs. Cotton's residence" or "Mrs. Cotton's apartment," ask "Who is calling, please?" and then summon you to the phone. The servant does not call or shout, but comes to where you are to announce that Mrs. Brooks is on the telephone. If you should be entertaining and the call is for the guest, the call will still be announced to you and you will tell your guest.

MAKING CALLS

Be sure first of all that you're calling the right number; and don't forget to dial the area code first if there is one. If you realize from the voice that you must have dialed incorrectly, say, "I'm sorry, I must have the wrong number." It is also courteous to say, "I'm sorry I troubled you."

Give the person at the other end enough time to answer. Twelve rings is not too many for a busy housewife who may be in the cellar or attic and perhaps doesn't even hear the phone until the fifth or sixth ring. As we all know, there is nothing more exasperating than to rush up or downstairs at risk of life and limb and find the line dead when we pick up the phone.

When you do have an answer to your call, identify yourself promptly. The "guess who" approach is a social liability. Say, "This is Marjorie Sparks," or if the phone has been answered by a servant or secretary, you might prefer to say that this is Mrs. Sparks. You would then ask to speak to Mr. or Mrs. whoever-you're-calling, using the last name.

Try to be considerate about the time of day you call. It's rude to call someone who works at night or keeps late hours at eight-thirty in the morning, even though you yourself may have been up since six-fifteen. And remember that if you call your attorney at five-twenty, you may, even though you are brief and businesslike when you get him, cause him to miss the five-fifty. The harassed mother of four would prefer to be called at a time when two are in school and two napping.

It is considerate to offer to pay for calls you make in another's home, but it isn't always easy to do this. It's simple enough if you are making a toll call. Dial the operator and tell her you would like to know the charges. After the call is finished, she will let you know the amount. Then you leave the money by the telephone. It is especially courteous to leave with it a little slip with the date, location, and amount of the call. This will prevent your hostess' blaming the phone company when the bill comes three weeks later and she *knows* she never called anybody in Kiplinger's Falls. If the call is a local one and your hostess, like most of us, is billed for these in message units, it is impractical and a bit patronizing to try to pay for it. Just keep such calls at a minimum and make them brief.

TELEPHONED INVITATIONS

Many of us extend and receive invitations over the telephone these days instead of using the most informal of notes. The invitation is extended simply and naturally as it would be in face-to-face conversation. Be direct—it is thoughtless and ungracious to begin with, "What are you and Jim doing Saturday night?" Instead say, "We're having a barbecue Saturday night—we do hope you and Jim can come."

If the invited guest cannot give a definite acceptance before consulting her husband, it is all right to say, "May I make sure that Jim hasn't made any plans? I'll call you back after dinner tonight." Then, of course, be sure you *do* call back when you said you would.

If you must refuse an invitation, remember it's always more polite to say why. In replying to a formal invitation, an expression of regret is enough, but over the phone as in face-to-face conversation, your reason—another engagement, forthcoming visit from relatives or whatever—ought to be given.

If you must leave a message about an invitation, be certain that the person who takes it has all the information: the date, the place, the time, the kind of party, and your telephone number. (Even if the person you are inviting knows your number as well as she does her own, having it right in front of her acts as an incentive to call it *now*.)

PARTY LINES

In heavily populated communities separate listings are the rule. In some rural communities and many summer resorts, however, party lines are common. It is, of course, very rude to talk at length on the party line, keeping two, three, or four families from making or receiving any calls. But it is unforgivable to refuse to get off the line when you are requested to do so in an emergency. In some cases and in some places, you may be breaking the law by refusing to let an emergency call go through, not to mention the burden of guilt you might have to carry should tragedy come about as a consequence of your selfishness.

11

Table Manners

TABLE MANNERS ARE MORE WORRIED ABOUT THAN THEY REALLY DE-
serve to be. Most of us have pretty good ones because we are considerate of others in the way in which we eat. It doen't matter if at a
very elaborate dinner party you are unfamiliar with some of the food
and some of the pieces of silver—you can always take your cue from
your hostess. But a pleasant table companion and a welcome diner-
out is one who eats with enjoyment and neatness. A messy or a
greedy eater may take away the appetite of others; a finicky, prissy
diner is not quite so hard on the appetite but may make others feel
stiff and self-conscious.

SITTING DOWN AT THE TABLE

If you are at a dinner party, wait for the hostess to tell you which
chair will be yours. The gentleman at your right will draw out your
chair. At informal dinners, such as those among close friends, the
seating may be more casual and the women will seat themselves.
In either case seat yourself as unobtrusively as possible, from whichever side of the chair is most convenient.

Unless you know the custom of the household, wait before you
take up your napkin or touch anything on the table to see if grace
will be said. In some families grace is said before every meal, in
others only on certain days. As a rule the head of the household says
the grace, but he may ask one of the guests to do so, particularly if
one of them is a churchman. Sometimes a child is asked to say it.
In Christian and Reform Jewish households, the custom is for the
guests at table to keep silent during the grace itself, bowing the

head, then each saying "Amen" at the end. Among Orthodox or Conservative Jewish families, everyone says the entire grace together, often at the end of the meal as well as the beginning.

NAPKINS

When the hostess unfolds her napkin, it is a signal for the guests to pick up theirs and put them in their laps. A small napkin is unfolded completely, a large one is half unfolded. The napkin shouldn't be tucked in the vest or neck of a dress. However, if you are wearing a gown of slippery material, it is better to anchor your napkin in some way that will be invisible above the table rather than forcing your partner to dive for it throughout the meal or finding it on the floor when you need it most.

Don't forget to *use* your napkin—not, of course, for taking something out of your mouth should that prove necessary, but for wiping your mouth frequently before drinking so that the glass will not show greasy smears. The napkin stays on your lap until everyone is finished, when you put it down casually, unfolded, beside your plate. If you are using a paper napkin, treat it as if it were cloth; don't crush it into a wad.

POSTURE WHILE EATING

Sit straight in your chair, but relaxed, not as if you were in the schoolroom. If there is not too much room between the place settings, you will of course be as careful as you can when you cut your meat not to jab your partner on either side with your elbows.

It used to be considered the height of rudeness to put elbows on the table. Nowadays everyone does it, but only *between courses*— it is still bad manners to have an elbow on the table while actually eating. And remember always that the food is brought to the mouth, not vice versa.

WHO IS SERVED FIRST

In the United States, there are three common ways of presenting a dish: to the hostess first, to the woman on the host's right, or to the guest of honor. *Good Housekeeping* prefers to serve the hostess first, in order to give a lead to any unsure guest. The other methods, however, are not incorrect. Of course, if the hostess is the only woman present, she will naturally be served first. If she is doing the serving herself from her place at the table, she fills her plate last.

WHEN TO START EATING

With four or six at the table, it is courteous and probably doesn't harm the food to wait until everyone has been served. If there are many people or if something has been served that ought to be eaten immediately, such as a soufflé, it is more considerate to begin as soon as two or three people have been served.

In a maidless household, it is incumbent upon those who have been served to use and pass on whatever is on the table for use with that portion of the meal, such as rolls, condiments for the curry, cream and sugar, and so on. If your neighbor holds the relish dish for you, help yourself and then hold the dish for him before you pass it on.

USE OF SILVER

If the table has been properly set, at a formal dinner always use the utensil farthest from the plate on either side first. After this course is finished, the silver is left on the plate neatly and securely so it will not drop off when the plate is removed to make room for the next course. The silver next in line from the plate is used now, but if you are in any doubt glance at your hostess to see which piece she is using.

It has long been the American custom to hold the fork in the left hand, the knife in the right, to cut meat. Then the knife is laid on the plate and the fork is changed to the right hand. Nowadays it is equally correct to keep the fork in the left hand and spear the pieces of meat with it, tines down.

The knife is only for cutting, spreading, or occasional use as a stop against which to push some elusive bit of food. The knife is never used to convey food to the mouth. When it is not in use, it is laid across the top of the plate—never propped against the edge.

At the end of the meat course, the knife and fork are laid side by side on the plate; the fork, tines up, nearest you; the knife beside it with its cutting edge turned toward you. Again, remember to place your silver firmly so it won't go clattering off when the plate is picked up.

Spoons are never left sticking out of cups. They belong in the saucer underneath. An exception to this is made in the case of soup spoons when the soup has been served in a soup plate. The spoon is then left in the plate with the handle to the right.

Occasionally, you may be served iced tea or coffee with the spoon in it and no saucer. In this case, you are obliged to leave the spoon in the glass, holding it between two fingers as you drink, or lay it on your plate.

Never put a piece of silver you have used into anything that is intended to serve others. Help yourself to the butter with the butter knife that should be there; use your own knife only if the proper utensil is lacking and then only if your knife is clean. It is perfectly proper to ask the hostess for a butter knife or other serving utensil if there is none. Sometimes the reason there is none is that an absent-minded guest deep in conversation has helped himself to something and unthinkingly kept the knife or spoon while passing on the dish. Try not to be one of these!

BUFFET MANNERS FOR THE GUEST

The buffet more and more plays an important part in our entertaining. Guests can do a great deal to make or mar the success of the meal. A woman guest will always be welcome if she can be counted on to help get the others moving into the dining room

when the hostess has indicated the meal is ready. Of course, it is impossible for everyone to help himself at once—though this surely does not account for the universal reluctance of buffet guests even to begin! Buffets are, or should be, arranged so that several people can move around the table at once. The others can chat in line just as well as in the living room, where the maidless hostess or her husband will be trying to clear away the cocktail things and swiftly set up little tables.

A buffet guest picks up napkin, fork, and plate, then helps himself to any or all of the various dishes arranged around the table. Then he carries his plate to the living room, selects a place to sit, and begins his meal. When he has finished, he goes back and takes a second helping if he likes and the hostess has suggested it. A spirit of informality and mutual helpfulness pervades a buffet dinner. Guests often serve each other as they take turns at the buffet table, and when it's time for seconds, men—and sometimes women too—may offer to replenish another guest's plate. After the main course is finished, each guest takes his plate and fork to wherever the hostess wants the used things—or she may take them herself—helps himself to dessert, and goes back to where he was sitting.

HOW TO EAT

To savor your food is not only good manners but also good sense. Eat slowly enough to give your palate time for the subtleties of the special sauce or the deliciousness of the sliced steak. Don't wash down your food with water. Don't take huge mouthfuls of food, and don't be overly genteel by taking tiny bits and nibbling. Chew your food quietly with your mouth closed, and don't talk while chewing.

Don't mess your food around on the plate with your fork or stir different things together. (If you like to eat turkey dressing and gravy at the same time, pick up some dressing on the fork and dip it into a little of the gravy on your plate.)

It is untidy and somewhat childish to cut up all your meat at once. Rather, cut a bite or two at a time. It is, of course, perfectly all right to cut up your children's meat for them, and all at once.

There is nothing wrong with eating everything on your plate if you want it, as long as you don't do this by attacking your food as if it were your last meal. If you want to mop up the last of something, like a delicious sauce or gravy, it is all right to drop a small piece of bread into it and then pick up the bread with your fork. But don't use your fingertips.

Soup served in a soup plate is eaten from the soup spoon, which you fill by pushing it away from you rather than toward you. It is all right to tip the dish a bit to help fill the spoon, but tip it away from you.

Soup served in a cup is drunk from the cup. A spoon is usually served with it (a bouillon spoon rather than a soup spoon, correctly). This is to use at the beginning when the soup may be too hot to drink, and at the end to reach the vegetables or noodles at the bottom of the cup.

MISHAPS AT THE TABLE

Mistakes or accidents can happen to anybody and have happened to most of us. We deal with them as best we can and try not to make them worse by repeated apologies to a company which is perfectly willing to forget and prefers to do so.

If you have to cough, go ahead and get it over with, using your handkerchief or napkin to cover your mouth. But should you have a real seizure of coughing or choke on something, just leave the table; your excuses can wait until you come back with a usable voice. The same applies to one of those whooping sneezing fits that allergies can bring on. If you are subject to these, do have some of your medication with you wherever you go.

If your allergy is caused by certain specific foods you must of course avoid them. By all means simply say, "No, thank you" to such a food. If it happens to be the main dish, you may *have* to take some or cause no end of consternation on the hostess' part, but you can always put it to one side of your plate and leave it severely alone. If you make no comment and busy yourself with the foods you *can* eat, it will probably pass without comment.

If you are on a diet, don't bring up the subject—just do the best you can and resolve to deprive yourself of those extra calories tomorrow.

If you have the misfortune to be served something that nobody would be expected to eat, such as a spoiled clam or a piece of bone or eggshell where none should be, get it out of your mouth (with fingers if it's small enough, otherwise with spoon or fork) and back on the plate as inconspicuously as you can, and hide it with a piece of bread or other food.

Olive pits, cherry pits, bits of bone, and so on you just take out of your mouth and put on the edge of your plate. If you ate the food with your fingers, take out the pit, seed or bone with your fingers; if you ate it with a spoon, you may use your lips to put it back on the spoon and thence to the plate, or you may transfer it from mouth to hand to plate.

WHEN A MAID SERVES

When the maid comes to your left side and extends the dish for you to help yourself, pick up the serving spoon in your right hand, the serving fork (if there is one) in your left, and pick up the portion nearest you, using the spoon to support it and the fork to steady it. If only the serving spoon appears, it means (or should mean) that you don't need a fork but can just dip the spoon in and help yourself. When things are served in pieces, such as chicken, it is a great temptation if you are dieting to scout around for a small piece, but this is just as bad manners as surveying the platter for the biggest; best take what's nearest you and don't eat it all.

Naturally, you don't ask the maid for anything yourself. If you need something, ask the hostess.

It is not necessary to say "Thank you" to the maid each time she serves you. It is more pleasant, however, when refusing a serving to say "No, thank you," rather than just shake your head.

CONVERSATION AT THE TABLE

It is obligatory at a dinner party and comes naturally enough at any meal to make agreeable talk with your neighbors. At a small dinner, talking across the table as well as to your neighbors on your right and left is easy; at a large table this is inconvenient, if not impossible. It is naturally expected that you will chat with your dinner neighbors each in turn. It's rude to try to talk more than very briefly across one of them to a guest several seats away.

THE ROLE OF THE HOSTESS

The hostess is also engaged in conversation with her neighbors to left and right. Nevertheless, she is always aware of the progress of the meal and alert to her guests' needs. She does not urge a guest to take more of the lamb, the wine, or anything else that he has refused. She times the eating of her own meal so that she finishes at about the same time as everyone else. If there is no maid, she sees that dishes, bread, and so on are passed to those who are ready for them. At the dinner's end it is she who suggests leaving the table.

DESSERT AND FINGERBOWL SERVICE

Sometimes when the dinner is served by a maid, the dessert silver is placed on the dessert plate and set in front of the guest before the dessert itself is passed. In this case, the guest simply picks up the fork in the left hand and the spoon in the right and sets them down to right and left of his plate. If, in addition to the silver, there is also a fingerbowl and doily on the plate, he lifts up bowl and doily and places them at the left of his plate above the fork.

If fingerbowls are served with any course other than dessert, such as lobster, they appear on a plate with doily but without silver. The guest places plate and bowl on his left and uses it as he needs it. At the end of the course it is removed.

After the dessert is eaten, the guest dips his fingertips in the water, one hand at a time, and dries them on his napkin.

FOODS THAT ARE DIFFICULT TO EAT

There is no need for any of us to be embarrassed when we are confronted with some food we don't know how to tackle. If out of cowardice we leave it practically untouched, we may be missing a real eating experience. It is never wrong to ask, "How does one eat this?" If you feel self-conscious about doing that, watch your hostess and follow suit. (See also How to Eat Difficult Foods in the section called Helpful How-to's at the end of this book.)

12

Dining at a Restaurant

AT CASUAL EATING PLACES SUCH AS DINERS, LUNCH COUNTERS, CAF-
eterias, our manners are informal and so is the service. We pick
our own table, hang up our own wraps, give our order, leave a
tip, and pay the cashier as we go out. In more elegant dining places,
we expect and get more service and by the same token more formality is expected of us.

CHECKING YOUR COAT

On first entering a restaurant, a man checks his hat and over-
coat or topcoat, together with rubbers and umbrella if any, plus his
briefcase and packages. A woman often does not check her coat,
although she may, but she will check her raincoat and umbrella
and any books or packages she may have.

FINDING A TABLE

This is something you don't do for yourself in a restaurant, as
opposed to a lunchroom or diner. You stand in the doorway expectantly and someone—a headwaiter or a hostess, possibly the pro-
prietor—will seat you. If the place is very busy, it may take you a
few minutes to catch this person's eye; when you do, he will come
over and, after asking you how many are in your party, will lead you
to a table. Once a couple has come under the headwaiter's pilotage,
the man lets the woman precede him.

If the table is unsatisfactory—right next door to the kitchen or
directly in a draft—it is perfectly in order for the man to ask for

another, although if there are only a few empty tables and those are reserved, he may have to take it or go elsewhere.

RESERVING A TABLE

If the restaurant you are planning to go to is popular, it's a good idea to spare yourself disappointment by telephoning and reserving a table in your name for your party of so many at such-and-such a time. When you do this, be sure to get to the restaurant quite close to the time you asked for.

SEATING

The headwaiter will usually seat the woman and help her off with her coat if she hasn't checked it; if he doesn't, the man should do it for her. If two or more couples are dining together, they should seat themselves so as to alternate men and women.

If a couple sits in a booth, they may sit across from each other or side by side. If they choose to sit beside each other, the man takes the outside seat. If their table for two has one sofa seat against the wall and one outside chair, the woman takes the sofa. If, as is often the case, the sofa seat provides room for both, they sit side by side, the woman entering first as the waiter pulls the table out.

THE MENU

It is important for the man to have some idea in advance of the price range in the restaurant he has selected. Unless he has plenty of money, if everything is à la carte and very expensive, his evening and possibly hers may be quite spoiled. If a couple should unknowingly choose a restaurant whose prices are far too high—or worse still, where no price mark is to be seen anywhere on the menu—there is nothing wrong with telling the waiter that they have changed their minds and are leaving.

The expression "à la carte" means that you pay for each separate item. Therefore a meal of many courses may be extremely expensive if ordered à la carte. On the other hand, if you want only the main dish, a salad, and coffee, you may very well get that à la carte for less than a full course dinner ordered from the table d'hôte selections.

"Table d'hôte" means that you pay a fixed price for the entire meal. There are usually a number of these meals with a selection among several items for the first course and for dessert, the price of the meal being indicated by the price of the main course or entree. On the menu these meals may be in a group headed "Dinner" or "Luncheon" or "Special for Today." If you like a number of courses, a table d'hôte meal is usually a good buy. Don't forget, however, that if you should want to substitute a shrimp cocktail, say, for the allotted fruit cocktail, you will probably have to pay extra.

ORDERING

When a man is taking a woman to dinner, he always does the ordering. If there are to be cocktails, he orders them before giving any meal order, and if it is likely there may be another round of cock-

tails, he indicates to the waiter that he will order the meal later on, probably doing so when the second cocktail is served.

When it comes to ordering the meal itself, the man always consults the woman's preferences. It is quite all right for her to ask the waiter questions about various dishes if she likes. (There's no need for anyone to feel shy because he doesn't know the meaning of every term on the menu. Just ask the waiter how the chicken Christina is prepared and he'll tell you. For your guidance, however, a list of terms you might find on a menu featuring French cuisine is given in the Helpful How-to's section at the end of this book.)

A woman should remember that while it is quite all right, especially where the cuisine is rather special, to deliberate over the menu, it is inconsiderate for her to ignore the subject until everyone else has decided and *then* begin her musings.

Once the woman has made her selection, she tells the man and he tells the waiter, giving first her order, then his.

The only time a woman escorted by a man gives her order directly to the waiter is when the group is so large that to avoid confusion the waiter takes all the orders individually. When women are dining or lunching together, each gives her order to the waiter, unless there is a hostess, in which case she takes over the ordering just as a man would.

Men dining or lunching together give their orders separately to the waiter. If one man is host, he usually limits his hostly efforts to suggesting a possible cocktail and being sure to get the check when it comes.

WINE

The man, of course, orders the wine, if any, from the wine list, which he asks for if it is not offered him. If he is not familiar with wines he may ask the waiter what he would recommend with the food that has been ordered. A half-bottle, if available in the wine of his choice, is generally enough for two. When the party is large, the same wine is usually drunk by everyone, even though some may be having meat (red wine is best) and some fish (white wine is preferred).

THE WAITER

In a well-run restaurant, shortly after the headwaiter has seated you, a waiter will come to your table to take your order. (He may be preceded by a bus boy, who fills your water glasses, sets the table if it is not already set, and brings the bread, but does not take meal or drink orders.) When you need the waiter's services after ordering, you catch his eye and beckon him with a nod or an upraised hand. Sometimes it seems impossible to catch that eye—in such a case you wait your chance and when he passes close to you, call "Waiter!" You don't call "boy." And if it should be a waitress who has served you, call "Waitress" rather than "Miss."

SERVICE

In any good restaurant you should expect and will get good service if you know what you want and show that you do without being unrealistic or overbearing. If you do have a complaint, make it quietly but firmly to the waiter or the headwaiter. It is not neces-

sary or desirable to raise your voice or make a scene. On the other hand, there is no reason to meekly accept the frogs' legs Marseillaise when you ordered the Provençal, or rare beef when you ordered it well done.

PAYING THE CHECK

When the meal is over the man gets the waiter's attention and asks for the check, which is then brought him face down on a small tray. Holding it in such a way that he does not seem to be showing the total to his guest, he quickly checks the addition. There is every reason why he should check it and none why he should not, but he shouldn't take so long over it that he looks like a penny pincher and makes his guests uncomfortable. If there is a mistake, in his favor or the restaurant's, he quietly calls the waiter's attention to it and when it has been corrected, puts the check and the money on the plate. He will leave enough money to cover or more than cover the tip for the waiter. (The bus boy is not tipped.)

If the meal is to be charged, after checking the bill the man either just signs it on its face (when he has an individual charge) or puts his credit card or charge booklet on the tray with the check after signing it. In these cases the tip is taken care of in one of three ways: the man has the necessary bills and change for the tip and leaves it on the plate when the credit card is returned to him; or he designates above his signature on the check the amount he wishes to leave as a tip and so charges the tip as well as the cost of the meal; or he puts a bill on the plate when signing and asks for change to be brought, out of which he leaves the tip.

Should the check say "Please pay cashier," the tip is left on the table; if the man is without proper change, he comes back to the table and leaves the tip from change the cashier has given him.

Bills or silver or both may be used for tipping. It is somehow patronizing to leave two or three pennies among the coins, but five is all right.

The amount of the tip to the waiter is a minimum of 15 per cent. In metropolitan cities and in very fine restaurants 20 per cent is expected provided you have had good service. If your party has been large or you have had an expensive meal, between fifteen and twenty dollars or over, 15 per cent is enough.

For tipping at counters, diners, lunchrooms, and so on, see the section on tipping in Helpful How-To's at the end of the book.

SEPARATE CHECKS

It is perfectly in order for several men or several women lunching or dining together to ask for separate checks. When there is only one check, try not to make too much of a production about who owes what. Each person should figure up mentally what he had (not forgetting drinks), add the tip and tax, if any, and hand his total to whichever companion is handling the payment. It's often easier to divide the check equally, after adding the amount of the tip. Whatever trouble arises in this operation usually comes about because someone has nothing smaller than a ten. In such a case, let that person take care of the check and the others pay him or her. If change making becomes an acute problem, the waiter may be asked to bring change and the check settled when that has arrived. It is very courteous, by the way, if you know you are going to be a member of a Dutch treat group, to make sure beforehand that you have singles and silver.

LEAVING THE RESTAURANT

When the meal is over and the bill paid, the man helps the woman with her coat, then follows her out of the dining room to the coat room or hat-check bar, where she waits while he claims his things, hers too if she left any. When they are ready for the street, he tips the hat-check girl and the couple leave together, the man holding the door open for the lady. If the weather is very bad, she may wait inside until her escort or the doorman has flagged a taxi.

13

Entertaining Away from Home

IN A RESTAURANT

Taking your guests out to dinner is often done nowadays. When you have house guests for the weekend, it makes a pleasant change of scene for them and gives the maidless hostess a breathing spell. To take guests from out of town to a special restaurant honors them as much as dinner in your own home. And, of course, restaurant hospitality is a godsend with unexpected dinner guests when notice has been short and the larder is not at its best.

Restaurant entertaining is perfectly acceptable as long as the host and hostess remember that they must be just as alert as they would at a formal dinner at home to see to it that the food and service are good and the guests are made happy.

In general, matters proceed as described in Chapter 12, but there are some additional responsibilities which the host in particular assumes. The hostess too, of course, will see that guests meet each other and that nobody is overlooked conversationally; and she will have done some of the initial planning with her husband. She may also have to call her husband's attention to some needed service so he can tell the waiter. But once in the restaurant, it is the man who for the most part is in command of the ship.

It is always wise to reserve a table when you are taking guests to dinner.

MEETING

The careful host will have made sure that guests who have been asked to meet at the restaurant are certain of its location, the time and the exact spot. Many excellent restaurants are small enough so that it would be hard for the guests *not* to find their host and hostess, but in a large hotel or other place where there may be one or more entrances, specify which entrance, which dining room, or which bar. The host and hostess will, of course, be there a good ten or fifteen minutes before the time set. If the bar is the meeting place—and this is often a good idea because it prevents the awkwardness of standing or sitting around waiting for the inevitable stragglers —the host orders for each arrival his choice of drink. If a drink is refused, the host does not insist. Most bars will serve plain tomato juice if wanted, or a "horse's neck"—ginger ale with a strip of lemon peel.

When everybody or practically everybody has come (it is impolite to keep the whole party waiting for a really late arrival), the host or the hostess will suggest that they all go to the table. A good moment to select for the move is when nearly everyone has finished his drink, because in many places guests are not allowed (aside from the looks of it) to carry their drinks to the table. The waiter will bring unfinished or just-ordered drinks to the table.

The host is in luck if everyone has come more or less on time. If someone still has not arrived it is up to him to wait by the door to the dining room unless he can keep it in view from the table, and go to meet the late-comers when he spies them.

SEATING

Seating as you might prefer it at home must often be disregarded in a restaurant because hardly ever will all the seats for a large party be equally desirable. If the seat to the right of the host or hostess is a good one—facing the other diners, on the banquette, or overlooking the ocean view—then the guest of honor will be asked to sit there. Otherwise, the women should be placed in the best seats and the men alternated between them as far as that is possible. The host or hostess may direct the seating.

ORDERING

It makes for a smoothly run party with the maximum of good conversation to order the entire dinner, with its wines if any, in advance of the party. (Predinner drinks, of course, are not so ordered —at bar or table the host asks what the guests would like and gives the order to the waiter.) Preordering has several advantages. If you know the restaurant's best dishes, you can be sure that every guest's meal is equally good, the flurry of many individual orders is avoided, and the wine is more likely to be just right. You can usually also pay in advance for a preordered meal and avoid the bother of check and tips. In such a case the host takes care of the bar bill just before the group goes into the dining room, or adds the proper amount, plus the bar tip, to his check.

A preordered dinner has an air of formality which may not suit a particular group. Then too some people feel that part of the fun of dining out is being able to choose. Should you, as host, feel this way, you will order the meal at table after giving your guests time to study the menu, making recommendations about special dishes if you want to. Then the host may give the orders to the waiter; if the party is large, it is just as correct and much easier for the waiter to go from person to person and take individual orders.

The host will give the wine order for the entire table once he knows what the prevailing choice of main course is. (It behooves him to listen to the orders if the waiter is taking them separately.) He would probably select a white wine or rosé if both fish and meat dishes have been ordered. If everybody is eating meat, he could select a red wine or quite properly the rosé. Champagne could also be served throughout the dinner. It is well to remember that in much continental cuisine chicken and other things which might ordinarily call for a white wine have been cooked in a red wine—if several people have ordered something like this (the waiter will know how it was prepared) a red wine would suit everybody's meal.

In some restaurants, the platters or serving dishes are presented to the host before they are passed to the guests. This is simply a gesture silently requesting the host's approval—he does not help himself, but simply nods or he may say, "very nice."

When the meal has been ordered at the table and the check is presented at the end, the host is supposed to deal with it as unobtrusively as possible. As always, if there is any mistake in the bill, the host will quietly straighten it out with the waiter, but if a real disagreement arises the host must not spoil the evening for his guests with a scene, though he may resolve to straighten out the matter with the management the next day or mentally blacklist the dining place.

LEAVING THE TABLE

The hostess is the one who gives the signal to rise by getting up herself when she has managed to attract the attention of the other women guests. The women join the hostess in leaving the dining room, the men following.

ENTERTAINING AT A NIGHT CLUB

When you are entertaining a party at a night club, it is usually wise to make a reservation in advance, mentioning the number of guests and making as sure as you can that the location of your table will be a good one. If you find that your table is well placed, it is prudent for the future to show your appreciation with a tip to the head waiter.

On the other hand, if you find your party has been assigned to a table by the service door or out of sight of the floor show, quietly ask to be changed to another table. Should your request be refused, you may leave and take your chances at another night spot. However, if some of your guests are to join you there, you have no choice but to accept the table, at least until they all arrive, and ask to be moved to a better location later. No doubt you will cross that place off your list for the future. As with any other reservation, you should plan to claim the table quite promptly at the time you set.

In seating, the women should of course be given the places where they can most comfortably see the floor show. The men, who may be faced away from it, can turn their chairs around or shift themselves in their seats with only the briefest apology for temporarily turning their backs on the ladies.

When there is dancing, it is important that the host dance with each woman guest. He starts with the woman guest of honor if there is one, and dances last with his wife.

ENTERTAINING AT THE THEATER

At this sort of party the host and hostess have the least responsibility at the event itself, but they will naturally have planned carefully by buying the tickets in advance, and by making as sure as they can that the party arrives at the theater before curtain time. Often you will have dined with your guests first and taken them to

the theater by cab. The host is of course responsible for the cab fare for the group he is with. If it is necessary to take several cabs to accommodate the entire party, male guests will take care of the fare in the other cabs. It is better for the host just to thank such guests than to offer to reimburse them.

If you are not dining with your guests first, you arrange to meet them in the theater lobby. You arrive there of course ahead of time. The guests should be ahead of time, too. They are guilty of very bad manners if they are not.

With tickets in hand, you collect your guests and let them precede you past the ticket taker. Then locate an usher, give him the ticket stubs, and let the party follow him down the aisle, ladies first, you at the end. There is no special rule about seating except that the host always takes the aisle seat (or the one nearest the aisle) and goes in last. If there is time, it is a good idea to alternate men and women. Should you have the misfortune to arrive as the curtain is going up, the courteous thing is to get everybody seated as fast as you can and, above all, silently.

If your seats are not all together, arrangements are made (in the lobby whenever possible) to divide the party into two groups, the hostess going with one set and taking charge of their tickets, the host with the other.

When you have a box, the women are seated in the front, the men in the back.

If the host and hostess think the evening still young at the play's end and want to go on for a nightcap nearby or perhaps to a night club, it is up to the host to suggest this. It is not any guest's prerogative to promote such an idea, because it would actually be a continuation of the party and the host would feel obligated to pay. There are occasions, however, particularly among close friends, where a guest may suggest to the host that the others be *his* guests for a drink somewhere and the host may gracefully yield.

14

When You Entertain at Home

ONE OF THE MOST VALUABLE KEYS TO SUCCESSFUL HOME ENTERTAINING is a very special sort of preparation, preparation that begins well ahead even of the guest list or the menu. It begins with you, the hostess! There are a few individuals who love to give parties, any time for any reason, or for no reason at all. Such people are perpetually prepared. But if like most of us you are more variable in mood, or are inexperienced and perhaps apprehensive about the responsibilities of entertaining, you need to help yourself into a party frame of mind. Assure yourself that *you* are going to have a good time at this party, that you're looking forward to getting ready for it, and can hardly wait for the people to come. Then *act* that way as you clean the silver and make your lists. Even though you may have to assume this attitude consciously in the beginning, it will take hold. As you go ahead with your invitations and your menu planning, you will find you really do look forward to the party— and the enthusiasm when you greet your guests will be real and contagious. You'll *all* have a good time!

The first step in actual party preparation is to decide what kind of party you'll have and make up the guest list. If you are having a cocktail party or a buffet, you can have as many guests as your living and dining room will accommodate comfortably; if it's to be a dinner at table and you have no maid, four or six guests probably should be the limit. At a large party you can mix many kinds of people; at a small dinner it is best to have people who know each other at least slightly, although it adds zest to have a new face or two.

Invite your guests by telephone or note for whatever hour suits you best—six-thirty or seven if that's easy for you, seven-thirty or eight if you have small children to feed and put to bed, if you are a working wife, or if you just like a late dinner. As to the date —well, impromptu dinner parties are fun, but if you have planned the mixture of guests quite carefully it's best to give them advance notice of a week or ten days.

Next comes your house. Several days in advance of the party give it a keenly critical examination for things that may need special attention. Newly washed plant leaves, gleaming andirons, and freshly polished furniture make a room sparkle. Make sure you have plenty of good-sized ashtrays. Check your flat silver and any silver serving dishes you will use and clean them if they need it. When you have planned your menu, check the plates for it. If they're seldom in use, they may need to be washed. Take out the linens you plan to use to see that your cloth and napkins are fresh and not dog-eared from lying in the drawer. Housecleaning will have to be done the day before the party, but it helps to have these time-consuming extras out of the way. Next in the planning comes the menu. What you have to eat depends, of course, on what kind of party it is and whether or not you will have help.

DINNER AT TABLE WITHOUT A MAID

If you are maidless, be sure that the menu is one that can be at least partly fixed ahead of time, with foods that need as little last-minute attention as possible and will stand waiting. Two courses are enough, especially if you plan to have several good things to eat with cocktails. You can have a meat-vegetable-and-potatoes-meal (but better select a meat that doesn't require gravy because this is a last-minute chore that takes you away from your guests) with dessert, or easier still and just as good, a casserole, salad, and dessert. Hot rolls buttered in the kitchen (like the butterflake kind, buttered before heating) or herb bread or garlic bread are all delicious and eliminate bread-and-butter plates. If you serve garlic bread, it is best to use plain butter on at least half a loaf for the people who do not like or cannot eat garlic in any form.

WHEN SPECIAL MENUS ARE CALLED FOR

Whether the party is to be a buffet supper for a crowd or a sit-down dinner or some other affair, such as a reception, there are times when some of the guests may present the hostess with difficulties in devising an appropriate menu. No matter how good the food may taste, no truly welcoming hostess wants ever, if she can help it, to set before a guest food which for medical or religious reasons he cannot or should not eat.

For example, food allergies are quite common these days. In most cases, the hostess doesn't know about an individual allergy and doesn't need to—the guest is his own censor. In other cases, the reaction to a particular food may be so devastating that the hostess is warned beforehand by the prudent—and considerate—guest. When Abby Bernhard, for example, alerts you that mushrooms are like pure poison to her husband Jim, without a second's thought you will naturally cancel the mushrooms flambés with wild rice you'd planned. Further than that, you'll scan every item of your substitute menu with an eagle eye, crossing out any casserole that calls for cream-of-mushroom soup and carefully checking the label of any other cans or freezer packs you might ordinarily use.

Many a gifted hostess keeps a record of what she served to whom —and when. This not only keeps her from giving the same people her curry dinner twice in succession, but also reminds her (or should) that mushrooms are out for Jim B., that Joe Daly carefully pushed aside the avocado in his salad, and that *everybody,* even the meat-and-potatoes men, seems to love that ham-and-bean casserole.

Most hostesses, when they know a guest is on a special diet such as that for diabetes, ask what he is allowed to eat at the time they invite him. In most cases the guest replies that he shouldn't have starches and sweets, say, but urges the hostess to go ahead and have whatever she ordinarily would, adding, "You'll understand if I skip the potatoes and dessert." (This in effect gives the hostess *carte blanche,* but if she is very considerate she will try to avoid serving very rich or creamed dishes.) When someone's diet is extremely restricted, no hostess is required to play the role of hospital dietician—the guest will either decline or decide to eat what he can—and say nothing.

A hostess isn't expected to pay obsequious attention to the needs of guests who are reducing, especially those who diet "off and on." The slimming guest is expected to do her own disciplining, and that without fanfare. At an informal meal, however, when several of the guests may be trying to shed pounds (perhaps even the host and hostess themselves!), it can be fun, as well as especially courteous, to see how good a meal you can put together with a minimum of calories.

Still other skills in menu planning are called for in entertaining guests from other countries, who are often of other faiths as well. In these times of widening world horizons, hostesses may with increasing frequency be called upon to entertain a visiting lecturer, an exchange student, a new delegate to the UN and his shy wife, who may come from the Middle East, the Far East, Africa—almost any spot on the globe. One wants to make them welcome, to make them feel at least a little bit at home in this bustling and somewhat frightening land of ours. Food, of course, is the age-old symbol of hospitality—but what shall we prepare for these new friends that will not violate their religious rules or upset the dietary habits of a lifetime, especially when so often we may not be sure just what those are?

Very few hostesses could unhesitatingly select an ideal menu for any national from a far-away place (except, perhaps, one who has for some years been accustomed to Western food as well as Western ways). So much depends on what part of his country he comes from, what his religion is, and how much of an opportunity he has had to orient himself. In many cases, especially with exchange students, the organization that directly or indirectly brought hosts and guests together will be able to give you sensible answers about what to serve and what not to.

If no such source of information is available, it is perfectly correct to ask your prospective guest. As a rule he will be so very polite that you'll have to pin him down with specific questions. "Do you eat meat?" "How about fish?" Either question can be answered by yes or no, and the replies give you something to go on. If both answers are in the negative, you know that your main dish should be a vegetarian one—that is, macaroni and cheese, a meatless chow mein, or a bean casserole.

If you have no opportunity to question your guest, or are entertaining a whole group of nationals of various countries, it's safe to follow the example of the diplomat's wife, who often gives parties of this kind. Her basic rule is to provide enough variety so that there will be *something* the guest can drink and *something* he can eat, no matter what the limitations of his diet.

Moslems and some others never drink anything alcoholic, and they almost invariably prefer fruit juice to tomato juice, though it might be best to serve both. Hindus and certain other sects eat no meat of any kind. Among those who do eat meat, certain peoples from the Middle and Far East are most accustomed to lamb, some from the Far East especially are more at home with chicken, and many eat both. Rice is, of course, a staple and usually a favorite food over much of the Eastern Hemisphere. Vegetables, fruits, and practically any dessert (minus alcoholic flavoring) are usually acceptable. So it's hospitable to provide *both* alcoholic and nonalcoholic drinks, one meat dish and one meatless dish, plus rice in some form, vegetable or salad, and dessert, with strong coffee, and possibly tea also.

And don't overlook the necessity of tactfully indicating to the guest what's in any dish whose contents are not obvious at first glance. For instance, at a buffet the host or hostess might escort a guest to the table and say, "This one is chicken and rice—and here's cold salmon. Or if you prefer a vegetarian dish, there's one down at the other end of the table."

When a hostess invites to her table American friends of a faith other than her own, then, too, of course, she wants to make sure that the food she provides is not only good to eat but violates none of her guests' religious observances or dietary laws.

Most non-Catholics know that those of the Catholic faith, as well as Anglicans and many other Protestants, eat no meat on Friday or on fast days in Lent. Therefore when they're invited to dine on a Friday or a fast day, you should either serve fish as your main course or provide the Catholic guest with a special non-meat portion—the former is, perhaps, more courteous since it makes the guest less conspicuous.

It sometimes happens that a hostess who isn't Catholic invites a Catholic guest for a non-Lenten Wednesday, but it turns out that that particular day happens to be an Ember Day, which also calls for fasting. In this case, the Catholic usually says, "Oh, I'd love to, but that's a fast day for me—won't you ask me another time?" This leaves the way open for the hostess to choose, with perfect propriety, between asking that guest another time or deciding to alter her menu. In the latter case, she not only urges the guest to come, but assures her that she will not have to break her fast.

Many Christian hostesses are uncertain about just what to serve their Jewish friends. This is partly because not all Jews observe the dietary laws with equal rigidity. Reform Jews are the most liberal in this respect and Orthodox Jews the most observant, with Conservatives taking a median position. The average Christian hostess is seldom faced with the necessity of serving a suitable meal to a guest who is strictly Orthodox, for Orthodox Jews know that it is all but impossible for any but an Orthodox household to follow the dietary laws to the letter, and so they more often than not decline the invitation.

Most non-Jews know that no pork in any form is permitted under the dietary laws, but they may not always realize that the emotional holdover of the tradition may make it somewhat distasteful even to those who no longer abide by many of the prohibitions. There are, of course, other foods that may come under this category—many sea foods, for instance, including shrimp, lobster, oysters, clams, octopus, and, in fact, any "fish" which has neither fins nor scales. Frogs' legs and snails are also banned. And insects too—which rules out "conversation piece" tidbits like grasshoppers and chocolate-covered ants.

Many Reform and some Conservative Jews, as we have said, no longer adhere to these prohibitions, or only to some of them. But in the name of true hospitality, a Christian hostess would not serve any of these foods to Jewish friends unless she is positive that they will be acceptable.

GETTING READY

Now make out your marketing list. Shop the day before the party, and do as much of the dinner preparation as you can, such as trimming the salad greens and making the dessert, on that day too. Many casseroles can be partially prepared the day before. So can some kinds of hors d'oeuvres, such as those that require chilling before slicing.

The day of the party, sally out early and buy your flowers. You can, of course, do this the afternoon before if you have more time then. Just cut the stems and plunge the blooms deep into cool water to stay there overnight. Unless you are a master flower arranger, you will probably want to make your table arrangement and any others you expect to use early on the party day while you are fresh and not rushed. Should some emergency arise so you run behind schedule, you can always ask your first-to-arrive woman guest to give you a hand with the hors d'oeuvres, but flower arranging is too demanding and too messy for a last-minute job.

Now lay your cloth or mats on the table, put your arrangement on it, and set the table. (See Chapter 19, "Table Settings.") Plan the seating and make a mental note of it or write it down on a slip in the kitchen for last-minute reference.

Many people find it helpful to make out not only a marketing list and a seating list, but also a what-to-do-when list with tasks written down in the order of doing. It might go something like this:

A. M. arrange flowers
tidy up house
set table
make garlic butter
prepare casserole
prepare salad greens
get out all plates and serving dishes
P. M. make salad dressing
fix canapés
butter garlic bread

Late-day chores such as tossing the salad and completing the cooking of the casserole you time by working backwards from the probable dinner hour, allowing, of course, enough time for cock-

tails. Not the least important part of your preparations is to plan some leeway—an hour if possible—for resting and changing before the guests arrive.

You or your husband or both will, of course, greet the guests at the door. While he mixes drinks for them, you talk with them; when he brings the drinks in, you can slip out and bring in the hors d'oeuvres. Pass the tray around once or twice and then put it down where it is not in the way but available for the guests to help themselves, which you encourage them to do. Sometimes guests just don't; in that case, you or your husband or the children may pass the tray at intervals.

Just before you are ready to announce dinner, check the table. Light the candles, fill the water glasses, see that butter is served if needed, and put the first course on the table. Then you go back to the living room, wait for a convenient break in the conversation, and ask your guests to come in to dinner. The women will follow you first, then the men.

SEATING

Seating at a maidless dinner follows the usual procedure—the most important woman guest (this may be the guest of honor, the oldest guest, or one who is visiting your house for the first time) will be placed at your husband's right, and the corresponding man at your right. After this, alternate men and women around the table, separating married couples when possible. This is difficult to do with eight people—you may have to sit elsewhere than at the end of the table to make the seating come out properly. See the seating diagrams below:

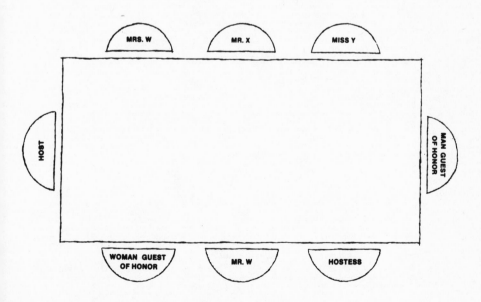

The drawing below shows the seating for a party of ten with guests of honor (who may or may not be husband and wife) alternates men and women and separates husbands and wives. It may be used for six as well as for ten, but not for any multiple of four. Using this arrangement for a party of eight or twelve, it would not be possible to alternate men and women.

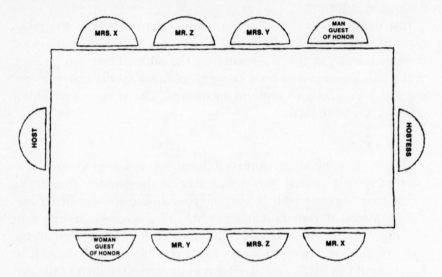

When there is no host. Both male and female guests of honor would be seated at the right of the hostess, even though they might be man and wife and would be sitting next to each other.

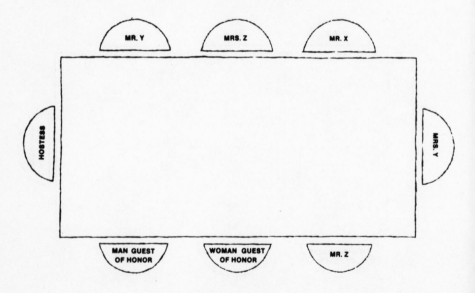

When there is no hostess. In this case the host places the guests of honor at his right whether or not they happen to be man and wife.

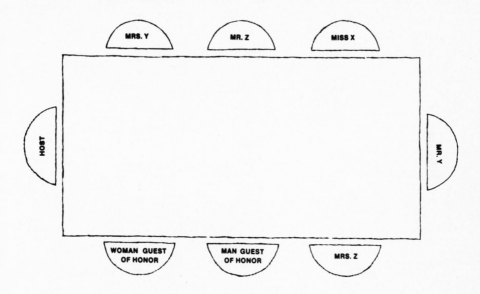

At the table below, Mr. and Mrs. Z (or some other couple) must sit next to each other. It would be preferable (from the point of view of seating only) to invite an unmarried couple, say Miss Y and Mr. X instead of the Z's.

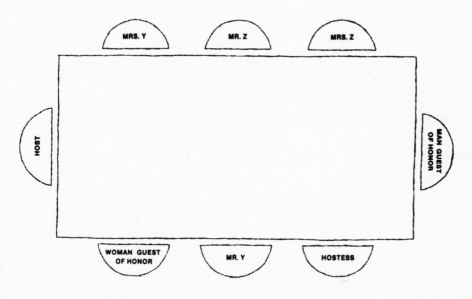

At a table which is to seat any multiple of four, the hostess cannot sit opposite the host but must sit at the side of the table, placing the guest of honor (or some other man if there is no guest of honor) at her right, which puts *him* at the end of the table opposite the host. (Note that it is always the hostess who gives up her place, never the host.)

If there are no guests of honor as such, the two honored places would fall to any couple.

Should there be only four at table, the hostess automatically places the male guest at her right, the woman at her left.

For a dinner of more than eight, it is helpful and appropriate to use place cards, For eight or six, place cards might look pretentious, though if you find it difficult to remember the seating plan swiftly and easily you *could* use place cards for eight. With or without place cards, it's a good idea to refer to your seating diagram privately just before you call the guests to the table.

The main dish, whether meat or casserole, goes in front of the host with carving fork and knife if needed or with serving spoons. The carving utensils—knife, fork, and steel—are placed to the host's right, fork nearest him with tines down, knife next, with blade-edge pointing left, and steel last. Many hosts prefer to sharpen the knife before the meal, in which case the steel won't be on the table. Others like to whet the guests' appetites by putting an edge on the knife, and there is a traditional appeal to this custom, especially at turkey time! If there are accompanying vegetables, these too may be set in front of the host. Some couples prefer that the host take care only of the meat and that the hostess serve the vegetables as the plates are passed down the table from him to her.

With the assistance of the guests, the meat-laden plate is passed down either side of the table to the hostess, who adds the vegetables. She then says to her neighbor on the appropriate side, "John, would you pass this to Betty?" Then John hands the plate to Betty if she is next to him or hands it to the woman who *is* next to him saying, "This is for Betty."

This method of passing is quite acceptable, and especially practical when the task of carving uses up much time and table space, as with a turkey.

The serving plates are stacked at the host's left, with one of them put directly before him for the first serving. If the main dish is a casserole and its accompaniment is a salad in one bowl, the bowl may be passed around from guest to guest as each is served. Bread, relishes, and gravies are also passed. Once you as hostess are seated, you do not rise to pass or serve things; you get up only to take away plates and bring on courses.

When it is time, the host asks each guest if he would like more of anything, and helps each plate separately, passing the plates down to the hostess if any serving is being done by her.

At the end of the course, you as hostess usually remove the plates, although there is no reason why you should not accept the help of one of your women guests if it is offered and if you want to. Whether or not your guests help you, they are likely to feel somewhat uncomfortable when you are working while they're talking, and so you may clear the table more informally than a maid would, just to expedite the chore. You may take plates from either side and stack them several at a time if they're not too messy. Maidless hostesses don't crumb the table, but you will, of course, pick up anything that has been spilled. Now is a good time to refill the water goblets if they need it.

In some households, the hostess saves steps by having a tea cart at her side and puts the used plates on the bottom shelf. The dessert service—and the dessert itself, if it is something that can be served at room temperature—may be already set out on the top shelf.

When the table has been cleared, bring in the dessert and the plates for it. Since this is a maidless dinner, the silver for the dessert will have been put on the table when it was set. Serve the dessert and proceed as you did for the main course. Or you may serve the plates in the kitchen and bring them in two at a time or on a tray.

AFTER-DINNER COFFEE

Coffee may be served at the table or in the living room. The latter way is becoming increasingly popular and is a bit more relaxing than continuing to sit at the table. However, if you decide to serve it at the table, you may have the service ready beforehand on a buffet or on your tea wagon, bringing in the hot coffee when it's time, or you may fill the cups in the kitchen and bring them in, serving them with the spoon on the saucer, at the far side of the cup and with the handle parallel to the cup handle. It is thoughtful to have both demitasse and large cups available, and to let each guest have his choice.

Then when dessert and coffee are finished, you may leave the table as it is and move back to the living room (you have taken away the cocktail things and emptied the ashtrays while the others are talking over their coffee, or your husband has done it earlier), or you may slip away to clear the table and see that the perishable things go in the refrigerator. How much more you do depends on your mood and the mood of the evening, and how well you know your guests. If one of them wants to help you, it is a comfort to have the dishes scraped and stacked, even if not washed up. On the other hand, if you would rather do the work after the guests have gone or in the morning. just thank everyone who has offered to help and explain you'd rather do the dishes later.

Should you prefer to have coffee in the living room, you will have to slip out quickly and clear away the cocktail glasses and empty the ashtrays, unless this was done just before dinner. The coffee is brought into the living room on a tray previously set up with cups and saucers, spoons, cream and sugar, and possibly strips of lemon peel. If the hostess wants to do a little clearing away in the dining room, it is perfectly all right for her to set the tray on some convenient table and ask the guests to serve themselves.

Of course as at any party your duties as hostess extend beyond the food and the serving. You see that no newcomer is left adrift in a sea of cross-talk about people he doesn't know. You draw out the shy ones and are on the watch for tactful opportunities to turn aside a monologuist. Above all, you make sure no guest can feel left out.

When people start to go, you rise to say goodby to each one. If they have already made their goodbys to your husband and he is in the kitchen making drinks, then you should see the guests to the door.

And of course you would say in reply to a guest's thank you, "I'm so glad you could come," or "We enjoyed seeing you so much."

WHAT THE HOST DOES

Because the wife has the responsibility for the meal, in most families the husbands help out by taking on various chores other than the hostly functions which are always expected of them. Often the husband puts the children to bed, and while they're still up, takes on at least part of the job of keeping them occupied and moderately quiet.

You as host are responsible first of all for drinks. This needs a certain amount of preparation—getting extra ice if you think you will not have enough, checking the liquor cabinet, and reminding your wife not to forget the grocery items you may need such as soda and mixes, limes, lemons, cherries, olives, and so on. Be sure you have a good recipe book for mixed drinks, clearly marked measures, and an adequate server for cocktails. If the latter doesn't have a closed lip to hold the ice back, you should get a bar strainer. An ice bucket is a very useful piece of equipment. Just before the company goes, get out the ice cubes, bottles, glasses, and all the makings.

Highballs and one kind of cocktail are all you need be ready to provide before dinner, although some energetic hosts serve manhattans *and* martinis, or in hot weather are ready to make a long cool drink like a Tom Collins if the guest prefers. Whatever your range of drinks, do be specific when you are taking orders for them. Say "Would you rather have a manhattan or a highball?" The host who just says, "What'll you have?" not only puts his guests in an embarrassing spot, but also is likely to end up with the chore of making one old-fashioned, a daiquiri, and two manhattans plus a highball— a time-consuming job even if he has all the ingredients. When someone asks for a highball, be sure to mention the choice of liquors if you have one, and find out if he prefers soda or water.

When you have made the drinks, take the tray into the living room and pass each guest his drink. It is up to you, of course, to watch for needed refills, and it is a big help to your wife if you pass the hors d'oeuvres now and then.

It is a very efficient and thoughtful husband who whisks all the empty glasses back on the serving tray when dinner is announced, and maybe even swiftly empties the ashtrays while his wife is seating the first of the guests. Then the tray is ready to be carried out at the first opportunity.

If wine is served at the table, this is also your responsibility as host. Unless the wine is served in a decanter, as red wine sometimes is, the bottle may be opened at the table. (If you serve wine often, a special opener which prevents cork splitting is well worth the investment.) If you are having champagne and the cork is likely to pop and the wine to drip, or if it has been chilled, be sure to have a napkin wrapped around the neck of the bottle. Pour a little wine into your own glass first. This is in case any bits of cork are left in the bottle. The wine is poured into a guest's glass first only if it is being served from a decanter; it is assumed that you will have tasted it for flavor before decanting it. Having poured this little bit into your own glass, you next fill the glass of the woman on your right and then go right around the table (not skipping the men) and serve each guest.

If by some misfortune bits of cork drop into your glass, you may excuse yourself and empty the glass in the kitchen, or pick out the bits of cork with a clean knife or spoon.

Wine is poured directly into the glass as it stands beside the guest's plate. After pouring, give the bottle a slight twist before raising it. This avoids spilling. Don't fill wine glasses full—a little space at the top allows the wine to breathe.

Liqueurs and any other drinks served after dinner are also served by the host. Liqueurs are usually served with the coffee, either at the table or in the living room.

As host, you escort your departing guests to the door after getting their hats and coats for them, and as you bid them goodby, express your pleasure that they came.

DINNER WITH A MAID

Whether you have one or choose to hire one for the occasion, a dinner party with a maid can be of any degree of formality that you wish. In other words, just because you are having help with the serving and clearing away, you don't need automatically to have many courses and very elaborate food unless you really want to. And unless the maid is a cook as well, you will probably prepare the food yourself as you would for a maidless dinner party. The great advantage of having a helper is that it frees you of some of your chores so that you can give even more attention to the guests. And of course a maid relieves you of the burden of washing up.

If you have a maid, you may want to serve one hot hors d'oeuvre, which she will pass, and you may also want to have a first course such as soup, or shrimp, or fruit cocktail. You can have hot breads and bread and butter plates and unless there is meat to be carved at the table, the maid can serve all the dishes. The host, however, serves the wine.

You will probably want to arrange the flowers and set the table or supervise its setting. If the maid is to do some or all of the cooking, then you will naturally plan to have things she cooks well. In any case, you will go over the menu with her; it's a good idea to write it down, in order of appearance. Unless you know your helper is experienced, it is a good idea to have a rehearsal with her. And if she has not worked in your house before, you should be quite explicit about what you expect. Go over with her the plates, glasses, serving spoons, and dishes, as well as the cooking equipment.

Be sure to put a bell on the table to ring for the maid when you want her. And don't forget to be watchful of your guests' needs and ring the bell for second helpings, more butter, and whatever else is needed.

When your guests arrive, the maid may answer the door, although in most homes the host and hostess do. If the maid does do it, she takes the guests' coats and hats and puts them away. If your coat closet is small, she may take just the men's things and direct the women to a bedroom.

The procedure during cocktails before dinner is just what it would be with a maidless dinner, except that the maid will bring in and pass any hot hors d'oeuvres you may have. You will probably want her to do this twice at least, presenting freshly made ones each time. It is well, though, to remember that she can't make too elaborate hors d'oeuvres or serve them too frequently and still handle the last preparations for the meal.

When dinner is ready, the maid comes to the living room and announces that it is served. Then you as hostess lead the guests in and seat them just as you would if there were no maid. At the end of dinner, you give the signal to leave the table by rising. At some point during dinner, probably during the dessert course, the maid will have cleared away the cocktail things and emptied the ashtrays. She will bring in the coffee service, but you pour it whether it is at table or in the living room.

For the service of the meal, see Chapter 20.

WHAT THE HOST DOES

With few exceptions, the host's responsibilities at a dinner served by a maid are about the same as those for the maidless dinner. The mixing of the drinks is done by the host, although he may call on the maid for some assistance, such as asking her to get out the ice cubes or bring the limes.

If the host is carving, he will help the guests to second servings of meat when they are ready. The hostess will ring for the vegetables to be passed again only after each guest who wants it has the second serving of meat on his plate.

THE BUFFET SUPPER

If you are maidless, a buffet supper is the ideal way for you to entertain a larger number of people than can sit comfortably at the table or be served easily there. You can also have buffet service for just a few people simply because you find it easier, and you needn't confine it to the evening. Buffet is very practical for breakfast for weekend guests, for brunch, lunch, late supper. And you can have it on the lawn or terrace when the weather's fine, just as well as in the dining room.

The fact that large numbers of guests can serve themselves from a well-stocked buffet misleads some hostesses into asking too many people. The governing factor in determining how many guests to invite is not the food or service, but the guests' comfort in eating. Nobody should have to stand to eat his dinner, of course, and having to use one's lap for a table is often privately deplored, particularly by men. Try to plan your party so that each guest has some place to put his plate—two may use the coffee table, one an end table, one the desk, and so on. Little folding tables may supplement some of these places.

If your living room is large or if you have two rooms available, you may want to set up card tables. In this case seat the guests, not forgetting yourself and your husband, in multiples of four.

Be sure you have or can borrow enough silver, china, and glassware for the number of people you plan to ask.

THE BUFFET MENU

In selecting buffet food the first consideration—after ease of preparation and the ability to stand waiting—is that you remember how it is to be eaten. Your guests, unless you have seated them at card tables, will be dining in a less comfortable position than at a dining room table, and will be eating from one plate, with a fork and no knife. This means that you plan on something that can be cut with a fork if it needs cutting at all, and rolls or bread that can be buttered in the kitchen.

Buffet suppers seldom include soup—it's hard to carry without spilling—and for this reason the eatables served with the cocktails may be something rather filling. A casserole as the main dish is espe-

cially convenient for a buffet as it may often be served in the same dish it was cooked in and will stay hot for a while. Curries, goulashes, sea food Newburg, turkey or chicken in a sauce on fluffy white rice—all these are good choices. A tossed green salad rounds out the main course. For dessert select something that can be made ahead of time, and again something that is easy to eat—no skiddy meringues or drippy chocolate sundaes. Finger foods like cheeses and fruit are fine.

THE BUFFET TABLE

If your dining room table is large, by all means use it for your buffet. If you extend it with leaves, make sure that there is room for your guests to move around it comfortably. If not, or even just because you prefer to do so, you may put it against a wall. Or you can use your sideboard. Or an aluminum folding table, or card tables—sturdy ones—pushed together. Your cloth will, of course, be large enough to hide any unsightly underpinnings.

One of the nicest things about setting up a buffet table is that you can really make a showpiece of your flower arrangement because you don't have to worry about being able to see over it. Put it in the center if people are going to move all around the table, against the wall if that is where the table is.

For details of arranging the table, see Chapter 19, "Table Settings." In general, place everything so that the guests can serve themselves in logical order: napkin, hot food, cold food, salad, bread, relishes, and fork. (It would seem to be and really is more logical to put the napkin as well as the fork last so it doesn't have to be carried around the table. But habit is such that if you do this guests make a bee-line for the napkin and so begin at the wrong end.) Don't forget to use adequate napkins—a little one doesn't do much to protect a guest's dress or suit.

Of course, the table setting is done before the guests arrive —including the serving spoons. Shortly before you think people are ready to eat, light the candles (if you have room enough on the table to use them) and set out any cold dishes and the salad, leaving the hot dishes and bread to be prepared and put on the table just before you announce dinner.

To announce it, you go among the guests and tell them dinner is waiting in the dining room—won't they help themselves when they're ready? Gradually they will start to go in. You might say to a group seemingly settled in their chairs for the evening, "May I get you some dinner?"—which will probably get them on their feet.

You, your husband, or a maid if you have one, may help your guests to the various dishes or they may help themselves. Afterward they take their filled plates to the living room and sit wherever they like. You don't seat them unless you know one of them to be a confirmed hater of lap eating, in which case you might want to give him an especially comfortable place such as at the desk.

When you see people are almost ready for second helpings, you quietly refill and refurbish the serving dishes, warming up the hot ones if they are not on any kind of hot plate, and invite your guests to come back for more.

When the main course is finished, you collect the plates and take them to the kitchen, and clear the table. This is something that a maid can do if you have one, a friend may help or you and your husband can do it together. Then arrange the dessert and dessert service on the table, with coffee and coffee service. You may serve the dessert plates in the kitchen first if you like. If the table seems crowded, you may put the coffee service on the sideboard or serve it in the living room.

When everyone has had dessert and coffee, you will clear away everything from the living room, including the used napkins and the folding tables if any.

THE HOST AT A BUFFET

Your duties as host are much the same as at any other dinner, except that since the guests are serving themselves you are freer to help things go smoothly by seeing that everybody is comfortably seated, by passing wine or water on a tray, by refilling the plates of women guests, and by helping to straighten up the living room after the meal. There is usually time, too, while the guests are at the buffet table with your wife, to empty the ashtrays, take out the tray of cocktail glasses, and set up the little tables if they are to be used.

A BARBECUE PARTY

This is another wonderful way for maidless couples to entertain. Everybody enjoys the informality of eating out of doors, the food always seems to taste especially good, and you can ask the children as well as their parents.

Invitations are extended by telephone, although if you are having a very large affair you may want to write notes. The most usual time is five or six o'clock. On a Saturday or Sunday, however, it can perfectly well be a midday affair if you prefer.

Even though informality characterizes a barbecue, careful organization is a must. In most households it is the man who does the barbecuing, so your main dish will be something he likes to cook and cooks well. This, whether steak, hamburger, chicken, marinated lamb, or something on a spit, will be the star of the meal. If he is very able and has a big grill, he may also want to do something extra like corn roasted in foil or roast potatoes. Everything for his part of the menu should be ready to his hand: asbestos gloves, tongs, pot holders, skewers, kitchen matches, long fork, spoon and spatula, foil, seasonings, materials for marinade or basting, carving fork and knife and platter if needed. Everything else—bread, hot or cold, salad, dessert and much of the serving—will be up to you as hostess so that he is free to cook. While the fire is building up, he may fix the drinks, but once he has things on the grill you should take over any refills necessary.

Synchronizing the readiness of the fire to cook with the readiness of the guests to eat is a delicate matter if you are serving drinks. Don't start the fire so late that too many refills of drinks must go round before you can cook on it. Remember that it takes from forty-five minutes to an hour for a bed of charcoal to come to the proper heat.

Service at a barbecue is always most informal. Buffet is the rule, although if you have only a few guests you may prefer to sit down at an outdoor table. Paper plates are acceptable, but if you use them be sure to get the strong, rigid kind. Have plenty of hot coffee, and if you serve it in paper cups use the kind with handles.

A gay colored or checkered cloth is better for the table than paper, which is likely to be skittish if there is any wind. You can use paper napkins; if the breeze is strong, use terry cloth dish towels instead.

If the weather is hot and muggy, don't forget to spray the area with an insect repellent well before the guests are to arrive, and be sure to include the space under the chairs.

LUNCH

Lunch is a pleasant way to entertain, whether it means sandwiches and coffee on the terrace with a neighbor or a more elaborate meal before an afternoon of bridge. The guests at lunch are usually women, since the men are away at business, but even a lunch on a weekend with men present is a less formal affair than dinner. Fewer courses are served, and often there are no drinks or just simple ones like sherry. (If you do serve either cocktails or sherry, be sure to have tomato juice for those who don't care to drink at noon.)

Guests are often invited to lunch by telephone, although informal notes may also be used. When you telephone or write, it is correct to say "lunch" and not "luncheon," even though it may sound some-what colloquial. The word "luncheon" is properly used in print, such as in a newspaper description, or when the meal is announced by a maid, who would say, "Luncheon is served."

The time may be set at whatever is most convenient for the hostess and guests. One o'clock is perhaps the most usual.

THE MENU

For lunch you may have one, two, or three courses. A one-course meal might have a casserole for its main dish—this can be of sea food; kidney beans, Mexican style; macaroni and cheese; or something with meat if you wish, although meat is not essential at lunch. With this you would serve salad, hot rolls, and coffee—iced tea or iced coffee in the summer if you like. The addition of dessert would make a two-course meal. A three-course lunch would include a first course, such as consommé or fruit or tomato juice.

THE TABLE SETTING

This is less formal at lunch than at dinner. A centerpiece should be used, but not candles. The table is often set with mats and match-ing or contrasting napkins, or a colored cloth. You wouldn't use white damask except for a very formal affair such as a wedding luncheon.

Unless you are having sandwiches, which is unlikely except at the most informal of lunch gatherings, your table will be set with bread and butter plates because you will always have bread or rolls.

Use a cup or bowl for soup served at lunch. If, however, the main dish is to be a thick soup like purée mongole, it is correct to use regu-lar soup plates, serving the soup from a tureen if you have one.

The plates for the main course are somewhat smaller than dinner plates.

BRUNCH

This portmanteau word while frowned upon by purists is so useful to describe a frequently served meal—half breakfast, half lunch—that it has passed into the language.

Brunch is most commonly served on Sunday morning any time between ten-thirty and three o'clock—on Saturday mornings a little earlier, say ten to noon, to give people the afternoon for shopping, golfing, or mowing the lawn. Since both the meal and the service are quite informal, buffet service is ideal. Or you can sit at table, with the hostess pouring the coffee while the host either serves the dishes or passes them around for the guests to help themselves.

THE MENU

It is to be assumed that your guests will have had at the most fruit juice and coffee before coming to your house, perhaps only coffee. So the food should be fairly substantial. Serve fruit or fruit juice first, and follow it with scrambled eggs and sausages, chicken livers and bacon, shad roe and bacon, creamed chicken on toast, or fried tomatoes and bacon, to name just a few of the possibilities. No dessert, but lots and lots of good strong coffee.

If drinks are served, one or two will probably be the limit. Whisky sours are always popular, and so are drinks with a tomato juice base, while some people will prefer the tomato juice plain.

TEA

Teatime is a time for relaxing, a time for friendliness and quiet talk. Usually, therefore, it is for a small group of people brought together for the sake of congeniality or to introduce a house guest to your friends. On occasion a tea may be given for a more special reason, such as presenting a debutante or a new daughter-in-law. In such a case, the group would be larger and the hostess will probably ask one of her friends to pour so that she may mingle with her guests; otherwise the food and service are much the same.

When you are having tea for just a few, invite your guests personally or by telephone; by note for a large tea, giving at least a day's notice. Four o'clock is the usual time, though you may ask people for any hour from two to six. The number of guests invited for a small tea is determined by the seating capacity of your living room, porch, or terrace. Tea guests are not expected to sit at the dining room table, nor, unless it is a very large tea, to stand. It's best not to drag in lots of chairs for extra seating capacity, as the whole idea of a small tea party is its coziness.

THE MENU FOR TEA

The most important item on the menu is the tea itself. First, it should be of good quality and for a tea party leaf tea is preferable to tea balls. Be sure the tea is made with fresh boiling water, and don't forget at the last minute to warm the teapot by rinsing it out with hot water. Measure scrupulously as indicated in the tea-making directions on page 126.

A large tray may hold all the things for tea: the teapot, a smaller teapot for the hot water, a tea caddy or bowl for the tea leaves, a bowl for waste, a pitcher of cream (actually it's generally milk), a plate of

thin lemon slices and a lemon fork, sugar and sugar tongs. If there is room, the cups and saucers may go on the tray too, with the teaspoons laid either on the saucers or on the tray. If there isn't enough room on the tray, the china and silver may be placed on the table from which the hostess is serving, within her reach.

There should also be a stack of small tea plates with napkins (you can use little paper cocktail napkins) placed between them. If your cups and tea plates match or make an agreeable contrast, it is much easier for the hostess and more comfortable for the guests to eliminate the saucers and put the cups directly on the tea plates.

Foods that are served with tea may be tiny sandwiches, or breads such as cinnamon toast, with cookies, tiny cakes, or tarts. Layer cake is often served with tea, but it shouldn't be a rich or sticky one. Pound cake sliced thin or slices of fruitcake are good. The sandwiches should be made of thinly sliced bread with trimmed crusts.

Fillings may be of sliced cucumber, watercress, cream cheese and olive, to name just a few. Thin bread and butter goes especially well with tea.

At any small tea you as hostess make and pour the tea yourself. You put the proper amount of tea leaves (a teaspoon for each two measuring cups of water) into the teapot, which will have been rinsed out with boiling hot water just beforehand, pour a little water over them, and let the mixture steep not less than three and not more than five minutes. The result is very strong tea, and as each cup is poured, you or the guest whom you have asked to pour will dilute the brew as each person expresses her preference. Each guest in turn is asked how she likes her tea, weak or strong, with lemon or sugar and cream and how much sugar. Then the filled cup is put on the saucer or tea plate with a spoon and handed to the guest, who helps herself to the food, which is set out on one or more large plates or serving platters. If cake is being served, don't forget to put a cake server on the plate.

COCKTAIL PARTIES

A cocktail party is such a comparatively easy way to entertain, especially for servantless couples and bachelors and women living alone, that it has become very popular. Your cocktail party may be quite large or you may ask just a few people. Make it a point to invite congenial people together, especially for a small party. Have at least as many men as women if you can. If you're having a small group, be sure you have enough chairs for everybody; if you're having a large number, you may want to move out a few of the occasional chairs so that the first eight or ten arrivals will move around and mix rather than sit sewing-circle style all through the party. Be sure the liquor is good, that you won't run out of ice, and that there is plenty of food.

Invitations to cocktail parties may be telephoned or you may write informal notes. Or you may prefer to use some of the gay cocktail-party invitations that the gift and stationery stores now carry in great variety. The usual time is five to seven.

Even though cocktail parties are easier to give than dinners, careful planning is just as important. Get yourself in a party mood, first of all! Then make your house as welcoming as you can with flowers and shining furniture. Have plenty of large serviceable ashtrays and make coasters available, especially if you have a piano and fine wood furniture. Provide lots of cigarettes and book matches; the matches in plain or colored foil covers look festive and are less likely to vanish into men's pockets than the ordinary kind.

If you have a record player, select some soft background music to start playing just before the guests arrive. It will add gaiety until the party has gained momentum of its own.

Be sufficiently organized ahead of the guests' arrival so that you can greet them at the door—this usually is the hostess' job, since the host will be mixing drinks almost continually. If you have hired a bartender to take care of the drinks, then you may take turns at the doorbell so that one of you is always available to talk with the guests and make introductions. At a quite small party you would introduce everyone; at a large one, you need only introduce new-comers to a few of the guests already there.

Beg, borrow, or rent if you must in order to have an ample supply of glasses—people are always putting down their empties and forget-ting them. Even though you may have hired a maid who will collect and wash the glasses from time to time, it is wise to allow two or three glasses for each guest. Correctly, you should have stemmed cocktail glasses for most cocktails, tall glasses for the long drinks, and old-fashioned glasses for whisky on the rocks, martinis on the rocks, and old-fashioneds. In practice, you can make do with substitutions of an appropriate kind, serving whisky sours in wine glasses, cock-tails or sherry in footed juice glasses.

Double the amount of ice you think you may need. Make quanti-ties of ice cubes ahead of time and put them in plastic bags in the freezer or in insulated coolers, borrowed if need be. Or buy several bags of ice cubes just before the party. Or guests who are neighbors may be called upon to bring you a few trays.

THE DRINKS

The host can easily handle the making of drinks for a small party. (A woman living alone can ask one of her men friends to take over the bar department.) He may make them in the kitchen and bring in a tray of filled glasses, or he may set up the essentials for making them on a side table in the living room. Each guest should be offered a drink as soon as he arrives.

For a large party a bar table is often set up in the dining room, the den or study, the sun porch, or any place away from the front door and living room. (Such a position makes for better mixing of guests, since they come to the bar table for refills.) Cover the table with a large cloth and arrange the glasses and bar equipment. Don't forget a large pitcher of water, and also a small cutting board and sharp knife if fruit is to be used. Be sure that your bar equipment provides enough jiggers so that drinks can be measured. Otherwise, some poor unsuspecting guest is likely to be bowled over with a drink far stronger than he wants or needs. After the first drink, it is perfectly all right to let the guests mix their own, but the host should be alert to see that supplies of ice, liquor, soda, water, and so on are renewed and that glasses are ready at hand.

The hors d'oeuvres should not be put on the bar table as the person who is mixing the drinks needs as much room as he can get. Rather put them, between passings, on a table in another room. Plates are not necessary, but have plenty of cocktail napkins available.

Whatever you serve in the line of cocktail accompaniments, be sure to have plenty of them. Trays or platters with crackers and spreads or dips can be left where guests can help themselves, but the hostess must see to it that they are kept replenished and attractive looking. If you have any hot hors d'oeuvres, they must of course be passed while they *are* hot and any left-overs taken back to the kitchen.

Do see that ashtrays are emptied often, and used glasses carried away.

Cocktail parties have one drawback for the host and hostess—they are often very hard to end. Sometimes the party givers and the last few of the guests go out to dinner together. Although this may be at the host's suggestion, it is generally understood that the meal itself will be a Dutch treat affair. Sometimes the host and hostess can plead an engagement at nine o'clock or so. If these stratagems are useless because of children who cannot be left alone or for some other reason, the wise hostess plans on some sort of simple buffet to serve the late stayers: a casserole, bread and salad with a bought pastry, for example, and lots of good strong coffee. The one thing you can't do is to shut down the bar—this is considered very rude.

DESSERT AND COFFEE

This is a very pleasant way to entertain without much work or expense. You simply invite your guests, by telephone as a rule, to "come over for dessert and coffee," setting the time for eight, eight-thirty, or nine, depending on the customary dinner hour in your community. You will, of course, have your own dinner early to give yourself enough time to clear away and prepare for your guests. You will probably plan to have some rather special dessert, such as a torte or a rich layer cake or angel food with fruit or ice cream. Be sure to have plenty of coffee, enough for several cups apiece, and you may want to serve liqueurs with it. It's wise to have whisky and soda available in case people want long drinks later on. You may serve the food and coffee buffet style or at the dining room table. Whichever you choose, don't ask more guests than can be seated comfortably in your living·room or at your table.

AFTER-DINNER PARTIES

To have friends come for the evening, for bridge, games, television, or just good conversation, is enjoyable for everyone and very easy on the hostess who works or who has small children. Because the conversational evening is the simplest, we shall deal with it first.

Your guest list for such an evening will be small to allow uncrowded seating for everybody and to make general conversation easy. You can invite people by telephone, saying, "We're having some people over on Saturday evening and we're hoping you and Dave can come." If the answer is yes, you will express your pleasure and you might add, "About nine, then?" making it clear that they're not expected for dinner.

After tidying up your living room, if it needs it, and the dining room, you or your husband get out the makings for the drinks. These will be long drinks, with beer ready in the icebox for those who prefer it and soft drinks available, too. The drinks may be made in the kitchen, or a tray with the ice, glasses, and makings may be set out in the living room.

THE REFRESHMENTS

If it is a week night or if your guests don't usually keep very late hours, no refreshments are necessary, although it is a good idea to have something for people to nibble, such as peanuts or mixed nuts, potato chips, cheese crackers, or the like. If it is a Friday or Saturday night when people are able to stay up later and often want to, it is a good idea to serve something more substantial around eleven or eleven-thirty. It is to be hoped that the conversation is going well, and if you don't want to put a stop to it, it's best not to make people get up for the food. You can arrange a platter with cheeses and crackers on it, perhaps fruit also, or one with the makings of

sandwiches. If the party is going to last very late, you may prefer to serve a simple cold supper at midnight, with plenty of coffee to go with it.

On evenings like these the conversation is more important than ever since it is the chief entertainment, and it is up to the host and hostess to see that it flows smoothly. You will first have asked congenial and interesting people, and then you will try to see that the talk is general and that everyone has a chance to be heard. You will steer the conversation away from depressing or unpleasant subjects or topics that might hurt the feelings of any of the guests. Although a little controversy makes for good talk, you won't let an argument go on if the opponents become heated. Try to avoid letting the men cluster for shop talk while the women all exchange house-keeping and child-raising problems. If this happens, the host can usually be more successful than the hostess in drawing the groups back together and launching a new subject of general interest.

AN EVENING OF CARD GAMES

When you have your friends in for bridge, canasta, or whatever card game is popular with your set at the moment, a little more planning is needed. Be sure you have the right number of guests for the game. Have firm card tables with a good light for each, ashtrays, coasters if needed. To keep the table clear of ashtrays and drinks, a little stack table on each side is very useful. Provide freshly sharpened pencils, new or reasonably new cards, and adequate score pads.

Drinks and refreshments you may handle as you would for a conversational evening. Card playing is thirsty work, so don't forget to have a pitcher of ice water and soft drinks for those who don't want an alcoholic drink.

And when you invite your guests, let them know that it is to be an evening of card playing, so that if they don't like cards or are momentarily surfeited, they can decline with thanks.

AN EVENING OF GAMES

Some people enjoy parlor games and some have a very real aversion to them, so it is only fair to let your guests know in advance what is planned for the evening. If any guest accepts your invitation with the proviso that he will not participate, you can let him keep score or just watch. Don't coax him to change his mind and join the game. The same applies when parlor games break out spontaneously at a party.

The host and hostess are in a delicate position when a parlor game is suggested by a guest. If the reaction of the other guests is enthusiastic, well and good; if it is lukewarm, it is best to discourage the idea as tactfully as you can. But if you do have games, don't force any guest to play.

TELEVISION PROGRAMS

A television party as such is rather rare, as few people watch television for an entire evening. However, you may want to ask friends to come in and watch a special program that you want to see and think they will too, such as a spectacular with big names or a special sports program. Here again, phrase your invitation so that the guests will know what is planned—"We're having some friends in tomorrow night to watch the horse show on television—can you and Henry come?"

When television watching is not part of the planned program, one of your guests may mention a particular offering he doesn't want to miss and ask if he may watch it. Or if the party is lagging and the host or hostess knows of a program that seems of general interest, they may suggest watching it. Some of the guests may want to watch, others may prefer to continue their conversation. In that case, the host would stay with one group, the hostess with the other. If your television set is in the living room, it is best to take your non-viewing guests into another room if possible. Otherwise, let the viewers huddle close to the set and keep the sound low. Don't forget to make these guests comfortable with their drinks and ashtrays and chairs or hassocks.

DANCES

Dances are not given so often as they used to be, simply because the main requirement for a successful dance is space and lots of it, and most of us haven't the room—or if we do, it is likely to be covered with a wall-to-wall carpet. If, however, you have available a large living room or sunroom with a smooth floor and rugs that can be taken up, or if you have a large basement room with an adequate floor, by all means give a dance. It is a delightful form of entertainment and need not be either troublesome or expensive.

First clear the room to be used for dancing of all its furniture— unless it is very large, in which case you can have small chairs in corners and against a wall for lookers-on. Sprinkle either powdered wax or fine-ground cornmeal evenly over the floor. The dancers will spread this about very quickly. (Be careful, however, not to throw on too much and make the floor slippery—it is easier to add more than to take any off.)

The music is just as important as the floor. If expense doesn't matter, get a four-piece orchestra. These can be quite expensive if they are professional, but often one can find a group of high school or college students who play more than adequately for a far smaller fee. Be sure, though, that you get one accustomed to playing for dancing—with consistent rhythm and a strong beat. If the group is unknown to you, ask where they have played lately and check on how people liked the music.

If the budget doesn't stretch to an orchestra, an evening of dancing to records can be just as much fun. In fact, it's better to have good records than a poor orchestra. But you must have plenty of good *dance* records—a few waltzes, a number of Latin American pieces if your crowd likes them, swing records and many fox-trots fast and slow, perhaps some square dance numbers for a change of pace. Be sure the record player is in good working order, and it's wise planning to enlist the aid of a friend or two to help with the record changing.

If you have a very large, finished basement, you may want to provide a place where those who aren't dancing can sit and talk. Card tables and chairs can be set up against the walls, and your refreshments can be arranged on a buffet table there.

INVITATIONS

As even a small dance is a rather formal occasion, you will probably invite your guests by writing a note or by card. The invitation should state not only the hour when you expect them to arrive, but also the time when the dance is to be over. Ten or eleven until two or three are usual times, although if the dance is for teen-agers you will probably want it to begin and end earlier. Ask as many extra men—or boys—as you can.

REFRESHMENTS

The usual refreshment at a dance is a punch, which may be alcoholic or not. The punch may be served in a large bowl with a big piece of ice in it to keep it cold. A large piece of sherbet will do the same thing and also lend a little flavor. Whether you use ice or sherbet, replace it often so that the punch doesn't become warm and diluted. The guests help themselves from time to time, using a punch ladle to pour the drink into small glass cups with handles. (It is possible to rent bowl, ladle, and cups if you don't own them and can't borrow them.)

A supper of some sort is usually served at midnight. This can be a fairly elaborate buffet with something hot, or it may be just cold meat and sandwiches. Although couples may and do go to the table together to fill their plates, it is also quite common for a man to seat the partner with whom he has just been dancing and fetch her a filled plate.

GREETING THE GUESTS

At an informal dance there is seldom a receiving line, but the hostess usually greets the guests as they come until nearly all have arrived. Her husband may occasionally join her in doing this, but as a rule he is on the dance floor dancing with the women guests.

The dancing usually begins as soon as ten or a dozen guests have arrived.

ENDING THE DANCE

If an orchestra has been engaged, the group stops playing at the time agreed on beforehand. Before putting their instruments away, they traditionally play "Good Night Ladies," which is the signal that the dance is over. If you have been dancing to records, it is harder to bring the dancing to a close. However, in all probability it can be managed by serving the supper late in the evening, about an hour before the departure time indicated on your invitations.

It is considerate for the extra men to offer to see home any unescorted women, or for couples to do so. Otherwise, the host must do so himself—no woman should ever be permitted to go home alone after a dance. In practice, however, if a lone female guest of an independent nature has come in her own car and intends to go home in it, there is not much the host can be expected to do.

DANCES FOR TEEN-AGERS

Time was when any dance for young people meant a cluster of chaperones lined around the wall. At a dance in a private home this is not necessary. The parents who are giving the dance are chaperones enough and even they need not and should not hover. They should always be on the premises, on call if needed. They will greet the guests with their child, dance a few dances, and help get the party started, if necessary, with circle dances or other ice breakers. And they will help with the refreshments, and say good night to the guests. But they need not be in evidence every moment.

15

How to Be a Guest

JUST AS THERE'S AN ART IN HAVING GUESTS, THERE'S ARTISTRY IN BEING one. It's a talent well worth acquiring, for if you have it, not only will many invitations come to you, but you'll always be sure that your welcome is a truly warm one. The guest who is considered by every hostess to be an addition to any group and fun to entertain alone as well, is the person who is charmingly pleasant, thoroughly appreciative, and outgoing to others.

The *rules* of good guest etiquette are not very hard or very many. They are the same rules you remind your children about when they are old enough to start going to birthday parties by themselves. Be on time. Greet your hostess. Be polite to everybody. Remember to say goodby to your hostess and don't forget to say that you had a nice time!

Of course, this is over-simplifying. The occasions where grownups are guests are more varied and more complex and so our responsibilities are a little more demanding. Then, too, when they know the rules adults can alter some of them from time to time with impunity. There are many communities where, if the dinner guests arrived on the dot of seven, as they were invited to do, they would find the host and hostess not quite ready for them. On the other hand, there are places where the guests when asked for dinner at seven are expected to start coming at six-fifteen or six-thirty for cocktails first. As a good guest, you will know or will find out just what is considered "punctual" in your community and observe the custom.

It is understood everywhere that a hostess is not expected to hold dinner—certainly not a sit-down dinner—much more than fifteen minutes for a late guest, unless the delayed one is the guest of honor. If you are the guest of honor, lateness is all but unforgivable and nothing but a real emergency can excuse you. Occasionally a guest of a less exalted variety will be unavoidably late and arrive after dinner has been started. If this happens to you, come into the dining room (after having shed your outer coat), go directly to your hostess, make a sincere but brief apology, and take your seat in the empty place, where you will be served with whatever course is then in progress. The whole idea is not to disrupt the party further by a lengthy recital to all the guests of the cause of your lateness.

If you have been asked to the party by note or letter, your obligation of punctuality begins with your receipt of the invitation. You should reply as promptly as you possibly can so that the hostess can invite other people if you are unable to come.

When you and your husband arrive at a large cocktail party or reception and are ushered in by a maid, you seek out your hostess and your host and greet them. If there is a reception line, you will join the group waiting to go through it before you chat with others or have refreshments. When you leave the party, find the host and hostess and make your farewells, telling them how much you enjoyed it.

At any kind of party, the good guest remembers that it is her—or his—responsibility to help keep the conversational ball rolling. In doing this, don't forget that half of good conversation is listening. Help your hosts draw out the shy ones or those new to the group. Don't worry if the beginning of your conversation with a stranger strikes you as banal—it may have to be while you're finding some common ground. The weather, the seasonal sport, the new cars, the woes of packing and unpacking if the shy one is a newcomer—any of these will do for an opener if you are alert to pick up any spark of interest and fan it.

Do make a real effort to remember the names of the people to whom you are introduced at a party—certainly you can remember them for the evening, and by consciously intending to, you can recall them weeks later. If you have a good memory for faces and a poor one for names, it often helps to write down the names of those you met for the first time that evening when you get home.

At almost any gathering except a card party or a television watching occasion, try to circulate. At a large tea or cocktail party, don't stand in one spot for hours like a room divider—make it your business to move around and talk with different people and different groups. After a dinner the talk goes much better if the guests don't all plump themselves down in the same chairs they occupied for cocktails but shuffle themselves around—some of them, at least—into different combinations.

A maidless host and hostess always appreciate any guest, man or woman, who quietly offers to help. If on this particular evening they prefer to have all the guests contribute to the general gaiety rather than help clear the table or mix the highballs, they will refuse your offer politely. When this is the case, don't press the point. Often, however, the host is grateful when one of his men friends helps to make the drinks, especially if there are several kinds, and the hostess is thankful for the guest who passes the hors d'oeuvres now and then, especially when people are slow about helping themselves. Women guests at a buffet can be a real help in getting the serving started by getting up and moving toward the dining room when dinner is announced.

It oughtn't to be necessary to say that the well-behaved guest of either sex is especially careful with cigarettes and drinks. To leave a cigarette so carelessly placed on the ashtray that it can slip off and burn the table is inexcusable, and so is putting a cold highball glass on a polished wood or marble table. If there is no coaster ready for you, ask your hostess for one.

Sometimes a guest unintentionally takes over the hostess' party by insisting on games or putting loud dance music on the record player or continuing to press an argument which has become too heated for a social evening. Don't be this bossy kind of guest. It is perhaps all right, if you know the hostess well, to suggest a new party game you think everybody would enjoy, but if she says she thinks now isn't just the time for it, drop the matter for good. It's selfish to drown out conversation with dance music unless it is part of the planned entertainment, in which case it is the place of the hostess to begin it. And it's rude to rant from your soapbox at the expense of everybody else's peace of mind. When you do any of these things you put the hostess in a most uncomfortable position.

Guests who drink too much are, of course, the kind of nuisance a host and hostess are not likely to welcome often. Less objectionable, but still trying, are guests who never know when to go home.

When you're dining in a restaurant as someone's guest, the ground rules are just the same as if you were at the hosts' table in their own home. There really are some people who, just because a restaurant is a public place, so forget their manners as to criticize the food or service or both. The hosts themselves may be deploring the long waits between courses or feeling compunction because the steak is not so tender as it has always been before. If things are really bad, they'll complain; if they don't, you must appear not to notice that anything at all is wrong. And don't squabble over the check—if you are invited guests this is especially poor taste.

Some otherwise well-mannered guests appear to forget their manners at a theater or night club. If the show or routine is truly a failure, allow the host a chance to say, "I'm so sorry this turned out to be a dud—I'd heard it was good . . ." before you downgrade it. And if the host and possibly most of the other guests think it's wonderful and you think it a bore or in bad taste, you can be diplomatic in your comments without hypocritically raving about it. You can nearly always find *something* to praise—and keep quiet about the rest.

HOW TO BE A GUEST FROM OUT OF TOWN

Let's suppose you and your husband are far from home, in a hotel in a big city. You have telephoned or perhaps written in advance to your old friend Mary Sarton in the hope that you and the Sartons can get together some evening. If they have a free evening, they will undoubtedly want to entertain you, either at home or in a restaurant. If they haven't, Mary will probably invite you to lunch or tea or take you to a matinee, or whatever fits in with her schedule and yours. Don't feel dashed if she and her husband are too involved to see you as often as all of you would like. Remember that those who live in big cities are always pressed for time—you may be on vacation, but they're not. This may be your first trip in four years—but they may have had four sets of old friends turn up within the past three weeks, not to mention business people to entertain—and they may have to do this frequently.

And don't lean on your city friends. Ask for advice, if you like, about what sights to see, what's the best shop for children's clothes, where to get your hair done, but don't burden them with commissions, such as getting tickets for the latest hit. It costs them just as much time to get them as it does you, and they can't get them at bargain rates either.

If you have been entertained by friends when you have visited their city, or if they have been helpful in other ways, of course you write from home and thank them, and it's even more gracious to send flowers or candy and a little note before you leave.

16

Having House Guests

IN TIMES WHEN HOUSES WERE FULL OF BOTH ROOMS AND SERVANTS, having friends come to stay meant a crowd. Often a visiting relative or old family friend occupied a corner guest room for weeks at a stretch and there was still room for a house party, even if someone had to be fitted into the sewing room after the second- and third-floor guest rooms had been filled up. In the establishments of the very rich, it was nothing to have a dozen or two dozen guests for Friday afternoon till Monday morning or even for a week.

Today, with space at a premium everywhere and servants even more so, most of us have house guests on a more modest scale and treat them informally. Long visits are the exception rather than the rule and, aside from putting up an occasional out-of-towner who needs a bed for a night, we are generally obliged to limit ourselves to one couple or two at the most, and have them for a Friday-Saturday-Sunday weekend.

Just as it used to be, the principal goal is still enjoyment—the pleasure of each other's company on the part of host and guest alike. And the secret of enjoyment, aside from having congenial people, people whom you really want to see, is planning. Well ahead of time plan all the meals you'll have with an eye to easy preparation. The food needn't be mundane, but save the very elaborate dishes for another time. After all, your guests will be coming mainly to see you and talk with you—they can't if you're always popping into the kitchen. And besides, they'll feel guilty that you're going to so much trouble. You invited them, didn't you, because you wanted to see them?

Have your marketing and house cleaning and as much of the cooking as possible done before the guests arrive, and naturally have everything in apple-pie order for their comfort in their quarters.

THE GUEST ROOM

It's been observed dozens of times that every hostess (host, too! say the men) ought to spend a night in her own guest room to see how it feels. We may be sure the idea originated in the mind of some forlorn guest with nothing to read and no light to read it by, tossing on a lumpy mattress and wishing there were an extra blanket and a pillow less like a tea bag. So give the room a very stiff inspection. Look at it with a guest's eye, for practicality and comfort as well as prettiness. Pretend you're unpacking, making up your face, dressing, writing a letter, reading and eating in bed. And at the same time try to recall the lacks that may have inconvenienced you when you were a guest in someone else's house. You'll end up with quite a checklist!

Beds come' first, for no amount of good talk and good food can make up for a restless night. Twin beds are ideal for the guest room. It's best not to assume that all married people can sleep comfortably in a double bed. If they are accustomed to twin beds at home, they probably can't.

Don't ask more guests than you can put up both comfortably and politely. A married couple can of course share a room, or two girls or two boys, or two youngish women or two bachelors. So may two older women, provided you know they're compatible and that neither is a fanatic about her privacy.

Bed springs and mattresses should be youthfully firm—certainly not senescent. There should be two pillows for each bed and they shouldn't be weak sisters. In wintertime, unless you use electric blankets, in addition to the blankets on the bed there should be a quilt at the foot or extra blankets in a drawer or on the closet shelf—don't forget to tell the guests where. In summer you would have a lightweight blanket on the bed and a slightly heavier one available for those occasional chilly dawns. Each night table should boast a lamp tall enough to read by, with a good strong bulb in it.

Now for the rest of the inspection. First the unpacking—where to put the suitcase? (And don't forget that often there are two suitcases.) It saves your bedding if you have a pair of luggage racks. Then where to put the clothes? Try to have at least one and preferably two bureau drawers emptied out. In the closet, move over the mothproofbag brigade to free at least a foot of hanger rods. Make sure there are plenty of hangers, not forgetting skirt and trouser hangers and one or two velvet-covered ones for off-the-shoulder dresses.

The dressing table should have a good mirror, an empty drawer or two, and should be as well lighted as possible, especially if this is where a guest might write a letter. A straight chair or comfortable stool should stand in front of it.

Don't forget an easy chair if there's room for one. A scrap basket. Plenty of ashtrays. A box of facial tissues. Aspirin. And some reading matter—not just the overflow from the living room bookcases, but something really interesting. Have a few new magazines plus, say, a mystery or a new novel or an anthology or cartoon book.

If the guest room lacks privacy or its windows face the sunrise, be sure to have venetian blinds or opaque shades and warn your guests to draw them at night—or do it for them when you come to turn the beds down.

A guest so provided for will be comfortable and at ease. Not strictly necessary but pleasurable for guests to find are such extras as a luminous alarm clock (the kind with a bashful tick), a small radio, cigarettes (the guests' brand if you know it), a freshly filled carafe with glasses, a plate of fruit with a knife and napkins. A supply of throw-away toothbrushes is good to have on hand for a guest who has forgotten his own or for people who stay over unexpectedly.

Flowers—just a small bouquet on the bureau or dressing table—will warm your guests' hearts in the same way a fire in the fireplace would. And if you're so fortunate as to have a guest room with a fireplace, by all means make use of it—except in summer, naturally. In the cool seasons, no matter how adequate your heating, gay flames crackling away say "Welcome!" to your guests.

THE GUEST IN SMALL QUARTERS

If you live in a house where your only extra room must double as study-*cum*-sewing-room, you may not have the space for such extra appointments as night stands and dressing tables. But you can provide the essentials: a bed that is comfortable even though it may pretend to be a couch in the daytime, plenty of blankets and pillows, a standing lamp to read by, a good mirror (on the closet door if need be), some room for clothes, a place, however small, for toiletries.

If you're an apartment dweller, you probably have no extra room of any kind and must bed down any guest on the living room couch. This is such a makeshift situation that it will occur only for emergency overnight stands, and both guest and host must make the best of it.

THE GUEST BATHROOM

If you are fortunate enough to have a bathroom for the guests' sole use, of course you will stock it with such necessities as large and small towels, washcloths, soap, tissues, scrapbasket, drinking glass, and bathmat. It's thoughtful to clear a shelf of the medicine cabinet and to set out a pretty jar of bath salts. If you're maidless, you probably keep a few pieces of cleaning equipment in the bathroom. If you do, leave them there, all ready for any helpful impulse that may seize your guests.

If the guests are to share a bath with the family, set aside one of the towel racks for their own use and tell both them and the family which one. Some hostesses buy and keep just for guest use towels and washcloths markedly different in color from anything in daily use—bright coral or turquoise, say—in order to warn the absent-minded adult or hurried child. Should your family be large, almost certainly there aren't enough towel racks to go round as it is. In this case it may be better to put a standing towel rack in the guestroom itself.

This may not add the decorator touch, but it does forestall the appearance of grimy little pawprints on the guests' towels.

If your supply of hot water is limited it's only fair to warn your guests about it. If you're country dwellers and your guests are not, tell them too what can and can't go down the toilet—it's not fair to expect them to know the limitations of country plumbing. If you don't tell them, think how mortified and embarrassed they would be if their inexperience resulted in serious trouble!

THE INVITATION

You can invite your guests by telephone or by note, as you like. A note is perhaps more courteous and is easier for both guest and hostess because it will cover all the details that might be forgotten in conversation. Your invitation should make clear who is expected (if you want the children or resident mother-in-law to come too, say so), when and for how long, information about how to get to your house, and mention of any special activity or entertainment so that the guest knows what to pack. Your invitation might read like this:

June 28

Dear Sally,

It seems so long since we have seen you. We do hope we can have you and Bob with us for a weekend. How about coming out on Friday the 11th? The drive from the city takes about an hour on the expressway. Get off at Exit 12—I've drawn you a little map showing the way from there. The lake is waiting for you, so don't forget your bathing suits. We thought we'd have a small dinner party here Saturday night and go on to the club dance, but that's very informal—just sports jackets and cottons.

Do come if you possibly can,

Love from both of us,
Beth

A departure time is not specified in this note because, although it is understood you will have an evening meal ready on Sunday, the guests may decide to leave in midafternoon to avoid twilight traffic. If your guests are coming by train, your note should mention several of the outgoing trains on Friday afternoon; you should indicate which of these are the fastest and enclose a timetable. If the trains are infrequent on Sunday, you might say, "I wish we didn't have to pack you off so early, but the only Sunday train between lunchtime and midnight is the six-ten."

If it's possible, it's the friendliest thing to meet your friends at the station. If for some reason you can't they won't mind taking a taxi for the average suburban haul, but you should explain this in your invitation.

ENTERTAINMENT

Friday night, especially after a busy week and a train trip or a drive in weekend traffic, the guests (and perhaps the hosts, too—almost certainly the male host) would probably prefer to be quiet. On Sunday evenings the prospects of packing and an early departure inhibit any festivities. So Saturday is usually the best night to arrange some lively and probably late entertainment for your guests—and it doesn't need to be elaborate if you feel certain your guests would prefer a quiet evening to a giddy one. You could have a buffet supper or take them to a club dance—or both—or give a small dinner party. An evening of cards, music, or just talk, with or without a few congenial neighbors coming in for coffee, may be what your guests would most appreciate. Indeed, if they are very old friends who moved away some years before, on such a brief visit they, as well as you, might like best to talk just with you or with a few other acquaintances from the neighborhood.

Friday evening, at bedtime, you indicate what the plans are for breakfast. You may suggest a tray brought to the guestroom or breakfast with the family, or if you think your guests may want to sleep late, show them where the bread and coffee and sugar are and how the stove and coffeepot function. It's the work of only a moment and very thoughtful to put guest trays in the kitchen the night before, set with silver, china, napkins, and juice glass.

Don't block out every hour of your guests' weekend with some activity, as though you were their camp counselor. If you belong to a golf club and your guests are golfers, it will no doubt be understood that golf will be the major daytime activity—in fact, the weekend is no doubt planned with that in mind. If your part of the country is new to your guests, take them for a short drive. Or take them to pay a short visit to some neighbors you know they'd like— after you've telephoned the neighbors, of course. But leave your guests, and yourselves, time in which to relax, read, talk, or putter. On trips you must make that they don't have to, it's pleasant to give them a choice: "Would you like to go to the village with me for the watermelon, or would you rather just sit and soak up the sun?"

If your guests want to help you, let them. When they want to help you cook and that's just too distracting for you, say you're the world's rattlebrain when it comes to cooking and talking at the same time—but it would be a big help if they'd cut some iris and put them in that pail in the laundry, or take the charcoal and the grill out to the barbecue, or fill the ice bucket and make more ice cubes.

In these maidless days most women guests, knowing two hands can do only so much, not only keep their room tidy and make the bed daily, but also on departing would really like to do something constructive about remaking or stripping the beds if they know which you want. If you'd like them made up as they are or stripped and the linens put in the hamper, just say so. If there's ample time and the offer to make the beds afresh is earnest, thankfully hand over the clean sheets and pillow cases.

YOUR CHILDREN

Presumably your guests don't expect you to put your children in solitary for the entire weekend or they wouldn't have accepted your invitation. All the same, it is up to you to see that your offspring do not make nuisances of themselves. Particularly if the guests are childless, try to discourage endless questioning and insistent bids for attention. In any case, make the children understand they are to respect the privacy of the guest room, and try to keep them as quiet as possible if the guests are sleeping late.

YOUR GUESTS' CHILDREN

Should your guests have children and bring them along, you can look forward to a more relaxed attitude toward what can and can't be expected of small fry—at least, one hopes so. Don't grind your own children down, but be ready to step in if they act up or are unfair to the other children. If there are disputes between the houses, don't take sides either way, settle the matter fairly by separating the parties or manufacturing a diversion. If the guests' offspring seem to be acting like bullies or spoilsports, don't forget that the visiting situation may have put them off base and make allowances for that. When the guest-parent stays aloof from the whole affair, your role is harder, but if you discipline your children along with hers in an unemotional and common-sense manner, she shouldn't take offense.

YOUR PETS

Always remember that your guests may not be used to animals. If you don't already know that they're not fond of dogs, you'll find out quite soon. Should this be the case, try to keep the dog out of sight as much as possible. And make your dog mind his manners— even people who truly love dogs don't care to be jumped on or nagged for tidbits.

Many people are almost pathologically afraid of cats. This is a real fear and they can't help it, so don't try to educate them or ridicule their fright. Instead, shut the cat away or ask a neighbor to take care of it for the duration of the visit.

17

How to Be a House Guest

THE PERFECT HOUSE GUEST IS, ONE SUPPOSES, ABOUT AS RARE AS THE perfect weekend and the guest room without flaw. But it isn't hard at all to approach the ideal quite closely.

First of all, answer your invitation promptly and arrive when you said you would. If you have visited your present host and hostess before, you know just about what to expect and will bring the proper clothes and sports things with you. If you don't know what sort of entertainment will be provided, there's no harm in asking, "What shall I pack?" This query should lead the hostess to indicate whether there'll be tennis or swimming or riding, and also probably to give you further clues by saying, for example, " . . . nothing dressy except for the club dance Saturday night." If you know the club and its customs, you're set; if not, you can ask, "How dressy?" The point is to come prepared, feeling poised because you have the right clothes and don't have to choose between borrowing from your hostess or turning up in an inappropriate outfit.

While you're a guest in the house, you should keep your room and the bathroom tidy, even if there is a servant. And, unless your hostess has a number of servants, you should make your own bed. When there are servants, always remember they're not yours. You may ask—not order—small favors, but make them small and make them few so they don't interfere with regular duties. Try to pack so that no pressing is needed; if pressing must be done, don't let it go until it's nearly time to dress. In a house with one servant, put your problem to your hostess, offering to do it yourself. If the servant can manage, the hostess will say so; if not, she'll show you where the iron and ironing board are kept. Naturally, in a servant-less house you will expect to do it yourself. Here again, though, don't leave the ironing until the last minute. A guest who needs such a chore performed half an hour before the party is a guest unloved.

In a maidless house, of course, and especially if you are sharing a bathroom with some or all of the family, you will want to keep everything as nearly spotless as you can. Equipment for cleaning the bathroom is usually in the bathroom somewhere—find it and use it and leave a gleaming tub and basin. On an extended visit of several weeks in a servantless house, it may be appreciated if now and then you ask your hostess for her duster and carpet sweeper or the vacuum cleaner and give your bedroom a going-over.

You'll naturally want to do whatever you can for your hostess without being more hindrance than help. Don't rush in. It takes a little time and tact to determine where she does and doesn't want you to tread. If she'd rather cope alone when she cooks, as those of us who can't chat and measure simultaneously often do, there are always little tasks around the house—emptying ashtrays, plumping up the cushions, gathering up last evening's papers, and so on. Vacuuming the living room and dining room, if there's to be company that evening and you know she'll have to do it if you don't can be a tremendous help—but not if she truly doesn't want you to.

If you use your eyes the first day to see where things are kept and take note of the habits of the household, you'll find dozens of small ways to save your hostess time and steps. If you like to arrange flowers and your hostess has a garden, she will no doubt love to turn you loose with the vases and scissors and let you do the flowers for the house, or at least some of them. (If there are flowers enough, don't forget a little bouquet for the master bedroom.) If the hostess is a flower arranger herself, best leave the party centerpiece for her unless she asks you to do it. When you've discovered she uses the straw mats for family dinner and have noticed where they and the table silver are kept, you can set the table. You can devote half an hour or so to reading to the children or otherwise keeping them amused while their mother rests or is busy in the kitchen. And, of course, you can always help with the clearing up and the dish-washing.

And house-guest husbands? Though they're really not called on to do much in the line of helping, the thoughtful things they find to do are always appreciated—assisting the host as bartender, collecting the stack tables, moving the garden furniture when it rains, and so on.

Just as the best-loved hostesses leave their guests some free time, the most popular guests are those who respect the family's privacy and withdraw from the activities now and then. Breakfast may be one of these times, especially if there are children and if the host has a train to catch. Then the considerate guest does not add to the congestion of kitchen and bathroom but sleeps late—or pretends to. If the hostess wants to bring your breakfast to your room on a tray, don't protest, "Oh, I wouldn't dream of letting you!" Maybe doing just that, after the school bus has come and gone and she has made the trip to the station, will give her a breathing spell and a chance to plan her day. If you loathe eating in bed, you can always put the tray on a table!

On the other hand, some gregarious families seem to thrive on confusion and commotion and would think it odd if you didn't join them for breakfast. You have to take your cue from the hostess on this. If at bedtime on the first evening she doesn't make any suggestion, ask her what time you should be up. When you do join the family at the breakfast table, be ready on time, fully dressed and neat. Don't come in bathrobe or negligée even on a Sunday unless you are old friends or know this to be the custom of the family. Whatever you do, don't arise very late and then plunk yourself down, expecting the hostess to drop everything and feed you. If you want to sleep, the best thing is to ask the night before if you may, get the hostess to show you where the bread and coffee and so forth are, and make it clear you'll get breakfast for yourself and your husband. And, of course, you won't forget to wash the things you use and leave the kitchen tidy.

Breakfast is not the only time of day when the family you're visiting may need a little privacy. Be aware of such occasions when they arise, and excuse yourself casually to retreat to your room. The wise guest always brings along something to occupy herself—address book (and stationery and stamps) for letters she's been meaning to write, a paperback or two, manicure things. Knitting is very helpful —it keeps the guest occupied and looks "busy" so that a hostess feels no compunction about leaving her alone with it.

A guest husband, especially if he's going to be there when the host is at his office, ought to be prepared, too, to amuse himself— with reading, a sports program on television, or some work he has brought along. A short stint of pitching ball for the children may benefit both him and them as well as the mothers. Or if he wants to, he can simply sit.

Guests shouldn't forget that sometimes people need mental privacy as well as physical. No need to talk all the time. Companionable silence is restful for the host who has been jammed into the 5:44 after a hard day. When he gets home he needs to relax in his own way, which for the first half-hour will probably not include being responsive to chit-chat or questions. And silence can be a boon to the hostess now and then, too. She may want to work on a private worry for a few minutes or just need to be quiet.

The ideal guest is friendly and pleasant, and agreeable to whatever is proposed. If you've been gadding much too much all week and your host and hostess have planned a brunch, a buffet, and a picnic, plus visits to neighbors' houses, go along with it all even though you're sure you'll be sanitarium fodder when you get home.

This doesn't mean that you must go along with every *suggestion* that is made to you. Planned entertainment is one thing—an inquiry if you would like to go along with the hostess to the supermarket or library is another. Here you may do as you like—go, or say with a smile, "I think I'd just as soon stay home and finish my mystery." If the family dines at what you consider an uncivilized hour—primitively early or too fashionably late—mentally resolve to eat less or more lunch accordingly and come to the table with a sunny face.

Flexibility is the greatest single asset a guest can have. Cultivate it. Try to adapt yourself to the household mores, especially the "thou shalt nots." Sneaking pretzels to the dog when it's been made clear that this is frowned upon will make you popular with the dog and nobody else. It's the same if you pretend the children are cute when they're really being fresh and know it. On the other hand, if the family is much more easygoing than you are, don't try to make them over or indicate your disapproval even silently. If you are compulsive about ashtrays and your hostess dumps them only when they're full, go along with her system even though you twitch inside; if you busily empty them throughout the evening, it will seem to be more a criticism than a favor.

CHILDREN

When you're asked to stay overnight or longer at anyone's house you would not bring your children unless you are specifically invited to, or unless you know from old friendship and custom that you are expected to. Even then, it's more polite to ask whether the children may come too.

When you do bring them, make sure you carry along, even if it means still another suitcase, all the paraphernalia they need—bibs, crib pads, rubber sheeting for the toddler, plenty of clothing changes plus toys and books for the older ones. It is well to remember that a hostess with children in the upper grades or in high school may have given away everything she once had in the baby department.

It is to be hoped that if your children and your hosts' are of an age to play together that they get along fairly well. If not, the exercise of a good deal of tact and firmness will be necessary, for here the guest's golden rule of "When in Rome . . . " may now and then have to be bent, though not, one hopes, broken. You can't expect your children to sacrifice themselves on the altar of good guesthood as you do for two whole days and nights. And if they did. they would probably grow up loathing the very idea of visiting! Leave them alone if they're not in danger of harming themselves or any of the hosts' property and not making too unearthly a racket. If the hostess referees any disputes, so much the better—if she seems unwilling to, do it yourself as tactfully as you can.

You will, of course, be constantly alert to check any rudeness on your children's part and to see that they do not do any damage to the house, the furnishings, or the lawn and garden. And this means damage according to the *hostess'* standards, not yours. If you don't already know, you can soon discover whether her attitude about her house and belongings is casual, fussy, or in between. Especially if she has no children or if hers are much older than your own, remember that while your upholstery is childproof or is considered so by you, hers may not be.

Make sure, for your children's sake as well as the hosts', that your children have a quiet period away from everyone else every day even if they don't nap. Don't let them disrupt any grown up gathering. Above all, don't let them roam the house before you are up in the morning, unless they are old enough to be both tactful and self-reliant.

Fortunately rare is the hardest role in the guest's repertoire—that of the parent-guest whose children are better behaved and better disciplined than those of the hosts. For one thing, childhood misbehavior is more catching than measles and gets progressively more virulent, so that managing your offspring takes more tact and dexterity than ever. Dispense these as best you can, together with as much justice as good manners will allow. Button your lips firmly over any maxims of child raising that threaten to pop out. And resolve that if there is a next time, you won't bring the children!

A FEW SPECIAL DON'TS FOR GUESTS

Don't bring pets unless you have made very sure they're welcome. Very often they're not. Someone in the household may be allergic to animals, the hosts' pet may be antagonistic to other pets, or the hosts just don't like pets in the house. When you do bring your animal, make absolutely sure it does no damage. You will, of course, bring the pet's food with you, prepare it with as little fuss as possible, and clean up afterwards.

Don't bring servants or employees with you unless your hostess, knowing that you never travel without your chauffeur or your secretary-companion, has indicated that she can put up him or her. This is practically never possible in a small house and often awkward even in a large one. If you must take along such a person—your chauffeur, for instance—try to make arrangements for him to stay nearby at your expense.

Don't make free with the hosts' telephone. Ask when you want to use it, and if you make a toll call, take care of the cost as suggested in Chapter 10.

Of course, you would not extend invitations to your hosts' house without permission, and neither do you accept any without consulting your hostess first. If you do go out to call on a friend in the vicinity, set a time when you'll be back and stick to it.

Don't keep your hostess picking up after you. Put back the book you took from the shelves, the magazine you took out to read on the terrace. Be tidy with those bulky Sunday papers—and never carry any sections off to your own bedroom unless you know positively that everyone else in the house has finished with them.

Don't keep your host and hostess up until all hours. If they want to stay up, too, well and good—but watch for the smothered yawns and the lag in conversation. If they are the ones who want to look at the late-late show, you may just say, "I'm so sleepy—I think I'll turn in now if you don't mind," and go off to bed.

A "don't" that should be emblazoned in flaming letters on the consciousness of every guest: Don't leave anything behind when you go. You may have been the perfect guest in every other way, but the gratitude and affection with which your hostess puts you on the train will curdle if she comes home to find your mules under the bed—which she'll have to find a box for, wrap, address, and carry to the postoffice.

GIFTS

It isn't ever necessary, but it is always gracious to bring a gift to your hostess. Most people bring something for the house—good things to eat like a special paté, cheeses, or preserves; some new

cocktail accompaniments, gay table mats, soap in unusual shapes and colors, little guest towels, or something for the garden. The gift needn't be expensive, but it should be something you know your hosts will like and something that fits in with their way of living. The gift is usually presented shortly after your arrival.

TIPPING

Most of us today are servantless at home and find ourselves servantless when we go visiting as well, so the question of tipping when we are house guests arises less often than it used to. If there's only one maid, you seek her out just before leaving and give her your tip with your thanks. Two dollars for a short weekend is all right—more if she has done you some special service, such as pressing a dress. If there is a cook as well as maid, you go into the kitchen and extend your tip and thanks there. You wouldn't tip the cleaning woman or the gardener, even though you may have seen and spoken to them.

In a house with a very large staff, you similarly tip only those who have personally served you. This need not include the cook and usually doesn't unless you have brought one of your own servants with you. In that case, members of the kitchen staff who have served him should be remembered. You should give two dollars or more to the chambermaid. Tips for men servants may be given to the butler for distribution, along with his own. He should get from two to five dollars, the other men servants a little less unless one of them, such as the chauffeur, has given you some special service. The amount would never be less than a dollar for any member of a large staff.

In some houses with a large staff of servants you will find a notice in the guest room asking guests not to tip. Such a rule should be observed by the thoughtful guest because it means that your host has settled on a system of extra benefits for extra work that suits everyone concerned.

BREAD-AND-BUTTER LETTERS

Promptness in thanking your hostess is a detail that helps to make a bread-and-butter letter memorable. You should write it within two days, three at the most, of your arrival at home. Your hostess will be appreciative of even the most conventional thank you, but it will give her a warm glow, which in all probability she has worked hard to deserve, if you are specific about the ways in which your visit was enjoyable. After all, your host and hostess did invite you and they did try to please you. After you left, if they're like most married couples, they said to each other, "*I* think they had a good time, don't you?" So mention whatever you remember with special warmth—the reminiscences, interesting new people you met, the new house or the new décor, the special attention to your wants. If it was a very gay visit, it stimulated and refreshed you; if it was a quiet one, you feel rested. Just a sentence or two of specific appreciation added to the routine "We had such a lovely time at your house" makes all the difference.

YOUR WELCOMING HOUSE

18

Your Linens and Silver, China, and Glass

WHETHER YOUR HOME IS AN APARTMENT, A SUBURBAN SPLIT-LEVEL OR a roomy, rambling Victorian, you want it to have that aura of welcome always. To family as well as friends it should speak of warmth and comfort. The curtains and color schemes and all the furnishings will, of course, reflect the personalities of you and your family. But no matter whether your taste is traditional or modern or both, your

favorite colors brilliant or muted, your pocketbook fat or thin, you want to be sure that your closets and cupboards come close to holding everything you need, not only for your family's comfort and enjoyment but also to extend the hospitality of a truly welcoming house. You want all of the essentials and at least some of the luxuries in china and sheets and towels, in silver and glassware.

What do you buy? How many? And *how* do you buy?

YOUR LINENS

Let's divide the household linens into two parts, one a list of minimum needs and the other a tally of all the things you may want to add to these, given sufficient funds and storage space.

BED LINENS

For each bed in your house, you'll need linens in the quantities listed below:

    6 sheets for each bed

    3 pillowcases for each pillow

    2 mattress pads (one may be enough if you launder them at home)

    1 electric blanket or a pair of winter blankets

    1 pair of summer blankets

    1 bedspread (you may want two, one summer and one winter)

BATH LINENS

    3 large bath towels for each person

    3 hand towels (terry or linen)

    3 washcloths

    2 bathmats for each bathroom

    1 shower curtain for each shower

    1 rug for each bathroom

For any guests who may stay with you, you will want at least one bath towel, hand towel, and washcloth. And, of course, you'll want a supply of small guest towels, terry or linen or both.

FOR THE KITCHEN

    6 dishtowels at least (more if you send laundry out)

    4 dishcloths

    2 or 3 potholders

FOR THE TABLE

    2 or 3 changes for everyday use, as a minimum

    A variety of practical place mats

    1 cloth and napkins for entertaining

    1 set of mats and napkins for entertaining, (or a second cloth with napkins)

ADDITIONS TO THE BASIC LIST

You may want to add to the bed linens a second pair of heavy blankets for very cold weather or to use when the other pair is being cleaned. Or you may, like many housewives who have the equipment to wash and dry blankets in a day, prefer a comforter for extremely cold weather.

A summer blanket cover, the simple, washable kind, protects your blankets and also can be used as a temporary spread if your bedspreads must be sent out for cleaning.

You will probably want to buy several more sets of sheets and pillowcases. The ones you have won't then be in the wash so often and will last longer. And it's very comforting to have more than one spare set of bed linens in case of illness or a series of overnight guests in rapid succession.

If there is more than one bedroom in your home, and especially if the sizes of the beds vary, it's a good idea to choose an identifying color or design for each bed size. For example, your double-bed sheets and cases might be in pure white, your singles for a boy's room might be yellow, your singles for a girl's room might be blue, and guest sheets might be in a figured design. This system saves your opening up a sheet to find out what size it is.

You may want to stretch the budget to buy more towels and wash-cloths for the bathroom. Assuming that the bathroom rug is wash-able, it's a blessing to have a twin to it so that the soiled one can be laundered at your leisure. If your basic list included only terry hand towels, you might add some linen ones.

When it comes to the kitchen, more dishtowels are never amiss, and unless you have a dishwasher, you will probably want to get some special towels for glassware. A reserve supply of dishcloths and pot-holders is good to have since the former are always wearing thin and the latter so quickly acquire stains and scorches that won't wash out.

Table linens, many of us think, are the most fun to buy. One can go on and on, funds permitting, acquiring not only more cloths, mats, and napkins for the dining room table, but also such extras as tray sets, doilies, and cocktail napkins. If you already have white damask—or even if not—you may select a damask cloth and napkins in shell pink or some other pastel.

While a white, off-white, or pastel damask cloth and napkins are eminently suitable to the formal dinner, it's quite correct to use place mats. In fact, because of today's laundering and storage prob-lems, place mats have become extremely popular, and can be found in a wide variety of shapes and colors and materials. For formal din-ners choose mats of fine linen or lace.

If you do much buffet entertaining, several matching cloths and napkins for bridge table service are good to have—you can always borrow the bridge tables. (Note that it's ideal for these cloths to match each other as well as their napkins.) There will be times when you need a tea cloth and napkins.

When you buy either mats or cloths in colors, try to get them in shades that will combine attractively with what you already have, so that not only will your new rose-red cloth and napkins be lovely used as a set, but its napkins, with a centerpiece of rosy gladioli, say, will enliven your gray cloth, and vice versa.

For your damask cloths, matching napkins in the largest size—twenty-four inches square—are always available in the better grades and are essential. Unfortunately, some colored tablecloths, even when quite large, are accompanied by napkins only a foot or so square, and they are really too small for formal use. So search for a cloth with large napkins, sixteen or eighteen inches at the least.

Be sure that any tablecloth you buy is long enough for a generous overhang of twelve to fifteen inches—more, if possible.

Don't forget a pad or "silence cloth" to go under tablecloths.

If your dining room table has a perishable finish, especially if there are children in your family, you may prefer to use a cloth rather than mats for most meals. It is possible nowadays to get very pretty, nonfancy cloths of various synthetics and plastics—some sheer, some in a linen-like texture—and a great variety of paper napkins. The use of any of these is a matter of personal preference. Certainly they are tremendous time-savers for the wife and mother who does all her own housework. Remember, though, that they are definitely for informal use.

HOW TO BUY LINENS

The prime rule in linen purchase is to get the very best that you can afford. One good thick terry towel will outlast at least two of the flimsier sort. Stay away from fancy touches like elaborate machine embroidery on pillowcases and towels. Not only are they not in the best of taste, but they also weaken the fabric. Hand embroidery or hemstitching on towels and bed linens is handsome and distinguished, but may shorten the life of the article.

For things that are used only occasionally, such as tea cloths, embroidery and even lace and drawn work are lovely provided they are done by hand. But one tires more quickly of the ornate than the plain for anything in frequent use—so when in doubt, choose the simpler of two designs.

White towels go with any bathroom color scheme, but there is an infinite variety of colored towels to choose from. A caution about deep shades—they have a tendency to bleed, especially when new, and shouldn't be washed with lighter colors.

MONOGRAMS AND INITIALS

Either of these can be used in marking linens. An initial is of course just a single letter; a monogram is made up of two or three. Most frequently it's three, because it is harder to make a good design with only two. Good monogramming is extremely expensive; initialing somewhat less so. If you use either, be sure to keep the initial or monogram in scale with the size of the article it marks—big for bath towels, small for hand towels, big for dinner napkins, small for tea napkins. When in doubt, choose the simpler of two possible monograms, shunning the very fancy scrolls and arabesques, especially those that are not part of the letters themselves.

WHAT INITIALS TO USE

For years it was the custom for everything to be marked with the initials of the bride's maiden name: E B H for Emily Borden Hall. Today practically everyone makes up the monogram from the initials of the bride's first and last names plus the initial of the groom's last name. Thus when Emily marries John Winter, her—or, more properly, their—monogram becomes E H W. If a single initial is used or if the design requires one initial to be larger than the others, that initial should be the W. Of course, whatever Emily bought before her engagement for her "hope chest" would be marked E B H.

Although it is not strictly correct according to some authorities, many young people today are combining initials in a different way, using the initials of the bride's first name and the groom's first name plus that of the groom's surname. This would make E J W the monogram for the Winters.

YOUR SILVER

Formal table silver used always to mean solid silver. When it is in the reach of one's budget, there is no doubt that there is nothing that so graces a table and so delights a woman's spirit as sterling. Moreover, if it is used regularly and properly cared for, it will last for generations. Nowadays, though, a bride has many other choices. If she does not wish to buy sterling a few place settings at a time, she may prefer to use a heavy silver plate. Or she may decide on a good quality of stainless steel, which is improving in design almost day by day.

STERLING

This means that the pieces are of solid silver, although they may be of heavy, light, or medium weight. The heaviest is the most expensive and the most nearly indestructible. The light weight is least practical, because it is liable to bend with hard and frequent use or over-energetic polishing.

Sterling flatware which is in constant use can be kept in an easily accessible drawer in the kitchen or dining room. Less frequently used pieces should be kept in tarnish-proof wrappings. Constant use improves the appearance of silver and reduces the amount of special polishing it requires.

PLATED SILVER

This is less expensive than sterling, since only the coating is silver, the base being of another metal. The price depends on the thickness of the plating. It is not economical in the long run to buy the cheapest except for short-term use. The cheaper sets are often too light in weight and the plating too thin. Also, the balance may not be good. Balance is important—if the weight is not properly distributed, the piece will seem clumsy in use.

Plated silver needs the same care and polishing as sterling.

STAINLESS STEEL

Stainless steel is both beautiful and practical. For the most part it is very well designed, and it doesn't need polishing, ever. Stainless steel isn't cheap—the very best grades often cost as much as the cheaper grades of sterling. It pays to buy the best quality you can afford. Many inexpensive sets are often too light in weight and not properly balanced. The design may be over-elaborate as well.

The only possible disadvantage of stainless steel is that at present it is not considered in very good taste for extremely formal dinners and usually does not harmonize when the glass and china are traditional. If, however, your home and its furnishings are modern, it is quite permissible to use a good quality of well-designed stainless, even for formal dining.

WHEN YOU SELECT YOUR SILVER

Plated and sterling silver come in hundreds of designs, ranging from the very plain to the very elaborate. Stainless steel is not adapted to the making of designs in heavy relief and so it usually comes in rather simple styles, either modern or colonial. The pattern as well as the material of your flat silver should express your husband's taste and yours. It need not "go with" your furnishings. It may do so if you prefer, but don't think that because you have quite a bit of traditional furniture you must have a traditional silver pattern.

Your silver need not match, either. Your main pieces should—your setting of knife, fork, and spoons. But if you have or are given some lovely antique silver or silver of a different pattern in the shape of serving spoons, salad forks, coffee spoons, and so on, use them with joy alongside your chosen pattern.

Don't make the mistake of rejecting a plain pattern when you really prefer it to an elaborate one, because you're afraid it'll scratch. It will, but the scratches will soon blend and the patina improve with use.

It has become the custom for the bride to register her selected pattern and monogram at the store where the silver is purchased. The flat silver is traditionally the gift of the bride's parents, and the store keeps a list of what pieces have already been purchased. Friends of the bride who wish to give flat silver as a wedding present go to the store, consult the list, and select other pieces in the bride's chosen pattern. Relatives and close friends may add individual place settings if only a few have been ordered, or they may elect to give a carving set or a serving piece or two. A few people feel that "filling in the bride's list" seems a bit cold and mechanical, but almost everyone—certainly the brides and grooms themselves—think it extremely sensible. The giver knows the gift will be just what the couple wants and that there are not likely to be duplicates.

MONOGRAMMING

In general the advice about linens earlier in this chapter applies to the marking of silver. But do try to select a monogram style in keeping with the character of the silver. Simple letters look best on simple silver, script may be more becoming to an elaborate pattern. If the pieces are very heavily ornamented, it's perfectly correct to put the marking on the back. The store where you buy your silver will give you good advice on the style and placing of your monogram.

WHAT IS A PLACE SETTING?

Literally and obviously, the term means eating utensils for one, not counting pieces used just for serving. The average bride starts with four or six of these, hoping to increase them eventually to eight or perhaps a dozen. Just what constitutes "eating utensils for one" depends on the bride's pocketbook. The number of pieces can range from four to a dozen or more if you include all the refinements such as oyster forks and iced-tea spoons.

Most brides start off with a five-piece place setting:

> 1 dinner fork
> 1 dinner knife
> 1 teaspoon
> 1 dessert spoon (these are bigger than teaspoons and
>   can double as soup spoons)
> 1 butter spreader

If the budget allows for six pieces, add a salad fork.

So much for the absolute minimum. Next you would increase the number of your place settings if you have only four. Or add more teaspoons, since you often use two at a meal. Or buy for each setting a smaller knife and fork, the luncheon size. Many people use this luncheon fork for both salad and dessert.

As you increase your supply of flat silver you add these:

> a gravy ladle
> more serving forks and spoons
> a pie server
> demitasse spoons
> a small ladle for sauces, a large one for soups or punch

From time to time you can add, if you like, rather special pieces such as a tea strainer, oyster forks, steak knives, fruit knives and forks, iced-tea spoons, a sugar spoon and/or tongs, cream soup spoons, salt spoons.

Since none of these last-named pieces need match the rest of your silver, you can often pick up charming pieces in secondhand and antique shops quite reasonably, and they will add interest to your table settings. When your selected pattern of sterling is also available in plate, as is sometimes the case, there is no reason why you shouldn't buy plate for those pieces that get only occasional use.

YOUR CHINA

Time was when china always came in sets, or seemed to. And a bride always started off with—or saved up for—a complete matched outfit of fine china for company, with dozens and dozens of pieces from butter chips (very small individual butter dishes) through covered tureens and platters in graduated sizes all the way to gravy boats. Then there was a small, less expensive set for most week-day and family meals.

Lucky those of us to whom some pieces of that everyday "blue onion" or Spode have descended, let alone the company Lowestoft or Crown Derby! But imagine the monotony of many of yesterday's

table settings—always white damask on the table, and course after course marching in on the same pink rosebuds or gold bands—as sure as death, and more sure, in those days, than taxes.

There isn't a thing wrong with white damask and gold bands. On the contrary, a white table with gleaming crystal and silver plus any kind of formal china is beautiful! Most of us glorify our entertaining with them at least occasionally. But today changing customs plus a wide range of choice among inexpensive china patterns have given us much more freedom. We can and do serve different courses on different plates. We enjoy making an adventure of each meal!

WHAT CHINA IS

In a book like this one and generally in conversation, the word "china" is used to mean all the dishes that we eat from and may include very fine china, earthenware and plastic.

Technically the word should include only the very fine grades—that is, bone china, real china, and porcelain. These are close-grained, not absorbent, and are often so thin you can see through them, though they are much stronger than they look. Fine china is manufactured both in the United States and abroad, and the price varies widely in accordance with the amount of skilled handwork needed for the design, as well as on the amount of gold (or silver) trim. Purists still believe that no part of any formal dinner should be served on anything other than these fine wares, but that custom is daily being modified.

Earthenware has a softer texture, is not translucent, and in some grades may be absorbent and therefore not resistant to staining. It's also heavier to handle. In quality it ranges from very fine to very coarse. Spode, Wedgwood, and others are beautifully patterned and durable. Mexican pottery and other peasant wares are softer and coarser, though very colorful and attractive for informal table settings.

Good plastic can be quite expensive. It comes, however, in beautiful solid colors and some excellent designs which are very decorative. And it is so nearly indestructible that it is an excellent investment for everyday use. Be sure to buy a good brand—some of the cheaper grades won't stand up to the temperatures of your dishwasher and will quickly absorb stains, especially from hot coffee. And do test the handles of the cups for comfort.

HOW TO BUY CHINA

After you have decided what kind, or kinds, you want, the wisest thing is to select your pattern from those carried in open stock so that replacements are usually available. Sometimes a "set" of china seems such a bargain that it would be foolish to resist it. But there are many disadvantages. There are always too many of some pieces and not enough of others. You can seldom replace anything that breaks and the most used pieces will fall like autumn leaves. Often, many of the pieces are impractical—the cereal bowls too small, the soup plates too deep.

So open stock is preferable. But be sure to pin the term down in the language of the store that's selling the china. A woman likes to take it for granted that when a pattern is marked "open stock" it means that the china will be there whenever she needs replacements or has saved up for additional pieces. And this is what it should mean. Sometimes, however, it may mean only that this particular pattern can be bought by the piece as well as in sets. This is fine at the time of purchase, but it may be "open stock" only for a season or two. In other words, when you go back eight months later for two cups, one salad plate, and a cream pitcher, the store may not carry it any more or the manufacturer may have discontinued the pattern. So make sure that *your* open-stock pattern will be available for some time to come.

WHAT TO BUY

Whether you are a bride starting out with everything new or a housewife enlarging her store of china, the kind and number of pieces you need depends on the number of people who sit at your table every day, the kind of entertaining you do and the amount of storage space you have.

A place setting for each person should include at a minimum:

> dinner plate
> luncheon plate
> butter plate
> cup and saucer
> bowl for soup or cereal

To this you might add—not necessarily in the basic pattern:

> salad plates (can be used also for dessert)
> dessert plates (for times when you serve both dessert and salad)
> soup plates
> egg cups
> demitasse cups and saucers
> place plates

PLACE PLATES

These (sometimes called service plates) may appear at formal meals served by a butler or maid. (For details of their use see

Chapter 19.) They are used less frequently in a maidless house but the hostess can avail herself of them if she likes and there is no denying they do enhance the welcome of a pretty dinner table. As long as they add a note of interest to the table and don't clash with the centerpiece, the pattern of the service plates may differ from any others used at the same meal. Dessert plates often double as service plates.

For serving pieces (omitting any you may have in silver) you'll want:

    gravy boat
    large platter for turkeys and roasts
    smaller platter
    cake plate
    2 or three vegetable dishes

MIXING PATTERNS

Such things as place plates, salad and dessert plates, egg cups, and serving pieces can be in a different pattern from that of your basic china. Or even in several different patterns—egg cups of one, plates of another. Glass plates—clear, frosted, or in color—make attractive salad or dessert plates, especially in summer. Demitasse cups and saucers practically never match anything else. Odd tea cups (as long as they are pretty and are still mated each to its matching saucer) make charming conversation pieces at the tea table and are rightfully treasured.

We do try to avoid, however, the rummage-sale effect that results from mixing too many kinds at one time and from mixing kinds that don't get along together. All the plates set on the table for any one course should match—"eating" plates, that is. (There is of course no reason why you shouldn't set gold-edged white soup plates on place plates with a solid blue border or even a flowered one.) We don't mix peasant-style pottery with porcelain at the formal dinner table. And all the parts of a tea set or coffee set should match.

Of course, as a woman of taste and discrimination you can break these rules on occasion. If you have a perfectly lovely but lone antique china teapot, don't relegate it to the shelf in favor of a new "set," but instead build a set around it, selecting a china that complements it in feeling, size, and color. And what could be more cheering at breakfast than gay provincial egg cups, whether they sit on plates of white plastic or fine china patterned in turquoise?

YOUR GLASSWARE

Just as with china, today we're seldom hampered with rigid conventions when it comes to glassware. Our choice of kinds, shapes, and even colors is all but unlimited.

Glassware is of two sorts—crystal (so called) and plain glass. Practically all glass is made with a base of silica. To this the makers of ordinary glass add lime and soda; the makers of fine crystal substitute potash for the soda. In lead crystal the lead usually replaces the lime. All crystal shines more brilliantly than glass, rings like a clear bell when struck, and is quite fragile. Lead crystal may have an even greater shine, especially if cut, and is a little stronger than regular crystal.

For the most formal use you may prefer crystal to glass. There's no doubt that its diamond brilliance puts the finishing touch on an array of damask, gleaming silver, and lovely china. It is expensive, however, and extremely fragile, so those of us who rarely entertain with great formality happily settle for the many beautiful pieces in ordinary glass.

Both crystal and ordinary glass come patterned as well as plain. Patterns may be etched into the glass or cut. Some of the cut designs with fluting or diamond-shaped patterns are beautiful and seem especially appropriate with early American or modern surroundings. It is often more practical, however, to get unadorned glasses; you'll tire of them less and you'll find they adapt themselves more readily to all kinds of table settings. An etched glass often looks faintly out of place with a table setting whose principal characteristic is color and gay informality.

Like china, glassware is often sold in sets. If the pattern is open stock, there is no reason not to buy it this way, but as with china sets, you may get very tired of seeing the same leaves or stars turn up each day for everything you drink from fruit juice to beer. Then, too, if every glass you have is patterned, you're limited in your imaginative adventures with table settings. It's more fun to have a variety—a few patterned if you like, but mostly the ever-adaptable plain.

HOW MUCH GLASS TO BUY

The quantities you purchase depend, of course, on how many there are in your family, your budget, and your storage space, as well as on the kind and size of the parties you give. Stemmed cocktail glasses, if you entertain often, are likely to suffer a good deal of breakage and chipping, and so an extra four or six of these will not be regretted. The same is true of the fruit juice glasses and others used every day. (If your budget is small and your children are too, don't overlook the practicality of plastic glasses for family meals and between-meal use.)

Most families find that six to a dozen of the following constitutes an adequate wardrobe of glassware. You can always rent additional glasses for any really big party.

> straight-sided beverage glass for iced tea, milk, water, highballs, beer, etc.
> stemmed goblets for water, for dinner and formal table setting
> straight-sided juice glasses
> an all-purpose wine glass
> old-fashioned glass which can also be used for soft desserts with sauces, or for juice
> finger bowls with matching glass plates (these will double as dessert dishes and plates can be used alone for dessert or salad)

Additional glasses for liqueur, champagne, brandy, sherry, and so on may be added, depending upon the amount of entertaining you do or the amount of use these pieces would get in your family.

COLORED GLASSWARE

Much glassware is available in colors—ruby or sapphire bowl with crystal stem, all blue or all ruby, pink cranberry glass, white milk glass, modern glassware in smoke and topaz, rosy antique goblets encrusted with gold. If you buy any of these, make sure that they harmonize with your china and other glassware, not only in color but in mass and above all in spirit. Therefore, unless you can afford several sets, it's safest not to buy such frequently used items as water glasses in color. And though some of the colored wine glasses are exquisite and may be used with discretion (the ornate goblets for a red wine at a very formal dinner, for example, or iridescent amber glasses for sherry), clear crystal is preferred by connoisseurs of wine and is invariably in the best of taste.

A SPECIAL NOTE ABOUT WINE GLASSES

The average person intending to buy glasses for several wine courses is completely bewildered by the endless array of shapes and sizes as well as by conflicting advice. Don't worry—even the experts feud among themselves about just which glass is proper for just which wine. You need only to stick to simple classic shapes, and when it comes to sizes, bear in mind that the wine is always supposed to come well below the top of the glass. The most useful size for an all-purpose tulip shape wine glass holds four ounces.

If you and your husband like wines and plan to serve them often, you may want to add other glasses to the basic four-ounce one, especially if you occasionally serve two or more wines at a meal, because a different size—and perhaps shape—for each wine makes the wine-glass array more interesting. A five- to eight-ounce glass is very useful for both red and white wines, and so is a long-stemmed glass holding five ounces, for Rhine wine. You might also want to consider special glasses for beer. Beer can be served in a number of containers, from steins to tall highball glasses, and among these you may select what most suits your taste and your table accessories: double old-fashioned glasses, Pilsener glasses short and straight or tall and flaring, brandy inhalers (the kind with a big bowl), antique mugs and tankards.

MIXING GLASSWARE

As is true of china, all the glassware for any one course should match, with the exception of the wine glasses. These should match each other for each wine served, but don't need to match the goblets or glasses for other wines.

Harmony is an important consideration. Use glasses that correspond in spirit with your table settings and the china for each course.

MONOGRAMMING

Marking glass is expensive and so ordinary glass is rarely marked. Crystal may or may not be. The monogram consists of the couple's initials or those of the bride's married name, and may be in a diamond or triangular shape or in some other arrangement that is in keeping with the size and shape of the glass. Many kinds of glasses, expensive or not, shouldn't be marked at all. Any store that has a large selection of quality glassware handles the engraving too, and will gladly advise you whether to mark—and how and where.

19

Table Settings

NOTHING SO DELIGHTS THE EYE OF A GUEST OR THE SPIRIT OF A HOSTESS as a beautiful and inviting table. No matter whether it's the glass-topped table on the terrace adorned with grass-green mats and yellow peasant ware, or an expanse of white damask gleaming with silver and crystal, candles, and camellias—the imaginative hostess has planned it to flatter the guests, the food, and the occasion. Setting the simplest breakfast tray can be an adventure—make it so!

Try, too, to be a hostess for your family and not just for your guests. Vary the table settings as you do your menus, and every now and then break the routine of dinner in the dining room, breakfast in the dinette. Have an occasional meal on the terrace even if you're not barbecuing. If you have a big kitchen, make it a social center, just for a change, and surround yourself with friends and talk while the delicious smell of your specialty flavors the air and whets the appetites. Now and then have a more formally set table than is your wont, not only for anniversaries and birthdays, but to celebrate a top notch report card, a promotion, a homecoming from camp. You needn't *have* a reason, for that matter!

COVERING THE TABLE

Many women think rather of *un*covering the table—and certainly, especially in a modern setting, a bare table can be very handsome. If your table top is resistant to stains, heat, and scratches, as well as being beautiful, you will probably not want to cover it except for very formal dinners. Should the table have a perishable finish and you want the bare-table effect, you can get it by using round mats under the plates, small enough not to show, and still smaller mats for the glasses. Such mats, of course, should be of some material sturdy enough to protect the table from dampness from the water glasses as well as heat from the filled plates.

Regular-sized mats, each large enough to hold table silver, plate, and glass, can be used at almost any table except that for a formal dinner or buffet. Some, such as cork and plastic, are plain and practical, some like appliquéd organdy or rounds of lacy straw, are more formal. When selecting table mats, you would, of course, avoid choosing a fussy, patterned mat as a background for your flower-sprigged china.

Mats are placed even with the table edge and symetrically spaced. A matching runner may be used unless it crowds the table, in which case it's better to use no runner or to substitute for it one of the place mats, provided that its shape and color are attractive under the centerpiece. Pads are not used under mats. If your table top is hypersensitive, use thick mats or abandon mats altogether in favor of a tablecloth with silence cloth or table pads beneath.

Mats can be very exciting to use, not only because they come in so many beautiful colors but also because they provide an almost limitless array of textures. And texture is almost as useful as color when it comes to making a picture of your table.

The napkins you use with your mats may match or contrast with them, and for informal meals may be of paper. Colorful kitchen towels make good napkins for many occasions, such as barbecues and informal buffets.

When you want to use a tablecloth, you have an almost unlimited choice in colors, though perhaps in textures you have less latitude than you have in mats. You will find yourself getting inspiration from everyday cloths in gay ginghams, printed linens, plain and patterned synthetics, as well as from your cloths of lace and organdy and damask for formal dinners.

It's important to remember that your cloth should be large enough to cover the table and allow for a generous overhang. Under most cloths, and certainly under damask for a formal dinner, you should use a silence cloth or felt-backed pads fitted to your table. A lace cloth is always laid on a bare table, unless for some special effect you want to use a colored cloth underneath and let it show through. Always lay the cloth straight on the table.

Napkins used with tablecloths may match or contrast, though for a formal dinner with a damask cloth they usually match. Dinner napkins ought to be large—twenty-four inches square in damask, as large as possible in other materials. They are usually folded in an oblong shape, sometimes in a triangle or a shield shape. For napkins smaller than the large dinner size, the oblong or triangle looks better than the shield.

THE CENTERPIECE

Fresh flowers are favorites for centerpieces and rightly so. Lacking them, however, with a little imagination and daring, you can create some stunning effects. You can use driftwood, skunk cabbage, eggplant, lemons, eggs. You can use a ring of growing plants in little pots or baskets. You can use coleus leaves, pussy willow, heaped-up fruit. You can use almost anything (provided it doesn't have a strong odor like the picturesque leek) if you suit the container to the material and suit the entire arrangement in color, scale, and character to the table setting.

No matter what the temptation, it's better not to use artificial fruit or flowers at a dinner table. The very best of them lose enchantment viewed at so close a range. But don't forget that other things that grew out of someone's imagination rather than out of the ground make beautiful centerpieces, too—an old covered tureen, a child's gay drum, a milk-glass hen, a piece of antique pewter, a little statuette. A touch of green, such as philodendron leaves or the foliage from some other houseplant, perhaps a spray of evergreen, may be needed to enliven these. And, of course, if your centerpiece is obviously a container it should, unless it has a decorative cover, *contain* something, even though it be only a host of ivy sprays masking the grapefruit into which you've stuck them, or a pile of lemons accented with lemon leaves.

When you're making a centerpiece for a seated dinner, remember to keep it low enough so that people won't have to play peek-a-boo with their fellow diners. A centerpiece for a buffet table is another matter entirely. Here you can make an arrangement as towering as the table's proportions will permit, because people don't have to see over it. If your buffet table is against the wall, you have the additional advantage of a background and can put together something very striking. Buffet centerpieces, however, must leave a good amount of room for all the serving equipment as well as the food— so don't get too carried away!

CANDLES

Here again visualize your guests as they will be sitting at table and don't have the flames at eye level. They should be well above it, or else well below. Candles may be white or colored. White or ivory candles are preferable for the damask-cloth dinner, but there'd really be nothing wrong with pale yellow ones complementing a centerpiece of miniature yellow narcissus. Very elaborate candles with colored and metallic ornamentation are not in the best of taste and would in any case detract from the effect of your centerpiece.

Candles are seldom used in the daytime—with the possible exception of a formal tea served in the winter dusk. At an evening meal they are flattering to the table and the guests and lend a romantic air. The idea is to provide enough light to see by without crowding the table. A candle at each end of a small table for four might be enough—and certainly would be if there were supplementary light such as wall sconces. But ordinarily four candles would be needed— more if the table is large, perhaps a candelabra at each end or a cluster of candles around the centerpiece. Or sometimes a large candelabra can itself serve as a centerpiece. It's safer not to use candles at all if you must choose between overcrowding the table and not having enough light. If the table is too crowded, serving will be more difficult and the table itself less attractive. If there is too little light, the food you have so carefully prepared will lose much of its attractiveness in the semidarkness. Moreover, most people, and particularly men, like to be able to see what they're eating.

MENUS AND COLOR

As an experienced hostess, you will have learned to keep color in mind when you plan your menus. First, the color of the food itself, for you know that color is one of the most important spices in a meal, and you wouldn't dream of serving such a combination—pastel in taste as well as color—as creamed fish with mashed potatoes and summer squash! But go a step beyond this in menu planning; consider each course with an eye to the sparkle that comes from a variety of colors and textures and picture it on the plates from which it will be served and eaten. Don't serve white things from a white dish if you can help it, and if you're using white dinner plates, do use colorful food. Remember the value of garnishes—don't overdo them, but don't forget how lots of finely chopped parsley and butter can change the looks as well as the taste of boiled potatoes. Whenever you have a choice of dishes, select the ones that will enhance a food's color or contrast strikingly with it.

SETTING THE TABLE

THE NAPKIN

Folded in one of the ways sketched on page 176, the napkin is placed either to the diner's left outside the forks, or directly on the dinner plate if there is no first course on the plate. (If the plate is

intended merely as a service plate, the napkin would go on it, too.) When the napkin is put next to the forks, the long edge of whatever fold is used goes closest to the forks. When paper napkins are used, it's better to put them by the forks—a paper napkin on a dinner plate seems somehow pretentious.

THE SILVER

Silver is placed symmetrically on the table, allowing the same distance between each setting. The bottom of each piece should be about an inch from the table edge, and right and left sides of each setting should be far enough apart so that no fork or knife is concealed by the plate. Forks are placed tines up, and with the occasional exception of oyster forks, they go on the left. The spoons, with their bowls facing up, go to the right of the knives. At any meal except buffet, when a main-course fork appears at each setting the knife must accompany it, whether the knife is to be used or not.

It is not incorrect to place the silver so that while the dinner knife and fork are set about an inch from the table's edge, the pieces for the next course are a little farther away:

In general, the silver for all meals is so arranged that the diner picks up the piece farthest from the edge of the plate on each side as the different courses are served. This is supposed to prevent the alert guest from using his dinner fork for his salad and so finding he has only the salad fork left for the main course. There is only one notable exception to this rule—at a maidless dinner or lunch, you may find your dessert spoon between the soup spoon and the knife— a placement which technically violates the "eat from the outside in" maxim, but is sufficiently logical so that no one would be confused.

Many people prefer to place the dessert silver above the plate parallel to the table edge. Or you may put the dessert fork nearest the plate and the dessert spoon on the right. Occasionally the salad fork will be placed at the left of the dinner fork.

Jams, jellies, sauces, gravy, relishes, and the like, whether on the table for the guests to pass or served by a maid, should be in appropriate containers, each with its own serving implement. When any of these is put on the table, the proper spoon or fork is set on the table next to it. Or if there is a saucer underneath the container (and with most things, especially jam, there should be!) the spoon should go on the saucer.

The coffee spoons are not set on the table as the dessert silver may be, but are brought in with the coffee, each spoon resting on the saucer with its handle turned toward the diner's right—as is the cup handle.

The oyster fork is a more footloose implement than most of the other pieces and may appear in any of these three positions, although that on the left is the most usual:

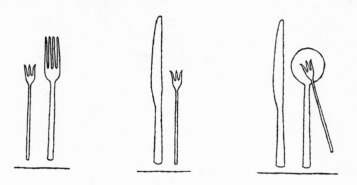

If butter is to be used at the table, the butter knife is laid on the butter plate in one of these three positions:

If there is a service plate, it goes in the center between knives and forks as would the dinner plates if true service plates are not being used. If you are using plates with scenes on them, remember to set them down so that the picture is right side up for each guest. The butter plate is placed directly above the forks, on the left; the water glass goes above the knives, on the right.

The formal ways of placing smoking materials, finger bowls when they are used, nuts and candies are discussed under "Formal Dinner" later in this chapter. What is outlined above is correct usage for most meals, the one you would teach your children (by degrees!) when they want to "help."

THE BREAKFAST TRAY

Breakfast on a tray can be anything from the most functional of arrangements for the members of a hurried family to the tray with eye appeal especially designed for the guest or the invalid. For any tray but the family-style one (which may be bare or covered with a paper napkin), a tray cloth or a mat or good-sized doily is a must. The necessary silver consists of a knife, fork, spoon for egg or cereal (or both!), coffee spoon on its saucer. A bowl with cereal, if needed. Juice in its glass, and a small plate from which to eat, plus a small butter plate with its knife. The toast should be in a domed dish or folded in a napkin. Individual salt and pepper, napkin, cream, sugar, and possibly jam or marmalade, must not be overlooked. If there's room add a glass of water.

Not everyone is fortunate enough to have a complete breakfast set for individual service, but it isn't hard to pick up extra small-sized pieces that harmonize with your regular breakfast china. And it makes tray service so much more practical. A small pot to keep the coffee hot until wanted, an attractive egg cup (for a nosegay if not for an egg), and a little jam pot with its own spoon are very useful.

If you can possibly find a little extra room on the tray for a tiny bouquet or even a fresh rosebud placed across a corner, the enjoyment a guest or invalid derives from this little touch far outweighs the extra trouble.

THE BREAKFAST TABLE

Ordinarily breakfast is the most simple of meals and the least leisurely, so the table setting is simple and practical. At each place a knife and fork (the luncheon size if you have them), a cereal spoon, coffee cup and saucer with coffee spoon on the saucer, butter plate with butter knife on it. A glass for water or milk. A small plate (lunch or salad size) at each place, a glass with juice set on that plate or beside or above it. Cold cereal in its bowl is set above the plate. (Hot cereal should be served from the kitchen.) The napkin is on the plate or at the left of the fork. Don't forget the cream and/or milk and the sugar!

LUNCH, INFORMAL AND FORMAL

The table for an informal lunch would be bare, or set with mats or tablecloth as the hostess prefers. A tablecloth if used may be quite formal—lace or organdy, for instance—but for lunch it would never be damask, although the napkins may be. At each place is a minimum of knife and fork plus a spoon for soup or for appetizer. If there is to be a dessert course, the dessert silver may be placed above the plate, or the dessert fork may be placed inside the luncheon fork, the dessert spoon outside the knife. Butter plates should be used, because some form of bread is traditionally part of a lunch, and as a rule, an individual ashtray, cigarettes, and matches are at each place. The water glass is set above the knife.

The napkin goes to the left of the forks, unless the first course is to be served after the guests are seated. (If water is served also, the iced-tea glass would go to the right of the water goblet and just a little bit closer to the table-edge than the goblet.) Most hospitably, the iced-tea glass is set on its own saucer and the iced-tea spoon goes on the saucer, too. If there are no saucers, the iced-tea spoon goes on the table to the right of the knife or knives.

The coffee spoon is usually brought in with the coffee.

A setting such as this would be adequate for most lunches of the informal sort, which today usually consist of only two or three courses. The table for a more elaborate lunch, which might include a sea-food appetizer, soup, salad, main course, and dessert, would be set like that for an informal dinner (see below) except that an iced tea or iced coffee glass might replace the wine glass, and you'd add the butter plate and butter knife.

INFORMAL DINNER

A setting for an informal dinner would be quite like that for lunch, except, of course, that with more courses you'd add the appropriate silver for each. Butter plates may or may not be used.

You will want a salad plate if the salad is to be served at the same time as the meat, and you will set it at the left of the forks, putting the salad fork inside the dinner fork and the salad knife if needed (either for salad or for cheese) inside the dinner knife. If there is a soup spoon, it goes outside the knives. The dessert silver may be placed on the table as for formal lunch or may be put on the dessert plates when they are served, with or without fingerbowls and doilies.

If not served in the living room, coffee—demitasse or otherwise —would be served as at an informal lunch.

The first course may be already on the table when the guests are seated, and if so, the napkin of course will be placed to the left of the forks; otherwise the napkin is on the empty place plate. (In the maidless house, as well as in many houses with a maid, the place plate or service plate is not often removed unused and replaced with another for the first course. Instead, the first course is already on it or is set down on it when it is served.)

If dishes are to be served at the table, you will of course place necessary serving implements on the table—the carving set at the right of the carver, the serving spoons at the right of the hostess or at her husband's right if he is to do the serving (See Chapter 14, page 102.)

Wine glasses are placed on the table in order of use, the first glass above the knives, the second to the right of the first and a bit nearer the edge of the table. At an informal dinner, you would rarely have more than two wines, most usually one.

As with informal lunch, salts and peppers, a set for each guest or several sets to be shared, are customary, as are matches, cigarettes, and an ashtray for each person. If possible, the salts and peppers should match and the ashtrays should be a set, too. Mixing two very similar sets or crystal with silver is perfectly allowable, but you would not combine colored pottery or enamel ashtrays with crystal or silver ones.

FORMAL DINNER

Even though you may not be able to manage it very often, especially if you must engage help for the occasion, there's nothing like the lift a formal dinner table can give a relaxed host and hostess and their guests. Prepare a beautiful snowy spread of damask, a colorful centerpiece, lit tapers, lovely china, sparkling silver and glass and add to these outgoing, compatible guests, a special wine or two, and good food imaginatively prepared and served. What better way to add to the world's store of enjoyment?

Your cloth for a formal dinner may well be damask in cream or white or ivory, but it need not be. Damask in a pale pastel is allowable too. It's best to stick to one tone in the cloth—in modern fabrics a two-color effect with the design in one shade, the background in another, is inclined to look tricky. The contrast in weave that makes up the pattern is really all the drama a lovely damask needs. Some antique damask cloths in deep colors make a stunning table. Then, too, you can use point de Venise, unusual lace, drawn work —as long as it is fine handwork and has a special, very festive look about it.

It is probably only at the formal dinner that most of us would have any need to bear in mind what is called "the rule of three," which forbids that more than three forks or three knives appear on the table at one time. In the days when eight courses were a minimum at any formal dinner worthy of the name, this mandate was necessary to keep the table from being cluttered with silver. Nowadays the rule is seldom needed, but it is well to be familiar with it.

A typical setting is shown below:

In setting the silver on the table, the general order we have already described for lunch and informal dinner is followed, except that there are probably more courses and therefore more pieces needed, and no butter plates or butter knives are used.

The first large glass is the water goblet. The wine glasses from left to right hold sherry, the wine for the entree, and dessert wine. Two wines, however, are adequate, and you may serve champagne throughout the meal if you prefer. In that case you need no other wine.

There would be no serving implements on the table, as the serving would all be done from the kitchen or pantry. Although it used to be the custom to ban cigarettes and ashtrays until they were passed with the coffee, today one often sees smoking accessories and cigarettes on the table in front of each guest. If these are used, they should be as formal as possible—small sterling or foil matchboxes with miniature matches, or narrow foil match packs, quite plain unless there is an initial or house name. Small crystal or silver cigarette containers may be set on the table, or two cigarettes may be laid across each crystal or silver ashtray.

Salt and pepper containers should likewise be formal in spirit. They may be individual open salt servers of silver or crystal with tiny salt spoons, accompanied by matching or harmonizing pepper shakers, or they may be little silver salt shakers with twin shakers for pepper. Or you might use larger salts and peppers, each pair of which will serve two or more guests. If these are to serve more than two people, it's better to place them symmetrically in some relation to the centerpiece rather than dot them here and there about the table.

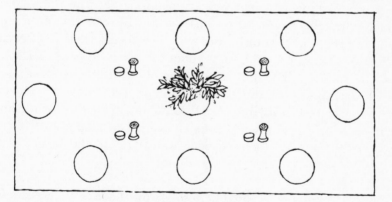

The dinner napkin is on the place plate. If a place card is used, it may be laid on the napkin or on the table cloth above the plate.

As we have said, there are no butter plates or butter knives at a formal dinner. Nor is butter passed, though bread may be. Often hard rolls are laid on the napkin or to the left of the plate, on the cloth. They are eaten unbuttered.

If you want to serve candy and nuts at your formal dinner and have room enough on the table, bonbon dishes (open bowls or compotes in silver or fine china) may be put between the candles and the centerpiece, one at each end of the table. Small nut dishes may be put on the table in some evenly balanced arrangement. The main idea is not to overcrowd the table and make it look cluttered; if there is any danger of this, it's better to pass the nuts and candy at the meal's end.

At a formal dinner, the dessert service is usually placed on the dessert plates, most often with doily and finger bowl. A finger bowl used at the meal's end (this is not the strictly utilitarian finger bowl used with lobster and similar foods) should be filled to the halfway mark with cold water. It's not necessary, but it is pleasant to add to each bowl a floating flower, a tiny curl of lemon peel, or a sprig of rosemary.

Wine glasses are placed on the table all at once and set to the right of the water goblet in the order in which they are to be used. Remember that you should use matching wine glasses for each wine, although the burgundy glass need not match the dessert-wine glass or indeed have anything in common with it except to be in harmony with the other things on the table.

Coffee may be served at the table in demitasse cups, the little spoon laid on each saucer, handle directed toward the guest.

Consider carefully, when you are planning your meal and when you are directing the maid or butler who will serve, the dishes and utensils from which your guests will help themselves. The serving platters and dishes should allow room for guests to help themselves without spilling. The implements should suit the food—that is, serving fork *and* spoon should be at hand for a course such as chicken breasts that need steadying as well as lifting, as well as for a course with sauce or gravy, when the spoon is used to help oneself to the gravy, once the main food has been transferred to the dinner plate.

BUFFET SUPPERS

The word "supper" is used here solely for the sake of convenience —the buffet style of serving can be employed for any meal, including brunch and lunch. It's easy on the hostess and the pocketbook, and flexible in its demands—you need a minimum of china (and a minimum of dishwashing!), your menu can be as simple as you like, and there are so many ways of serving it that you don't even have to have a dining room table! You can arrange the meal and the accompaniments on a sideboard, a buffet, a bookcase top, a living room table, the top of a chest of drawers, or on a folding picnic table. You can even have a combined buffet and sit-down dinner by setting the table as usual but having dinner plates and food arranged on the sideboard, so that the guests help themselves and then bring their plates to the table.

A buffet dinner can and should look quite festive. You usually have room for a striking centerpiece, and it will set off a tablecloth that may be as dramatic and colorful as you like. If your china and linens are beautiful, use them, and make your table rather formal if you want—a buffet table doesn't *have* to be in rich color! On the other hand, if you have some interesting pieces, such as an ironstone tureen, a huge turkey platter, a copper chafing dish, use them all and plan your table around one or two of them. To cover the table itself, give your imagination free rein. You may decide on your ruby-red linen, but then again you might feel like using inexpensive

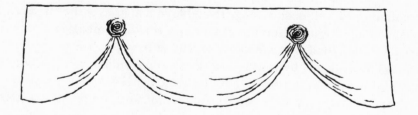

striped sateen or other cotton, or straw mats placed end to end to make a runner the length of the table. Or a paper cloth. Or a pastel or printed sheet!

Often, especially when a table is set against the wall, it adds a festive note to catch the sides up in a swag effect. Whether or not you do this, remember to have the cloth, whatever the material, large enough so it doesn't look skimpy or reveal too much of the table's underpinnings.

SETTING THE BUFFET TABLE

Just how you do this depends on several factors—how big your party is, how large your dining room, whether or not the table is set against the wall. There are a number of other ways of setting out a buffet table: in the middle of the room; or several complete duplicate settings in several places to expedite traffic if you have a big crowd.

Try not to overcrowd the table. Put water and glasses, coffee and cups, spoons and so forth on a side table. The food itself is of course all fork food except for dessert. This may be finger food like fruit and cookies, but it can be something that is eaten with a spoon so long as it isn't soupy or drippy—or skiddy, like a meringue. Bread or rolls are buttered, ready to eat.

Arrange food, china, and silver so that they can be picked up in the proper order: napkin, dinner plate, hot dishes, cold dishes, salad, bread, relishes, fork. Don't overlook the serving implements!

Since the food is on display, as it were, and part of the entire setting, make sure it is attractively arranged. Use good-sized platters and bowls, and fill them so that the platter edge shows. The edge makes a frame for the food, and you run less risk of difficult and untidy serving.

If you can possibly manage it, it's considerate to leave enough room beside each serving dish so that the guest can set his dinner plate down while he helps himself. If you can't manage this for the main dish or dishes, do arrange the table so that at least the salad bowl has this area beside it; one *can* manage a shrimp jambalaya with one hand, but a salad is so much easier with two.

Keep foods hot by setting the dishes on a radiant tray or over a candle-lit warmer. Or serve them in a chafing dish.

The plates should be heated, too, as for any dinner. Some hostesses, however, prefer to let the plates stay at room temperature, making sure that the entree is piping hot, rather than have people set the beautifully chilled salad on a warm plate.

Napkins should harmonize with the cloth in general degree of formality; otherwise, ingenuity has practically no limits. Colored cloth, paper, dishtowels—almost anything as long as it's large enough to be of some real use.

At a quite informal buffet, you may want to use paper plates and cups instead of china. If you decide to, be sure to get the very best quality so that the plates are quite rigid, and make sure you serve only things that are *extra* easy to cut with a fork alone. And get the cups with the fold-back handles—much pleasanter and safer for hot black coffee than the ordinary kind without handles.

CARD TABLE BUFFETS

If you decide now and then to have a buffet party where the guests serve themselves but are seated for the actual dining at a series of card tables, you will put up the card tables before the guests come. In a maidless household, the card table plan would probably be followed only if you had an extra room such as a screened porch, sunroom, library, or den where the tables would not interfere with free movement of guests past the buffet table. Individual tables would be set with cloths, napkins, and silver. The cloths may be formal or informal, white or colored, but it's best that they harmonize with each other even if they don't match. All red and white check or all white or pastel linen, for example, but not an assortment. Napkins may range from white or cream damask to white or pastel linen or paper.

The silver setting is as simple as it would be for a non-sit-down buffet, except that for the sake of appearances knives as well as forks should be provided, whether or not they are needed. Bear in mind, though, that one of the advantages of providing tables for your guests is that you need not limit yourself to fork foods for the main course.

It quadruples the attractiveness of the tables when there is some sort of centerpiece on each. It must, of course, be kept rather small lest it overpower the table. If there is room, and sufficient other illumination to help out, a candle or two is charming. Those small combination candle and flower holders can be especially pretty on card tables.

OUTDOOR ENTERTAINING

Barbecues or just "eat outdoors" parties, although they require thorough organization, are among the simplest as far as table setting is concerned. At very informal affairs, especially where there will be young children, you may prefer stacked trays and paper plates and cups, with the minimum of silver wrapped in a gay napkin. If your party is small, you may want to seat the guests at a table on the terrace—but still informally. Checked tablecloths, paper tablecloths, gay mats with napkins of equal informality, are suitable. If the day is breezy, you may prefer cloth napkins to paper ones because they're less likely to take off in a sudden gust. On such a day it would be wise not to use a paper tablecloth too—and if you use a lightweight cloth one, slip a small lead weight in the hem at each corner.

You probably won't want or need a centerpiece unless you're all sitting down at table. It's hardly essential even then—but if you use one, keep it simple and rustic—zinnias in a bean pot, cherry tomatoes in a white soup plate (and this is one time when the guests should be encouraged to nibble on the "flowers"!) or even dessert cheeses on a pewter plate.

Uncovered candles aren't practical at an outdoor table. But don't forget the special magic of candlelight at the hour when the trees turn from green to black and the fireflies come out. Have hurricane candles and patio or lawn lights ready to be lit as dusk falls, whether the meal is finished or not.

FORMAL TEAS

How to set the table for a small tea has already been described on page 125. At a formal tea, of course, the table will be larger—your dining room table, no doubt. And it should be set with all the elegance you can muster—a beautiful cloth and napkins, the tea tray, tea set, and spoons polished to within an inch of their lives, and as a rule a partyfied, feminine centerpiece rather than a smashing one. Exceptions: special events or holiday parties, such as a football or Christmas tea or one for a wood or paper anniversary, might well call for a special centerpiece in keeping with the party theme rather than an ordinary floral one.

The tea tray, set up as described on page 125, is set at one end of the table, a similar tray for coffee at the other. The space between will be taken up by the dessert plates and napkins, plus the cookies, sliced cake, or other snacks attractively arranged on good-sized plates. Behind the tray, arrange the cups on their saucers, complete with spoon, within easy reach of the pourer. Ditto for the coffee cups.

Although not strictly part of the table setting, for a big tea the pourers are as essential as anything except the tea itself. Pouring is not an easy job and it is sometimes difficult for the shy, so the hostess should select the kind of person who enjoys meeting others and can maintain her poise and remember about lemon and sugar without strain. (How to pour is described on page 126.) The friends who are asked to pour should be invited to do so in advance. Another guest should be asked to act as a floater, standing ready to help the pourers by providing fresh tea, hot water, or other supplies as they are needed.

The pourer is supposed to stay at her post until she is relieved. At any sizable tea the considerate hostess will see that someone takes her place after a reasonable interval. The relief pourer will be brought to the table by the hostess, introduced if necessary, and the hostess will thank the first guest for her help as she rises to leave the table.

OTHER PARTIES

Most parties would follow one of the patterns described in this chapter. For many helpful suggestions about table settings for all sorts of seasonal events, children's birthday parties, bridal and baby showers, need we say that you have only to refer to the *Good Housekeeping Party Book*.

20

How to Serve

THE "HOW'S" OF SERVING TO BE DESCRIBED IN THIS CHAPTER CONCERN the duties of a maid (or manservant) at a meal where the guests are seated, whether for lunch, dinner, or any other meal. (How the maidless hostess serves is described in Chapter 14, "When You Entertain at Home.") At other functions, such as teas and cocktail parties, the maid or other helper should be an alert passer and fast clearer-upper. At a cocktail party she should pass the hot appetizers (the others being placed where the guests can help themselves) and make sure that all the hors d'oeuvres platters are kept filled and attractively arranged. It is part of her duty to empty ashtrays, collect empty glasses from time to time, and wash them. She will refill the ice bucket when necessary and fetch fresh soda or cut fruit or other supplies needed by the bartender, but only when the bartender is the host or a friend of the host. If the party is so big that a bartender has been hired, he is shown where things are kept and then usually prefers to run his own department. Be sure, however, that this point is clarified when you hire him—if he must have assistance, you should forewarn the maid and remember that perhaps you may not be able to demand so much of her in making and serving hot hors d'oeuvres.

At a tea, the maid may pass sandwiches and cakes or they may remain on the tea table, in which case she will keep the serving plates filled and looking pretty, will keep used tea and coffee cups cleared away, and will see to it that hot water, fresh tea and coffee, sliced lemon, and so on are available when needed.

At a buffet, whether or not the maid fills the guests' plates at the buffet table, she will see to it that the serving dishes are replenished for second helpings and that the hot ones are reheated if they need to be. She will also accomplish the clearing away between main course and dessert—although the hostess may help by bringing out used dinner plates from the living room—and she will do the general clearing away at the meal's end. She will bring in the dessert and the dessert service, if it is not already laid out on a side table, and will bring in the coffee tray whether she sets it on the buffet table or carries it into the living room for service there. At the buffet table, she may pour the coffee for the guests; if coffee is served in the living room, the hostess usually does the pouring.

The host of course always serves the wine, although the maid may bring in the decanter or bottle, with its neck wrapped in a white damask napkin, and a corkscrew if needed. The wine glasses will already be on the table.

When a maid is employed especially to serve a dinner, the hostess usually has done most of the cooking and it is understood that the maid just finishes things off, popping hot hors d'oeuvres into the oven and cooking last-minute things like asparagus. Very good cook-waitresses are sometimes available. In this case the hostess provides the makings for a menu which she knows the helper cooks well and easily. She may still do some of the preparation herself—start the roast, make the dessert—and will probably set the table.

Many communities are graced by one or more couples who have made a business of catering and serving for cocktail and cocktail-buffet parties, the woman doing the cooking and the serving, the man doing the bartending, carving, and helping in an all-around capacity while dinner is being served.

Whether you employ such a couple or get in a maid for the evening or obtain the services of a cook-waitress, make sure that it is understood well before the party what the menu is, how much of it will be cooked by you, how many guests there are to be, and in detail what dishes, glassware, and serving dishes are to be used for what foods and drinks. If this is your first experience with her or them—and theirs with you—make sure they know how you want the serving done and exactly what their duties are. If it is to be a sit-down dinner, don't forget to have a bell to summon the waitress from the kitchen.

Above all, be reasonable in planning duties. Remember that one person can accomplish only so much. So if you want the maid to clear the living room of the cocktail debris while you and your guests are having the first course, put the celery and olives on the table instead of expecting her to pass them. If she is a cook-waitress and must cope with a fairly elaborate meal, she can't be making and passing countless piping-hot cheese puffs at cocktail time.

HOW A MEAL IS SERVED

Before announcing dinner, the maid fills the water glasses, lights the candles, and sets the first course on the table. If service plates are on the table and the first course is to be served, she may remove the service plates, one or two at a time, after the guests are seated, or she may set the first course directly on the service plates. The latter way is more sensible and perfectly correct because there will probably be no reason to replace the cold service plates with hot ones —either hot soup or a cold dish would be in its own bowl.

In announcing the meal, the maid simply appears at the living room door and says, "Dinner is served."

When the guests have been seated and while they are eating the first course, the maid can clear the living room, but she will be alert for the sound of the hostess' bell, indicating that it is time to serve the next course. Then she sets a heated plate in front of each guest, and passes the dishes, including the meat (passed first) if it has been carved in the kitchen.

If the host is carving at table, the maid puts the platter in front of him. In this case, she will probably have put the heated plates in front of him as well (rather than one in front of each guest), and will serve each plate as he fills it. It's equally correct, however, for the heated plates to be put on the table one at each place. If this is done, the host fills the plate in front of him, the maid takes it and serves it to the woman at his right, at the same time picking up her empty plate and bringing it back to the host to be filled. She continues trading empty plates for filled ones until everyone has been served. This process is often speeded up by having two plates rather than one set in front of the host—he fills the top one, and while the maid is taking it to the guest and bringing back the guest's empty plate, the host has already filled the other plate and it is ready for the maid to take to the next guest. When everyone has been served, the maid takes the left-over empty plate away with her.

When the meat is on the diners' plates, the maid passes the vegetables, not forgetting any special sauce that may go with them. (The sauce should either accompany or immediately follow the dish it was prepared for.) If there is to be a salad course, the main course plates are cleared before the salad plates (not heated, of course) are put on the table and the salad passed. When it is time for the dessert course, the table is cleared completely, except for water and in-use or to-be-used wine glasses and dessert silver if it is on the table. The maid also crumbs the table, empties the ashtrays if they have been used, and fills the water glasses if they need it. Then she brings on the dessert plates—with the dessert silver on them if it isn't already on the table—perhaps with finger bowl and doily, too. Or the dessert may be served already on its plate—an individual Bavarian cream, for example, may appear in its own amber sherbet dish on a decorative dessert plate. (In this case, the finger bowls will be omitted or passed to the guests between dessert and coffee.) Usually, though, the dessert plates are set in front of the guests and the dessert passed around, or plates and dessert are set in front of the hostess, who serves it while the maid passes the filled dishes.

If coffee is to be served at table, the maid, after clearing away the dessert service and the finger bowls if any, sets the coffee service in front of the hostess. If liqueurs are to accompany the coffee at table, she sets the tray of bottles and glasses in front of the host and then disappears into the kitchen until the guests have left the table.

There's no doubt that when a maid is serving, it's preferable to have coffee and liqueurs in the living room. Not only is it more elegant and partyfied, but also it adds to the enjoyment of both host and guest to be able to linger over it without the feeling that the maid would just love it if you'd finish up so she could take off the tablecloth. Unless arrangements have been made to the contrary, if she has been hired simply to serve dinner, it's usually understood that clearing up for after-dinner coffee and evening drinks not served at the table is her employers' responsibility rather than hers.

ORDER OF SERVING

The maid serves first the woman guest on the host's right and then goes around the table counterclockwise, serving men and women as they come—*not* all the women first. If there are no guests, she would serve the lady of the house first and then go round the table.

RIGHT AND LEFT

Food is served from the guest's left, water and other beverages are served from the right to avoid reaching *across* the guest. Dishes most properly should be cleared from the left, but today's less rigid serving etiquette permits us to take them from whichever side is more convenient—as long as you don't reach across the diner. Similarly, it is quite allowable, especially when one maid must do all the serving, for her to take out a plate in each hand rather than to make a separate trip for each. Plates should not be stacked for clearing, however. The maid may pass two serving dishes at the same time, provided she is able to handle them easily. She may well make just one trip with the asparagus and its sauce—but she'll need both hands to manage a big meat platter gracefully and safely.

SOME NICETIES OF SERVING

When the hostess is planning her meal and going over the details of its service with the maid, it is her responsibility to allot serving dishes and platters of proper size for each course; and she must be sure that none of them is so huge as to be hard for the maid to balance and make the food look skimpy, or so small as to cause a guest to run the risk of spilling.

Unless she is quite experienced and you have used her before, it is a good idea to go over the details of service with the maid. If she seems at all uncertain, you may need to practice with her—a few moments well spent for the peace of mind of both of you—and also simplify the serving for her as much as you can. You may have to remind her to drain the vegetables thoroughly. And to hold the serving dishes low enough so that the guest can help himself comfortably—it's impossible to accomplish this even neatly, let alone gracefully, when the platter is held level with one's nose!

The maid should hold the serving dish on the palm of the left hand, with a folded napkin underneath it if the dish is hot. If it's a big platter she may use her right hand to steady it. Serving utensils

(one or more) are placed in the dish so that their handles point toward the guest.

Plates (both serving and dining) should always be heated when hot food is to be placed on them.

Serve hot food as hot as can be managed—and cold food really chilled—not just coolish.

21

When You Have a Servant

IF YOU'RE LIKE MOST WIVES AND MOTHERS, THE "SERVANT" IN YOUR house may well be you—if not all of the time, very likely some of the time, for today's busy women must serve the house as well as the children, the car, the committees, and the commissary. A staff of helpers is the exception rather than the rule, and indeed the woman who has a single full-time houseworker considers herself fortunate. Many get along with someone to do the heavy cleaning weekly, plus an occasional baby sitter. Whoever and whatever your help, choosing and managing them successfully is an important part of running your house.

When you decide to employ someone, you must first determine just what jobs you want done by an outsider and what you are prepared to pay. If you live in a small apartment, a weekly cleaning woman who can also handle much of the personal laundry and a bit of silver cleaning now and then may give you all the help you want. In a large suburban house your needs may best be served by a woman (or a man) who cleans thoroughly at least once a week, with extra time occasionally for window washing and floor waxing. You may find that a weekly team from a house cleaning firm suits you best. Or if you have a large family, and particularly, of course, if you work, you may discover that a sleep-in, full-time houseworker saves you priceless time and energy as well as giving you a good many free evenings without the baby sitter's fee-plus-transportation.

Should you be hiring for the first time or in a new community, it's wise, once you have decided on your requirements, to do a bit of investigating. Ask some neighbors or call a few agencies to find out what is the going wage scale for the kind of worker you want, the customary time off and vacation arrangements, and any special factors that exist in the local labor market. Then make arrangements to interview several possible people. The candidates may be the products of discussions between you and an agency or may be sent to you through friends, or both.

There are certain specific traits to look for in anyone you hire. Naturally, you want someone who is sober, capable, and trustworthy. It is to be hoped that you will succeed in finding someone who in addition to these essentials has a pleasant personality and a temperament geared to your own and your family's. However industrious and competent a live-in maid may be, if her manner is glum or surly she'll cast a pall over the whole house. The matter of disposition is not so vital in the case of a part-time worker, but even her sullenness or an antagonistic attitude can be very trying.

THE INTERVIEW

It is not easy to judge a servant's personality in the initial interview—you just have to do the best you can. Keep in mind that this talk is probably harder for her than for you. Try to put her at ease, and remember that if she seems downcast and taciturn or giggles and fidgets, she may only be timid and self-conscious. Use your insight in deciding what is naturalness and what is indifference, what is a permanent chip on the shoulder and what is temporary self-protection.

Whenever it is possible, it is more satisfactory to conduct the interview in your own home, especially when you have young children. An on-the-scene talk gives everybody a chance to do some real exploring. The worker can see her room (if she is to sleep in), can evaluate your automatic equipment, and get some idea of the amount of work to be done. You too can judge better than you could in an agency office whether she thinks she can handle the work and really wants to, and whether she will be good with the children and they with her. Arrange the interview so that the children meet her briefly—give worker and children a few minutes to take each other's measure, and then see that the children retire from the scene.

Whatever the settings of the interview, be on guard lest the applicant take over the reins—you're interviewing *her*, not the other way around.

Most people begin the interview by asking the worker to tell about her experience. Her answers will illuminate her intelligence and her disposition as well as her capabilities. Meanwhile, you can assess her personal cleanliness and make a rough guess at her age. You may want to ask her for her references at this point. Then when you have clearly outlined what you expect, forestall any later misunderstanding by being clear and specific, not only about duties but also about what and when she will be paid, time off, and paid vacations if they are included.

Many women, even though they may have done a good job of outlining the required duties in their own minds, are inclined in the actual interview to paint too rosy a picture for the prospective employee. Beside being unfair, it will ultimately work against your own interest to represent a good-sized weekly ironing as "a little pressing now and then" or to say that you do "all the cooking" when you expect her to fix the children's lunch and early dinner.

When the worker comes to your home for the interview, you pay her carfare both ways, whether or not you decide to employ her.

At the end of half an hour, perhaps less, you will have a fairly good idea whether this is the worker for you. If not, you end the interview by rising, and dismiss her as tactfully as you can without hurting her feelings. If there's a concrete and special reason, it is kinder to be frank about it. For example, if she's well past middle age, tell her that although you think she could probably handle either job alone very well, the house *and* the children might be too hard on her. If, on the other hand, the qualifications are fine but her personality is one you feel you couldn't be happy with, there's no point in needlessly wounding her self-esteem. You can say, and truthfully, that you are interviewing others and will let her or the agency know very soon.

If you're definitely interested, tell her that you would like to follow up her references and that you will let her (or the agency) know very shortly, say by the end of the week. Then check the references as promptly as you can and follow your decision with a call to the agency—or to her, if she came independently. It's as well, by the way, not to seem to go overboard until you *have* checked the references, no matter how much she has impressed you. If you have practically promised to engage her and the written references are not backed up by the former employers, you must then retract and let yourself in for an uncomfortable discussion.

REFERENCES

Unless the worker you are considering comes to you highly recommended from a personal friend, always ask for and check on her references. These should be recent, checkable, and specific. At the very least, they should appraise the worker's reliability, industry, and honesty and should give the reason for her leaving the employ of the writer.

Always bear in mind that a letter of reference almost invariably lists all the worker's good points, but that any faults she may have will probably be obvious only by the omission of any mention of them. If she is characterized as sober, sober she almost certainly is, if there's no mention of sobriety, it may mean (although it doesn't have to) that she tipples occasionally. When you call the writer of the reference, make specific inquiry on that point. Again, if she says she took care of the children in her last place, but the letter not only doesn't say she was good with the children but in fact makes no reference to any children, make a note to question the former employer about this.

In checking a reference, it is better to telephone than to write. It's much easier over the phone to pick up the hesitant note that tells you that while Mary cooked like an angel, her cleaning was haphazard. And oftentimes an employer who can't bear to set down on paper unfavorable comments about a person who must earn her living in the only way she knows, will be more frank in speaking, certainly about such serious matters as intemperance or incompetent care of children.

When you telephone the writer of the reference, tell her who you are and that you've been given her name as a reference by so-and-so. If the reference has been full and enthusiastic, you may immediately learn that Mary really is a jewel with whom her employer is truly sorry to part. You may, however, find that the voice at the other end is guarded, in which case you'll have to probe a bit to find out what Mary's drawback is. If you have children, it's a good idea to indicate that to the former employer. But remember to use your own common sense. If the person you're calling sounds very rigid and says her only complaint about Mary was that she had to keep *after* her about the cleaning, it just could be she's a perfectionist whom no Mary could succeed in pleasing. If she grants that Mary was good in every other way, she may be worth your trying.

Naturally, you would not call any former employer in the presence of the prospective employee.

HEALTH CERTIFICATE

If you have children, it is essential that any servant who is with them daily and prepares food for them have a clean bill of health.

Even if you are a family of adults, it is only common sense to make sure that your worker is free from any communicable disease. Many workers have up-to-date health certificates, and an agency, if requested, will see to it that they get them. If the worker you want to employ does not have one, you may want to send her to your doctor (at your expense) for an examination. If the noncertificated worker is young and inexperienced, be tactful about the matter. Be sure she understands that this is simply a common-sense precaution taken by employers and agencies—not to mention restaurants—as a matter of routine.

THE FULL-TIME WORKER

Don't forget that a maid who works for you full time needs both help and supervision. It is you who must see to it that the work is systematized and properly carried out. No doubt you will help her with much of it, particularly when there are children and when most of the washing and ironing for the family is done at home. You will probably plan the meals and do the marketing, or at least the major part of it. Unless you yourself work, you will probably help with some of the housework—making the beds, putting away clothing, perhaps doing most of the cooking. And even if you do work outside the home, there'll be many things you must do in your spare time to keep things running smoothly.

When you have young children, bear in mind that you can't expect her to keep up with the housework if she has to be a nursemaid all day. You should take the children off her hands some of the time each day. As you yourself know, one pair of hands can do only so much. If she was hired to be a nursemaid, you'll have to do correspondingly more housework; if she was hired to be a houseworker, you can't handicap her with the constant care of the children.

It is probable that your full-time worker "sleeps in," although some prefer to go home at night just as an office worker would. If she does have a room in your house, it is very important to her and to your interest in her that her room be both comfortable and attractive. Don't yield to the temptation to furnish it with Mother's bird's-eye maple dresser that you never liked and that wobbly bedside table from the attic. If you must use furniture that you have retired, mend it and paint it so it looks attractive and the pieces harmonize with each other. A good small radio is practically a necessity. And these days a modest television set does a great deal toward keeping a houseworker contented.

A comfortable mattress and two sound pillows are also a must. There should be a comfortable chair to relax or read in and a desk for writing, each well lighted. The closet should be adequate and unencumbered by any of the family's stored blankets, clothing, or white elephants. Put up gay curtains and use a matching or harmonizing bedspread. The carpet or rug ought to be pretty and in good condition. Add a good mirror, a dash of color and imagination in a few pretty ornaments, perhaps a plant—and you have taken a very important step towards a good worker-employer relationship!

It's a good thing to have it understood from the beginning that she is expected to keep her room both clean and neat. If it's pretty, her pride in it will almost always insure this. Unless you have good reason to expect that she habitually keeps the room in a horrible state, trust her and respect her privacy. Don't enter without knocking, don't examine her bureau drawers when she isn't there. The room should be definitely off bounds to the children, too, except by express invitation.

TIME OFF

The amount of time off differs in various parts of the country. It may be a weekly day off or two afternoons off; it may be a full day plus an afternoon. Whatever the agreement is, it is up to both of you to honor it. Many otherwise fair and considerate employers unthinkingly behave as though it does not matter when the day off comes as long as the employee gets it. This attitude can be productive of a great deal of resentment, and needlessly so. If you and your worker have settled on every Sunday off, for example, it is Sunday that she should have. When the Curtises are having a cook-out on Sunday and you want to go, it's all right to ask Mary well in advance (and politely) if she minds taking Saturday off instead. But if she seems reluctant, cheerfully drop that idea, and plan to bring the children if that's possible or start calling baby sitters. Mary has a right to make engagements, too!

Besides the agreed-upon times off, a full-time helper, especially if there are children, should have an hour or so each afternoon to be by herself in her own room to rest and read and relax in private. The children must be made to respect this time and not impinge on it.

In most communities a full-time worker is given a paid vacation of two weeks. If she has worked for you only a short time—say six months or somewhat less—she often gets for her first vacation a week at full pay or two weeks at half pay.

WAGES

These are paid either weekly or monthly, whichever was agreed upon at the time of hiring. If for your own reasons you are paying her a weekly wage of so much but prefer to make actual payment on the first of each month, don't forget that some months have five weeks in them. Your payments must be so figured that she is not penalized by the arrangement.

Naturally, your servant will eat the same food that you do. Neither meals nor room and board are deducted from wages these days, although of course she pays for any meals she eats away from the house. The employer supplies the uniforms.

UNIFORMS

For doing the housework a maid customarily wears an outfit known as "morning dress." This consists of a simple dress with short sleeves, in a solid color—blue, pink, gray, or light green. Or you may like a fine candy-stripe in pink, blue, or red on white. In any case, look for colors and materials and workmanship of a grade that will take plenty of tumbles in the washing machine. If they need only a minimum of ironing, so much the better. And when you're buying uniforms for the summer, remember to get a cool weave and a very simple style.

Some morning dresses are designed to be worn without collar and cuffs; others are improved by these, which usually come in a set with cap and small apron to match. They're white, and plain except for the borders, which may have a self-piping or some other decoration, also white.

These little aprons, though they look most attractive, don't really do much to protect the dress, so it's wise to get some good-sized aprons for heavy or messy work.

For informal family meals, the day uniform (a fresh one, of course, if the one that was worn during the day is soiled or wrinkled) can be worn for serving, and the formal uniform reserved for company. The formal uniform is also a simple dress, but of a plainer cut. It's often black, but may be gray or maroon, in silk or a synthetic. It is worn with the white collar and cuffs and little apron. The sleeves may be long or three-quarter length, but the latter is much more practical when one is dishing up and serving a meal!

The shoes worn with both uniforms may be black. White shoes can be worn, if preferred, with the morning dress.

The little caps that often come with the collar, cuff, and apron set are not so much worn today as they used to be. Cap or no cap, your maid's hair should be conservatively arranged and tidy, supremely so when she is serving.

A minimum supply of uniforms consists of four morning dresses, with at least four work aprons, and two or three of the cuff, collar, and apron sets if they're to be worn. If the maid is to wear the dinner uniform every night, she'll need at least two, plus a spare for emergencies. If she wears the dinner uniform only when guests are present, one should be enough.

THE PART-TIME WORKER

Many women today, especially those whose children are of an age to be in school most of the day, do their own cooking and light housework and employ a helper to come in once or twice a week to do the heavy cleaning and perhaps a weekly ironing. Usually such a worker comes for a full day or two days, though sometimes a schedule of half-days works as well for a house that is small and easy to keep. Though the customs vary in different localities, it is the usual practice to pay such a worker each work day and to include transportation costs. You also provide lunch for a day worker. Remember that this kind of employee works hard—she needs and deserves a substantial meal. So don't expect her to be happy with the health salad you've made your noonday fare so you can struggle into that beige knit! It isn't fair, either, always to foist leftovers on her. A meal consisting of half a custard cup of creamed carrots plus a dab of spinach with the heel of the meat loaf just doesn't make anybody's heart lift up and sing to the glory of work! Take your day worker's meals into consideration when you plan the menus—naturally leftovers should be utilized, but not invariably, and not a meal of "nothing but" unless they are imaginatively disguised.

Who prepares the worker's lunch is a matter of choice. Some women prefer to get the meal ready and call the worker when it is on the kitchen table. Others prefer to tell her what she is to eat and let her prepare it. In either case, give her enough time to relax and enjoy it.

The greatest mistake most women make with their part-time workers is to make too many demands on them. When the cleaning is consistently well done within the allotted time, the temptation is to say, as you leave for the supermarket, "If you could just press this skirt and these few napkins for me . . . ," or "I didn't have time to do the oven last night—will you. . . ." Unless some ironing and oven cleaning are parts of her scheduled jobs, this isn't fair. She has a lot to do in little time. If small extras are slid in here and there, something is bound to be skimped unless she has your permission to omit some regular chores to make up for them.

Remember, too, that if you're out of the house and the children in it, her efficiency is likely to be impaired. Even if she is not supposed to be "taking care" of them, when they are underfoot she may not be able to work as fast as she otherwise would.

Don't keep your part-time worker overtime unless she has agreed to stay an hour or so longer for extra pay. On the other hand, don't allow yourself to slip into laxity if she is chronically late to arrive and early to leave.

Day workers usually don't get paid when they don't come, even though the reason may be illness, and for them paid vacations are the exception rather than the rule. However, many considerate employers whose part-time helpers have given them faithful service give them a week or two weeks' pay when the family goes away in the summertime. Such employers may pay the worker all or part of wages lost through illness when they are aware that the illness is a real one and works financial hardship.

WHAT YOU CALL THE SERVANT

In very formal households with large staffs, the servants are often called by their last names, men and women alike. In today's informal America, it is more usual to use first names, although sometimes a male worker is addressed by his surname. In communities where your helper is a housewife like yourself and never thinks of herself as a "servant," the customary form of address is "Mrs. Hawkins" rather than "Sarah."

WHAT THE SERVANT CALLS YOU

Your worker calls you and your husband Mrs. Jones and Mr. Jones and refers to you in that way when she is answering the door or the telephone. In brief conversation or when taking orders, she may use "sir" and "ma'am." The worker usually calls the children by their first names, and if they grow up while she is still with the family she may continue to do so until they are in their middle or late teens, when she will address them as Master John and Miss Susan.

YOUR SERVANT AND YOU

Family needs and local customs vary so much that it's hardly possible to lay down a set of rules for the management of servants that will meet every circumstance. Day in and day out, however, the good management of household help should always call into play the basic meaning of good manners—consideration for others. In this area as in most, this is a two-way street. You will have the best relationships with your helpers and will readily earn their loyalty by being considerate of their rights and needs as employees and as human beings.

WRITE IT RIGHT

22

Your Stationery

Once upon a time no lady ever typed a letter, and one who used tinted paper labeled herself definitely not a lady. Paper printed with one's name and address would have been frowned upon even had it been available, and engraved paper was too expensive for all but a few. Uninspiring stationery awaited the letter writer, and the address of the sender was written each time on envelopes devoid of any cheerful lining—with a scratchy pen, no doubt!

These days we're never limited to white paper—we can select pewter gray and Wedgwood blue and other pastels. More often than not, the envelopes are lined with smart stripes or rich solids or gay flowerets. We can choose not only satin or linen finishes but also dozens of other interesting textures. We can brighten up and individualize our stationery with name or monogram in scarlet or sapphire. On many occasions, it is perfectly permissible to type our letters. And we can find papers in a practical size for every need, whether it be a formal invitation, a business letter, or three pages of news to our distant friends. If all this doesn't make us better correspondents, it ought to!

WOMEN'S STATIONERY

Practically every busy woman finds that a plentiful supply of paper printed with name and address, plus matching envelopes and correspondence cards, is invaluable for all but the most formal of correspondence.

Such stationery comes in double sheets as well as single small sheets and single large sheets. The double sheet, folded down the left side and printed on the first page only, is liked by many who write letters in longhand. It folds crosswise once to go into its envelope. The usual size is 5 inches by 7¼, although this, like all other sizes mentioned in this discussion, is to be thought of as average.

Single sheets are popular too, especially with those who type many letters. The smaller single size, 6 x 7, is easy to handle and adequate for most social and business letters. It fits into its envelope with one fold. The large single sheet, which measures about 7 inches by 10½ and folds twice into its envelope, is good for people who write long letters or have a large, sprawling handwriting.

The envelopes for any of these papers match the paper in color and finish. If the stationery is marked with name and address (or address only), so is the envelope—on the flap. If the paper is thin, the envelopes are lined so that the writing doesn't show through. The flaps should be straight across or come to an even point; any fancy shape, such as a diagonal closing, is frowned upon.

If the paper is monogrammed, the monogram doesn't appear on the envelope, which may have no marking at all or may carry your name and address (or address only) on the flap.

If in your household it is you who write the checks for the butcher and the baker as well as the beauty parlor, it's convenient to have extra envelopes with name and address for those tradesmen who don't enclose return envelopes with their statements.

A most useful adjunct to the writing-paper wardrobe is the correspondence card. This is used like a postcard for brief informal messages. Though made from a heavier stock because it needs no envelope, it often matches the rest of the stationery in color and finish, although this is not necessary. Such cards may be printed across the top with the name and address of the sender or the address only. A popular size is 3¼" x 5½".

Many people like to use what is called a note or semi-note instead of, or in addition to, the correspondence card. This is a sheet about 4″ x 5″, folded at the top. It goes into its matching envelope without further folding. Like the correspondence card, this serves for brief messages and may also be used for informal invitations.

Then there is the calling or visiting card, a small white or ivory card (about 2¼″ x 3¼″) which most properly should be engraved. Time was when these were used by the dozens on rounds of formal calls. Nowadays, unless you move in military or diplomatic circles or in those of official Washington, you "leave cards" very rarely indeed. If you have them, you'll use them much more often to enclose with gifts or flowers and now and then to extend and answer invitations. (All the details about calling cards and their use will be found in Chapter 25, "Greetings by Card.")

If in your community the custom of formal calling has passed completely from the scene, you may choose to substitute for the visiting card what is called an "informal." These informals are folded like the notes mentioned above (in fact, notes are also sometimes called informals) but are a little smaller, about 3 by 4½. They may be used like visiting cards for informal messages and invitations, but never *as* a visiting card.

While your notes and informals and/or visiting cards may be used for sending and answering many invitations, there are some occasions that demand severely formal paper. It's wise, therefore, to have at hand some plain white or ivory notepaper of very good quality to use for handwritten acceptances (or regrets) of formal invitations, handwritten invitations to formal affairs, and letters of condolence. The double sheet is best for this purpose, often in a slightly smaller size than used for ordinary correspondence. No marking is necessary. If a marking is used, it may consist of a monogram or of the address with the name, in a subdued rather than brilliant color.

Now that our world grows smaller every day, and more and more of our friends move about it, it's a good idea for every household to have airmail stationery ready to hand—special lightweight paper and envelopes with the attention-getting red and blue edge, plus some airmail stamps. Most people, unless they have a heavy overseas correspondence, don't bother to have airmail stationery printed with name and address, but there's no reason not to do this if you want to.

MONOGRAMS AND NAME AND ADDRESS

It is never necessary to have your paper marked, for unmarked paper is always acceptable, but monograms *are* pretty. And a name and address line is a time-saver to your correspondents as well as yourself.

Monograms when used are put at the top of the paper, either on the left or centered, except in the case of notes or informals, when they are centered on the front page.

For formal correspondence a monogram *or* address may be used— not both, and not the name. For everyday and business letters your name as well as the address may be used, although on notes and informals people often use just the address in order not to crowd the rather small page.

According to the strictest etiquette, this name should consist of your given name and surname plus your husband's surname. If you were Elizabeth Preston before you married David Evans, your stationery should be marked Elizabeth Preston Evans. Since in a business letter this would necessitate your writing Mrs. David Evans in parentheses below your signature, it is becoming acceptable to have informal stationery marked Mrs. David Evans.

A single woman may use either Elizabeth Preston or Miss Elizabeth Preston.

The address without the name may be used on any stationery.

COLOR AND FINISH

The paper for your formal correspondence should be white or ivory. For informal letters your safest choices, after white and off-white, are light and medium blues and grays. Ecru and pale green are also acceptable; most authorities still say no to pink, lavender, and turquoise. Very deep shades are neither smart nor practical for paper, but they may often be used in monograms, borders, and envelope linings.

Monograms and names and addresses are commonly applied in a color that will contrast with the color of the paper, for legibility as well as looks—scarlet or charcoal on pale gray, deep blue on light blue, and so on. White on blue and mulberry on gray are attractive combinations. Black is often used too, although many people think a colored ink is not only gayer but also makes the sheet look less like a business letterhead.

Decorated paper, too, may be used for informal correspondence, and correctly so provided the decoration is restrained, not gaudy in coloring or overpowering in size. Most authorities feel that a single initial is not in the best of taste, especially the ready-bought cutout kind.

There's a wide, wide choice of finishes today and practically all of them are acceptable. You may like a matte surface, usually called vellum or kid, or you may prefer a satin or linen-like finish. Many papers show a shadowy pattern in the form of barely visible parallel lines; these are called laid papers. Good papers are often water-marked. If you hold the paper up to the light, you can see the maker's trademark on each sheet.

The weight of the paper is also a matter of choice. As long as it's of good quality, it may be of any weight that suits you.

If you like a paper bordered in color, use a narrow border and match its color in the envelope lining and the monogram if any. (There is nothing actually incorrect about a printed name and ad-dress with a bordered paper, but usually it just doesn't look right —as if you were to wear a wristwatch and pendant watch at the same time.)

Some people like to include the telephone number along with a name and address. This is practical on the stationery for a country house, perhaps, but the increasing complexity of the dial system de-mands a long string of digits that is in no way decorative and might even be said to make the paper seem first cousin to a strip of ticker tape. If you do decide to print your telephone number on your household stationery, remember to include the area code number if you have one. In the interest of maintaining your telephone privacy, it's wisest to omit it from envelopes and correspondence cards.

It's not in good taste to strive for attention-getting effects in any of your writing paper. Naturally, your stationery represents you and should reflect your taste, but if you go to extremes to shout that it's yours and yours alone, the result is likely to be obtrusive and tire-some. So it's better to avoid such obviously contrived combinations as, for instance, a bottle-green imprint on light green paper with the message inscribed in green ink.

Every store that carries a good stock of stationery has books from various manufacturers showing samples of many different papers, inks, and styles of imprints. Jewelers and the better department stores do engraving as well and will advise you about it.

One last caution: Today's experts agree that scented paper is not in good taste, and ruled paper, of course, is only for small children.

STATIONERY FOR MEN

A man uses a large sheet of severely plain paper—not for him the dainty sheets or colored borders or fancy linings. A common size is seven by ten inches or even larger; the sheet folds twice across to fit into its rather long envelope. If the paper is not white, it may be off-white or gray, preferably rather heavy, with a dull finish. It's better to have cut edges, although a deckle (rough) edge is acceptable, too.

The printing, if any, is in black, dark blue, dark green, or maroon. The most common marking is an address across the top of the sheet. His name (always without *Mr.*) can also be used, alone or with the address, and if his signature is hard to read, this is advisable. Initials or a monogram are all right too, as long as they are very plain and not too big.

The unlined envelopes match the paper, of course, and the flap should be cut straight across or in a symmetrical point. Name or name and address may be printed on the flap.

STATIONERY FOR CHILDREN

Many attractive papers are designed especially for children, and there's no doubt that a gay row of red balloons or a bowing clown does more to tempt a child to write than does a blank white sheet. Even teen-age girls may like to make use of name-imprinted paper further glorified by a little cartoon showing a young miss in the throes of telephonitis! In the middle teens, though, both boys and girl appreciate the dignity of regular stationery, either plain or name-imprinted to make it all their own.

HARBORVILLE STATION

R. D. 5, GREEN BAY   MILL HOUSE

SHOREPORT 6-1212

STATIONERY FOR A COUNTRY HOUSE

Although special paper for a house in the country may be something of a luxury, it can be diverting and attractive, and in some cases a real necessity. For instance, if your house is in Shoreport

Village but your friends are met at the railroad station at Harbor-ville and write to you at the Green Bay postoffice, it does avoid a strain on their memories and your pen to get stationery which clues all three places.

A good way for country hosts to avoid lost guests is to draw—or persuade a gifted friend to draw—a good clear map of the route to your place, and have the local printer reproduce it on informals, together with your phone number. Such a map would go on the front flap, your invitation inscribed inside.

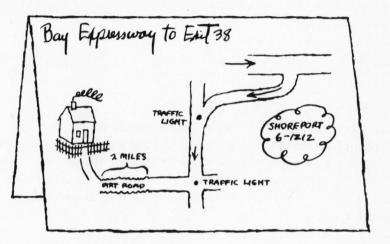

MOURNING STATIONERY

Like other outward signs of mourning, this special stationery is less used today than formerly. There is every reason, however, to use it if you want to. The very wide black border that was once considered proper for the first six months or the first year is seldom seen any more; a narrow border a thirty-second of an inch to a quarter-inch wide is customary. The paper of course is white. The envelopes are bordered also (in the same width) and are unlined.

23

Your Social Letters

That desk drawer full of all the needed kinds of paper is a good morale builder and takes you a long way toward the goal of being a really good correspondent—the kind that people love to hear from! But, of course, for your letters to make the best impression the paper isn't everything—you want your letters to be in the proper form.

THE FORM OF A SOCIAL LETTER

If your address isn't printed on the paper, you will probably want to write it in; and if so it should go at the top, over at the right. Underneath that (or by itself if your paper is imprinted with your address) goes the date. Just "Friday" spelled out will do if the letter needs no reply and probably won't be kept. However, it is more considerate to set down the date, month, and year (October 17, 19—). The month should be spelled out although the date may be written in figures or semiabbreviated (October 17th instead of seventeenth). The dateline can also be placed at the end of the letter, on the left-hand side below the signature. This is usually where it appears in a formal note.

Now, a few spaces below the address and/or date and starting from the left-hand side of the page, comes the salutation, formal or less formal, depending on how well you know the person you're writing to. A few examples: "My dear Mrs. Osborne," "Dear Mrs. Osborne," "Dear Betty," "Betty dear," "Dearest Katie"—or even "Hi, Katie!" Most properly the salutation is followed by a comma, but to a dear friend like Katie you could just as well use a dash or exclamation point if you feel that way.

Next comes the body of the letter—the message—and then the goodby or the closing, followed by the signature.

CLOSINGS

Just like salutations, the forms that signatures take depend on your mood and the relationship between you and the addressee. "Sincerely," "Sincerely yours," "Cordially" or "Cordially yours"— any of these would be appropriate expressions with which to close the letter to Mrs. Osborne. There's nothing actually wrong with "Yours truly" or "Very truly yours," except that they sound the least bit cold and perfunctory, perhaps because they are so often used in business letters. After carrying on at length about all the family news to Betty or Katie, you would probably say goodby with "Love to all of you," "Devotedly," "Lovingly," "Affectionately"—or whatever seems comfortable and natural. Try not to yield to the temptation —even if the laundry man is banging on the door and the phone is ringing its head off—to set down "Yours in haste" or "hastily yours."

The closing "Respectfully yours" is no longer used for the average social letter, although it is occasionally employed in business letters, as for example in a letter from a tradesman to his customers, and this expression may also be used in writing to certain high government officials, churchmen, and diplomats. "Gratefully" or "Gratefully yours" should be used only when the whole purpose of the letter is to thank someone for a very real favor or benefit.

It's better to stay away from the ornate phrases that were proper in our grandparents' day, such as "I beg to remain," "I have the honor to remain," "Believe me, I am," and so on.

SIGNATURES

The signature is written below and a little to the right of the closing. When you're writing to close friends like Betty and Katie, there's no problem about what signature to use—your own given name or the nickname they associate with you goes under the closing. One important thing to remember about a signature is that it should *always* be written by hand even though the letter itself is typed. Another is that the middle initial shouldn't be used; either write out the middle name or omit it altogether. And when your handwriting is so hard to read that you type nearly all your letters, it's considerate to type out your name underneath your written version of it in any letter sent to someone who doesn't know you well.

Remember, too, that letters should never be signed Miss, Mrs. or Mr., unless one of these is really necessary for identification, and then it should be set off in parentheses. For example, a man who has a given name that could be mistaken for a woman's and is writing to someone who doesn't know him, puts Mr. in parentheses before his signature, Marion Kendrick.

Miss requires no period after it because it isn't an abbreviation. Mr. and Mrs. do require the period.

A single woman signs herself Elizabeth Preston. If she wants to make it clear she is a Miss and her stationery affords no clue, she may write Miss in parentheses before her name. Or she may type Miss Elizabeth Preston (in parentheses) below the handwritten Elizabeth Preston.

Should Elizabeth marry David Evans, she signs her social letters Elizabeth Evans or Elizabeth Preston Evans. Mrs. David Evans in parentheses may go below the signature when she feels this is informative to her correspondent.

A married woman's signature on a note to an employee or to a tradesman like the milkman may be signed Mrs. Evans, and so can a note to the housekeeper. It wouldn't be incorrect to sign it Elizabeth Evans with Mrs. David Evans underneath, but as a matter of common sense, just Mrs. Evans is quicker and simpler and less pretentious.

No title such as colonel, commander, Dr., or reverend should precede a signature. A military officer may, however, put his rank and service in parentheses below his signature—(Rear Admiral, U.S.N.)—and a doctor may follow his signature with M.D., a churchman with D.D. or whatever may be the appropriate initials.

MR., MRS., DR., JR., ESQ.

The titles Mr., Mrs., and Dr. precede the name and are *always abbreviated* when used as part of the name (doctor is lower cased and spelled out in general references): Mr. Appleton; Dr. DeVoe. Names followed by "Jr." (Jeremy Snowden, Jr.) indicate that the man's name is just the same as his father's. A letter to him is addressed: Mr. Jeremy Snowden, Jr., with a comma before the junior. It is most correct for a man to drop the junior after the death of his father, but some people continue to use it. It is sometimes considered a courtesy to the widow if she is allowed to keep her husband's name and both her son and daughter-in-law continue to be Mr. and Mrs. Jeremy Snowden, Jr.

When you *refer* to a junior, by the way, the word is always spelled out and begins with a small letter. The abbreviation used in addresses and signatures always begins with a capital "J" and is followed by a period. A woman never signs herself Jr., although she may be a Leslie or a Marion named after her father.

Even when a man has a grown son who is a junior, he never in writing attaches the word "senior" to his own name, because the son is always junior to the father. As a practical matter, he may be referred to as senior in conversation and may be asked for on the telephone in that way. When the son is married and both families live in a small town, people get into the habit of distinguishing between them with the lavish use of senior and junior even in writing, particularly if they live in the same house or on the same street. This is a matter of taste governed by common sense. If there is seldom any real confusion, it's more proper for the wife of the older man to sign her name without any Sr. and for the son's wife to sign herself Mrs. Frank Carter, Jr.

The abbreviation "Esq." stands for esquire, an old English word which originally meant a candidate for knighthood and is now a courteous synonym for gentleman. Though it is still in common usage in Great Britain, it isn't much used in the United States except for certain personages. (See "Forms of Address.") If you do use it, remember that it replaces Mr. and so is never used *with* Mr.—moreover, it follows the name instead of preceding it. The proper form is David Evans, Esq., or David Evans, Jr., Esq., or David Evans, III, Esq. The abbreviation is preferred to the spelled-out word except in diplomatic and extremely formal correspondence, and is used to address the man only, never for man and wife. In American usage it is never employed in the addressing of engraved invitations.

"Messrs." is the abbreviation of *messieurs,* the French word for misters, and is used to address two brothers in the same family, but never father and son. In other words, if you want to invite certain members of the Haynes family to your daughter's wedding, widowed Howard Haynes and his sons James and Grant, you could address one invitation to the Messrs. Haynes—or the Messrs. James and Grant Haynes—but the father should have an invitation of his own. Technically, any invitation sent to the the Messrs. Haynes indicates that all the brothers in the family are invited, no matter how many there are or what the age range. (If, by the way, one of Mr. Haynes's sons is a junior, addressing the sons' envelope to the Messrs. Haynes is a convenient way of managing a joint invitation, since it avoids the awkwardness of writing the Messrs. Howard, Jr. and Grant Haynes.

"Master" is traditionally the form of address to a boy under twelve, though many feel it sounds just a little too quaint when it's applied to today's live-wire independent youngsters. If it seems so to you, just use the boy's name without either Master or Mr., adding Jr., of course, if that is applicable.

"Miss" is the proper form of address for any unmarried woman and for all female children. To be strictly correct, the oldest daughter of several is addressed by just the Miss and her surname. She is (the) Miss Evans and her sisters are Miss Dorothy Evans and Miss Claire Evans. Any invitation intended to include all three could be addressed to the Misses Evans.

SEQUENCE OF PAGES IN A LETTER

When you're using single sheets, do number them if your letter covers more than two pages, particularly if page two is on the back of page one. (It's really better *not* to use the other side of a page, especially in typing—it makes it much harder to read.) Your opening page really needs no number, but *count* it as page one.

When you're using double sheets, numbering is important, too. Different people have different ways of doing it. A two-page letter goes directly from page one to page three—which is the right-hand page inside the fold—and if that's the case, you really don't need to number at all. For a letter of three pages, the most logical method is to proceed in sequence, leaf by leaf, numbering as you go. When you think you will fill all four pages, there are three ways of numbering possible. You can go straight through—one, two, three, and four. Or, after completing the first page, you can turn the paper around, open out the fold and write across the paper over the whole inside, labeling it page two, and then turn it around again to put page three on the last leaf. An older form, which many people still use, is to put page two on the very last page and then unfold the sheet to write crosswise inside, labeling the whole inside page three.

The method you choose is not important—the numbering is. On any long letter, write out your numbers large and clear so your friends won't have to flip pages madly to figure out what's happened when a wedding party suddenly turns into somebody's tonsillectomy.

TYPING VERSUS HANDWRITING

An adult's handwriting is as much a part of him as the way his hair grows and almost as difficult to change, unless more effort is put into it than one usually cares to give. Your penmanship may or may not be beautiful or striking—but legibility is a real necessity. It's worth taking a little time and pains to achieve. If this truly seems beyond you, then resort to typing every time you possibly can.

These days you may type many, many kinds of letters without running the risk of hurting a friend's feelings because you didn't take pen in hand *just* for him or her! There are still a few letters that must be handwritten: most letters of condolence and their acknowledgments, many letters of congratulation and most invitations. The exceptions to this rule are governed by common sense. You could, for example, send a typed letter of condolence from your office expressing your sorrow at the death of a person whom you knew mainly in business. And there's no reason why you shouldn't type a note to the daughter of your oldest friend Katie to congratulate her on winning a scholarship. Of course, you would never type any invitation (or acceptance or regret) that is formal enough to be expressed in the third person, but you *could* type informal invitations to a cocktail party, a buffet supper, a cook-out. But it usually turns out that it's really easier to write and address these by hand, because you're probably sending them on small-sized notes or informals, unhandy for the typewriter. Besides, handwritten ones look so much more festive! And so we still write out most invitations, except the informal ones that may be embedded in a typed letter, such as an invitation to spend the weekend.

A good general rule is: when in doubt, write it out. There's no denying that a handwritten message seems to speak more from the heart.

THE LOOKS OF YOUR LETTER

Naturally, you want any letter that goes out into the world as your representative to look as neat and stylish as possible. The attire, so to speak, you've already taken care of by selecting attractive and appropriate stationery. Next make sure that your letter is well groomed. The proportion of writing (or typing) to white space is an important part of that grooming. Leave good margins all around. And a moment's consideration about the probable length of your message can save you from having to choose between exasperated rewriting or sending out an unlettered-looking letter. If you need only a few words—"Looking forward to Tuesday lunch—but I forgot about the dentist! Could you make it one-thirty instead? Unless I hear from you, I'll see you then."—remember to start it far enough down the page so the words "Fondly" and "Celia" don't come smack in the middle of the page.

THE ENVELOPE

You address the envelope for a social letter in the same manner as the letter itself—that is, typed if the letter is typed, written out if the letter is in longhand. The address starts just below the center of the envelope and each line is indented from the one just above it. Take special care with long, complex addresses: if your correspondent lives at Waggoner House, Somerset Road, Head of the Harbor, Oaks County, Virginia, start writing far enough to the left and high enough so that you'll have plenty of room for both Harbor and Virginia.

According to the strictest etiquette, no abbreviations should be used in the addressee's proper name—if you're writing to Miss Frances Hamilton Knox, you write the whole thing out or address her as Miss Frances Knox. In writing, however, to a person who habitually hides his first name under an initial, you have to address him as Mr. W. James Byron.

Commas are not used at the end of lines in addressing an envelope for a social letter. The names of states should be spelled out in full. It is perfectly proper to spell out short numbers like six and ten, but when we consider the millions of envelopes that must pass through our postoffices, it seems more efficient as well as more considerate to put *all* numbers into figures—legible figures.

City and state should be on separate lines.

Don't be in too much of a rush with the stamp—stick it on properly in the upper right-hand corner. Sending out a letter with a crooked, mangled, or upside-down stamp is akin to letting your lingerie straps show.

THE USE OF "PERSONAL" AND OTHER DIRECTIONS

You may write in the lower left-hand corner of an envelope the word "personal" when, and only when, you're writing on a confidential matter to someone in an office and want to make sure that no employee in what would be a daily routine opens this particular letter. But it's most discourteous to put "personal" on a letter addressed to anyone at his home. You're implying that the members of his family would be mannerless enough to open it unless warned off.

When you want to have a letter forwarded to someone who is away, put the phrase "Please forward" on the lower left-hand corner of the envelope. Or if you're addressing your letter to a hotel where you know your correspondent is to arrive in a day or so, you put "Please hold" in the lower left-hand corner.

HOW TO WRITE LETTERS THAT PEOPLE LIKE TO GET

The adage goes that letter writing is an art. And so it is, in a sense, at least. Few people have the talent and the time to send through the post little masterpieces worthy of being collected and bound for future generations. But no need to use this as an excuse for not writing; your friends and family aren't awaiting lyrical descriptions of the October leaves or a brilliant critique of the play you saw last night. They just want to hear what's been happening in your world—whether you've been having a gay time or a quiet one, whether the dreamed-of trip to the West is still on, how Mary's making out with the piano lessons, how you all are. And not the least of what makes your letter meaningful to them is that it shows you have been thinking about *them,* with love, and missing them.

That's what a letter should show. That's what you *want* it to show. But sometimes it doesn't. Why?

The thing that most frequently sours a well-intended letter is the necessity to apologize for not having written sooner. All too many epistles divide themselves like Gaul into three parts, and these in the case of letters are: the apology, the assorted excuses, and the classic closing, such as, "I have to dash now to pick up Tommy from Scouts." And so the message could just as well go into a ten-word telegram: SORRY HAVEN'T WRITTEN NO NEWS HOPE YOU'RE WELL MUST DASH. The recipient of such a letter, tearing open the envelope in hopes of the nearest thing to a visit with you, feels as if you'd invited her over for a cup of coffee, poured it out, and then gone back to bed.

Of course, this doesn't mean that you shouldn't apologize for a delay in writing—all too often one must. But do avoid an ungracious opening like this, for example: "I suppose I ought to have written sooner, and I would have, but I haven't had a minute. First I had the whole flower show on my hands and then Bobby got a sore throat and after that the people came to remodel the kitchen and they had to take up part of the floor. . . ." This implies that writing to your old friend is positively the last straw in a harried existence. So when you must begin with an apology, take care to make the tone outgoing and friendly rather than complaining: "You don't know how often you've been in my thoughts, but the letter just hasn't gotten from my head onto the paper until now. So much has been going on on top of the daily scramble!" Or, "You must think I'd forgotten you completely, but each time I got what I thought would be a chance to write, something interrupted. . . ." You could follow such an opening with some interested comments on her long-unanswered letter and perhaps a question or two about her doings. *Then* try to imagine you're talking to her, right in your own living room, and be fine and funny about the string of disasters in setting up the flower show and about the balancing act that's required to slide a heavy turkey into the refrigerator when there isn't any floor in front of it. Stir in any family and local news you think would interest your friend, add at least a heaping tablespoon of affection and interest in her affairs— and you've written the kind of letter people like to get!

The best way, of course, to avoid the apology struggle is to answer letters promptly. It makes writing a good letter so much easier, too

—when the news in the one you're answering is still fresh and when the pleasure of having received it hasn't had time to fade.

BREAD-AND-BUTTER LETTERS

When you've stayed overnight or longer in anyone's house, it's the tradition that a note should fly practically by return pigeon to your hostess. Well, that *is* a bit of exaggeration! But it's true that no more than a few days should pass before you write your thanks. Technically, you can do this by writing "Thank you for a delightful weekend" on a visiting card. How much more appreciative, though, and how much more warming to the hostess' heart, to write a brief note that mentions specifically your enjoyment of some of the doings she arranged for your pleasure.

As with other thank-you letters, you write a bread-and-butter letter for both you and your husband. You alone sign it, but you make it clear that you're writing for him, too, by concluding with some such phrase as "Dick and I enjoyed it all so much."

The bread-and-butter letter is considered an informal one. It needn't be on formal stationery and it may be typed. It is always written to a woman. If you're a college classmate of Penny Taft and have visited her at her family's home, you direct your letter to her mother. If you and your husband visit newly married Jean and Joe David who make their home with the groom's mother, you write to the senior Mrs. David. The only time when a thank-you for a weekend would be written to a man is when you and your husband visit a bachelor.

It's not at all necessary, but a courtesy that is always appreciated is a thank-you note for entertainment other than a weekend, especially when the hostess has been particularly thoughtful of *you*— when you've been to a dinner party where another guest was asked especially for you, or to a concert selected because the performer is one of your favorites.

Bread-and-butter letters need not be answered.

THANK-YOU LETTERS FOR GIFTS

When you're thanking anyone for anything by mail, you should write a note even if only a brief one. Printed acknowledgment cards aren't really the same thing at all.

It isn't, of course, ever essential to write a note to someone whom you thanked in person at the time the gift was presented—though you can hardly hurt the donor's feelings if you do! Other gifts should be acknowledged as soon as you can—within the week gives you top marks for appreciation. Such a letter may be typed if you like, and written on regular notepaper or on an informal. There's no need for it to be a long letter, but its sincerity is enhanced enormously when you make some specific reference to the gift. No matter how promptly it reaches the donor, a note that says only "Thank you for the lovely present" is bound to be somewhat disappointing to the one who spent time and thought as well as money to find something she felt sure you would especially like. So do recognize and praise this thoughtfulness: "The color is perfect with my new blue coat and I did so need a pretty scarf. . . . "

An aside to donors: It's very hard for a recipient to be specific in thanking someone for a gift when she doesn't know what to call it or what it's supposed to be for. Certain accessories—antique china pieces, some imports, a few kitchen gadgets—may baffle the uninitiated, especially the bride. When you're sending something of this sort, do write on your gift card a word or two to identify it and its use or uses. "I thought this Victorian cheese box would be lovely for flowers if you don't like cheese!"

THANK-YOU'S FOR WEDDING GIFTS

It's the bride who writes all the thank-you notes for wedding presents and signs her name to them, though of course she always makes mention of her husband's pleasure in the gift. (Or of her fiancé's pleasure, if she wisely decides to write as the gifts come in rather than letting the thank-you's pile up until after the wedding.) The notes don't have to be long and may be written on informals. Some authorities say they shouldn't be typed, but when there are a huge number to be written and the new wife has a job as well as a home to run, surely it's better to type some of them whenever that's faster and the alternative is letting months go by before the gifts get acknowledged at all. The thank you should say what the present was and why you like it, and if possible, how you're going to use it. Here's a sample:

Friday

Dear Katie,

I wish you could have been here to see our faces when Ben and I unwrapped the beautiful tray and stand that came from you and Joe. We haven't any coffee table, so this will be a joy in front of our sofa—the gold and red is a beautiful accent for its lime green. We want you and Ben to come see it and us—we'll call you soon.

With love,
Irene

LETTERS OF CONGRATULATION

In these busy days, congratulatory letters are perhaps not characterized as obligatory—but to your friend who has just become engaged, graduated from college, had a baby, or landed an impressive new job, a letter from you expressing your delight in the event is the icing on the cake!

Letters of congratulation are among those that in the best usage are handwritten, but certainly you could type one to a close friend.

Remember when you write a letter to a girl on the occasion of her engagement, you don't congratulate *her*—you wish her happiness and congratulate her fiancé. You might write something like this:

Wednesday

Dear Marian,

A letter from Mother just gave me your wonderful news, and I'm writing to wish you everything that is happy. Mother says Bob is a wonderful person. I'm looking forward to meeting him when I come home in December—meanwhile do congratulate him for me.

With much love,
Doris

To a newly fledged lawyer you might write:

November 16th, 19——

Dear Ben,

More times than you know, I've thought about your stick-to-it-iveness throughout the long grind and admired you for working so hard and so cheerfully. I congratulate you heartily on passing the bar exam. And when you hang out that new shiny shingle may people flock to you in droves—they will, I know!

Sincerely,
David

ANSWERING LETTERS OF CONGRATULATION

No policeman is going to give you a ticket for not answering a congratulatory letter, but surely you really want to say thank you to the people who were kind enough to write you. Again, your letter needn't be long, and it may be typed if need be. The main thing is to express your appreciation of the other person's warm interest in this important development in your life. For instance:

November 20, 19——

Dear David,

It pleased me very much to have your letter. It doesn't seem possible that at long last I can call myself a lawyer, and believe me, there were plenty of times I thought I'd never make it! I'm busy making plans—I've been lucky enough to find not only a minuscule office but also two small cases with which to launch my ship. So we shall see what we shall see! Thanks again for your letter.

Sincerely,

Ben

LETTERS OF CONDOLENCE

It won't come as news—certainly not if you have ever had to send one—that letters of condolence are just about the most difficult to write. But you must somehow express your sympathy to the ones left behind, and that promptly—as soon as you hear of the loss. This expression may take other forms than that of a letter. You may, for instance, send a visiting card with "Deepest sympathy" written across it. Though this is quite correct, it does seem to lack warmth. Sometimes people turn it into a more thoughtful gesture by enclosing such card with a small bouquet of flowers already arranged in a container, sending it directly to the house.

You may also express your sympathy in a telegram: JOHN AND I DEEPLY SHOCKED AND SEND HEARTFELT SYMPATHY AND ALL OUR LOVE. Or: JUST HEARD TRAGIC NEWS YOU AND GENE HAVE OUR DEEPEST SYMPATHY. Or: THINKING OF YOU MY HEARTFELT SYMPATHY AND LOVE.

When you do write a letter, according to the strictest etiquette it should be on your formal writing paper. However, many people use good quality informals, which are all right provided their tone is subdued—white, ivory, pale blue, or gray paper, monogram in a conservative shade (not red) and the envelope lining, if any, plain and in a quiet tint. And unless they come from a business office, such letters should be handwritten.

It doesn't matter whether your letter is a lengthy one or quite short as long as it is sincere and indicates your real sympathy. There's no need for philosophical flights—you aren't required to explain the meaning of life and the inevitability of death, and at this particular time it wouldn't be of much comfort if you tried. By the same token, it is better not to refer to the death as a blessing even though it may have been. When the final illness was long and marked by suffering, rather than call its end a release, sympathize instead with the tragedy of the illness' striking at all, and praise the courage of the deceased while he had to endure it. So many times, of course, those nearest and dearest to the one who has died will have suffered and endured, too, if not in the same way. A reference to this may be comforting, provided you do not appear to make martyrs of them or seem to attach more importance to their brave endurance of the strain than to the patient's own suffering or the family's loss. "Of course it must be a comfort to you now to know that you never let up and never complained . . ." is a dangerous sentiment for the theme of a letter of condolence, for it implies that a clear conscience makes up for everything. Make such a reference only after you have expressed your sympathy, your own sense of loss, and some appreciation of the qualities that will make the deceased mourned by those who knew him. Then stress the fact that the courage *they* showed helped *him*: "What a tower of strength you have been—such a tremendous help to Bob's morale all along."

Whenever you can—and you almost always can—say something about what the dead person meant to you—to you personally, perhaps to the community, perhaps to your children—and how much you will miss him. If you knew him only slightly, pass up the trivialities, the superficial memories of social occasions where you occasionally saw him, and rather stress the loss of those he left behind and your sympathy with it.

Even when you yourself have suffered the identical loss, in writing your letter of condolence be wary of dwelling on the fact. While it is true that you can identify with the bereft one's feelings more than someone who has yet to suffer this particular loss, in the rawness of first grief the one you're trying to comfort feels as if no one else can know what *his* loss is like. What you want to put down is not a reminder of how much you suffered a year ago, but an assurance that you feel with him, that your heart is aching for him. And if you even thus obliquely refer to your own loss be sure it is a comparable one. It is, of course, always a very sad thing when a parent dies albeit peacefully and full of years, but this is not quite the same thing as losing a husband or wife.

Letters of sympathy aren't written by rule, of course. All of the above pointers simply mark morasses that are easy to fall into. When it comes to you to write such a letter, write what you feel. Always, if the sympathy comes from the heart, with the intelligence doing just a bit of censoring when necessary, no awkwardness of expression can dilute the comfort that the letter is intended to give.

Here is a brief note from one who is an acquaintance rather than an intimate:

Tuesday, May 10th

Dear Jane,

Bob and I were inexpressibly shocked when we heard about Tom —we did not even know he was ill. Our hearts and thoughts are with you. We liked and admired him so much, and were always sorry that time and distance seemed to prevent our spending more time with you both.

Our deepest sympathy goes to you and young Tom.

Sincerely yours,
Ellen

From a college friend of Jane's who never met Tom:

July 16th

Dear Jane:

I was so very sorry to read in the alumnae magazine of your husband's death and I have been thinking of you often these last few days. I know that words can't be much comfort at such a time, but I did want to send you my sympathy.

Sincerely,
Agatha Day Winston
(Mrs. John W. Winston)

This letter is from a widowed friend who knew both Tom and Jane:

Monday

Dearest Jane,

I was so shocked on my return from Chicago to learn of Tom's death and can hardly believe that it has happened. He was such a warm person—and he accomplished so much so young that for him to go in his prime is all the more poignant. I shall miss him, and so will many others, for he had such a capacity for friendship.

My heart goes out to you, dear, for I know so well every inch of the way you must travel. But the same strength that meant so much to Tom throughout that tragic illness will help you now. If

I can help please call on me—I mean physical help. I know better than to offer any other kind just now. My thoughts and sympathy are with you always.

Lovingly,
Marjorie

And this is from a business associate of Tom's who had not met Jane:

June 21, 19——

Dear Mrs. Harris,

The sad news about Tom has just come to me, and I am so very sorry to hear of it. In my association with him I developed a great deal of respect for him as a lawyer and as a human being, and for whatever comfort it may be, I should like you to know that he will be missed by his brothers at the Bar as well as by his other friends.

Please accept my deepest sympathy.

Sincerely yours,
Edwin Pierce

Everybody knows that grief and shock plus the burden of adjustment to an emptier world make it impossible for a newly bereaved person to carry on briskly. Therefore no one expects a lengthy answer to a letter of sympathy nor a very prompt one. All the same, such letters should be answered and by the one who owes them— unless that person is so ill that writing is out of the question, in which case a relative can do it for her, explaining why.

Printed acknowledgment cards, though occasionally used, are not to be compared to a handwritten note, however brief. They may have to be used, of course, in cases where the deceased was such a public figure that thank-you notes could run into the thousands.

In reply to a letter of condolence, just a line or two is enough. For instance, Jane may write to her friend of college days:

July 23rd

Dear Agatha,

Thank you so much for your sympathy—it was so thoughtful of you to write.

Sincerely,
Jane Weiss Harris

And to Mr. Pierce she may say that his thoughtfulness in writing her has meant a great deal to her, and thank him for his sympathy.

To her closer friends Ellen and Marjorie, she would indicate how much comfort their letters gave her and thank them for writing, and she would probably indicate that she will get in touch with them as soon as she can.

THE LETTER OF INTRODUCTION

In the past, when your friends were bound for distant cities you wrote several letters of introduction to people you knew out there—and handed all these to the travelers for them to present to the natives. No matter how pressed for time, the travelers felt obliged to make use of the letters, and the busy friends in Seattle or Chicago not only felt but *were* obliged to show hospitality. Nowadays introducing our friends from here to friends elsewhere is done much more sensibly. When May and John Boswell are headed for Chicago, say, you write directly to your Chicago friends the Stantons—and don't mention to the Boswells that you're doing so. Then, if the Stantons aren't tied up and want to see some new faces, they can call the Boswells at the hotel and make a date. On the other hand, if Jack Stanton happens to be working day and night on a big advertising campaign or his wife is worn out after the twins' bout with measles, with a clear conscience they can let the whole thing go because the Boswells' feelings *can't* be hurt—though you'll undoubtedly get a note from Peggy Stanton regretting that she couldn't get in touch with your friends and explaining the reasons.

The letter that you write to the Stantons might go like this:

May 20th, 19——

Dear Rosemary,

A couple whom we've grown to like so much—May and John Boswell—are planning a trip to Chicago. They're going to stay ten days and will be at the Ambassador, arriving there the afternoon of the tenth. If you and Jack happen to have some free time while they're in town, I'm sure you'd enjoy meeting them and they you. They're green-thumbed gardeners, both of them, and play good bridge, too. Please don't feel that you must see them—I haven't said a word to them about writing you. But if you should want to get in touch with them, I know it would be a highlight of their trip.

Fondly,
Lillian

There are still occasions when we revert to the old style in giving letters of introduction. Perhaps the Boswells are driving across the continent, sightseeing as they go, and don't know just when they'll be where. In that case, give the Boswells the Stantons' address and write the Stantons to say you've taken the liberty of suggesting that the Boswells let them know when they get to Chicago; if it's convenient for them all to meet, you're sure they'd enjoy each other.

You could also use this method to introduce the Boswells to your American friends the Joneses who are now living in Switzerland— *if* you know them well enough. Bear in mind that you're not the only friend the Joneses left behind in America and that these days everybody travels—if all the home-towners aimed their touring friends at the poor Joneses the latter might soon be bankrupt both emotionally and financially. Be sure, therefore, to extend this privilege only to intimate friends whom you are quite certain the Joneses would enjoy.

In trying to provide for the Boswells a rather special pleasure by enabling them to meet a European whom you know (and it must be one whom you know very well indeed), you would again go about it in the old-fashioned way, giving the Boswells a note to present. A letter to your friend Charlotte Prunier might say:

July 20, 19——

My dear Charlotte,

   This will introduce two dear friends, May and John Boswell, who are to be in Geneva for a week en route to Athens, where he is to begin a fascinating new job reporting on some new archaeological finds. I know you will enjoy each other—how I wish I could see you too!

Fondly,
Lillian

It's a good idea to write these formal letters of introduction on your best white paper and by hand, presenting the letters to the Boswells unsealed, with a separate memo of the Joneses' address and that of Mme. Prunier. The envelope containing the letter bears only the name of the person to whom it is to be presented, plus a conventional phrase identifying those who are being introduced: Courtesy of Mr. and Mrs. Boswell.

When someone has given you a letter of introduction, you may mail it with your visiting card (or a brief explanatory note) bearing your address in town. Or a couple or a single man may go to the house and leave the letter and the visiting card with a servant. A woman traveling alone would forward the letter by mail with a note on her hotel paper, reading something like this:

Friday
September 20th

Dear Mrs. Jones,

Jane Stark has given me this letter of introduction to you. I am to be here in Geneva until a week from Monday. I should like so much to meet you and hope that it may be possible.

(Miss) Marian Andersen

Always remember, when you give anyone a letter of introduction you are in effect sponsoring the friend who bears it—are yourself guaranteeing the acceptability of his behavior. What's more, the presentation of a letter of introduction, whether by mail or in person, puts an all but inescapable obligation on its recipient. Unless there is illness or a death in the family, these people *must* entertain the visitors in a fairly formal way or run the risk of being very rude.

Therefore, never let anyone talk you into providing a letter of introduction for some friend of *his,* whom you know slightly if at all, and be chary indeed of dispensing them on your own without due thought, lest you lose at least one friendship and maybe two!

24

Your Business Letters

STRICTLY SPEAKING, THE CORRESPONDENCE OF THE WORLD OF BUSINESS, those millions of letters that sally forth daily to and from banks and stores, lawyers and clients and manufacturers, isn't a matter of etiquette. But it's surprising, when you stop to think about it, how many business letters are written at home in the course of a year—ordering things, returning things, making reservations or ordering tickets, writing a reference for a servant. Here are the "how-to's" for the commonest of these communications.

THE FORM OF A BUSINESS LETTER

If the paper you are using isn't imprinted with your address, you must put it there—on the right-hand side of the page near the top—and then write the date below it. When your address is already on your letterhead, then you just put the date on the top right-hand side. Somewhat below the date line but over on the left-hand side you set down the name and the address of the person you're writing to. This part of your letter would look like this:

> 170 Avon Road
> Oakmont, Texas
> June 19, 19——

Mr. Harold Johnson
Johnson and Atterbury
105 Broad Street
Arcadia, New York

Note that the month and the state are spelled out and so is the word "street." Organizations vary when it comes to spelling out such words as "and," "Company," "Incorporated," and the like. Their letterhead, advertisement or brochure will give you the firm name in its exact form; if you are writing from memory, or otherwise out of the blue, just do the best you can—it isn't a matter of life and death except in published bibliographies if you write "and" when it should be "&." Don't forget to include the zip code in the firm address if you know it, and also indicate your own if you have one.

There are no periods at the end of the address and date lines, as you see, and the commas are there only to separate the date of the month from the year or the name of the town from that of the state.

In today's usage the block form shown above—each line coming directly under the line above it, lined up on the left—is preferred to the older indented style and fortunately it's easier to achieve on the typewriter.

Several spaces below the address on the left and lined up with it, comes the salutation, followed by a colon. If you're writing to a store or a hotel or a company impersonally, you will write "Sir," "Dear Sir," "Dear Sirs" or "Gentlemen." When you're writing an individual in the company, you'll say "Dear Mr. Johnson" or "My dear Mr. Johnson." Should you be writing to a woman or women impersonally, you would use "Dear Madam" or "Dear Madames"— not "Mesdames" for the plural.

The closing of a business letter goes two or three spaces below the last line and to the right of the center of the page. Correct closings are: "Yours truly," "Yours very truly" or "Very truly yours," "Yours sincerely" or "Sincerely yours."

The form of a business letter is important, of course, but so also is the content. Make your message as brief as you can and your meaning as clear as you can. Don't ramble. Don't use "I" any oftener than you have to. Be direct.

Type your business letters if you can. If you can't, take extra pains to write legibly, not only out of consideration for the busy addressee but also to be sure that your order or question or reservation can be taken care of accurately. If your handwriting is commonly considered very hard to read, don't hesitate to print, especially your name, address and specifications of your order.

ORDERING FROM A STORE

When something in an advertisement or a catalogue offering has caught your eye and you send away for it, don't be so eager to get your order in the mail that you leave out essential information. You must let the store know not only just what it is you want (its name and description and its catalogue number if any) but also how many, what size, what color. (It's often wise to give a second color choice if you can.) Set down the price also, and specify how it's to be paid for, and in cases where this information is necessary, how it's to be sent. Check before sealing the envelope to be sure you haven't omitted your address. Here is a typical letter:

101 SYCAMORE DRIVE, OTISBURG, WYOMING

September 21, 19——

William Deere
Fifth and Main Street
Otisburg, Wyoming

Dear Sirs:

Please send me at the above address one long-sleeved cashmere slip-on sweater as advertised in the *Times* yesterday at $17.90. The size is 38, and I want it in heather beige if possible. My second color choice is camel. Charge to my account.

Sincerely yours,

(Mrs. Howard F. Felton)

MAKING RESERVATIONS

Although in this case you want rooms instead of merchandise, in effect you're ordering by mail, so don't forget to be specific here too about what you want and exactly when you want it. You may make reservations by letter or by telegram. A letter would read like this:

4 OWENS PLACE, CHESTER, NEW YORK

April 3, 19——

The Manager
Black Point Inn
Brookfield, New Hampshire

Dear Sir:

Will you please reserve a double room with twin beds and private bath for my husband and myself for two weeks? We expect to arrive on the afternoon of June 14th and leave the afternoon of the 30th, and would prefer to be in the lodge. Please confirm the reservation to the above address.

Yours truly,

(Mrs. John Osgood)

And a telegram (if you're on the tardy side in making your plans:

PLEASE RESERVE DOUBLE ROOM BATH FOR HUSBAND AND SELF JUNE FOURTEEN TO THIRTY LODGE PREFERRED REPLY COLLECT MRS. JOHN OSGOOD FOUR OWENS PLACE CHESTER NEW YORK

LETTERS OF COMPLAINT

Disappointed and angry though you may be when a long-awaited piece of merchandise arrives and is the wrong size or color or is broken, do cool off before you send an ill-tempered complaint. You're annoyed that somebody's carelessness has inconvenienced you and rightly so, but after all it isn't vengeance you're after—you just want what you ordered. You're much more likely to get it, and get it quickly, when you skim off the indignation and simply take it for granted that the error will be corrected, and that promptly.

17 Pine Road
Alta, California
May 6, 19——

H. Andersen Ltd.
1234 Prospect Street
Los Angeles, California

Dear Sirs:

On May 4 I selected at your store a dozen ruby-and-crystal goblets. You can imagine my disappointment when on their arrival this morning I found two of them broken off at the stems. These two were not protected by corrugated paper like the others.

The sales slip number is 7533-16, Dept. 60, clerk 1857.

Please let me know what is the earliest date I can expect replacement of the damaged glasses.

Sincerely yours,

(Mrs. John C. Bettman)

LETTERS OF RECOMMENDATION

More and more often these days men and women are asked to write a letter for a friend's offspring who is madly compiling a sheaf of documents to be forwarded to the colleges of his choice. For a male student, a man usually writes the reference. He may choose to write

on his business letterhead, especially if his name appears on it or the firm is well known—or he may use his personal stationery. (What he must never do is to write on stationery bearing a business letterhead which he crosses out.) When the applicant is a girl, a woman is often the one who writes (on conservative stationery, plain or imprinted with name and/or address), although she may include her husband in expressing their good opinion of the girl.

Any of these letters should be directed to an individual whenever possible—and it nearly always is possible, because the person asking for the reference usually gives you the name and title of the person to whom it's to go. (It's always best to avoid the expression "To whom it may concern." If by some mischance the applicant is hazy about just who should get the letter and time is of the essence, simply address your screed to Director of Admissions, so-and-so college, and use the salutation "Dear Sir.")

When you're called upon to write one of these letters, it's to be hoped that you know the student well and have a good opinion of him in general. You may know little of his academic abilities except what he tells you about his scholastic standing, but when this appears to be average or better you don't need to evaluate it. The college has or will have his marks, can judge these better than you and is prepared to do so. What the college people want to know is how you see him as a person—his integrity, his perseverance, qualities of leadership, poise, ability to make friends, and so on. If the boy (or girl) has been not only academically strong, but also a leader in school activities and popular with grownups and schoolmates alike, you haven't much of a problem. You no doubt admire him, approve of him, like to have him around, and hope he'll make the school he wants. So all you do in writing is to imagine you're speaking face to face with the admissions man and write the way you'd talk. Be friendly, be warm, be sincere. But don't gush—don't imply that your candidate's admission will put so-and-so university on the map. Nobody's all that perfect, and an effusive letter is always suspect. It will do your friend's son little good and may even prejudice his case.

When the student is one whose marks you know are nothing to boast of, perhaps even below average, who hasn't played any stellar roles in school activities and is, in fact, something of a loner, your task is a little harder. In such a case, if you like the boy and believe in him, the thing to do is to stress the potential you think he has, without glossing over or ignoring the spotty academic record or other negative qualities. Bear in mind that many colleges will consider an academic record that shows an upward climb as carefully as one with straight A's all the way, because it shows effort, the courage to meet a challenge, and above all, growth. Educators are also aware of the fact that it takes some young people more time to adjust to the difficulties of adolescence than others. Many people —and some very famous ones—have been slow starters. Maybe this boy is one of them.

If your thinking and feeling is along these lines, your letter should point up the good qualities you have observed in him and others perhaps have not. This can be done without seeming to brush off signs of uncertain or inadequate personal adjustment or the existence of a poor or fluctuating academic record. What really counts is the integrity of your message. Your honest recognition of past or present shortcomings lends credence to the positive statements you feel you can make.

Here is a letter written for a friend's son by a lawyer, on his firm's letterhead:

September 8, 19———

Mr. J. Henry Abernathy
Director of Admissions
Westport College
Deming, Ohio

Dear Mr. Abernathy:

I am writing to recommend Duncan Anderson, who is applying for admission to Westport College from Bronson High School in Westbury, where I live. I have known young Duncan since he was ten, when his family became neighbors and friends of ours. As an only child, he has in the past seven years spent a great deal of time in the company of our children. (Our oldest boy is Duncan's age; our other boy is fifteen and our daughter thirteen.) My wife and I have grown to know Duncan very well and we have always enjoyed having him at our house.

His academic record was, I know, quite spotty during his first two years in high school and he has not gone out for school activities or sports with the exception of swimming in his freshman and sophomore years. This was, I feel, because he then preferred to stand on the sidelines. He seemed at that time not to be quite at home with himself. In the past two years, however, he has been much more outgoing not only with us but also with his schoolmates. He wanted to take part in extracurricular activities and was especially tempted by debating, but he decided that it would take all of his time and energy to pull up his marks. This he has done with consistent hard work and a tenacity of purpose that we think is quite remarkable. The fact that he has succeeded in improving his academic standing seems to have given him the confidence he so sorely needed. Study is still not easy for him, but the will to work and the desire for learning are there.

I strongly feel that Duncan has real potential. He looks forward to the challenge of college, and in our opinion will prove himself there.

Sincerely yours,

LETTERS OF REFERENCE FOR SERVANTS

When your Mary is leaving and you're giving her a letter for some future employer, let's hope that she was a jewel while she was with you! When that's the case, sad as you may be to part with her, at least the letter will be a pleasure to write. If she's been so far from flawless that you're not sorry she's leaving—perhaps have even had to discharge her—then you're faced with the task of writing a reference that is honest without being altogether damning.

A letter of reference should cover everything that an employer wants to know about a worker: the length of time she has worked for you, her sobriety, her honesty, her capability, her reliability, and the reason she left your employ. In the case of a somewhat incompetent worker, you tell no lies but simply omit any mention of the qualities wherein she's deficient—it's the omissions that warn the next employer that Mary hasn't been *your* cup of tea, at the least. By the same token, in the case of a practically faultless worker you want to be especially careful not to omit any of the categories a letter of reference is supposed to cover, and you'll no doubt want not only to mention any special gifts she has, but also to write warmly enough so that there's no doubt of your high opinion of her.

Unlike other business letters, a letter of reference for a servant should not be addressed to anyone at all, not even "To whom it may concern." It should be on stationery printed with your address or with your address given below your signature. It has a date, of course, but needs no closing. It is given to the employee in an unsealed envelope.

The reference for a real jewel might read like this:

110 Horman Street
New York, N. Y.
March 12, 19——

Mary Ward has worked for me for five years as a general housekeeper. I have found her always honest, sober and capable. She is a thorough and systematic cleaner, and an imaginative cook. She has a most cheerful disposition and has been wonderful with my girls aged ten and twelve. We hate to lose Mary—but she must leave us now because of my husband's transfer to the West.

I shall be glad to answer any questions about Mary at any time.

(Mrs. Howard Simmons)

Although Mrs. Simmons is leaving New York, she means every word she says about backing Mary up in the future as well as now —and so she thoughtfully adds her new address, if she knows it, in parentheses on the left side a little below the level of her signature: (After April 1: 15 Clover Lane, Roswell Park, Arizona).

When it comes to the reference for Jane, with whom you've decided to part company because she was much too tolerant of dust and stomped about dressed in gloom, you might write this kind of letter:

220 Jaynes Avenue
Millertown, New York
January 10, 19——

Jane Wilson has been in my employ for four months as a part-time houseworker and occasional cook. I have found her sober and honest. She is leaving us now because we need a sleep-in worker and Jane prefers part-time work.

(Mrs. Harold Stern)

When a prospective employer, having detected something less than enthusiasm in your note, calls about the nonjewel Jane Wilson and asks you about Jane's cleaning abilities, you can truthfully say that her cleaning needs to be supervised. If the woman on the other end of the line sounds like a gourmet and pries into Jane's skill with sauces, you may observe that she was a competent meat-and-potatoes cook, but was never trained for anything more.

Don't forget, though, that there is an element of human responsibility in recommending workers. While a Jane Wilson who didn't work out for you might fit quite adequately into some households, there is no excuse for even seeming to stand behind someone whose failings could be dangerous to the physical or emotional safety of children. If you have had the misfortune to engage a worker who has been cruel to your children in any way or has proven irresponsible in caring for them, you have no recourse but to refuse her a reference.

25

Greetings by Card

CARDS OF ALL KINDS—BIRTHDAY, CHRISTMAS, AND GET-WELL CARDS, calling cards and informals—are used today with the briefest of messages to show our friends we think of them. In more leisurely times and in smaller places we used to visit in person for friendship's sake, but nowadays busy lives and widely scattered dwelling places often make it necessary for cards to be our messengers.

CALLING CARDS

In military and diplomatic circles, calling in person and leaving cards still plays a large part in social living. Cards are "left" and calls made and returned according to a strict protocol—or rather protocols, because customs may vary with career and with locale. Diplomats and military officers and their wives are usually briefed in these matters.

If, however, you're like most United States dwellers today, your grandmother's silver card tray hasn't peeped out from its maroon flannel in years and her tortoise shell card case is in an attic trunk. The custom of calling has so diminished in recent years that you may not want to bother with having any calling (or visiting) cards made. If you do, you'll probably be using them for greetings of various kinds.

For every purpose except that of actually calling, informals may be used just like calling cards. Still, many people like to have calling cards, and they can be most useful. They're small enough so you can carry one or two with their little envelopes (all kept fresh in another envelope or a bit of tissue paper) right in your billfold or handbag.

And when you spy a little gift or plant that would brighten Aunt Ellen's convalescence you have your own card to tuck in with it. Of course, almost all shops and florists have cards available and these are always acceptable, but using your own implies a little more forethought. Calling cards may also be used to accompany more important gifts; in fact, probably their commonest use today is enclosing with wedding, birthday, graduation, and other gifts, as well as flowers. When cards are used in this way or in any situation where your full name all done up in engraving seems too formal for the friend and the occasion, you may cross out the whole name or any part of it and (on the front of the card) write the appropriate message —"Hope you're feeling better," "Bon voyage!" or whatever you like. When you do cross out, however, of course, you leave your Christian name uncanceled or write it (or perhaps your nickname) underneath the message. The envelope flap should not be sealed, though it's best to tuck it in to keep the card from sliding out.

Visiting cards are also often used for invitations and replies (see Chapter 26). The visiting card is often used also to bear special messages through the mail: to say "Thank you—it was a wonderful party!" or to congratulate someone: "Congratulations and best wishes." And sometimes they're used for messages of condolence: "Our deepest sympathy"; "My heartfelt sympathy." Often such messages accompany flowers sent to the house or to the funeral service, or both.

It's also convenient to mail calling cards to friends whom you wish to notify of a change of address.

In all of these cases except the last named, a brief note is usually preferable to the card, because it's warmer and more personal no matter how brief the message. But you may use cards if you wish.

In mailing any visiting card, be sure to enclose it in a regular-sized envelope, as its own tiny one is banned by postal regulation.

Calling cards are also useful for enclosing with letters of introduction—see Chapter 23.

If you do decide that you'd like to have cards, they must accord with traditional form even though their original function is passing from the scene. Social cards should always be engraved—not printed —in black ink only. The paper should be nonshiny, rather like a very thin parchment. The type is most often Script or Shaded Roman, but a number of other styles are acceptable too, as long as they're not bizarre or attention-getting. Any good stationer or jeweler who does engraving can advise you competently on type, paper, and the size of the cards. Matching envelopes are convenient to have on hand for times when your card is used as an enclosure, even though the envelopes are too small for mailing.

WOMEN'S CARDS

In size these can be anywhere from 2″ to 2½″ from top to bottom and from 3″ to 3½″ in width. (The shorter width fits better into a billfold, but if your name is long you may need more space.) A woman's name appears in full on her card—no abbreviations except for "Mrs." or possibly "Dr." (see below) and preferably without initials. A single woman's card will read "Miss Harriet Bennington" or "Dr. Janet Hawkins." A married woman's card should read just like that of her husband except that Mrs. is substituted for Mr.—"Mrs. James Duncan Boswell." (The exception to this rule may occur when Mrs. Boswell is a doctor and Mr. Boswell isn't. In such a case her card might read: "Doctor Mary Boswell." On a social card it is better to spell out "Doctor" unless the name is very long, in which case it may be abbreviated.)

If your name is very long, you may also use an initial, even though as a rule the spelled-out name is preferable. When a woman's husband customarily uses an initial as part of his signature, however, so that his cards read "Mr. F. Harrison Roberts," her cards as well as their joint cards must follow suit.

The name form for the cards of a widow or divorcée follows the usage indicated in Chapter 4. The widow of Herbert Stone will continue to be Mrs. Herbert Stone unless she remarries. The former Jane Atwood, now divorced from Harrison Berling, calls herself Mrs. Atwood Berling.

Addresses are seldom used on cards any more, probably because people move around so much more than they used to and engraving is expensive! If you decide to use yours, however, the street address should go at the lower right. It can be spelled out—Ten Kingsbridge Drive—or all numerals may be used: 66 East 72nd Street. State and town don't appear as a rule, though for convenience sake they may if you travel widely and often enough so that there may be need to identify your locale. Your telephone number should never appear on a social card; if you want to include it at any time, write it in.

MEN'S CARDS

Men's social cards are usually narrower than women's—a common size is about 3 inches wide by 1½ inches high. If he uses an address

252 · GOOD HOUSEKEEPING'S BOOK OF TODAY'S ETIQUETTE

it is his home address and appears at the bottom right, unless he is a bachelor living at a club—a club address goes on the bottom left. Initials and abbreviations aren't much used, except Mr. and Jr. (The preferred usage on a calling card is to spell out "Junior," but frequently, especially with a long name, Jr. appears instead.) Roman numerals may follow the name when applicable; a comma goes between the surname and the Jr. or II or III.

CARDS FOR HUSBAND AND WIFE

These are often useful for things you do together—paying calls if you do that, and also enclosing with wedding presents, flowers, letters of introduction. They are wide enough to include the "Mr. and Mrs."—about 3½″ wide and 2⅜″ high. They may include the home address (see the section on women's cards for placing) but need not.

The Boswells' joint card would read "Mr. and Mrs. James Duncan Boswell." Should Mrs. Boswell, as we suggested earlier, be a doctor and her husband is not, she either decides to be just "Mrs." socially, or to do without joint cards. For "Mr. James Duncan Boswell and Dr. Mary Boswell," if not actually incorrect, is not only clumsy but makes Dr. Mary seem more than a little aggressive.

CHILDREN'S CARDS

Very few parents these days get cards for their teen-age children, although some do when it's being done in their social circle. A young girl's card is like any unmarried woman's: "Miss Jennifer Robbins." Her brother's card, however, would read just "Paul Robbins," because traditionally he does not use the "Mr." until he is twenty-one.

When young people do have cards, a very practical use for them is as an enclosure with formal invitations to graduation exercises.

BUSINESS CARDS

A business card should be larger than a social card—about 3½″ x 2″ or 2¼″ and it should be printed in a conservative type that's easy to read at a glance. (Script and fancy shaded types are not quickly legible.) The man's name, most often without the "Mr.," appears on the center of the card. On the card of a salesman or some other firm representative who is not an executive, the firm's name would appear on the center of the card with *his* name at the bottom left, the firm's address at the bottom right. His position or department—"Personnel" or "Glassware"—may be printed immediately under his name.

An executive's card shows his name in the center, his title on the bottom left, above the firm name, and the firm's address (if it is necessary, as in a large city) at the bottom right. The telephone number of the company may be included if it seems advisable, and should go under the firm name. Sometimes the "Mrs." seems to present a problem. When a woman has used her maiden name throughout her business career, on her business card she continues to call herself "Miss Jane Post." The fact that she is Mrs. Walter Latham in private life has no bearing on the matter. Suppose, however, that since her marriage she has become widely known in her field as "Jane Post Latham." She certainly won't want to preface this name with "Miss." Fortunately, while it would never be allowable on a social card, in the business world she may identify herself as "Mrs. Jane Post Latham."

Business cards, men's or women's, are never used except in connection with business. They may be enclosed with Christmas cards or gifts sent to a firm's customers, but they would never be sent to a business associate who is also a friend, or used in any other social way.

CHRISTMAS CARDS

Whether the card you choose to send to your friends is inexpensive or costly, quite conservative or very sophisticated, is a matter of taste and finances. Most husbands insist that selecting and ordering cards is the wife's job. If this is your husband's position, off you'll go

to look over the racks and albums—well ahead of time, especially if you want the cards imprinted! But when you choose, keep in mind your husband's taste as well as your own, and if some of these cards are to be mailed to business connections of his, whom you may or may not know, you'll probably try to find something that hews to the conventional line but is still a bit fresh and different, avoiding the bizarre and the humorous. (By the same token, cards with snapshot photographs of the family, while they're always a treat to people whom you know quite well, had better be reserved for these. Order others to send to those you know only slightly. A Christmassy photograph of your house is a little different—no reason why it shouldn't be sent to anyone on your list.)

The question often arises in the minds of non-Jews whether to send Christmas cards to their Jewish friends. In the case of extremely Orthodox Jews, it is a gesture perhaps best omitted, for they themselves will not be observing any of the Christian holiday. But many, many Jewish people today do adorn the holiday with Christmas trees, gifts, and cards. It is better not to send a Jewish friend a card with a picture of the Nativity or other religious scene, and when the number of your Jewish friends is large and you're not sure of the degree of orthodoxy of many, "Season's Greetings and Best Wishes for the New Year" might be a more generally appropriate message for the inside of your card than "Merry Christmas and Happy New Year."

If your Christmas card is rather sophisticated, one which stresses merrymaking or wassail rather than the holiday's spiritual meaning, you'll of course remember not to send it to any clergyman. Select a card for him which is at least dignified even if not explicitly religious in character.

Be careful, too, about any card you send to a friend who's been bereaved within the year. That first Christmas is always hard. No need to emphasize the fact with commiseration, but avoid the over-hearty "'tis the season to be jolly" kind of message. It's always appreciated, too, when you take the time to add your own message. You need only say you are all thinking of him or her and send your love.

SIGNING CHRISTMAS CARDS

Card sending these days is more often than not an informal procedure, and so cards are usually signed informally, although some people prefer to have their cards engraved with the full name under the greeting, just as it would appear on a calling card. Some prefer to engrave both name and message in a more formal style: "Mr. and

Mrs. Harold Comstock wish you a Merry Christmas" or "send you Greetings of the Season."

If you're the more informal type of sender, you would omit any Mr. or Mrs. or Miss. When names are imprinted, the wife's name comes first: "Louise and Harold Comstock." Sometimes the children's names are included (though preferably only on cards sent to personal friends) and in this case the husband's name comes first: "Harold, Louise, John and Emily Comstock."

When the cards are signed by hand, whoever signs them puts his own name last.

Christmas cards may be both signed and addressed in colored ink if you like.

Although it's time consuming, it's proper and in fact recommended to put your return address on the envelope, either handwritten or on a sticker. This keeps peripatetic acquaintances who perhaps write only at Christmas-time in touch with each other and is a big help in keeping Christmas lists up to date.

When you send cards to a family, it's in better taste *not* to put "and family" on the envelope. Rather address the card to the parents and if you want to, add a note of greeting to the youngsters on the card itself.

Of course, you can write a message on your card if you want to— and if, as so often happens, you're sending it to someone you haven't written to for a long time, it may even turn out to be a letter before you're through. And none the less welcome for that! But never use a Christmas card for a thank-you note.

Any card with a handwritten message must go by first-class mail. However, as long as there is no writing on the card *other* than your signature, it's perfectly all right with the postoffice, and socially acceptable as well, to send it under second-class postage, provided also that the flap is tucked in rather than sealed.

Do, do mail early! Early enough to be sure that recipients who live across the continent get theirs on time as well as your local friends. Some people who have a large list of widely scattered address-ees make a file classified by destination in such a way that the cards which travel farthest get written first. A New Englander, for ex-ample, may have her file box alphabetically arranged, but will use red cards for Europe, pink for the West and Middle West, yellow for the East Coast, making it an easy matter to write and mail her Christmas cards in logical order.

If you should receive a card from someone who didn't and can't now get one from you, it's pleasant and acceptable to acknowledge it with a brief thank-you note. This may be, if you like, written on a New Year's greeting card bought for the purpose, but it shouldn't be written on a Christmas card.

BIRTHDAY AND OTHER CARDS

Of course, you know (but sometimes when you're in a hurry, you forget) that you should read the printed message on any card very carefully, particularly on any that you're sending to a shut-in, to one recently bereaved, to anyone in a situation where for the time being the future can't present a joyful prospect. All too often a card with a pretty and perfectly appropriate picture may carry inside a message which may be cruelly inapplicable to some particular case.

26

Invitations and Replies

INVITATIONS, LIKE GARDENS, FALL INTO TWO MAIN CLASSES—THE courtly kind, laid out in geometrical beds edged with privet or box, and the more informal plantings in which the flowers, while not allowed to run riot, are given room to be themselves. Formal invitations are for rather special affairs and whether engraved or handwritten are set out in a time-honored symmetrical way. Informal invitations, on the other hand, may take almost any shape provided a few boundaries are observed.

SOME GROUND RULES

When you accept or decline any invitation that comes to you, you follow as closely as possible the style of the invitation—reply very formally if the invitation came to you that way, informally if that was its nature.

Some invitations—that is, those in the third person—are sent and answered on fine white paper. (They are occasionally telegraphed.) In the case of informal invitations, notes, informals, and calling cards are equally acceptable for your reply, no matter which one the hostess used. So is a telephone call or a telegram.

When you accept any invitation, it is mannerly to repeat the date and time so your hostess knows there isn't any misunderstanding— the place, too, if the party is being given away from the hostess' home.

"R.S.V.P.," as you know, is French for "Answer, if you please" —but the "please" is really just a politeness. Any invitation that bears those four letters means that your hosts need to know how many people are coming, and therefore you must accept or regret—and that promptly. An invitation to a large party such as a tea or "cocktails 5 to 7" may or may not have R.S.V.P. If it doesn't, no acceptance or regret is called for. (Though, of course, a hostess' feelings have never been known to be hurt when a guest who knows she is coming or is sure she can't telephones or drops a line to say so!)

The expression "R.S.V.P." may be written all in capitals or "R.s.v.p." Either is correct. Occasionally, in the case of formal invitations, you will see: "The favor of a reply is requested" or a variation.

The people who do the inviting may not cancel a formal invitation for anything short of a catastrophe—never for a whim or a domestic complication. If you have sent out formal invitations for a dinner and the plaster falls in the dining room the morning of the party, you should go ahead even if that means setting up card tables in the living room. On the other hand, if there is serious illness or a death in the family, you may understandably cancel the party. You may cancel, too, if your husband suddenly is sent abroad on business and wants you to go with him. The point is that it takes something major to make the cancellation of a formal party possible without raised eyebrows.

The cancellation of an informal affair like a Sunday brunch or small cocktail party is a somewhat less serious matter, but it still shouldn't be done except for a fairly cogent reason.

When you're the invitee, you're not of course under the do-or-die sentence, whether the invitation is formal or informal—you may decline or accept just as you please. Once you've accepted, however, you shouldn't afterwards decline except for some compelling reason, certainly never because you've been invited to another party you'd rather go to! In originally declining any invitation it is not essential to give a reason, although regret is usually indicated, and you may feel it's a little warmer to explain, if that's the case, that a previous engagement stands in the way. Of course, when you find you can't go to a party after you've accepted, it behooves you to write or call as promptly as possible and explain the compelling reason!

When the words "black tie" or "white tie" appear on a formal or informal invitation, you know that black tie indicates dinner gowns and dinner jackets, and white tie means that the guests are expected to turn up in full evening dress for the women and tails for the men.

Never, never ask for an invitation to somebody's party for yourself, even though you may know that it's a cocktail affair where you think one or two more wouldn't make any difference. When, however, you yourself have already been invited and would like to bring a house guest, it's all right to ask the hostess if you may. You may also do this if the occasion is a dance or even a buffet supper, but don't embarrass a hostess with such a request when you've been asked to a sit-down dinner, unless you know her very, very well and are certain that the guest (or couple) will really fit in. The extra single guest especially is bound to throw off her seating arrangement at the dinner table—although much can be forgiven if the extra is a man!

When you are the hostess, don't be a thoughtless one by extending an invitation in front of others whom you're not including in this particular party. Even though you entertained your friend May Atwood at cocktails just last Friday, and the Cruikshanks a few weeks ago at a rather special dinner, ask *this* party's guests at a time when neither those three nor other acquaintances can possibly overhear you and feel left out.

INFORMAL INVITATIONS

Informal invitations may be given in person, by telephone, by telegram, by note or informal, or by calling card.

When you telephone invitations, the most important thing is to be sure, should you be unlucky enough not to reach your guest in person, that the message you leave includes the kind of party, the date, the time of day—and you'll do well to include a request that you be called back. (For even if yours is such a big party that you don't need to know exactly how many guests there'll be, you *do* want to be certain the invitation was received. Don't forget to make sure that your name is clearly understood, and your telephone number.

In replying to a telephoned invitation, you simply call your hostess, express your pleasure, and say you'd love to come—or express your regret that you cannot come. If you prefer, or if you get no answer on a few telephone tries, you may send an informally written acceptance or regret by note, informal or card. If you can't come, it is polite to give a reason—and practically essential to do so over the telephone.

In telegraphing an informal invitation, all you need to say is: PLEASE JOIN US FOR DINNER FRIDAY TWENTIETH AT SEVEN JOSEPHINE BENSON.

In accepting (or regretting) such an invitation, you'd wire: DELIGHTED TO ACCEPT FOR FRIDAY TWENTIETH AT SEVEN MAXINE VOGEL.

Or: REGRET WE CANNOT COME FRIDAY BECAUSE OF PREVIOUS ENGAGE-
MENT.

For written invitations of an informal kind, you may use calling
cards, writing paper, notes, or informals. The last three may be
color-bordered, monogrammed, decorated in color, engraved with
your name, or printed with name and address, just as long as they're
not garish. You may type them if you like. The way in which you
phrase them depends on your mood, the party mood, and how well
you know the guests. If you want to be chatty, go ahead, but it's just
as correct simply to put down the details of the occasion. In either
case, be sure you've included date and time—and place, if necessary.

How you know when it's necessary to include the name and address is a question to which common sense dictates the answer.
Friends and neighbors don't need to be told where you live, but
including the street address will save trouble for newcomers to
town and anyone writing an acceptance. Naturally, if the party's to be
at a club or hotel, you indicate that name and address.

INVITATIONS TO COMMENCEMENTS

Commencement invitations are practically always formal and engraved, in the name of the President and Faculty of the college, and
are sent out with the student's visiting card or a brief handwritten
note. The invitation rarely says "r.s.v.p." Unless it does, you need
not reply to it, but it is thoughtful and polite to write or call the
student to accept or regret his invitation. If you write him, it's perfectly proper—and warmer—to do it in informal rather than formal
style.

"STORE-BOUGHT" INVITATIONS

These days many gay invitations for informal affairs, like cocktail
parties and showers, may be found in department, jewelry, and stationery stores, and it's perfectly all right to use them for any but
formal affairs. They're so festive they're a pleasure both to send and
receive, and they often have "what, where and when" blanks to fill
in, which makes it easy for a very busy hostess.

INVITATIONS WRITTEN ON INFORMALS

The message here is usually limited to the front or first page—
unless you are using an informal whose front page bears a large
centered monogram, in which case you write on the page directly

below the monogrammed page. You may put the information in note form or just indicate occasion, date, and time. The note form is often used when there's an extra bit of information you want to include, as here:

When your notes or informals are on the small side and your handwriting not so small, you may omit the "Monday" at the top. You may add "R.S.V.P." at the bottom left if you like, but in this case the expression "a few friends" and the query at the end ought to be a tip-off that a reply is expected.

More often than not, your invitation (let's pretend you are Mary Coxe) would read this way:

Ordinarily an informal carries only the name or the name and the street address, but the Coxes, who apparently live just outside our national capital, add the town and state for the convenience of their guests.

Let's say that among other friends of the Coxes, Helen and George Upham have received a dinner invitation from them. Their acceptance can be in the form of a brief note from Helen to Mary (especially in the case of the dinner for the cousin from New Orleans), or it can be simply a repetition of the details and notification that they'll be there, on one of the Uphams' engraved or name-imprinted informals, thus:

> *Accept with pleasure*
> Mr. and Mrs. George Upham
> *Friday, May 6, at 7*

Or, more warmly, Helen Upham might substitute for "Accept with pleasure" the words "We'd love to come."

If they must decline:

> *So sorry we can't make it on Friday*
> ~~Mr. and Mrs. George Upham~~
> *We'll be out of town*
> *Helen*

Note that in declining an invitation you don't have to repeat the hour; you don't even *have* to mention the day, although when you include day and date, the hostess is assured you had it all straight and didn't decline because of any misunderstanding on your part. Note, too, that it's always permissible to cross out the engraved name and write in a first name.

INVITATIONS ON VISITING CARDS

Except for the limitations of space, invitations and replies on visiting cards are used the same way as informals or notes. However, they are practical only for very simple invitations, such as the following:

Linen shower for Jeanne—
Friday, June 20, 1 o'clock
Mrs. John Coxe
Do hope you can come!
Mary
119 Wilmot Street
Riverton, Virginia

BIRTH AND ADOPTION ANNOUNCEMENTS

When a baby is born, the mother often writes personal notes to close friends and so lets the news spread as it may. Or the parents may choose to send out printed announcements to a larger list. These can be bought in stationery stores. Many are attractive and in perfectly good taste, but it pays to be selective because there are always a few that are too waggish or "cute."

In addition to these personal announcements to friends and relatives, parents may wish to send a notice to the local newspaper or newspapers. Such an announcement may read:

Mr. and Mrs. Philip Burke of 24 Clover Drive announce the birth of a son, Thomas Lee Burke, on December 14 at Community Hospital.

Adoptions are not announced in the newspapers.

Another kind of informal announcement, which may be ordered at any kind of store which handles engraving, is the tiny visiting card with the baby's name, tied to the parents' card with ribbon (pink for a girl or blue for a boy). Sometimes the baby's card—but not the parents'—has a narrow border of pink or blue to match the ribbon. This is the form:

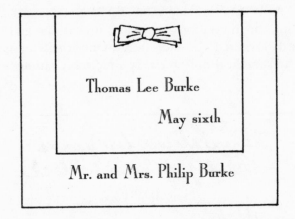

Thomas Lee Burke

May sixth

Mr. and Mrs. Philip Burke

The most formal type of birth announcement is just like that above, except that no colored border is used and the ribbon is white.

While birth announcements are usually sent out quite promptly after the baby is born—within two weeks, at most—an adoptive couple waits until the legal formalities of the adoption are completed and they know the baby will be theirs forever after. Many people write personal notes, but if an engraved card is used, you follow a special form rather than copy the traditional birth announcement. The (single) card will read:

Mr. and Mrs. Arthur Silverman

are happy to announce

the adoption of

David

aged eight months

RECALLING INVITATIONS

If you must do this, it's easiest to call the affair off by telephone, and in most cases the emergency arises too late for you to do anything else. But when time allows, notify your guests-to-have-been on a visiting card or an informal, like this:

> *So sorry we must cancel our dinner*
>
> Mr. and Mrs. John Coxe
>
> *for Friday, May 6*
> *We hope to see you soon!*

If you have no choice about having to call off the party for the date you originally set, but wish very much to have it as planned on a later date (a date you feel you can be sure of, this time) you may issue invitation B in the process of cancelling invitation A:

> *Sorry we must postpone our*
> *dinner Friday, May sixth —*
>
> Mr. and Mrs. John Coxe
>
> *to Friday, May 27th instead.*
> *We do hope you can make it.*
> *7 o'clock*

While you've implied that you would like an answer, it might be best to include "R.S.V.P." at the bottom left.

A postponement of any kind should whenever possible go out in ample time for your guests to make other plans if they like. Written cancellations, then, should be sent to arrive several days before the party date.

Cancelling a *formal* engraved invitation is never a casual matter in any sense of the word! (See page 258.) The method of doing so depends on the time that's left between the emergency that makes it necessary for you to change your plans and the date specified on your invitation. There's never enough time to order any engraved form for this purpose, so even if the originals were engraved, the cancellations must be hastily printed or they may be handwritten in formal style and on formal stationery like this:

Owing to the sudden illness of their son
Mr. and Mrs. Paul Robertson
are obliged to recall their invitation
for Friday, the tenth of October

FORMAL INVITATIONS AND THEIR REPLIES

Most engraved invitations that come your way these days are likely to be for weddings, commencements, or charity functions, but from time to time you'll get and perhaps want to send invitations in formal style for other events, such as luncheons, dinners, teas, receptions, debuts, or formal dances. (Wedding invitations and announcements are dealt with in Chapter 33.)

All formal invitations follow some rather strict rules, no matter what the event. They are very often engraved, especially for large official or ceremonial affairs like balls or debuts, but they need not be, and for such affairs as formal dinner parties and teas, generally are not. People who do a great deal of entertaining of the formal sort sometimes keep a stock of partially engraved invitations, to be filled in by hand for each occasion. Whether invitations are entirely handwritten or filled in, the writing should be in black ink and as carefully spaced as if the whole thing were engraved. Handwritten invitations should be on formal white or ivory writing paper of very good quality. They are always written in the third person, and should go out not later than two weeks before the event; occasionally, as in the case of those for debuts and charity balls, for example, they are sent even earlier.

When formal invitations are sent out by a married couple, they should be in the full "Mr. and Mrs." name of the host and hostess.

If the wife only is the hostess (as at a tea or luncheon where only women are to be the guests), she of course uses her full married name, "Mrs. John Coxe." Invitations sent out by a single individual include the appropriate Miss, Mr., or Mrs. When a group is the sponsor, the full name of the organization, school or college appears.

For engraved or partially engraved invitations to affairs other than weddings, a white or ivory card is often used, which may be headed with a small monogram but not with a name or address. The size varies, but should be oblong and as a rule it is about as large as an informal, often a little larger. 3½ inches by 5 is one of the standard sizes. Envelopes match.

The form is like this:

> Mr. and Mrs. John Coxe
>
> request the pleasure of
>
> *Mr and Mrs. Upham's*
>
> company *at dinner*
>
> on *Wednesday the first of June*
> at *eight o'clock*
>
> 119 Wilmot Street
> Riverton, Virginia
>
> R. s. v. p.

Some people prefer to use the phrasing: "request the pleasure of/the company of . . . ," in which case, of course, the guest's name would be written in without the apostrophe and its *s*. Your engraver can advise you about acceptable sizes, styles and spacings.

(Occasionally you will see "Regrets Only" instead of R.s.v.p. This is perfectly correct but risky as some of those invited may be away.)

The fully engraved invitation looks this way:

Mr. and Mrs. John Coxe

request the pleasure of your company

at dinner

on Friday, the ninth of May

at eight o'clock

119 Wilmot Street
Riverton, Virginia

R. S. V. P.

A formal invitation written by hand follows the same form as that
of the partially or fully engraved one, except that the address is
written at the bottom of the sheet on the right rather than centered.
Use a double letter sheet of fine quality in white or ivory and write

Mr. and Mrs. John Coxe
request the pleasure of
Mr. and Mrs. Upham's
company at dinner
on Friday, the ninth of May
at eight o'clock

R.S.V.P.

119 Wilmot Street
Riverton, Virginia

in black or blue-black ink. The message should be spaced on the front page just the way an engraved one would be.

In replying to formal invitations, whether engraved, partially engraved, or handwritten, you use—besides promptness—your best white paper and black (or blue-black) ink, and you always copy, in the main, the style and spacing of the invitation. (You don't always have to play back the whole thing word for word. You'll see some customary variations and omissions in the sample acceptances and regrets below.) But be sure to address the envelope to the host or hosts exactly as their name appears on the invitation: "Mrs. Gordon Mather" or "Mr. and Mrs. John Coxe."

> Mr. and Mrs. George Upham
> accept with pleasure
> the kind invitation of
> Mr. and Mrs. Coxe
> to dine
> on Friday, the ninth of May
> at eight o'clock

Regretting, you need neither repeat the time nor name the occasion, but simply say:

> Mr. and Mrs. George Upham
> regret that because of a previous engagement
> they are unable to accept
> Mr. and Mrs. Coxe's
> kind invitation
> for the ninth of May

The Coxes' formal invitation to a dance might read:

Mr. and Mrs. John Coxe

request the pleasure of the company of

Mr. and Mrs. Upham

at a small dance

on Saturday, the twelfth of May

at ten o'clock

Riverton Country Club

R. s. v. p.
119 Wilmot Street
Riverton, Virginia

Mary Coxe is modestly and no doubt truthfully labeling their affair a "small dance." But Helen Upham, if she accepts the invitation, will politely leave out the "small" and simply accept for "a dance." In sending a regret to this and to most affairs, the occasion—dance, dinner, tea—needn't be mentioned. Referring to the "kind invitation" for such-and-such a date is enough.

For a really big dance in the most formal style, the event is often labeled on the invitation as an "At Home," with a capital A and capital H, plus the word "Dancing" in the corner.

Of course the occasions for these formal invitations are rather few and far between in the lives of most of us. The Uphams and the Coxes happen to move in more ceremonial circles.

Now, however, the Coxes, having so far in this chapter given three or four formal dinners (not counting the cancellation), a small dance, a cocktail party, and a shower, are virtuously resting on their laurels, and it is the Uphams who feel inspired to do some entertaining. Let's suppose they decide on a gala evening of dancing with lots and lots of people. They may use engraved, partially engraved or handwritten invitations.

The wording and spacing would look like this:

Mr. and Mrs. George Upham

At Home

Monday, the tenth of September

at ten o'clock

Hotel Shoreham

Kindly send reply to
22 Wagoner Lane   Dancing
Riverton, Virginia

In replying to an invitation like this one, Mary Coxe will, of course, follow the formal style and spacing, but would simply accept (or regret) the Uphams' "kind invitation/for Monday the tenth of September"—no need to include the expressions "At Home" or "Dancing."

Should the Uphams or the Coxes send out formal invitations for a dinner in honor of a special guest, the words "to meet Mr. Harvey Bannister" are added to the last line of the invitation, and while it's not essential, the very courteous guest in replying repeats the line, whether accepting or declining the invitation.

INVITATIONS TO ANNIVERSARY PARTIES

Most anniversary parties, especially in the early years, are informal in nature and informal as to invitations. The "big" anniversaries are a different matter—the twenty-fifth and fiftieth are very festive.

So when silver and gold anniversary years roll around, it's usually an occasion for a celebration. Sometimes the couple gives the party on their own. In other cases the children give it for them. (It might be well to note here that if the parents are quite elderly, it is the better part of discretion for the children *not* to make it a surprise party—being taken unawares plus the emotional excitement of the occasion might be just too much for them.) The invitations may be handwritten, or if the party is to be very gala, they may be engraved.

The children's invitation might read like this:

In honour of the

Twenty-fifth Wedding Anniversary of

Mr. and Mrs. Hugo Bernauer

their sons and daughters

request the company of

Mr. and Mrs. Henry Pauling

on Saturday, the sixth of June

at nine o'clock

Western Hills Country Club

R. s. v. p.
Mrs. Hugo Bernauer, Jr.
10 Essex Avenue
Western Hills, New York

In replying guests will "accept with pleasure/the kind invitation of/the sons and daughters of/Mr. and Mrs. Bernauer" and repeat the date, time, and place. Or they will "regret that they are unable to accept" etc., including the date but omitting the time and place.

Note that the expression "sons and daughters of" is used when there are so many that it would be awkward to include all their names on the invitation. If there are only a few—an unmarried daughter and a married son, say—their names will head the invitation, like this:

Mr. and Mrs. Hugo Bernauer, Jr.
Miss Charlotte Bernauer
request the pleasure of . . .

When Mr. and Mrs. Bernauer, Sr. send out the invitation to their anniversary party alone, the wording is a bit different. Nobody gives a party "in honour of" himself, so instead the guests are asked to "celebrate" the occasion with the host and hostess. Their invitations would read:

Mr. and Mrs. Hugo Bernauer

request the pleasure of

the company of

Mr. and Mrs. Henry Pauling

to celebrate their golden anniversary

on Saturday, the sixth of June

at nine o'clock

R. s. v. p.
15 Byron Place

Of course informal invitations can be used instead of formal ones, particularly if the affair is limited to close friends, is of small cocktail-party size, and is given in a home. The invitations may be telephoned or written on plain white notepaper or on informals. In written invitations, Mr. and Mrs. Bernauer, Jr. might ask their parents' friends to a "silver anniversary party for Hugo and Aline at our house" on such-and-such a day. When other children are also hosts, Mrs. Bernauer, Jr. could say: "With Alice and Tom, we're giving a party (or buffet supper, dinner, or whatever) here at home on Friday, the twenty-seventh at eight. We do hope you and Sidney can come."

If the senior Bernauers should be giving the party and wish to send informal invitations, Mrs. Bernauer would write them just as she would any other invitation. She may specify the occasion or not, as she and her husband wish, but if she does mention it the phrase "in honor of" should not be used. Instead, the guests should be asked to "celebrate" the anniversary with them.

INVITATIONS FROM MORE THAN ONE HOSTESS

Sometimes several women want to give a party together, usually a tea, perhaps a bridge or other event. In this case, all their names appear on the invitation, in alphabetical order unless there is some reason, such as marked seniority, for a particular hostess' name to head the list. Since the replies, unless otherwise indicated, will be addressed to the name first on the list, that address must be shown on the invitation, as well as the place where the party's to be given if it's not the same.

Mrs. James Bartlett

Miss Amelia Fitch

Mrs. Frederick Hodgson

request the pleasure of

the company of

Mrs. Howard
at tea

Friday, the tenth of December

at five o'clock

10 Harbor Avenue

R. s. v. p.
Mrs. James Bartlett
16 Farrell Place

The acceptance or regret should list all the hostesses, referring to "the kind invitation of/Mrs. Bartlett, Miss Fitch and Mrs. Hodgson," but the envelope is addressed only to the woman specified under the R.s.v.p.

ORGANIZATION INVITATIONS

Organization invitations vary widely with the size and kind of organization, but in general they follow the same rules as those sent out by individuals. Here is a sample invitation:

The Haverhill Press

cordially invites you to meet

Miss Samantha Brooke

on the occasion of the publication

of her new book

"In The Palace Garden"

Hotel Cranford

1542 East 57th Street

New York

Cocktails
May 8th
5 to 7 p. m.

Note that occasionally such invitations may strain or even break the rules of formal etiquette, as when, for example, a party is built around a special theme in order to achieve news value. Those in charge, usually the publicity chairman (or the publicity department) may even use color to make the invitations attract attention. Whatever the form chosen, the date, time, and place must be crystal-clear.

INVITATIONS TO A DEBUT

Perhaps when the next autumn rolls around the Uphams want to present their daughter to society. If they plan to present her at a ball, the invitations would read in either of two ways—like this:

Mr. and Mrs. George Upham

Miss Constance Upham

request the pleasure of

the company of

Mr. and Mrs. John Cope

on Saturday, the fifth of November

at ten o'clock

Hotel Madison

Kindly respond to
22 Wagoner Lane   Dancing
Riverton, Virginia

or like this:

Mr. and Mrs. George Upham

request the pleasure of

the company of

Mr. and Mrs. John Cope

at a dance in honour of their daughter

Miss Constance Upham

Saturday, the fifth of November

at ten o'clock

Kindly send reply to
22 Wagoner Lane
Riverton, Virginia

In the first instance, a guest would accept "the kind invitation of/ Mr. and Mrs. Upham and Miss Upham/for Saturday, the fifth of November/at ten o'clock" or would "regret that (guest name) is unable to accept/the kind invitation of" etc., omitting the hour and the name of the function. And the envelope should be addressed to parents and daughter in the order in which their names appear on the invitation:

> Mr. and Mrs. George Upham
> Miss Constance Upham
> 22 Wagoner Lane
> Riverton, Virginia

Of course the reply to this or any formal invitation must be written in blue or black ink on a sheet of your very best formal notepaper with its matching envelope. Once again the lines must read exactly as they do in the invitation. This takes some doing so by all means practice on a piece of scratch paper to be sure your writing appears at its best—no letters squeezed to fit into their line and none stretched out to twice their ordinary width. The reply must be spaced as nearly as possible to match the spacing of the invitation.

The name and address on the envelope should be indented as in the sample above.

For the invitation which says that the Uphams are giving a dance *for* their daughter, the regret or acceptance would acknowledge "the kind invitation of/Mr. and Mrs. Upham/to a dance in honour of their daughter/Miss Constance Upham/Saturday the fifth of November/at ten o'clock." The regret would read ". . . will be unable to accept/Mr. and Mrs. Uphams' kind invitation for/the fifth of November." And the envelope would be addressed to Mr. and Mrs. George Upham.

Notice that the word "honour" when it's used in formal invitations is spelled in the British rather than the American way—that is, with a "u."

If the Uphams decide to present Constance at a reception, their invitations, engraved or handwritten as the case may be, would read like this one:

Mr. and Mrs. George Upham

Miss Constance Upham

At Home

Saturday, the fifth of November

at five o'clock

R. s. v. p.   22 Wagoner Lane

Riverton, Virginia

A guest who is planning to come will "accept with pleasure/the kind invitation of/Mr. and Mrs. Upham and/Miss Upham/for Saturday, the fifth of November/at five o'clock." One who must refuse simply "regrets that she is unable to accept/the kind invitation of/Mr. and Mrs. Upham and/Miss Upham/for Saturday, the fifth of November."

YOUR MANNERS

IN SPECIAL SITUATIONS

27

Some of Those Special Situations

A STUFFY-SOUNDING TERM, PERHAPS, IS "SPECIAL SITUATIONS," BUT IT'S only a convenient handle for a miscellany of occasions and places that aren't covered elsewhere in this book. The situations aren't actually special in the sense in which a wedding, the service of a formal dinner, or the wording of a formal invitation are special, for in all of these you follow a set of rules governed by strict convention as well as courtesy. In other situations, there are few rules as such, but people may unconsciously show thoughtlessness at best, or positive rudeness at worst, without intention. They are all situations in which it is easy to overlook the golden rule of etiquette: consideration for others. Hardly anyone commits all the blunders—but almost everyone is guilty of some of them some of the time. When haste and worry incline your feelings inward, or when you're concentrating on errands that must be done, it's all too human not even to see "other people."

IN PUBLIC PLACES

On the street and walking in and out of buildings, remember that others are bound on their errands, too. So don't walk with your friends in a group that takes up all the sidewalk space, or block a doorway while you discuss club plans with a fellow member you've happened to meet. If you're laden with bumpy packages, don't knock them against passers-by; and if you do so accidentally, apologize. Keep to the right on the sidewalk and on stairs. The best umbrella manners require you to maintain enough visibility from under your shelter to avoid colliding with other pedestrians or jabbing them.

If you're a woman, please remember to be polite to the man who holds a door for you. Don't just sweep through with your chin in the air as though it were his job to do so—instead, say, "Thank you" with a smile. And nobody, man or woman, should thoughtlessly let a door bang back on the person behind him.

Be careful about litter. Don't just toss away cigarette or candy wrappings or checked-off shopping lists. There's practically sure to be a bin or basket nearby to catch these nuisances; if not, ball up your paper or candy foil and put it in your pocket or handbag until you can dispose of it. Chewing gum, of course, should never be disposed of anywhere other than a trash container.

Of course, it isn't good manners to be noisy on the street—but many people who wouldn't think of being actually clamorous in the daytime forget how laughter and chit-chat carry at night. When it's late enough for many people to be in bed, keep voices low!

Avoid confidential conversation in any public place, particularly about personalities, unless you are positive you cannot be overheard.

IN CHURCHES AND SYNAGOGUES

First of all, remember that a place of worship must be a place of quiet—it's not for enthusiastic greetings and chatter. The place for any social gathering is in the vestibule or outside the church building. Indoors, you greet your friends with just a nod, and if you speak at all, it is in low whispers.

Well-mannered people try always to be prompt at church and to stay through the whole service. If you know you must leave early, take a seat in the back so that when you go you can make your leaving inconspicuous and disturb nobody. Always sit quietly in your seat, and don't crane about to find out who's come today.

Clothes for church should, of course, be quiet and restrained. Bare shoulders are out of place in church, even at a wedding. Remember that women of *all* faiths cover their heads in Catholic, Episcopalian, or Orthodox Jewish places of worship.

In a church of another faith than your own, you do as the rest of the congregation does, except in instances where the ritual may conflict with your own faith. For example, a Protestant (unless he is Anglican) or a Jew would not make the sign of the cross in a Catholic church because that is not part of the ritual to which he subscribes. A man who is a non-Jew would wear a hat, however, when he is attending a service in an Orthodox or Conservative synagogue.

At funerals, it should go without saying, church conduct is even more stilled and solemn than at a Sunday service. And promptness is even more important—fifteen minutes early is far, far better than one minute late.

A wedding, of course, is a joyful occasion, even though it too is a sacrament, and there is usually an undertone of whispered greetings and a limited amount of very quiet conversation between near neighbors. Everybody not only stands up but turns around to look at the bride at her entrance. Promptness at weddings is very important—it is most discourteous not to arrive in time enough to be seated before the hour set for the ceremony. (Seating at weddings is discussed in Chapter 34.)

AT THE MOVIES

As your own common sense tells you, quietness is the essence of movie manners. Nothing is more frustrating to a rapt movie-goer than to miss essential bits of dialogue because of the couple who can't settle down without an overture of giggles, whispers, and the crackle of cellophane. So even if you came only to see the feature, and the travelogue strikes you as unimportant, remember that others have a right to see and hear it without disturbance.

When you buy your tickets (the man usually does this while the woman he is escorting waits beside him in line or in the lobby), select them, if you smoke, in an area where smoking is permitted; this is usually the loges or balcony. And when you enter your seats (ladies down the aisle first, ladies into the seats first), you are of course careful to disturb the people already seated as little as possible. As you enter the row, face the seats in front of you and make yourself as thin as possible while you are squeezing by. It's nice to whisper "I'm sorry" (you're bound to distract them) and to say "Thank you" if they rise or move out for you, as quite often they are gracious enough to do.

There are a few special customs for drive-in movies that may not be obvious to those going for the first time. Dim your lights as soon as you enter the parking area, and keep them dim when you leave. You don't have to be quite so quiet as in an ordinary movie, but remember that in many of the cars around you there are small children sleeping, so in summertime particularly, when car windows are open, keep your voices low.

AT THE PLAY

Here the initial virtue is promptness. Being on time for the performance is not only considerate but also practical, as some theaters won't seat latecomers until the first act is over.

If you have to pass occupied seats to get to your own, the procedure is the same as that for the movies described above.

Should you come in just as the curtain is going up, don't make any more fuss than you can help in getting settled. Just take off your hat and lay your coat back. Don't rattle your program or talk. When intermission comes, you may take the coat entirely off and arrange it over the back of the seat—with the help of your escort if you have one. (When you've arrived in good time, of course he helps you take it off while both of you are standing.)

You may check your coats in the lobby checkroom, and many men, with their bulkier coats, prefer to. This usually means, however, a wait to retrieve them when the play is over.

Tickets are almost always bought in advance—if not, the man stands in line to get them. Then, the woman going before him, he hands them to the ticket taker at the door and locates an usher to whom he shows the stubs. (Sometimes there is no ticket taker; in that case, the usher takes the tickets and returns the stubs.) The usher first leads the way to the seats (or directs you to your section and its usher). The woman precedes the man and enters the designated row first, her escort following. The usher usually hands the stubs to him or to the last member of the party to enter the row, along with the appropriate number of programs.

Men are supposed to rise to let people reach their seats; women may sit and just turn their legs sideways. Sometimes women do rise, however—when they're quite long-legged or when they'd prefer to stand rather than have their shoes scraped in an especially narrow space. When you do rise for latecomers, sit down again the instant you can, because you're blocking the view of those behind you.

Should you have to leave before the play is over, make your departure as quiet and inconspicuous as possible. Clasp your coat tightly to you (you'll put it on in the lobby or foyer) and slide out with a murmured "Sorry."

Naturally a woman takes off a hat of any size so as not to hide the stage from those behind her. If she has left her hat on because it's only a scrap of veiling, but she is nevertheless asked to remove it, she does so graciously. When a woman with an escort is bothered by some other woman's hat, it's up to the man to ask the offender to take it off—which he does politely: "Would you mind . . ."

Theater audiences are not as dressy as they used to be. It is perfectly correct to wear street clothes at evening performances. On opening nights, however, men often appear in dinner jackets and women in formal or semiformal dresses. Of course, if you have dressed yourself in evening clothes for an occasion before or after the play, it's quite proper to wear them to the theater.

AT RESORTS AND HOTELS

These operate as a rule on either the American plan or the European—a few offer both. American plan means that all meals are included in the price of lodging—European that the price you pay includes your room only. When you make a reservation in advance (as it is always wisest to do) you specify, if there is a choice, which plan you prefer. (See Chapter 24 for letters making reservations.)

When you arrive, a bellboy or doorman carries your luggage into the lobby where it stands while you're registering at the desk. You identify yourself, mentioning that you have a reservation if you do, and the desk clerk gives you a card or book in which to sign your name and your home town or city. A woman signs "Miss Laura Ford" or "Mrs. Douglas Ford." A man omits the Mister, signing himself just "Douglas Ford." For himself and his wife he signs "Mr. and Mrs. Douglas Ford"—never "Douglas Ford and wife." If there are children they are registered by name, unless they're very young, in which case the father would write "Mr. and Mrs. Douglas Ford and two children." Most registration forms call simply for the home town of the guest, but some call for the street address as well.

When you've registered, the desk clerk hands the room keys to the bellboy, who picks up your bags and leads the way to the room. He opens luggage racks and puts the bags on them, shows you the bath and closet, turns on lights where necessary, you tip him. (See section on tipping in Helpful How-To's at the end of the book.)

In the desk drawer or bureau drawer or under the glass top of some piece of furniture, there's nearly always a list of services offered by the establishment—laundry, cleaning, room service of meals, and so on—with directions for taking advantage of them. Often in American hotels there is a recess in the outside door in which, after calling on the phone for valet service, you hang the garment you want cleaned or pressed—no need then to wait around until the man comes, for he can pick it up and deliver it without bothering you.

Room service is something of a luxury, for there's an extra charge for it, but for many people it puts the icing on the vacation cake, and women especially love to have breakfast in bed. There's no need to be fully dressed for breakfast—in fact, you needn't even be out of bed. Order by telephone, put on a negligée or bed jacket, make sure the door isn't locked, and soon the waiter will bring your meal. You can enjoy it in peace and quiet together with the morning paper, which you may have ordered if it wasn't left at your door as a hotel courtesy. In due course the waiter will come back for the dishes— and to present the bill. If you choose to sign for it and have it added to your room charge, and you are short of change for a tip, write on the face of the check "Please add—for waiter." Otherwise you tip him in cash.

A hotel's reputation depends on that of its guests. For this reason a good hotel frowns on any conduct, no matter how innocent in intention, that may be considered questionable. A woman traveling alone is looked on with suspicion if she receives a man in her bedroom, especially in the evening. If, however, even though you are traveling alone you have engaged a suite, you may ignore this unspoken rule and entertain in your sitting room, although a noisy party, as you might expect, will perhaps bring unwelcomed attention from the staff as well as fellow guests. You can, of course, always receive gentlemen callers in one of the hotel sitting rooms. There is one exception to this Noah's ark convention which applies to single women and women alone: when a man and his secretary are traveling together on business, they may often need to work together in the evening as well as throughout the day. She, however, should always go to his room to work—never he to hers.

When you as a woman alone go to a hotel, always take a small piece of luggage if possible. (If you're unexpectedly stranded, go to a good reputable hotel, explain what's happened, and offer to pay in advance.) In nonemergency situations, however, it's best to take a small case of some kind, even though it would be much easier to put a toothbrush, nightie, and change of hose into your capacious handbag. The hotel detective, as well as the desk clerk, is suspicious of any woman arriving without luggage.

A man, too, should carry something, if only an attaché case. This is not so much a matter of allaying suspicion about his morality; men without baggage have been known to walk out without paying.

The matter of dress in a city hotel isn't bothersome, as the general rules of appropriateness hold here. Only rarely is formal wear called for, except, in *some* places, on Saturday night in certain dining rooms. When this is the case, there'll be a notice to that effect posted somewhere in your room. Dinner jackets for men and dinner dresses for women will serve. With anything other than formal gowns, a woman may wear a hat in a hotel dining room if she likes—but if she is staying in the hotel she doesn't need to.

Resorts are as a rule less formal than hotels, but still are not places where you throw the rules overboard. If you're going for a stay of a week or more, find out when you make your reservation (or through your travel agent) what the customs are at that particular place. At a camplike lodge-and-cabin type of resort, for instance, you may see both men and women diners at all three meals in slacks or shorts and sport shirts—but most places require that at least at dinner men wear coats and ties and women appear in simple dresses. A large resort hotel would certainly expect this, and at many you might even see dinner clothes on Saturday night. Sunday dinner (usually in the middle of the day) practically always calls for coats and ties and dresses, but you would not have to be so formally attired for Sunday night supper.

All hotels have a check-out time (most usually in early or mid-afternoon) when the guest is supposed to vacate his room unless he is staying for another night. On the day you are leaving, you notify the desk a bit ahead of time—an hour or so—and ask them to get your bill ready. (When check-out time is 2 P.M. and the steamer for the mainland doesn't leave till 5 P.M., you can avoid paying for another twenty-four hours by removing yourself and your belongings from the room and stowing your bags in the lobby checkroom or at the desk until it's time to leave.) When you're all packed, you call the desk for a bellboy to take your bags, follow and pay your bill, turning in your key at the desk.

At a hotel the people whom you tip are fairly numerous, especially if your stay has been longer than a few days, and much of this may be done as you leave. You will have tipped the waiter at meals, of course, but you may in addition want to leave a tip (at your last meal) for the headwaiter if he has been specially attentive. There's the chambermaid: you give her her tip personally at the end of your stay or leave it on the bureau. The bellboy who takes your bags down and puts them in the car or cab; checkroom attendants who may have served you. Also, any doorman who has called cabs for you —either as he does it or at the end of the visit. (Most people prefer the former as there may be several shifts of doormen on duty.) If the pageboys have been busy in your behalf, they should be remembered too, if they haven't already been tipped as they performed the service. When your stay has covered a week or more, you often tip the elevator starters and operators, especially if the hotel is a small one with a friendly atmosphere.

At a resort hotel, doormen and elevator starters are often lacking, but to take their places are grooms, boatmen, and caddies whom you may want to remember. Custom varies as to when you tip your waiter. If the place is more like a hotel than a lodge or inn, you may tip at each meal, but in many places the dining room staff and often the whole inside staff pool the tips, which are left in a lump sum at the desk when the guest departs. If there's any doubt in your mind, ask the manager when you register what is the custom at this particular place. (For how much to tip, see the tipping section in Helpful How-To's at the end of the book.)

HOSPITAL MANNERS

Almost all hospitals have visiting hours, which should be strictly observed. When a hospital has no special hours, at least for private patients, it is especially considerate to find out when meals are served and to come before or after them. Very often an appetite which is only beginning to come back is put completely to rout with the distraction of a visitor. And when you come at night, as some hospitals allow you to do, keep mouse-quiet in the halls and keep your voice down in the patient's room—many other patients are asleep.

Before you come, make sure not only that the patient is allowed visitors but also that he wants them. Find out, too, whether or not food would be a welcome gift and if so, what kind—in some cases the rigors of a special diet may force your friend to give away the mints or grapes or cookies you'd thought of bringing.

Flowers are almost always welcome, but remember not to select those with cloying odors. Many hospital vases are undistinguished, are intended for tall flowers, and are often at a premium; it's thoughtful, therefore, to send arrangements in their own containers. Potted plants (not too big) are a good choice, too, especially when your friend's stay is likely to be a long one. And if on a visit you notice that flowers are coming in by the dozens, you may decide *you'd* prefer to send a plant or bouquet to the house the day after your friend's homecoming.

There are many other little gifts besides flowers and food to take to a friend in the hospital, of course. Books which you know are to his taste (bypass the very heavy ones, so tiring to hold when you're in bed); crossword puzzles, magazines. Women, especially new mothers, appreciate things like lipsticks, bedjackets, and glamorous versions of the open-backed hospital gown.

Some hospitals limit the number of visitors. When this is not the case, remember that two or three at a time are plenty, and if you make a fourth, wait in the lounge or corridor until one of the others leaves. And no matter how much a patient may seem to be enjoying them, visitors are tiring. So make your visit short—twenty minutes to a half-hour. If he's been quite ill, ten minutes is enough.

It's best not to smoke in a hospital unless the patient is smoking and suggests that you do. And even then, when there are other patients sharing the room, it's only polite to ask them whether *they* mind your smoking.

Telephone calls can be as tiring to an invalid as visitors—just holding the receiver may be an effort. So make your telephoned inquiries short as well as cheery.

Worse than rude, it's really cruel to pay a hospital visit when you have a cold or suspect that you're coming down with one. Don't forget that though he may be much improved, your friend is still there because he hasn't regained his strength and ordinary resistance —a tiny germ that you donate may well keep him in the hospital another week. And even if *he* is healthy—is there just for X-rays or a broken leg—the nurses and the other patients are vulnerable.

Considerate friends won't pay visits to a new mother on the first or second day after delivery, husbands and close relatives of course excepted. No matter how easy the delivery and how well both mother and child are doing, the new mother needs all the rest she can get. Of course you're dying to see the baby, but nurses have a million chores besides displaying the small bundles at the nursery window, so don't ask to see it except at the time when the showings are scheduled.

On your way to the hospital, especially when your friend is or has been seriously ill, in his interest prepare yourself for your visit by nailing down in your mind a few cheerful topics of conversation—amusing things that happened to you, news of the neighbors, good books you've read or new movies you've seen. It's not that the conversation has to be entirely impersonal or that there has to be a lot of it, but a mental preparation will help steer you away from the pitfalls that perversely await the kindest of us, the unfortunate turn of thought that brings to mind only lugubrious subjects!

Don't talk about your operation or be inquisitive about his. (It's another matter if the patient *wants* to talk about his ordeal—then, of course, you let him.) Don't volunteer medical advice or criticize the treatment he's getting—the last thing you want to do is to make him anxious and dissatisfied.

It's difficult for anyone to visit a friend whose illness is very serious, with an uncertain or perhaps an all too certain prognosis. About all you can do is to steer a middle course between Pollyanna and Calamity Jane. Be honest—don't insult his intelligence by telling him how well he looks. He undoubtedly knows better than this, even if he doesn't know quite how ill he is. Don't, on the other hand, pull a long face and drench him with pity. He doesn't need or want that. He does need the infusion of hope that your calm warmth gives him. Your attitude means far more than your words.

Remember to sit where the patient can see you and talk to you without contorting himself—and never sit on the bed!

When a wife or husband of the patient is there at the same time you are, it's tactful to be the first to leave so as to give them a little time alone before visiting hours are over.

It's seldom wise to bring children to a hospital unless they're teen-aged, and then only to visit a close relative who really wants to see them. Most hospitals admit as visitors no children under twelve.

HOW TO BE A PATIENT

It's moderately easy to be a mannerly patient in a private room—although some people can manage to be objectionable even then!

(They achieve it by constant complaining, treating the nurses like slaveys, fussing about *all* the food, and in general making themselves and everybody who comes near them miserable.)

It's a little harder to be an ideal patient in a semiprivate room, where you really must consider the comfort and feelings of the other patients, some of whom may be quite a bit sicker than you are, or perhaps not very compatible even when they're on the mend. Remember that smoking may really upset them, and loud and excited conversation almost certainly will, as will a radio or throngs of visitors. On the other hand, if you're on the receiving end of consistent lack of consideration on the part of a roommate, it's not bad manners but just plain common sense to speak to the doctor or to the floor nurse about it—without acrimony but with firmness.

In a ward, smoking and radios are almost never allowed. Your visitors you should monitor yourself—remind them to keep the conversation at a low pitch.

It's a sign of ignorance as well as bad manners to treat a nurse in word or tone as if she were a servant. To be sure, you're paying for her services, but she is a professional person and as such commands respect. Never call her "Miss" and don't hail her as "Nurse" unless you're in need of her immediate services and don't know her name. Find out her name—she usually tells you at your first meeting, or you can ask her—and call her by it. It's bad manners too to quiz her on medical points—she's not supposed to tell you what your pulse rate or temperature is, or whether you might need another operation. If you want to know, *ask your doctor.*

When you have private nurses, their bills are often presented by them as individuals rather than added on to the hospital bill. In a long case they are presented weekly; if the service has been needed only for a few days, they'll be presented to you at the end of that time. Needless to say, such bills should be paid promptly.

Nurses are never tipped in money, but very often patients give them small presents on leaving—a box of candy, a scarf, handkerchiefs, books, or cigarettes. Patients who have been in private or semiprivate rooms usually tip the maid or maids who have cleaned their room, and sometimes the porter, too, if he has done some special service like bringing in a television set. Often patients give the books they have finished to the hospital library (whose book cart service is volunteer financed) and send any flowers that are still fresh to the wards.

No gifts are expected from ward patients, but often they give a box of candy to be shared by all the nurses on the floor.

WHEN THERE'S A NURSE IN THE HOME

The registered nurse, remember well, is a professional person employed to do her job of nursing and nursing only, whether in a house or a hospital. She is always addressed and referred to as "Miss Johnson," never by her first name. She is in no sense a servant, and takes her meals either with the family or on a tray in the living room or in her bedroom if their dinner hour doesn't jibe with her nursing duties. (She's given the guest room to sleep in.) Her time off is sacred, as it should be if she is to conserve her energies for the patient's care, and when she is off duty some member of the family takes over the nursing or a relief nurse is employed. It is no part of her job to perform any household duties and she shouldn't be expected to. Though some kind-hearted nurses will help out now and then in a servantless house, this is very definitely a favor to the family.

When you do have a servant, you must be a diplomat and occasionally a helper as well, to smooth the ruffled feathers often caused by the presence of a registered nurse in the home. Try to explain to the servant that she's a *"hospital* nurse," trained especially for that, and is there to help the patient get well faster. Meanwhile, to minimize complaints about any "extra work" Miss Johnson may make, you'll probably want to pitch in and ease the burden by taking over a few chores when you can.

When the illness is not too serious, a practical nurse is often the ideal answer, especially in a house without servants. Practical nurses are not highly trained, as are RN's, but a good one has many nursing skills and the word "practical" means what it says—it is *part* of their duty to take over the practical aspects of the patient's care as well as the medical ones, and when time permits, to help a bit with the housework or even to run the house, as best she can, when it's the mother who's bedridden. This doesn't mean that a practical nurse is a glorified servant or house cleaner—only that she can and will help out with such essential chores as vacuuming the patient's room, preparing or helping to prepare the invalid's meals, and so on.

Any nurse you engage, registered or practical, should be paid promptly, usually by the week. Terms and times should, of course, be agreed upon before nurse takes over.

MANNERS IN SHOPS, STORES, AND SUPERMARKETS

All of these are places where concentration on the errand in hand and a sense of haste often make us behave rudely without even realizing it. So no matter how much shopping you have to crowd into a limited time, bear in mind that other shoppers have the same problems—and the same rights—as you do. In the supermarket, "drive" your cart so that you don't graze the heels of the slower paced woman just ahead, or collide head-on with another cart while you're frowning over your shopping list. Watch out for the small fry. You don't take your children, of course, unless they are little enough to ride in the cart, or are sufficiently well behaved to stay with you instead of racketing around, and to ask you before they take anything from the shelves. But there are mothers who are sublimely indifferent while their yelling offspring play tag through the aisles—so be wary of the racers and the floor sitters.

And do be a good sport at the check-out counter. Most women are. When your cart is full, you will of course graciously allow the woman behind you to go through first with her lone loaf of bread and box of tissues. And you won't get acrimonious (even though you feel like it inside!) when someone shoves in line ahead of you.

In store elevators don't be an immovable object making all the other people go around you! When you get in, go to the back of the car and stand facing the doors. When a crowded car is about to stop at your floor, start to work your way out gently, saying meanwhile, "Getting off, please." (If you should meet a stubbornly immovable force on the way, it's easier to go around her than to argue the point!) When the elevator is really jammed and you're standing near the doors, it's very courteous to step off temporarily to let people out.

Remember that getting on and off escalators should, for the sake of courtesy as well as good manners, be accomplished expeditiously. It's rude as well as unsafe to block the platform while you decide whether to head for the luggage or the lingerie. So when you have to pause to get your bearings, step *off* the landing section while you're looking around.

When you go to the beauty shop try always to be punctual. When you're not, the whole day's schedule of appointments is thrown off and other clients who *are* on time are forced to wait. Remember, too, that your voice under the drier, though it doesn't seem so to you, is amplified—this above all is not the place to make personal remarks or ask questions about other customers. It's best not to bring your small children with you to the hairdresser's unless you absolutely must—they get restless and noisy and are disturbing to the operators and the other customers, much more so than the drier-protected mother realizes. When you have to bring them, be sure they're provided with a toy, a coloring book, or something else to keep them occupied—it's not fair to expect a child to pass a couple of hours quietly with just some grownup magazines to look at.

In any shop or store, be polite to those who serve you. One of the trademarks of bad manners is a haughty or arrogant way of speaking to salespeople. Remember that they're paid to *sell* the merchandise, not to select or manufacture it. If what you want isn't in stock, it is not the saleswoman's fault, and it's thoroughly rude to take out your annoyance on her when she can't supply that cardigan in coral simply because the corals in your size have all been sold.

The politest and most effective way to get waited on when the salesperson doesn't see you is to approach her and say, "Will you help me, please?" If she's busy with another customer, then of course you wait until that transaction is completed.

When, as sometimes happens, the salesperson is rude to you, it's no excuse for being rude in turn, however great the temptation. Just withdraw in good order and find another salesperson or another store.

BEHAVIOR WITH A DISABLED
OR HANDICAPPED PERSON

Bear in mind always that a person is no less a person just because he is blind or otherwise disabled. Many kindhearted people unintentionally act as though the handicapped individual were not quite bright or were more helpless than he is, even though it should be obvious that he has exerted brains, patience, and courage to overcome his handicap to the extent that he has. On the other hand, don't marvel openly at his accomplishments—they no more make him an Einstein than his handicap makes him stupid.

Obvious pity is deeply wounding to the handicapped. Their pride and their feelings are often hurt by the whisperings, starings, or tongue clucking of thoughtless observers. And, of course, you'd never question any one of them about his injuries or how he got them.

A truly sympathetic attitude takes no special note of the handicapped person unless he asks for help or plainly needs it. And when
you do help, you do it as inconspicuously and efficiently as you
know how. If at a dinner you are sitting next to a one-armed guest
who has been served (quite inconsiderately, it is obvious) with
meat that needs to be cut, you could say quietly, "May I help you
with the meat?" Similarly you might hold open a heavy door for
the spastic making his slow progress behind you *if* you can do so
naturally and gracefully, but not if you are so far ahead of him that
you call attention to his difficulties by waiting for him.

Those who work with the blind suggest that you need not hesitate
to offer help to a blind person who is walking in your direction or
is hesitating at an intersection. He can no doubt manage by himself,
but it is always a strain (unless he has a seeing-eye dog) and the
right kind of help is often appreciated. You might say, "I'm going
your way—may I help you?" Then, if he accepts your offer (and
don't be hurt if he doesn't!) you let *him* take *your* arm. Never grasp
his and try to steer him that way. If you come to a place too narrow
for the two of you, you go first and extend your hand backwards.
Be on the watch for possible trouble spots, such as a curb or a ramp,
and warn him. When you help a blind person to cross the street,
you of course help him all the way over and make sure he is safely
deposited on the other curb, out of the way of such obstacles as
fire hydrants, mail boxes, or open cellar doors, and out of the path
of hurrying pedestrians crossing in the opposite direction.

When you help a blind person onto a bus or streetcar or into a
cab, again don't drag or push him and don't try to use his arm as

a lever. Put his hand on the door railing and if necessary tell him how many steps there are. When you're guiding him to a seat, put his hand on the arm or back of it, or if you're approaching the seat from in front, just walk up to it with him and tell him he's facing it.

In a group, always speak directly *to* the one who is handicapped, unless he is entirely deaf or without speech. It's very rude, for example, to say before pouring a blind friend's tea, "Does he take lemon or cream?" "He" knows perfectly well which he takes and is quite able to answer for himself.

The disadvantages of deafness, especially of partial deafness, are commonly quite misunderstood. Shouting seldom helps, and if the deaf one wears a hearing aid, it may even be painful to him. It's better to speak clearly in an even tone of voice, and it helps a great deal to keep looking at the listener so that he can gather clues from your lips and your expression. In any group, it is advisable to gently attract his attention before you speak to him—it is often hard for a person with hearing only in one ear to figure out where a voice is coming from.

MANNERS WITH FAMOUS PEOPLE

It's only human to feel tongue-tied, at least at first, when you meet a celebrity. Be as natural as you can. When conversation is required (as opposed to those occasions when you're there to look and listen and just say "How do you do" with a word of appreciation as you go through the receiving line), you're not expected to be a paragon of brilliance, and don't try to be if you're not. Above all, don't parade a superficial knowledge of his specialty or gush about his books if you haven't read them. Genuine admiration of his accomplishments and intelligent questions about his profession, his travels, and matters of general interest—*not* his personal life—will get the conversational ball rolling. And try to stay away from the cliché questions: "How do you get your plots?" or "Do you write the words and then the music or the other way around?"

Don't invite a famous person to your house just as a drawing card to lure other guests or impress them. You should know him well enough, or have some special interest in common, for the invitation to be a natural one and the occasion should provide for him not only good food but also interesting and congenial companions. Of course, if he is a singer or musician or any sort of entertainer, you would never ask him to perform for you and your guests, any more than you would ask a guest who's a pediatrician to check the children as soon as he's had his dinner!

MANNERS WITH PROFESSIONAL PEOPLE

In making or continuing an acquaintance with a professional person such as a doctor, a lawyer, an architect, an interior decorator— anyone, in fact, who makes his living by dispensing a specialized knowledge—it's a prime rule never ask or seem to ask for professional advice at a social occasion. If you can't decide whether your living room will look too busy if you redo the wing chair in a print, resist the temptation to corner Amy Cushing at your cocktail party. Go to her office and consult her. If your husband doesn't know whether such-and-such transportation expenses are deductible, he shouldn't tackle Harry Barnes at a dinner party—he should see him during office hours. Although professional people get somewhat resigned to being asked for free advice and are usually courteous about it, they inwardly resent it, and rightly so. When the professional person is one whom you regularly consult on a fee basis and is a close friend as well, there's nothing wrong with asking a simple question when you happen to see him in the evening. But it's better not to make a practice of it.

A doctor or lawyer is properly resentful when you quiz him about other patients or clients. Their business with him is strictly confidential—as you expect your own to be—and his professional ethics do not allow him to discuss it with anyone. By questioning him you put him in a very awkward position; he has no choice but to refuse to discuss the matter.

When you keep an appointment at the doctor's office, be punctual. The tardiness of earlier patients, a hospital emergency, or an unexpectedly lengthy examination may force him to keep *you* waiting occasionally, but that's no reason for you to be late. When you have to break an appointment, give his office notice the day before if possible, or at least several hours beforehand.

When you come for an appointment, it goes without saying—or ought to—that you and your underthings are clean and fresh.

When you telephone your doctor, try to do it during office hours. Nighttime and holiday calls are part of a doctor's life, and you shouldn't hesitate to call him in any real emergency. But don't be one of those universally unloved patients who suffers malaise Thursday, Friday, and Saturday—and then late on Sunday decides to give the doctor a full run-down on the symptoms right this minute.

Sometimes patients forget that *they* have certain rights. One of these is the right to request a consultation in any critical situation when having one would make you feel more comfortable. Naturally, you won't do this for a whim, to "pull rank" on your physician or for some minor ailment. But if you have contracted a serious disease or are facing a major operation, you may want another medical man's opinion. You are entitled to this and it isn't rude to ask for it. It's perfectly all right to say to the doctor, "Do you mind if we get another opinion on this? I'd feel more comfortable about the operation if a neurologist (or an eye man, or whoever is a specialist in the field) confirmed the diagnosis." Usually your doctor will agree, and often will suggest a specialist. You may even, if you know of a good man, suggest the specialist yourself. The one thing you shouldn't do is to go trotting off on your own for a consultation, without letting your doctor know. Not only is this very rude, but if the second physician is ethical, he'll have to refuse to treat you without your own doctor's knowledge.

Sometimes it happens that you don't feel at home with the doctor whom you have seen a few times—although Mary and Jake Greene swear by him, you aren't drawn to him. It could be simply a personality clash or it could be that he hasn't convinced *you* (no hypochondriac you, it's to be hoped!) that he is as thorough a diagnostician as you'd like. Whether you're right or wrong, when you decide to change physicians, do it in an ethical way. Don't just drop him and start in with a new one. Both you and he will feel more comfortable if you write him a friendly note, pleading inconvenience of his location, a misfit of his office hours with your business ones or some other excuse.

Such a note might read:

Friday, November 8

Dear Dr. White,

Now that we've moved farther out, it seems all but impossible for me to bring the children to your office without interfering with school and school activities. Although they and I regret it, it seems necessary to go to a doctor nearby. I should appreciate it if you would send their records to Dr. Albert Jones at 3 Ridge Road, Seabright. Thank you.

Sincerely yours,
Evelyn Deane

If there has been some disagreement between you and the doctor that has come out in the open, you'd probably prefer to be direct rather than try to pretend to a good will which may not exist. Then you'd simply "regret" that you feel you would prefer to go to another physician, and ask him to forward your records.

28

Manners for the Clubwoman

CLUB MEMBERSHIP PLAYS A PROMINENT PART IN THE LIVES OF MANY American women today. Most women belong to at least one club, and not a few belong to several. If you have children of school age, you're almost certainly involved with the PTA and its activities. You may also belong to a church guild or temple sisterhood, a garden club, a bridge club, a hospital auxiliary—there's an almost endless list of organizations serving every interest from hobbies to philanthropy.

If you're not now a member of any club and would like to be, decide first what kind of organization you really want to belong to. It's a waste of everybody's time including your own to join a club because you feel it would lend you prestige, because a friend belongs, or just because you're lonely. For the most fruitful results, you and your club should each have something to offer the other.

Ask yourself what you want most out of your club membership. Are you looking for people and pastimes? Or will your needs be most deeply satisfied by working with other people toward a common goal? If your interests are mainly social, then local women's clubs and special interest groups (garden clubs, art clubs, chess clubs, and so on) are for you. If, on the other hand, you believe in goals, then you will want to associate with one of the service groups —educational associations, health agencies, political groups, groups with religious affiliations, and those which make a specialty of youth service. Some of these may be purely local; many may be local affiliates of a large national association—such as, for example, the

League of Women Voters, the American Red Cross, the Boy or Girl Scouts of America.

There is, of course, much overlapping between social and service classifications, and many local differences. Some service organizations are more "social" than others. On the other hand, many a special interest club devotes some of its time to community service of one sort or another.

HOW TO JOIN

There are two ways of joining a club, depending on what kind of club it is that you incline to. A great many you can join simply by filling out a membership blank and paying the dues or membership fee. This is practically always true of the groups organized around educational, philanthropic, or community service projects and which welcome volunteer workers. Look up your chosen organization in the telephone book and call to ask if membership is open to everyone. If it is, a membership application will be sent you in the mail, often information leaflets as well. If you're applying as a volunteer worker, they will no doubt ask you to come in for a talk so they can work out with you what use can best be made of your skills and interests and experience.

In most communities, it is often a little harder to join the local social clubs, often originally formed for fellowship, perhaps around a common interest such as bridge, gardening, or sewing. These groups usually started small and have been kept that way for (convenience's sake, rather than snobbery) because the meetings are held in the members' homes. (Even somewhat larger groups with a clubhouse or other outside meeting place must limit membership to the capacity of the kitchen and the assembly rooms.) Admission is almost invariably by invitation only, and when openings do occur friends of the original members naturally come first. If you're a newcomer to the community, there isn't any special reason why they should invite you—you may be every bit as charming and congenial as the others, but they don't know that because they don't know *you*. In such a case, by all means join one or more of the open organizations and make friends there. This participation may turn out to fill your time and your needs; if it does not, it can be the entrée to other groups.

When you *are* known in the community or become so, then it is probable that you will number among your friends one of the members of the smaller group in which you are interested. Simply express to her, in a tactful way, your interest in the group *and* in the things they do. If there's room for another person, she'll probably take you to a meeting and (at that time or later) propose you as a member. If, however, she says they'd love to have you, but unfortunately there's a long waiting list, or if she makes no overt response to your hint, you must let your inquiry drop. It will be very bad manners to pursue it and will in the end be embarrassing to both of you.

WHAT IS EXPECTED OF THE CLUBWOMAN

In general, of course, a clubwoman is expected to conform to the standards of taste and manners of any charming woman. And it always helps to have or to acquire extra helpings of tact, poise, and discipline.

Once you have become a member, certain duties are incumbent on you, as they are or should be on all the other members. In any club it may now and then seem as if these duties are honored all too frequently in the breach, but the more the members conform to them the more enjoyable and successful is the club.

One of your prime obligations is to be regular in attendance at meetings *and* to be prompt.

Another is to pay your dues on time.

You should get a copy of the club's bylaws, learn them and obey them. You should also make yourself thoroughly familiar with the policy and purpose of your club and with the special house rules, if any. If your club's meetings proceed in formal order, as most of them do, it would be well to get a copy of Robert's *Rules of Order* and familiarize yourself with the rules of parliamentary procedure.

A good clubwoman should also know the functions of the officers in her club, their techniques of program planning and fund raising, the degree of formality with which they serve refreshments, and so on. These always vary from club to club. The new member, besides studying the bylaws, looks and listens for a while to get the "feel" of the way in which her club is run.

These are the basic ingredients of competent membership. But just as you wouldn't consider yourself a real cook if you knew only how to boil eggs, make coffee, and serve just one dinner menu, you won't become an effective member of your club or get the most out of its activities unless you also put your mind to acquiring a few skills necessary when you work with groups. You don't have to have any special talent or training for these—just a little fore-thought, a little tact, and the will to give as well as to receive.

First, make up your mind to participate. Vow that you won't be a piece of deadwood that drifts with the stream—it doesn't take many of those to block up the club's creativity! So don't be one of those who sits wordless in a corner and then *after* the meeting deplores practically all the decisions that have been made. Be prepared to give generously of your talents and your time. When volunteers are being called for to serve on the fund raising committee and you've had some experience in that line, you really ought to speak up. If you don't, don't carp later at the efforts of little Sally Jones, who wanted to be helpful but never tried to raise a fund in her young life before.

On the other hand, don't be over-eager and bite off more than you can chew. Volunteer for only one job at a time until you've explored both your capacities and your limitations.

Sometimes new members who have been active in clubs in other communities and actually have a great deal to offer, make the mistake of trying (or seeming to try) to rout the old order and establish a new one. Even though there may be a real need for reorganization or reform in certain ways, it isn't becoming, mannerly, or even effective for a new member to be aggressive about this. For example, the members of a long-established group may never have adhered to strict parliamentary procedure, but are used to conducting their meetings quite informally. Perhaps eventually they may welcome the saving of time and the gains in efficiency that more business-like methods bring about. On the other hand, sociable get-togethers and leisurely chatter may have always taken precedence over competence and that's the way they want it. In any case, it isn't up to you as the new member to whip the meetings into shape according to your ideas. In proposing any changes, go slowly and use the utmost tact. If some of your suggestions are accepted, fine. Should you meet with stubborn and continued opposition, relinquish your stand gracefully—or, if your ideas proved to be of overwhelming importance to you, it might be best, after an interval, to resign. You will, of course, have maintained pleasant relations with the other members, and in resigning may prefer (particularly if you were sponsored, and at your own wish, by a friend) to give some polite excuse quite unrelated to the real issue.

When a vote is called for, cast the most intelligent and well-informed vote you can. And when the result goes against you, accept the decision of the majority gracefully and uphold it in your actions, both at that meeting and afterwards. You won't, of course, run down any policies or actions of the club to outsiders, no matter how much you may occasionally disagree with them. All the representatives of a club should be its good-will ambassadors in the community and in so doing must present a united front. If you consistently feel yourself wanting to express disapproval, it may be this is not the club for you.

In working with a group as with an individual, there is no more heart-warming reward than receiving sincere praise for a job well done. When you have enjoyed an especially interesting program or a particularly stimulating speech, it will warm *your* heart as well as that of the program chairman or the speaker to express your appreciation sincerely and specifically, over and above the routine thank you that you would naturally extend.

THE CLUBWOMAN AS HOSTESS

In the case of a new member on her first visit or two, her sponsor is her technical hostess and takes the responsibility for seeing that she is introduced, shares in the refreshments, and in general is made to feel comfortable and at ease. All the club members, however, are hostesses whenever the group entertains a guest, whether that guest be a prospective new member or a participant in a special program. Usually a special hostess (often the chairman of the program committee) is appointed to take care of the platform star and other visitors of importance, such as visiting officials or flower show judges.

When such a guest lives in the neighborhood and is known to have transportation, club hospitality may begin and end at the meeting, though it is always polite to offer to pick up the guest and take him home afterwards. When the guest is from out of town, he should (except in very large cities) be met at the station or airport, and then taken directly to the meeting or, if he is to stay overnight, to the hotel where a room has been reserved for him. If a mealtime intervenes between his arrival and the meeting, it's customary for the special hostess to invite him to have lunch (or dinner), sometimes at her home, or perhaps at a restaurant, often with one or two of the club officers. She also acts as his hostess at the meeting, introducing him to the officers and to all or some of the members (depending on the size of the group) and takes him back to the hotel or to his point of departure as the case may be. (If he *wants* to be taken back, that is—many an exhausted speaker would rather take a taxi by himself and rest his weary larynx!)

When the guest has come from a distance, there may be several hours to fill in even when a luncheon or dinner interlude has been arranged. Very often the travel-tired one is only too glad to spend the time resting in his room, particularly if this is just one stop on a demanding lecture tour. Sometimes, on the other hand, he is energetic and gregarious, in which case he might enjoy being taken on a brief tour of the sights and scenes of your town, or to the art museum. The tactful hostess plays it by ear, as it were. If he wants to rest, so be it, but she will always have some entertainment planned for him which he may take advantage of if he cares to.

Naturally the plans for a speaker from afar will have been made by letter far in advance. The very first letter (usually the program chairman is the one who writes) should tell him what kind of club yours is, and how big. It should tell him why your members want to hear *him* speak on *his* subject (or on the subject you are suggesting), and how long you would like him to speak. Also ask him his fee; if it is your understanding that he charges expenses only and no fee, be sure to mention this. Tell him the date and time of the meeting and where it is to be held. Give him instructions for getting there and offer to meet him—at the plane or train, or perhaps (as is the custom in very large cities) in his hotel lobby. If he is to stay at the home of one of the members you of course tell him this and indicate that he will be taken there. It's polite then to ask him if the arrangements you have made are agreeable to him; or if he is making his own arrangements, ask him his time of arrival.

About ten days before the date of the meeting, the first letter should be followed by another confirming the arrangements. Of course, after the meeting a letter should go to him promptly to thank him for speaking to the club and to tell him how much his talk was enjoyed.

At the meeting itself, if you have not accompanied him there, you'll be alert to meet him at the door, introduce him to the president of the club, show him to the platform, and sit with him there. The platform should have been made ready in advance, with a reading stand (unless you know positively that he doesn't want one) and a light on the stand that shines on—and only on—the rostrum surface. If there's an amplifier, make sure beforehand that it works, and have someone appointed to stand by to adjust its height if that proves to be necessary. (It's considerate not to leave this up to the person who is introducing him.) There should, of course, be a glass of water, or glass and pitcher, at hand.

After the speech and a brief appreciation of it (not a rehash!) by you or whatever officer is responsible for that, see to it that the speaker gets tea or coffee and/or other refreshments. It's up to you to keep him from being so immediately besieged by his well-wishers that he gets no chance to take a breath or a sip, let alone a bite!

And don't forget, when you leave him, to pay him his fee!

Club teas, like teas at home, may run the gamut from informal to quite elaborate, depending on the occasion and on the member's wishes, plus the limitations of the club's facilities and its treasury. Seated meals such as luncheons and dinners are usually more elaborate and occasionally are given at a local restaurant. In a small club, however, a simple luncheon at a member's home or a casserole, salad, and dessert on the terrace can be just as satisfactory, even when there is a special guest.

THE CLUBWOMAN'S CLOTHES

Except for rare occasions, such as a big dinner for visiting officials or an important evening program where dinner dresses (or, rarely, even more formal wear) might be called for, a clubwoman dresses simply. You will find suits and wool dresses always appropriate in cool weather, and when cottons are worn for the few warm weather meetings, just see that they don't partake too much of the beach or picnic spirit. Generally speaking, in large cities and at meetings of big clubs you will usually wear a hat; in the suburbs you often go without—but clubs and communities vary widely about this, and if you're a new member, you'd best ask your sponsor what *your* club custom is.

When you are a speaker, you will find that for platform confidence it's best not to wear a brand new dress or suit, but one which you have worn before, so that it is used to you and you are used to it. This doesn't mean an innocuous garment whose only virtue is that it's comfortable. On the contrary, while your outfit shouldn't be inappropriate for the time of day and shouldn't in color or ornamentation be so striking as to distract the audience's attention from your speech, you always please the group when you dress as if you too think that this is an occasion.

The woman speaker practically always wears a hat (unless the affair is one calling for dinner or evening dress), which shouldn't be distracting and doesn't have to be spanking new, but ought to be as devastatingly becoming as possible.

29

Traveling

At all seasons, by all routes, to all the corners of our own country and the world, Americans are on the move. Gone are the times when for the average family a trip to the nation's capital was a milestone, when only the rich went to Europe for the "grand tour" and only the very rich embarked on a world cruise. Nowadays fast transcontinental trains, planes whizzing along the airways and dependable modern automobiles, plus travel plans to fit almost any budget, have for most of us all but eliminated the hurdles of time and money.

All the practical "how-to's" of travel—kinds of transportation, itineraries, costs, you will find in the many comprehensive travel books to be found in bookstores and libraries. Travel agents, too, have at their fingertips such a vast store of knowledge that it is well worth your while to consult them for any lengthy trip. It saves you time and often money, as well, and it usually costs no more than if you yourself made the arrangements.

In this book we're concerned not with costs and itineraries but with the manners and attitudes of the good, happy, and relaxed traveler, who whether he goes by ship or train, plane or car, knows what to do and what not to do. A few procedures and customs do vary according to the type of flying carpet you select for your trip, and with those practicalities we'll be dealing, always with the reminder that etiquette's favorite maxim—be considerate of others—applies just as much to the traveler as to the stay-at-home, and sometimes even more so.

An almost universal uncertainty about customs away from home centers around tipping. In Helpful How-To's at the end of the book, you'll find a complete schedule for all kinds of tips. In this chapter, tipping is discussed only when some special aspect of it seems to call for mention.

TRAVEL ON TRAINS

Except for daytime coach travel, which is on a first-come-first-served-basis, all train accommodations in the United States are reserved. These range in price and privacy from the daytime parlor car seat to the reclining overnight coach chair, and after that through upper and lower berths to the various separated accommodations such as roomettes, compartments, and drawing rooms. Only these "apartments" have private toilet facilities. In all of the others the traveler depends on the public dressing rooms—one for men and one for women—at the end of each car.

In berth accommodations, the convention is that the person who has bought the more expensive lower has the privilege of riding forward. Riding backwards unsettles many people, so when you have the favored seat, it is very gracious to ask if the other passenger would like to sit alongside you—if you're of the same sex, that is, since for a woman to suggest this to a man would be inappropriate. Often a man who has the choice seat and really doesn't mind riding backwards will offer to change places with the woman opposite him.

When it's bedtime, the berth occupants agree to ring for the porter to make up the beds. In a trice they're made, one up and one down behind the swaying curtains, each bunk complete with hangers and a mesh hammock for clothing, plus a ladder for access to the upper. While the porter's at his work, it's a good time to go to the dressing room, taking along a robe as well as toilet articles. Since the dressing room is small and often crowded, it's best to undress there only partially and wear your robe back to the berth to finish undressing inside it. If you're the occupant of the upper, you should do your planning well, for once the ladder's taken away you're stuck up there unless you ring for the porter to bring it back again.

If you're not ready to retire when your fellow occupant suggests having the beds made up (ten-thirty or so is a reasonable hour to suggest this) you should agree, but indicate you'll go to the observation or club car.

When you're in a compartment or drawing room, you will still call the porter to transform the various seats into beds. In a roomette, you just push a button whenever you're ready and the ready-made bed folds down from overhead.

When the diner is open, the porter or dining car steward announces the fact, as well as the location of the diner. (Walking through the train, a man precedes the woman who accompanies him so he can open the heavy doors for her.) When you get to the dining car, you wait until the steward comes forward to seat you. The procedure from then on is just as it would be in any restaurant, except that you almost always write your order. There is also a bit more informality in that it's perfectly allowable, even for a woman alone, to make impersonal conversation with table companions. A woman, however, will not allow a strange man to pay for her meal any more than she will in a restaurant.

While on a trip of any length, tipping of other employees may be done at the journey's end, you'd tip your dining car waiter at each meal. And don't forget to tip an extra amount, just as you would in a hotel, when you have meals served in your compartment or roomette.

Remember that on a train space is at a premium. Don't spread your luggage in the aisles or on the seats or where it will be in anyone's way. The luggage of berth and parlor car passengers is usually stowed away by the porter in a special location. You may keep with you an essential overnight bag, dressing case, or briefcase, which can go in the overhead rack when there is one or put on the floor out of the way of your seatmate. Day coaches have racks for the luggage.

If you know that all the trains you'll be on are air conditioned, you can wear anything you'd wear for daytime in the city, including hat and gloves. To be on the safe side, in case of windows open to dust and soot, it's best to wear something that doesn't show soil too readily. And since you'll be sitting so much, select in either case something that doesn't wrinkle easily.

There is, as among travelers everywhere, a sort of camaraderie among the passengers, but it isn't good manners to persist in chatting away to someone who wants to read or doze or just contemplate the passing scenery. And if you're traveling alone, it's the better part of wisdom to have a book handy with which to discourage, politely, any monologuist who bothers *you*.

If you're returning from the club car late at night, do remember that all around you people are sleeping; so be as quiet as you can. And when you reach your destination at daybreak, don't arouse the lucky ones who can sleep until just before the train pulls into Des Moines at nine. It's customary, by the way, and prudent too, to ask the porter to call you at such-and-such a time if you must be dressed and ready to get off at an early hour.

Washroom manners on a train as elsewhere are very important. Don't spread your cosmetics and toiletries all over the shelf, don't strew powder about, and don't leave the place looking as if a small hurricane had been through it. Above all, obey that small sign in the toilet which cautions you along the lines of that earthy common-sense rhyme: "Passengers will please refrain. . . ."

TRAIN TRAVEL WITH CHILDREN

Remember that the inactivity is hard on the youngsters. Take advantage of even a five-minute stop to walk with them up and down the platform. Bring plenty of things to amuse them—crayons, games, and books. (The dining car steward almost always provides special menus for children and very often gives them souvenir coloring books.) When the children get hungry, which they often do between meals, the porter will often supply a glass of cold milk or a soft drink. It's as well to have a supply of cookies or hard candy to supplement this.

Don't let the children hang over the backs of your seats, distracting and sometimes annoying the passengers behind you, and keep them from kicking the seat in front. Let them take a trip to the water cooler now and then—but only now and then, and a walk-not-run expedition. Make it a rule that they mustn't chase up and down the aisles.

On any long trip, the inactivity and the necessary discipline are so hard on children that it is far better, if you can afford it, to buy a compartment or drawing room space rather than berths.

Remember that there is (as a rule) only one observation or club car to serve many cars full of passengers, each of whom is entitled to a turn at looking at the scenery and relaxing there. Don't be one of those inconsiderate few who make a practice of spending the entire day and evening in it.

TRAVELING BY CAR

Motoring is one of the best ways to see any country thoroughly and intimately. Thousands of families crisscross our United States each summer—and many in other seasons as well—while a great many choose car travel on a trip abroad too.

When you're going on any extensive car trip, thorough preparation is a must. Your service station, the AAA and experienced friends can be of great help in route planning. It's up to you, however, to have your car thoroughly checked, to see that your insurance and driving licenses are in good order, and to get good maps for the sections you'll cover. Don't overlook a complete set of car tools and accessories, including flares, flashlight, first aid kit, and a good spare —two spares if you're going across the continent.

Travel in clothes that are as comfortable and creaseproof as possible. *And* remember that customs in dress vary from place to place. In your home town, well-tailored slacks plus shirt and jacket may be a perfectly acceptable woman's costume at roadside dining places and for casual shopping on Main Street. In other parts of the country, they may well cause an epidemic of raised eyebrows. Shorts are not in good taste anywhere as a traveling costume and may be quite uncomfortable to drive in. Haltered sun dresses may keep you out of some famous church or shrine that you want to see. So it's safest to dress conservatively and carry a scarf to cover your head in case of church visits. It's a good idea, too, to pack a simple but somewhat dressier dress, in case at the end of a day's driving you want to dine in a hotel or at a sophisticated country inn. If your husband wants to drive in shirtsleeves and slacks, there's no earthly reason why he shouldn't—but he should have within easy reach a jacket and tie to don for meal stops.

COURTESIES OF THE ROAD

In general, these are what you would observe in driving anywhere. In particular, remember that regulations vary from state to state and city to city, so be aware constantly of the signs which indicate traffic turns as well as those showing local speed limits. Courtesy and safety too demand that you signal your moves, keep to the right except when passing, and use your rear view mirror. Be on the lookout for drowsiness or thruway hypnosis so that you can pull off the road and rest or shift drivers before you get into trouble.

Always dim your headlights for approaching cars. Don't be a roadhog—if someone wants to pass, slow up a little, and if the road is clear wave him on. Don't set up an unrealistic miles-per-day goal. If you do, instead of being a relaxed driver—and therefore both courteous and safe—you'll fume and fret behind the inevitable combination of slow truck and narrow winding road.

Don't throw lighted cigarettes out of the window at any time. You could be responsible for starting a brush or forest fire. To empty an ashtray while the car is in motion is hazardous to you as well as to other drivers. And the people who dump their ashtrays in parking lots are extremely rude—it's easy enough to carry some sort of litter bag for this purpose.

Being neat and tidy in the restrooms where you stop en route is a basic "road courtesy" that ought to be more widely observed than it is.

OVERNIGHT STOPS

Experienced motorists find it restful and in the long run efficient to start driving early each morning and to stop for the day about four. This schedule gives you a chance to look for accommodations (if you haven't reserved them) in the revealing daylight, as well as time to rest and freshen up when you've found them.

At motels and cabins, the procedure is to drive up to the main entrance, get out, and register. You are directed to room or cabin number so-and-so and given the key to it, whereupon you drive the car to the parking space marked out directly in front of it and unload your luggage at your new front door. When you're ready to check out, you reload your luggage and drive to the office to pay the bill and leave the key. This is the routine at most such places. At unpretentious country cabins the parking may be on the grass or in a nearby clearing, and at the de luxe motels attendants may do the parking and luggage removing for you. In the latter case, you will tip for this service just as you would in a hotel, and also for any special services such as bringing ice. In the average motel you get no special personal services and aren't expected to tip, at least not for a one-night stay. On a longer visit you will probably want to remember the chambermaid.

MOTORING WITH CHILDREN

As in any traveling with the small fry, your aim will be to anticipate and prevent boredom and restlessness. Take along a selection of games, coloring books, and crayons, little puzzles, a pack of cards for games like Go Fish and I Doubt It. A small compass with which the children can follow the car's direction is fun, and for the littlest a favorite small stuffed animal helps to provide security. Some scratch pads and plenty of pencils are useful for scoring when the children play one of the many counting games that help pass the time: collecting license plates (by states, by colors, by lowest and highest numbers), compiling a complete alphabet from signs (one letter to a sign), spotting rarities like hay wagons, white horses, fire engines. Word games such as Twenty Questions or Ghosts can relieve the monotony, too.

Let the children change seats now and then, including an occasional turn in the front seat, and keep the driving day shorter than you might if you were traveling without them. A lot of energy can be released by having a picnic for the midday meal. It helps, too, to let them stretch their legs whenever you stop for gas; this is an opportunity for them to buy postcards and have a soft drink. It's wise to carry fresh drinking water in the car as well as nonsweet snacks. Chewing gum may help to ward off car sickness, but if any of your brood is especially susceptible, your doctor can prescribe medication.

When you're traveling with small children, it's always wisest to telephone to secure accommodations for the night rather than to leave the matter to chance.

Like the grownups, the children should wear easy-care clothes that don't show wrinkles or soil.

TRAVEL BY PLANE

While there's always a chance you may pick up space at the airport through a cancellation, it's a slim one, and it's much wiser to make reservations for a plane trip at the airline office or through your travel agent. Airports, of course, are usually located beyond the city limits and getting there must be part of your planning. If no kind friend offers to drive you, there's nearly always an airline bus or limousine you can take. The charge for this is not covered in the price of your ticket, but as a rule it's cheaper than a taxi would be.

The clothes you'll take must be carefully selected, for there is a limit to the weight you're allowed. You may be permitted to pay for overweight, but this can be riotously expensive! A bit more than forty pounds is the average allowance; it may be more in first class accommodations. Inquire about baggage allowance when you get your ticket.

For wear on the plane, a nonwrinkling suit of summer or winter material is always good. Carry a lightweight coat (it's safest to have one even if you're going to tropical climates). Travel books and travel agents are good sources of information about what else to take, depending on your destination and the length of your trip. In general, lean heavily on drip-dry underthings and a drip-dry dress or two, and good travelers such as knits. And don't take too much. Experienced travelers suggest laying out everything you think you'll need and then leaving half of it at home.

When you arrive at the airport, have your ticket verified at the counter and put your bags on the weighing slot nearby. The ticket clerk weighs them, gives you checks for them, and away they go on the moving belt to be taken out to the plane. When your flight is announced over the loudspeaker, go to the proper gate and get aboard the plane. Your reservation entitles you to a place on the plane, but not to a particular seat as a rule. However, there are certain flights where specific seats are assigned. (When you find an "occupied" sign in the seat you fancy, it means that it has already been claimed by a passenger who boarded at an earlier stop, and you must choose another seat.)

Generally, your flight bag is the only piece of luggage you're allowed to take with you to your seat. (If you don't own one, they can be bought at the airlines office; and on some overseas flights a flight bag is given to each passenger with the compliments of the line.) Besides toilet articles and nightwear, a light sweater should be tucked in here, and a pair of soft folding slippers will coddle your feet on a long trip. For safety's sake, nothing is allowed in the over-head racks except soft things like coats and hats, so your flight bag goes on the floor—it can make a comfortable foot rest.

The stewardess will hang up your coat or suit jacket for you if you ask her; and she will also supply you with a pillow and blanket for naps.

When a flight is so scheduled as to be en route during mealtime, the meal (or meals) are served aboard, free of charge, on trays brought to the passengers by the stewardess. (No tips expected or allowed!)

On overnight flights, sleeper service is sometimes available. This is much like having a berth on a train and the bedding-down procedure is much the same.

The dressing rooms on a plane, one for men and one for women, are usually quite tiny and only one person at a time can use them. Be patient about waiting for your turn. Of course, you'll leave the place tidy. For reasons of safety, no smoking is permitted in the rest rooms.

Manners on a plane are in general the same as manners on a train, except that certain aspects of plane etiquette are more binding on the passengers for reasons of safety as well as courtesy. It's rude *and* reckless to attempt to flout the safety belt and no-smoking directions. And it's unsafe as well as inconsiderate to block traffic by standing in the aisle to chit-chat with a friend.

Talking to your seat mate (or seat mates) is perfectly permissible, so long as you don't insist on conversation when the other person wants to nap or read.

On airlines everywhere, there is no tipping of the plane or airport personnel. The porter who takes your bags from the terminal entrance to the ticket counter, however, as well as the one who at the end of the flight takes them to your bus or taxi, should be tipped. (While in theory you don't have to, at the end of a flight it sometimes helps you retrieve your luggage more quickly if you slip a quarter to the airport baggage handler who sorts out the suitcases as they come from the plane.)

On leaving the plane, a courteous passenger always gives an appreciative smile to the stewardesses and steward—to the flight personnel as well, should they appear—and says, "Thank you for a pleasant flight!"

CHILDREN ON PLANES

Most children like plane travel and behave well. Of course, on any long flight they do get restless and it's well to have some diversions planned, because it's unsafe for them as well as inconsiderate of the tray-laden stewardesses to let them wander up and down the aisle.

On most airlines, families with children get thoughtful attention. Very special consideration is given to infants. As a rule, the stewardess will prepare a simple formula for you (it's safest to inquire about this when you make your reservations) and she will always warm the formula you have brought along. Many lines provide disposable diapers, standard brands of baby food, and even bassinettes.

WHEN YOU GO BY SHIP

Reservations for ship travel are not only essential but should be made weeks, if not months, ahead of time.

Accommodations on ships vary widely in price and spaciousness. First class is the costliest and roomiest; second class, available on some ships, less costly and less roomy; third class (sometimes called "tourist") offers the least room. A few ships, notably those designed for cruises rather than transocean travel, have only one class.

It's best to arrive at the pier a good hour before sailing time. A dock steward will carry your luggage aboard and show you to your cabin. He should be tipped for this when he leaves you, as you may not see him again. Next you will want to find the purser or the dining room steward and arrange for your table as well as the time when you wish to eat. There are usually two meal "sittings" (on some ships three), and families with young children not only prefer, but are expected to prefer, the first. At this time you may also want to locate the deck steward and reserve a deck chair for the voyage. If you haven't a private bath, then see the bath stewardess or steward, who consults a schedule and reserves a daily bathtime for you. You'll make a mental note always to be prompt for the bath engagement—if you're not, your lack of consideration will hold up everybody who comes after you.

Having attended to those chores, you'll probably want to unpack (shipboard life is so busy you'll be glad later that you did), check any large sums of money and valuable jewelry with the purser, and acquaint yourself with the layout of the ship.

It's by no means essential to be fluent in sea-going terminology—

in fact, you don't need to know any of it. But it may make you feel a little more at home to learn that the ship's front end is the bow and the rear is the stern, and that the port side is to your left as you face the bow, starboard to your right. Toward the stern is aft, toward the bow is forward.

Manners on shipboard are quite informal and you may speak to anyone you like. Experienced travelers, however, like to proceed warily toward friendship. If you wait until you've been at sea a day or two and have had a chance to observe everybody (and to be observed yourself), you'll avoid the embarrassment of having to withdraw tactfully from companions who turn out not to be so congenial as you thought they'd be, and who assume you'll all do everything "together" from now on.

Be wary of seeming to force yourself on any person or group who make it politely plain they don't want to be mixers. Naturally, you won't insist on talking to anyone who isn't at the moment inclined for conversation. Nor will you keep coaxing someone into making a fourth at bridge who just wants to soak up the sun and meditate or read.

Should you receive an invitation to sit at the captain's table (and this *is* by invitation *only*), remember that this honor carries with it certain obligations. You will be expected to be on time for meals, most especially prompt at dinner. And you're not supposed to leave the table until the captain does. If it happens that you'd really rather not be thus fettered with protocol, you may decline—but this must be done with supreme tact. You may explain to the dining room steward (who is usually the one to extend the invitation in the captain's behalf) that you have already arranged to sit with friends, or that you plan to take many of your meals in your stateroom; in other words, give him a reason, while indicating that you are appreciative of the honor and most regretful that you must decline. Needless to say, your reason must be a good one, and your later conduct must not give the lie to it.

On shipboard you must be especially careful about tossing a lighted cigarette overboard—the wind may carry it back into some open porthole.

CLOTHES ON SHIPBOARD

Some ships call for more gala attire than others—your travel agent or the offices of the line itself will tell you what your needs will be for your particular ship. In summer you wear much what you'd wear at a resort—in winter you dress with somewhat the same informality but in warmer clothes, of course. Suits and skirts and sweaters are always suitable. In the daytime, slacks are perfectly proper for women on most ships. Men are most comfortable in slacks and sports jackets during the day, but change to a business suit for dinner. And they should always wear jackets in the dining room.

Even though your baggage allowance on shipboard is liberal, it's still best to travel light, for you *are* limited to the amount of luggage you can keep in the cabin itself (extra bags may be taken, but are not reachable during the voyage); besides, the care of a lot of fussy clothes can spoil some of your fun. So take things that are easy to care for and not too many of them. Don't forget a bandeau or head scarf of some kind to keep your hair out of your eyes on the windy deck. (Stay away from big-brimmed hats for deck wear—you'll feel like a circus tent in a high gale!) And do take a coat as well as a sweater or two even on a summer cruise; nights at sea can be chilly.

Evening dress on shipboard is always optional. In the air age, it is seen even less than it used to be because so many people must travel light in anticipation of plane hops after landing. You'll be adequately prepared with a dinner dress and a cocktail dress, or perhaps a long skirt with two dressy blouses.

Cruise ships are a little different. The ship is usually your hotel at the various stops and there is no problem about transporting luggage. So most people bring along several dinner dresses, an evening gown or two, and the appropriate bags and shoes. A man often takes a dinner jacket for especially festive occasions, but a dark business suit would serve as well, unless he expects to be entertained ashore by people of prominence in the port.

In general, the degree of dressiness on a ship varies not only with the type of ship but also with the class you're traveling in. Dinner clothes are frequently seen among first-class passengers, but they are never mandatory. In second class, more people don't dress than do. In third or tourist class, you hardly ever see anyone in formal wear.

Nobody dresses on any ship the first or last night out, or on a Sunday night.

On one night of the cruise or crossing, on some ships there is an event called the captain's dinner, which is the big "party night." Occasionally this is a masquerade, and the passengers appear in all sorts of impromptu disguises. Masks and various accessories are often made available through the purser or cruise director. If it's not a costume affair, long evening dresses and dinner jackets may appear, in first class especially, although dinner dresses and dark suits will be seen as well.

On any other conveyance, party giving is the last thing on a passenger's mind, and even if it were not, how impractical if not impossible on a plane or in a car to give a party! On a ship, however, parties may be easily arranged and are all but effortless for the host and hostess. You may of course as at any hotel stand treat for drinks at the bar for certain friends, or may entertain at your table in the dining room, with advance notice, of course, to the dining room steward. (At first glance, this may seem to be a dilute form of hospitality, since in actuality your guests are paying for their own meals. But you can always glamorize the occasion with drinks and hors d'oeuvres in your cabin beforehand and by ordering some special wines with dinner.) To give a cabin cocktail party you need only to speak to the dining room steward, who will make all the arrangements. This is a special service on his part and calls for an extra tip, given either that evening or added to his end-of-voyage gratuity. The steward who does the serving (probably your own cabin steward) should also be tipped. The amount depends on the size of the check —not less than 15 per cent and a bit more if the job was very well done or if he must divide his tip with an assistant.

Bon voyage parties, nowadays, may not as a rule be "catered" in this way. Since few ship's bars are open while the ship is in port, you must take aboard your own liquor for the friends who are seeing you off. The cabin steward will provide glasses and ice and soda, nothing more—unless you are traveling first class in one of the big luxury liners, in which case a few hors d'oeuvres could no doubt be arranged with notice a day or so in advance.

On most ships, special attention (in all classes) is given to the needs of children. Sports events are arranged for them daily. On large and medium-sized ships there is nearly always a supervised playroom which operates during certain hours for children under ten. Menus especially designed for the appetites and tastes of children are often available. Ingredients for the most common formulas are on hand, and if you request it well in advance of sailing date, the material for your baby's very own formula will be stocked and made up daily according to your schedule. (The dining room steward will, of course, deserve an extra tip for this service.)

For children, traveling on shipboard is perhaps the most fun of all, and it's not too hard on their parents, because there's lots of fresh air and room to be active, plenty of diversions, and no need for a baby sitter. Naturally, however, well-mannered parents don't allow the children to racket around the decks, to be noisy at meals, or otherwise make a nuisance of themselves.

TIPPING ON SHIPBOARD

With the exceptions already noted in this chapter, tipping is usually taken care of at the end of the voyage. The bar steward may be tipped when you are presented with your total bill for the trip. You never tip any officer—and this includes the purser and the chief steward.

Tips should be given in dollars. For amounts see the tipping chart in the section called "Helpful How-To's."

TIPS ON TIPS IN FOREIGN COUNTRIES

Any uncertainties you may have about tipping are certainly compounded when the problem is translated into unfamiliar currency, especially if mental arithmetic isn't your strongest point. It's impossible to be specific about the "who, when, and how much," because customs and economies vary so widely. Travel books (in up-to-date editions!) and travel agents are good guides to the average in each country. Here are a few special pointers.

In any strange country, as you're familiarizing yourself with the currency, try to fix firmly in your mind the look, the feel, and the name of the coin that most closely approximates the American quarter and plan to have some of these always on hand for tipping porters, taxi drivers, bellhops, and so on. It's very useful also to be familiar with the coin equivalent to our dime.

There are certain people whom we never tip and Europeans always do. For example, in theaters in continental Europe, the British Isles, South and Central America, the usher (more often the usherette) who guides you to your seat expects a tip—whatever would be ten or fifteen cents in our money. In Britain you buy your programs; in France and some other countries, you are given the programs but are expected to pass on a small tip in return.

Whenever you're in doubt about tipping procedures abroad, you can always ask the concierge (known in Britain as the hall porter) —that ultracompetent soul who stands *in loco parentis*, as it were, to the guests of European hotels. He is the man with a world of know-how in every field, from getting theater tickets on short notice to suggesting a good hairdresser, and all but the very small hotels has one of these paragons on duty day and night. He will usually be quite willing to tell you what is expected in the way of tips. In many countries, especially when the service has been excellent, you may want to give just a little more than he says—not because you're a tip-flinging American, but because you're a shareholder in one of the most prosperous of the world's economies. Don't forget the concierge himself. (And his relief man if he has aided you.) He should get somewhere between two and five dollars a week, depending on the grandeur of the establishment and the number of times you have needed his assistance.

In many countries there is a service charge added to hotel and restaurant bills, but this by itself is not as a rule enough to cover the diner's liability. You are expected to round the figure off by a little, at least, and if the place is elegant and the service very good, you may do this by 5 per cent, sometimes more.

Don't overlook your special guides. When you're taken through a church or museum or castle by someone other than your regular tour guide, he should get about twenty-five cents from each member of a group, fifty cents from the lone visitor. And he may deserve more if he took pains to make his talk interesting, was well-informed and receptive to your questions, and in general acted the gracious host. A guide whom you have engaged for a whole or half-day should get a quarter of his fee, perhaps—at least a dollar or two dollars. The tour guide who's with you every day should be remembered at the trip's end, too, with how much depends on so many factors that you'd best ask your travel agent directly. The members of such a tour often pool their tips to the guides.

The tipping of house servants, if you spend the night in someone's home, is a custom infallibly observed abroad. Many European hostesses complain that Americans sometimes overlook this, and so unwittingly add to the domestic labor difficulties which are now pronounced almost everywhere. When in doubt as to how much to leave, ask your hostess outright—she knows and she'll probably be glad to suggest an amount which will keep her maid-of-all-work contented *and* unspoiled.

A FEW POINTERS ABOUT "WHEN IN ROME . . ."

Not just in Rome, of course! These are some pointers about attitudes and customs in various countries that may be unfamiliar to you.

In Latin America as well as on the Continent, manners in general are far less casual than our own. For example, you always shake hands on being introduced, and more than that, you shake hands at every greeting and every parting. Men are punctilious about rising whenever a woman is on her feet, lighting cigarettes, and other small courtesies. Women, too, very often rise when they are introduced to other women.

In the United States, we're accustomed to first names on short acquaintance; this is not so in most other countries. Even though you've met the Powells a number of times and seem to have much in common, best keep on addressing them as "Mr." and "Mrs."— no Grace and Basil unless *they* suggest it.

Another thing to remember is that the dinner hour in all Latin American countries, and in many of the great European capitals, as well as throughout Spain, Italy, and other countries of southern Europe, is far later than the average American dinnertime. In Spain and Mexico, for example, people often don't sit down to the evening meal until nine or ten. Unless you wish to sit among empty tables, the safest hour for dining in most restaurants abroad is eight—and even that may well be on the early side.

When you're invited to dine at a private home in the Latin American countries and southern Europe, you're not expected to arrive promptly at the hour stated, even though that hour may seem late to you. In the Scandinavian countries, however, you're expected to ring the doorbell at *precisely* the hour set. In Britain, Switzerland, and France you can be five minutes late, but not more than ten. In Britain, by the way, our elastic cocktail hour is quite uncommon —there's time for one brief drink, at most two, and dinner is announced promptly.

The custom of writing a thank-you note to the hostess with whom you have dined is practically obligatory abroad, and much more often one sends flowers. Your bread-and-butter letter, whether or not it's followed up by a gift of flowers, is sent promptly.

If you smoke, your smoking manners abroad may need a little watching. There is far less smoking at the table, and at any formal dinner in Britain no one, man or woman, smokes before the toast to the Queen has been given. When you're in a restaurant and on your own, you may, of course, do as you please; if you're dining with Europeans, especially in a private home, it's best not to light up until you see others do so.

Coffee *after* dinner is the custom in most foreign countries— to have coffee with a meal is considered eccentric.

HOW TO HAVE A GOOD TIME

Here's an opportunity—get ready to make the most of it! The kind of getting ready that makes travel rewarding is not just the tickets, the clothes, and the suitcases. The most valuable investment you can make is a mental and emotional preparation.

Read up on the places you'll see—not just travel guides, but history and travel sketches and personal reminiscences. Anything that stimulates your interest and adds to your knowledge *before* you're on the scene will enrich your visit and strengthen the memories you carry away with you.

Try to learn some of the language, too. Even if your stay is to be short, get a phrase book and try to learn at the very least the words for "please," "thank you," "how do you do," and "excuse me." Learn to count—this will come in very handy for shopping, making change, finding street addresses, and so on. "Where is . . . ?" is a useful phrase, too. (And while you're at it, learn the exact word for toilet, because in many countries when you inquire for the "ladies' room," you'll be shown to a powder room with a wash basin, the toilet being somewhere else, perhaps even in another part of the building.)

Most important of all—sail, fly, drive, walk, or run to your destination with the firm resolve to take things and people as they are, to enjoy what you can and ignore what you can't. The good and the happy tourist not only shuns arrogance, loudness, and the giddy sports shirt, but also is not handicapped by the notion that in every aspect of living the American is the best if not the only way. He remembers, too, that courtesy will stand him in good stead where-ever he goes.

So leave your prejudices (if you have any) at home, but don't forget to carry along your manners. Pack your lightest heart—and have a wonderful trip!

OCCASIONS OF CEREMONY

30

The Debut

MAKING ONE'S DEBUT IS A CUSTOM FAR LESS GENERALLY OBSERVED than it used to be. In the past, young girls were completely sheltered until they put up their hair and came out of the schoolroom to be "presented" to their parents' friends and to marriageable young men. Ours is an age in which most eighteen-year-olds have for a year or more been squired by various young men to dances, dinners, college proms and even night clubs; so a debut has lost much of its original purpose and is often passed over altogether, particularly by girls who are in a hurry to complete a college education and go on to a career. It is included among our ceremonies, however, because it *is* a ceremonial and as such should have an aura of dignity and formality, whether it is a small affair at home or a dance given at a hotel.

Today's debutante rarely marks her "coming out" with an elaborate ball complete with name bands, marquee, favors, supper, and breakfast, although of course she and her family may properly do this. More and more, however, parents even of wealth and social prominence elect to present their daughter at a dinner party given before a mass debut, or on the evening of a club dance, at a small private dance, or at an afternoon reception.

THE MASS DEBUT

This term simply means that at some large affair, such as a charity subscription dance, a number of young girls are presented together. The father of each girl makes a generous contribution to the charity, often in addition to the purchase of the tickets for his wife and himself, his daughter, and the dinner guests. The parents give a dinner for the debutante before the affair, at home or at the club or hotel where the ball is being held. Many cities have their annual cotillions or assemblies, a number of which are very famous, very old and exclusive. Other cities and smaller communities have within the past few years founded their own cotillions or assemblies for the specific purpose of providing a setting in which twenty, thirty, or a hundred girls may have their presentation at a cost which, since the parents pool the expenses, is quite moderate compared to that of a large private ball. Of course, dinner parties beforehand are the custom.

At the dinners the guests are mainly the debutante's contemporaries, since the ball itself with its receiving line is supposed to provide the opportunity for her to meet the older people. It is, of course, considered essential by the girls that "extra men" be present at the ball in abundance—one extra man for every ten girls is minimal, three is far better.

SMALL PRIVATE DINNERS

Perhaps you, like many American parents today, will prefer to present your daughter at a dinner before one of the regular dances which your country club or a similar group gives from time to time. You may give such a dinner party at home, at the club where the dance is to be, or at a restaurant. The guests are the debutante's friends, plus one or two couples who are close friends of the parents —and, of course, those extra men to fill out the stag line! Often the older people sit at a small nearby table while the young people have a big table of their own.

THE SMALL PRIVATE DANCE

You may like the idea of a small dance in your own home or at the country club (or a hotel) as an occasion for launching your daughter. Your guests will be your daughter's friends—not forgetting the extra young men—and also an assortment of *your* friends—not too many, for this is after all the debutante's party, but enough to indicate that she *is* being presented to society. You needn't give a dinner beforehand, but of course you may if you want to.

RECEPTIONS AND TEA DANCES

These are, of course, late afternoon affairs, held at home or in a hotel. Most of the guests are friends of the debutante, though some of the parents' generation will be invited, too. Among very conservative people a reception may be just that—a quiet affair with a receiving line and without dancing (unless the young people put on records at the party's end). You would serve a formal tea, or perhaps punch with tea sandwiches and cookies. The guest list would include many of your friends as well as friends of the debutante.

Needless to say, everybody at a "tea dance" would be quite surprised if tea were served! Nearly always it's cocktails (though it's thoughtful to provide something nonalcoholic as well, for the teetotaler guests), and sometimes champagne is the drink of the afternoon. Hors d'oeuvres are served, too. The music can be provided by a small dance group, or by records if the party is at home (see "Dances," page 132). If the party is at a hotel, the music must, of course, be live.

THE INVITATIONS

You may write personal notes for small affairs; large ones usually require engraved or partially engraved invitations. (See "Invitations to a Debut," page 275).

THE RECEIVING LINE

At mass debuts, the manner of handling the receiving line and other conventions is usually decided by a committee. At private affairs, the debutante and her mother (or whatever woman relative is sponsoring her, should she be motherless) stand just inside the entrance to the room where the party is being given, the older woman closer to the door. Officially, the father stands on the other side of his daughter—usually he chooses to "hover" rather than adhere to a mental chalkmark. Naturally, the guests pass through the receiving line before they join friends inside. A smile, a handshake, and "So happy to be here" is enough, but it's never amiss to compliment the parents on their daughter's charm and to tell the girl how pretty she looks.

Often the debutante asks a few of her closest girl friends to "receive" with her. Beyond the honor and compliment of being asked, it doesn't mean a thing—all they're supposed to do is look charming, be polite, and have a good time. They don't stand in the receiving line. Occasionally a few young men friends are invited to be ushers, but they won't be called upon for any special duties.

The debutante sometimes sends corsages, matching her own, to the girls whom she has asked to receive with her.

THE DEBUTANTE'S FLOWERS

The debutante's own flowers usually consist of a bouquet, though sometimes she wears a corsage or, particularly if she's to be dancing, she may prefer a wrist bouquet. The flowers she wears or carries are sent her by her father. The other flowers, which she receives from friends of the family and from young men friends, are arranged near or behind her as she stands in the receiving line.

Not every young man who's invited to a debut need send flowers, but if he is a close friend of the family, he really should. Women and girls don't, of course, have to send flowers to the debutante.

THE DEBUTANTE'S DINNER TABLE

At her party, the debutante is the guest of honor. It is her privilege to choose which of her guests will be her dinner partner, and he will be seated at her right. If the party is large and there are a number of tables, hers will be the most prominent and at a club or hotel it should have a "reserved" sign on it.

DANCING CONVENTIONS

The dance music may begin while the debutante is still receiving and whatever guests have been through the line may start dancing whenever they want. When the debutante is finally free, she usually dances first with her father; after that, the rush is on! For, of course, every young man who's been invited should ask her for dances and cut in on her. The very politest ones also remember to dance at least once with her mother.

WHAT TO WEAR

Traditionally the debutante appears in white, and many still do; many others wear pastels. Black, red, or any color that smacks of sophistication should be bypassed on this occasion. And the dress itself should be pretty, youthful, and gay. For an afternoon party, it would be short; for an evening party, a long one, full-skirted to look beautiful when she's dancing. She never wears a hat at her party, but does wear gloves, which she takes off or tucks in when she's eating.

At a mass debut, the committee usually has a say about what the girls are to wear.

The girl guests wear dresses of the same degree of formality as that of their hostess, and they too should stick to the pastels rather than more dramatic colors. At an at-home affair, they might not wear gloves even though the debutante does; at a ball they would.

The debutante's mother wears a dressy afternoon dress for a tea or reception, with gloves but no hat. For an evening affair, she chooses a formal evening gown and goes hatless, of course, but with gloves. Her dress, day or evening, should never be black.

Women guests dress for afternoon or evening as they would for any similar affair—with gloves, but without hats.

The debutante's father and the other male guests wear whatever they would ordinarily wear—a dark business suit for a reception or tea dance and evening clothes for an evening affair, dinner jacket or tails according to the invitation.

31

The Engagement

UNLIKE CHARITY, ENGAGEMENTS DON'T BEGIN AT HOME—AT LEAST not in the way that they used to, when the would-be fiancé proposed in the parlor on bended knee *after* he had bearded papa in his lair to paint a rosy picture of his prospects and formally ask for daughter's hand. Today the young people "engage" themselves and then tell the families about it. They do, however, tell their families (usually the girl's parents first) before they tell anybody else. It would be both rude and unkind to do otherwise. And while the girl's father may have a fair idea of his future son-in-law's financial standing, he deserves the courtesy of being told what the plans are for his daughter's support. If father doesn't know and young man doesn't volunteer, then father can hardly be blamed for asking him!

CALLING

The elaborate calling ritual between the two sets of parents is rarely observed any more, but it is customary and expected for the man's parents, especially his mother, to make the first move in acknowledging and welcoming the engagement. If she lives at a distance, she writes an affectionate letter to her future daughter-in-law and perhaps sends her a small gift. (A gift is not in any sense required, but it is often appreciated, particularly if it is some piece of china, jewelry, or silver which has family associations.) When the families live in the same town or within a reasonable distance, they arrange to get together before the engagement is officially announced. Most formally, the man's parents call on the parents of the young girl or ask them to dinner, but this cut-and-dried formula is not always adhered to and need not be. The important thing, after all, is for the two sets of parents to meet, if they haven't already done so, and to join forces in celebrating the happy event.

THE RING

An engagement ring is by no means essential to an engagement, and many young people, especially when the man is just starting to make a living—or perhaps is still in college—prefer to see that money go toward a honeymoon trip or furnishings for the new home. If, however, you do decide to have a ring, there are two things to keep in mind: decide beforehand how much you can afford to spend for it, and make sure that it will harmonize with the wedding

ring that is to be worn with it. If you can't buy both rings at the same time, often you can at least choose (and perhaps put a deposit on, if necessary), the wedding ring which makes a good companion in style and in fit with the engagement ring. As for the price element, many fiancés go beforehand to the jeweler and with budget in mind select three or four rings from which his fiancée may choose. This is perfectly acceptable practice—the only drawback is that when the fiancée has rather positive tastes and possibly a preconceived idea of what she wants, she may not really admire any of the group and, not wanting to hurt her young man's feelings or seem to criticize his taste, must select by a process of elimination the ring which she is to wear day in and day out. Young people today are so practical and clear-sighted, so honest about money matters in general, that there surely can be no objection to his telling her exactly what his limit is. Then both together may go to the jeweler and ask to see rings at that price; if nothing he has really suits them, they can go somewhere else.

If the fiancé is giving his bride-to-be a family ring, it will in all probability need to be reset. She should be consulted about the style of the setting, and here again, the style of the wedding ring should be considered at the same time.

The engagement ring doesn't have to be a diamond solitaire by any means, and especially when the budget is small, it's well to remember that a less expensive stone such as an aquamarine or amethyst, perhaps the bride's own birthstone, can make a more impressive ring than a minute diamond.

Engagement rings are seldom engraved, because there usually isn't room. If the band is wide enough, the ring may be marked with an abbreviated date plus the couple's first initials.

The engagement ring should not be worn in public until the engagement is announced, if it's going to be announced, or until the families have been informed and the couple is ready to let their friends know.

THE ANNOUNCEMENT

This may be in the form of a newspaper announcement, an engagement party, or both. Neither is essential, and many couples, particularly those who are earning their livings in a city away from home, just let the news leak out to their friends and coworkers, although the parents of the bride-to-be may want to insert an announcement in the home-town paper.

If the engagement is to be a long one—more than six months—it is wisest not to make a formal announcement, although the ring may be worn. It is, of course, in the worst of taste either to announce an engagement or wear an engagement ring if either one of the couple should be in the process of getting a divorce, and therefore not legally free to marry.

A local paper usually carries every announcement it receives; the papers in very large cities often restrict their coverage to couples one or the other of whom is prominent either socially or professionally.

It is the girl's family who sends in the announcement. The wording includes, besides their names, those of the engaged couple, the approximate date of the wedding, the schools that both went to, a mention of the girl's debut if she had one, and the man's profession or position. A typical announcement would read like this:

Mr. and Mrs. Aldon Jenkins, of Westbury, Long Island, announce the engagement of their daughter Susan Coleridge, to Mr. James Weldon, the son of Mr. and Mrs. Richard Weldon of Haverton, Pennsylvania. Miss Jenkins was graduated from the Shipley School in Bryn Mawr and is attending Bennington College. Mr. Weldon, who is an alumnus of Harvard College, is now associated with the Bankers Trust Company. The wedding will take place in June.

When one parent is dead, announcement is, of course, made in the name of the living parent, with a sentence to identify the one who has died:

Mr. Aldon Jenkins, of Westbury, Long Island, announces the engagement of his daughter. . . . Miss Jenkins' late mother was the former Althea Coleridge. . . .

When both parents are dead, the announcement may be issued in the name of the fiancée's grandparents, brother or sister, other relative, or guardian. Such an announcement would begin: "Mrs. Grady Holmes announces the engagement of her niece, Miss Susan Coleridge Jenkins," and would conclude with a sentence to further identify the niece: "Miss Jenkins is the daughter of the late Mr. and Mrs. Aldon Jenkins of Westbury, Long Island."

When the parents are divorced, it is the mother who makes the announcement, but always some mention of the father is included:

Announcement is made of the engagement of Miss Susan Jenkins, daughter of Mrs. Coleridge Jenkins of Westbury, Long Island, and of Mr. Aldon Jenkins of New York City, to. . . .

Or the announcement may read like this:

Mrs. Coleridge Jenkins of Westbury, Long Island, announces the engagement of her daughter, Susan Coleridge, to. . . .

Miss Jenkins is also the daughter of Mr. Aldon Jenkins of New York City.

A street address is given only when the family lives in the same town in which the paper is published.

The engagement of older widows or of divorced people is not as a rule given to the newspapers. The engagement of a young widow, however, usually is, and the announcement would be written like this:

Mr. and Mrs. Aldon Jenkins of Westbury, Long Island, announce the engagement of their daughter, Mrs. Ernest Walker, to. . . .

Mrs. Walker, the widow of the late Ernest Walker, was before her marriage Miss Susan Coleridge Jenkins. . . .

It is never correct to announce an engagement by means of an engraved or a printed card. Informal notes or letters to friends and family from the bride-to-be and/or her parents are an entirely different matter.

A picture of the bride-to-be may be sent to the paper along with the announcement, which the paper may or may not use depending on the space available. (Pictures of prospective grooms are almost never used.)

When you do send pictures to a newspaper, it helps to be professional about it. Don't send cabinet photographs, which reproduce badly, but instead glossy prints (8 by 10 inches is a good size) which the photographer will be able to supply if you ask at the time the picture is taken. Identify the picture plainly on a separate typed sheet the same size ("Miss Susan Coleridge Jenkins, whose engagement to James Weldon has been announced"), and enclose the picture, this identification, and the typed copy for the announcement itself, together with a sheet of cardboard to keep the photograph from being bent, in an envelope and mail it to the paper. It's a wise precaution to pencil "Miss Susan Coleridge Jenkins" *lightly* on the back of the picture lest it get separated from its caption. And don't ask for the picture to be returned!

THE ENGAGEMENT PARTY

The combination celebrating-and-announcing engagement party is given just before the newspaper announcement appears or on the same day. If there is to be no printed announcement, it should be given as soon as possible after the engagement has been made and the ring bought. ("As soon as possible" doesn't in this case betoken a rule of formal etiquette as much as the couple's impatience to let everybody know!) Such a party may be given at home or in a restaurant. The guests include relatives and close friends of the couple. It may be a reception or a dinner, or perhaps a small tea dance. Rarely is the party a big one and rarely is it extremely elaborate, partly as a matter of taste and partly because most brides-to-be prefer to save up the real partying for the wedding.

Often the "news" isn't actually news to many of the party guests, but all the same, some sort of announcement (beyond the girl's first public appearance wearing her engagement ring) is made. Sometimes the man stands in the receiving line with his fiancée and her parents, which pretty well tells the story. Sometimes the girl's father proposes a toast: "I'm very happy to announce that today Susan and Jim are engaged to be married, and I ask you to join me in a toast to them both. To many years of happiness!"

WHEN AN ENGAGEMENT IS BROKEN

A broken engagement is a sad state of affairs indeed, but far better a broken engagement now than a bitter divorce later!

When a couple does decide they must break with each other, it's wisest to proceed slowly, with dignity and circumspection. Slowly, because not all lovers' quarrels are irreconcilable—if you do make up, how embarrassing if you've spread it around that all was over between you! If, however, the engagement is definitely terminated, the girl should return the man's ring—legally she doesn't have to, but she'll look more than a little grasping if she doesn't! (When the engagement has come to an end because of the man's death, she may keep the ring, though she will not wear it on her engagement finger. But if it was a family ring her fiancé gave her, she should at least offer to return it to them.)

It's wisest not to go into *any* discussion of the whys and wherefores of the split; certainly no recriminations should be loosed for gossips to spread. To close friends and to relatives the couple simply says (or incorporates in letters), as casually as possible, some such phrase as, "I'm sorry to have to tell you that Jim and I (or Susan and I) have broken our engagement."

It is not absolutely necessary, either, to send an announcement of the breach to the newspapers, although it is often done, especially in a community which is small enough for the paper to have carried a lengthy engagement announcement, but large enough so that word-of-mouth may not reach everyone who read it and awaits the wedding with avid interest. If it is sent, the announcement should be brief and factual: "Mr. and Mrs. Aldon Jenkins announce that the engagement of their daughter, Miss Susan Coleridge Jenkins, to Mr. James Weldon has been broken by mutual consent." (Some people feel that just "Susan," rather than the formal full name, is preferable because it seems to emphasize the changed nature of the announcement and of their daughter's status. (See page 355 for the return of gifts.)

HOW TO BE ENGAGED

No, not how to *get* engaged, but how to act when engaged! Although engaged couples have somewhat more latitude than those who are still playing the field, as it were, you should both remember to conduct yourselves with dignity and to remember some of the rules that still apply. Neither of you should go out on dates with other people. (Not as a rule, that is—if Jim is out of town and young married friends ask you to go out with them and the wife's brother, that's one thing. To let the brother "date" you several times is another.) Nor should you go on overnight trips unchaperoned. And while the whole world loves a lover and would be disappointed if the two of you weren't in a perpetual glow, keep it on the light side. You make people uncomfortable when in acts or words you get *too* glowing, or too mushy, in public. So save your tenderer endearments and your prolonged kisses for the times when you're alone.

32

Planning for the Wedding

EVEN THE SIMPLEST WEDDING TAKES *some* PLANNING, AND A LARGE church wedding followed by a reception takes a great deal, plus plenty of time to execute the myriad details. So the first step is for the bride and groom, together with the bride's family, to decide on just what kind of wedding it's going to be.

(The word "wedding" as used in this book means a ceremony with invited guests—whether few or many—held in a place of worship, at home or in a hotel, with the ceremony performed by a clergyman. And "church" is intended to mean the place of worship of any faith.)

No wedding *need* be elaborate or expensive. The ceremony which a clergyman performs in the bride's home before half a dozen relatives and close friends, with punch and cake served afterward is just as beautiful as the most formal of church weddings. And such a ceremony doesn't necessarily indicate that economy is the main motivation. It may be—and many a considerate daughter has chosen it for that reason. Just as often or oftener, the couple *prefers* a simple ceremony to the many pressures of a large wedding. It's to be hoped that if for this or any other reason a small wedding in church (or at home) is the heart's desire of bride and groom, their elders won't for their own gratification bring pressure to bear for "a big wedding."

Traditionally it is the bride's privilege to choose the where, when, and how of her wedding. The practical engaged couples of today, however, usually do this together. For the broad planning, you must decide whether the wedding is to be large or small, formal or informal, where it is to be held, what kind of reception there's to be

341

if any, and an approximate date. The larger and more formal the wedding, the more time must be allowed for all the arrangements.

Formal daytime weddings are full-dress affairs, usually in a church. Semiformal weddings may be held in church, too, or at home, hotel, or club; what makes them "semiformal" is that while the feminine members of the wedding party can wear the traditional gowns and headdresses and carry bouquets, the men may be dressed less formally. The informal wedding, whether it's at home or in church, is just what its name implies—small and simple, yet warm.

TALKING WITH THE CLERGYMAN

As soon as a tentative date is set, the couple goes to see the clergyman to secure religious sanction for the marriage as well as to consult with him on details of the wedding. When both bride and groom attend the same place of worship and are known to the clergyman, his approval is almost always a foregone conclusion. When, however, the two are of different faiths or when one of them has been divorced, there may be certain conditions to be met by the parties. The clergyman will explain what these are and if he can, help to work them out.

The clergyman must also be consulted about the date and place of the wedding, for he will be the final authority, for a church wedding, on the regulations about floral decorations, dress, and details of the ceremony which may vary somewhat not only with the religious and local customs, but with the size of the church. He will also be able to tell you what the organist's fee will be and suggest appropriate music. (It ought to be noted here that even though a friend or relative is called on to play your wedding music, the organist should receive his fee just as though he had performed.) Even when the wedding is to be at home, or in a hotel, it is not only courteous but helpful to clear with him details of the procedure, the placing of the altar or canopy, and so on.

Of course you must also get legal sanction for your marriage in the form of a license. The regulations about these vary from state to state, but nearly all states require health certificates, and it's wise to find out the requirements well in advance of the wedding.

After the conference—or conferences—with your clergyman, you will have the date firmly fixed and you'll be in a position to judge whether your ideas for the place, the degree of formality, the number of attendants and guests, are workable. It remains now to decide on the size and kind of reception you'd like—many other details, as we shall see, must also be attended to in the early days, but because invitations must go out and caterers if necessary must be engaged, wedding and reception are at least roughly planned in tandem from the beginning.

THE BRIDAL CONSULTANT

In many communities there are bridal consultants (sometimes called "wedding counselors") who will for a fee take over *all* of the details of both wedding and reception. These can be of great help in the initial planning and in helping you reconcile your ideas with your budget. With very little work on your part, the counselor will organize and supervise all the rest, from mailing out the invitations to arranging for picture appointments, transportation, shoe dyeing, and rose petals. At the reception, too, you and your mother and father can relax. Everything will be efficiently and unobtrusively taken care of at the right moment.

For a large wedding, such a service may run to two or three hundred dollars—less, of course, for a more modest affair. If you can afford it, it's well worth the cost for the peace of mind of you and your family. Naturally this is true only if the people you engage are competent and experienced. It is also important that their taste correspond to your own. Therefore, unless the service has been recommended by friends of yours who have used it, ask for references and investigate carefully.

Where wedding counselors are not available, many shops have bridal services which are glad to help out in *some* of the chores. Stores which sell bridal gowns and bridesmaids' dresses are happy not only to assemble these and trousseau items for you and to get shoes dyed and so on, but also to dispatch an authority to the house on the wedding day. This kind of help is given without charge, but the family usually plans on a small gift or a suitable gratuity.

THE RECEPTION

A reception can be large or small, simple or elaborate, at a hotel or restaurant, in the church or temple if practicable, or at home. The food and drinks may be catered or homemade, and formally or informally served, depending on the size of the party and the degree of formality of the occasion. If a restaurant or hotel is to be the scene, you must make a reservation early, and the same is true if you're having it catered at home. (If your house is too small for the number of people you want to invite, it's perfectly proper for you to use that of a relative or friend.)

Morning weddings are usually followed by what's called "breakfast," which is more like a luncheon. Afternoon weddings proceed to a tea or cocktails or both, or possibly a buffet supper, and evening weddings may be followed by a supper. None of these need be elaborate affairs unless you want them to be. The wedding cake and punch or some drink other than coffee or tea with which to toast the bride are the only essential ingredients of wedding party fare. In fact there's no must about having a reception at all, unless you're having a home wedding, in which case all the guests present at the ceremony must be offered some collation, however simple. And there's no rule about the number of guests you ask to a reception. You may decide to ask just a few friends to the house, and "receive" the other guests informally in the vestibule of the church immediately after the ceremony. You may invite everyone whom you invite to the wedding, or just some of them. Or you can elect to have a small wedding and a bigger reception.

If the reception is to take place in a hotel or restaurant, the manager can be of help in arranging for floral decorations, music, seating, and many other details. You should consult him early. But do be careful in selecting the establishment. In some places, managers try to run off so many affairs in a single day that the assembly-line handling is likely to ruin the atmosphere of warm hospitality you're looking for. Some managers, too, if the planning is left entirely up to them, will turn the reception into an "entertainment," with a master of ceremonies introducing you and your bridegroom to the assembled guests (when you've probably never set eyes on him before!), a plethora of fanfares from the orchestra, and perhaps even an "act" or two.

Your reception *is* an occasion for gaiety and rejoicing, but you'll want it to be memorable for dignity too, in keeping with the beautiful and moving wedding ceremony in which you participated. Check to be sure you're getting the type of reception you've dreamed about. The hotel or restaurant stands today in place of your home, and you'll want the reception to run along the same lines as it would if you could have it at home—a receiving line to greet and welcome the guests, drinks ready for them on arrival, courteous service with no overtones of haste.

Select an establishment that you know or that has been strongly recommended to you by someone whose opinion you trust. Most places have a variety of plans and prices, which govern not only the menu, but also the amount of service, the amount *and* the quality of the liquor, the length of the interval between drinks and dining, and the number of rooms used. Make sure exactly what you're getting for what you're paying. Cut down the guest list rather than compromise on quality. And if the suggested party plan includes features that don't fit in with your ideas of what is in good taste, be firm about omitting them. For more details about receptions, see Chapter 35.

THE INVITATION LIST

Next in order of planning is what comes to be known (a prime topic in pre-wedding households) as "The List." You've already decided about how many people are to be invited for the ceremony and how many for the reception. If you want engraved invitations, your family and the groom's must get down to brass tacks right away and find out what quantity of invitations and reception cards are to be ordered, for they should be mailed three to four weeks before the wedding day and it may take six weeks for the engraving. And the hand-addressing takes time too, don't forget! If you can, allow three months for Operation Invitation.

Engraved invitations would be suitable for any large or middle-sized wedding. For a very small, informal wedding, you would use handwritten notes, telegrams, or telephone calls to go out ten days or two weeks ahead of time. (See Chapter 33 for details, not only about invitations and reception cards, but also announcements, which you may wish to send after the wedding, especially if it's a small one.)

The guests for a very small wedding would consist, of course, of close relatives and the very closest friends of the bride and groom. When anything larger is contemplated, however, the list always tends to swell like rice in too small a pot! The most practical plan is for the bride and groom and both the mothers to make up a tentative list and for the bride to combine these into a single list, which is then broken down into those who are to receive invitations for both wedding and reception, the wedding only guests and those, if any, who are to get announcements. Technically bride's and groom's family share the guest list equally, but very often—as when, for example, the groom comes from a distant city the bride's guests will be in the majority. In such a case, friends and relatives of the groom who are not likely to come to the wedding may be sent invitations without reception cards.

THE TROUSSEAU

The trousseau used to be considered incomplete unless it consisted of a whole year's wardrobe and a great chest full of linens. Today's bride considers the limitations of space and the fleetingness of fashion and prefers not to be quite so stocked up. Nevertheless the selecting and fitting of her wedding dress, her going-away costume, and even a small wardrobe of clothes and underthings all take time which must be allowed for in the wedding planning. (The groom, too, remembers to be sure not only of his wedding and going-away outfits but also of any necessary wardrobe fill-ins like new shirts and underwear.)

THE ATTENDANTS

Another thing which should get under way as soon as the wedding plans have taken shape is selecting and inviting the various attendants. For a simple at-home wedding, or a ceremony in a tiny church, you may prefer just to have a maid or matron of honor. For a very large formal wedding, you can have *both* maid and matron of honor, and eight to ten bridesmaids—plus junior bridesmaids, flower girls, pages, train bearers, and a ring bearer, if you like! For the average wedding, though, even a formal one, a maid (or matron) of honor and two to six bridesmaids is customary. A bride usually asks her sister or her closest friend to be her maid or matron of honor, and other young relatives or close friends to be bridesmaids. (It's nice to ask the groom's sister, if he has one, to be a bridesmaid, too.)

For best man, the groom usually selects a brother or a best friend, or sometimes his father or a brother of the bride. It doesn't matter whether the best man is married or single, but it does matter whether he's stable or flighty, for short of the bride herself, to the groom he's the most important member of the wedding party, as we shall see.

It should be borne in mind that except for the flowers they carry, the bride's attendants pay for their own outfits, including shoes and accessories, and so you would be kinder not to ask anyone on whom this would place a financial burden. (Ushers can after all rent their outfits, and at large formal weddings may be given their ties and gloves by the groom, so it doesn't mean much outlay for them.)

WHAT THE ATTENDANTS DO

The maid or matron of honor has more responsibility than the bridesmaids. In common with them, she is fitted for and pays for the outfit you've selected and goes to all the parties given for you immediately before the wedding, but more than that, she should be a sort of extra helper to you and your family. She addresses invitations and announcements, helps with last-minute errands and phone calls, and is a sort of wardrobe mistress to the bridesmaids if necessary. She often gives a prewedding party for the bride—sometimes on her own, sometimes with the bridesmaids. She gives a handsome present to the bride. At the wedding she precedes the bride and her father to the altar, arranges the bride's train if necessary, and holds the bridal bouquet during part of the ceremony. At the reception she stands in the receiving line, and at the bridal table, if there is one, is seated at the groom's left. Afterwards she helps the bride with her going-away outfit and last-minute packing.

The bridesmaids are more decorative than functional, but they *are* responsible for being dressed and ready well ahead of time on the day of the ceremony. They should be sure to attend rehearsals (and to be prompt!) so that they know exactly where they move and stand at the wedding itself. They, too, give nice presents to the bride.

A junior bridesmaid is a seven- to fourteen-year-old girl, usually a relative, whom the bride specially wants to be in the wedding party. At a very formal wedding there may be more than one. They do what the bridesmaids do, though probably they would not be included in the evening parties.

When the family—or families—are large and the wedding quite elaborate, the small fry younger than seven may be pressed into service as flower girls, pages, and train bearers or ring bearer. The little flower girls carry baskets full of flowers. The pages are little boys, who just walk along in the procession. The train bearers—usually two—hold the bride's train, and the ring bearer, littlest of all, carries the ring on a small white pillow. (Naturally, the precious ring had better be inconspicuously anchored to the cushion!)

THE RING

Unless the ring was bought or arranged for at the time an engagement ring was purchased, selecting the wedding ring is another detail that should be attended to in time for it to be engraved. Bride and groom usually go together on this exciting errand. Inside the ring are engraved the initials and the date, groom's initials first: J.W. and E.H. April 15, 19—. When the ring is ready, the bridegroom-to-be picks it up and keeps it for the wedding day.

If there's to be a double-ring ceremony, the couple may select his ring at the same time, though there's not much to the selecting, as the man most usually wears a plain gold band, a little wider than a woman's ring would be. His ring is similarly engraved. The bride pays for it and keeps it for the day.

THE GROOM'S ATTENDANTS

It is the best man who takes on the heaviest responsibilities by far. The average groom leans on him for moral support as well. The best man may be the groom's brother or his closest friend. Or he may ask his father, or the brother of the bride. The best man sees to it that the ushers have the right clothes and that they attend rehearsal and are on time for it. He makes sure that they are at the church well ahead of the hour set for the ceremony and that they know what they're to do.

On the day of the wedding he attends the groom some hours ahead of time, to help him dress and pack his bags, to make sure that the marriage license is in his pocket, and to take possession of the wedding ring so that he can quickly hand it over to the groom when it's needed. If he hasn't dressed himself appropriately before coming, he does it now. He also gets from the groom the clergyman's fee in its sealed white envelope and pockets it until time to give it quietly to the clergyman, usually before the ceremony. Thirty minutes before the wedding hour he steers the groom to the appointed place, and stays with him there.

When the ceremony is ended, he accompanies the maid of honor down the aisle, if there's to be a recessional, or he meets the groom outside and helps the couple get into their car. At the reception, though he doesn't stand in the receiving line, he hovers near the groom, and sits at the bride's right at the bridal table. He proposes the first toast to the couple, and, if they wish it, reads aloud the congratulatory telegrams that have come in. When the groom makes his exit to change his clothes, the best man goes too, once again helping him to dress and pack. Then he sees to collecting the couple's luggage and putting it in the car or cab.

The best man, of course, gives the couple a wedding present.

The number of ushers varies with the size of the wedding. If yours is to be a large church wedding, you must have enough of them so that the guests can be seated quite speedily—one usher, say for every fifty people. (It's wise to appoint one of the ushers to be a sort of supervisor, called the head usher.) There need not be the same number of ushers as bridesmaids—very often there are more of the former.

The ushers may include, as well as brothers, cousins, and close friends of the groom, the bride's brothers or the brothers-in-law of either bride or groom.

Like the bridesmaids, the ushers wear the outfits that have been selected, and pay for them whether they are bought or rented, except gloves and tie which the groom provides. They may entertain for the couple as a group or individually. They send wedding presents and attend the rehearsal. They go to all the parties, and they make a special effort to see that all the bridesmaids have a good time.

On the wedding day they make it their business to get to the church an hour early, wearing their boutonnières—and gloves if they're called for. As the guests arrive, each in turn offers his right arm to the woman, asks (unless he already knows) whether she is a friend of the groom or of the bride, escorts her down the aisle, and seats her either on the bride's side to the left of the center aisle, or on the groom's to the right. If several women arrive together and there aren't enough ushers at hand for them all, an usher gives his arm to the oldest (or to the nearest, if there's no *marked* difference) and the other women follow them. With a couple, the man follows the usher who escorts his wife. A man alone just accompanies the usher down the aisle.

If there are pew cards or within-the-ribbon cards, the guests present them and are seated accordingly.

Even though guests may occasionally arrive in clusters and the ushers have their work cut out for them, they're not supposed to run off the seating like a track race, but appear to walk unhurriedly and to exchange a word or two with the guests, even if only to comment on how lovely the weather or to introduce themselves.

When everyone is seated and it is time for the wedding party to make its entrance, the head usher escorts the groom's mother to her place in the front pew on the right, the groom's father following. Then he goes back to escort the bride's mother to her seat in the left-hand front pew. The bride's mother is always the last to be seated.

At the reception the ushers don't stand in the receiving line, but they do sit at the bridal table. They're assiduous about their dancing duties, being sure to dance not only with the bride and all the bridesmaids, but also with the mothers and a guest or two.

WHAT TO WEAR

First of all, naturally, comes the star of the occasion—you, the bride. What you wear depends on how formal your wedding is to be, as well as on your personal preferences and pocketbook.

At a formal daytime wedding (before six o'clock) you will wear a long white, off-white or pastel wedding gown, which may or may not have a train. You may wear a veil, if you like, attached to some sort of headdress such as a cap, tiara, or floral wreath, and gloves to match the gown if it has short sleeves. (Don't forget to have the wedding-ring finger slit along the stitching so you can get the wedding ring on without taking off the glove.) Your slippers will match your dress. For flowers, you'll carry a large white bridal bouquet, or if you prefer, white flowers attached to a white prayer book.

For such a wedding, the maid of honor and the bridesmaids will wear colored gowns with harmonizing hats or floral headdresses. Usually the dress for the maid of honor is of a different color from that of the bridesmaids. Matching slippers, of course. Gloves may be worn with short-sleeved dresses. The flowers usually contrast in color with the dresses or are of a deeper shade of the same color. The idea is for the bridesmaids, as a part of the pageant, to look alike, so one should not wear any jewelry that the others do not, except wedding and engagement rings.

The groom, the best man, the ushers, and the fathers should wear cutaway jackets, striped trousers, and light waistcoats, or Oxford jackets and striped trousers. (Note that the striped trousers don't have to be identical, but should be similar.) With these go black shoes and socks, stiff white shirts, and wing collars with gray silk ascots or four-in-hand ties. Gray gloves, too—the ushers wear these throughout, but the groom and best man either wear none or remove them just before the ceremony. And let's not forget the boutonnières—these are small and always white.

The mothers of the bride and groom will wear very *dressy* dresses —long, ballerina, or street length. If they're décolleté, a wrap or scarf should cover the shoulders at a religious service. Aside from black or white, these dresses can be of almost any color but should not clash with each other or with the bridesmaid's dresses. Gloves (not black) and dressy hats are worn, as well as corsages.

The women guests should wear quite formal street-length dresses, hats and gloves, of course—usually no woman guest wears flowers, except close relatives to whom the groom may have sent corsages.

The men guests dress like the groom's attendants—minus the boutonnière—or may wear dark blue or dark gray business suits with black shoes and socks and conservative ties.

For a formal evening wedding, the bride, her attendants and the mothers dress the same as for the formal daytime wedding just described. The groom, best man, the ushers and the fathers wear white tie and tails, white gloves and boutonnières. Women guests wear long or short dinner dresses with some sort of head covering (with wrap or scarf for the church ceremony), and the men guests may appear in tails or may wear dinner jackets with black ties.

At a semiformal wedding, you will select either a long or ballerina length gown without a train, in white or in color, with a matching headdress but no veil. Your attendants would have dresses no longer (though possibly shorter) than your own, with headdresses, and the men would wear business suits of navy or dark gray (one or the other, not mixed) with white shirts, black shoes and socks, and the white boutonnières. At a summer wedding, the men may wear navy blue jackets and white trousers or white suits. (With white suits the boutonnières are often colored; if so, they should match each other.)

The women guests will dress like the mothers, except that they won't wear corsages, and the men guests will wear business suits in dark blue or gray with white shirts. In summer, like the ushers, they may wear white trousers with navy jackets or white suits.

FLOWERS

It's a good idea to consult your florist fairly early, especially if your wedding is to be formal. You must decide whether you want decorations of greens or flowers or both for the place where the ceremony is to be. You'll also want to decide on your own bouquet and the bridesmaids' flowers, as well as the boutonnières for the male attendants, and on the corsage for your going-away outfit. Then, too, the corsages for the two mothers must be included. Don't forget, after you've talked to the florist and know what the charges will be, to tell your bridegroom how much his share will come to. He's always responsible for the going-away corsage, usually for your wedding bouquet, and often for the mothers' corsages.

THE WEDDING CAKE

Conventions about the wedding cake are few, but the cake is important and you should plan now whether it's to be homemade or catered, how simple or elaborate it's going to be. The inside can be white or yellow, can be sponge or pound cake, or if you feel splurgy, let it be the time-hallowed fruitcake. Whatever the inside, the outside's always white, of course, and often very elaborately decorated, with flutings and sugar flowers, or, especially on the top of a tiered cake, a wedding bell or a miniature bride and groom. (There's never any inscription on the cake, though.) Having cake in boxes for the wedding guests to take home is a charming custom but so expensive nowadays that it's seldom done except at elaborate weddings. If it is done, however, the cake is usually fruitcake, and the whole scheme must be planned with the caterer well ahead of time.

FAVORS AND MONEY BAGS

At many receptions the wedding guests receive gay favors as a memento of the occasion, and while these are not essential and may sometimes be omitted when there are wedding cake boxes to be taken home, it's a pleasant and festive custom. Almost always the guest tables boast at each place a match pack in white or a pastel color with the names of the bride and groom (often the date also) printed in silver or gold. Sometimes there are instead, or in addition, personalized paper cocktail napkins or drink stirrers. And at some receptions each guest receives a traditional favor of white Jordan almonds in a white net bag which is tied to a small souvenir such as an ashtray or a glass slipper.

Another derivation of a folk custom adhered to in many communities is a money bag—a drawstring purse, harmonizing with the bridal gown, which the bride carries in the receiving line. In it she puts the gifts of checks or cash which the wedding guests have brought to the reception. Some guests will have sent a gift or a check to the bride *before* the wedding day—if so, there's no need for them to feel embarrassed. On the other hand, if you know that this is the custom in the bride's circle and you wish to make a money gift, bring your check with you. (You would naturally not *take* a gift other than money to the reception.)

A time-honored custom still occasionally observed is for the traditional candied nut and ashtray favors to be arranged on a table beside the bride so she can hand one to each guest in the receiving line. Do this if the tradition is important to you and your family.

TRANSPORTATION

Another important part of the wedding plans is to arrange for cars to get the bridal party to and from the place where the ceremony is to take place. The groom, the best man, and the ushers get there on their own, but cars and drivers must be provided for the bride, her father and mother, the maid of honor and the bridesmaids, as well as any relatives or other guests staying at the bride's home. For the wedding party proper at a formal wedding, cars and drivers are usually hired; less formally, or to help out with the overflow, some of the bride's male relatives may be called upon.

In leaving the house, the usual order is for the first car to take the bride's mother with the maid of honor and one or two of the bridesmaids. The other bridesmaids follow them. Last to leave are the bride and her father. The bride's car stays in front of the church during the ceremony, ready for the newly wedded couple when they come out.

THE WEDDING PICTURES

Most brides have their bridal photographs taken at a studio a few days before the wedding, since this involves far less rush and confusion than trying to get it done at home just before the ceremony.

If you want a series of candid camera shots of the great day, be sure to engage the photographer very, very early; for shots inside the church, make sure you have the clergyman's permission.

WEDDING GIFTS

The groom doesn't have to but usually does give his bride a present, usually jewelry. Sometimes the bride gives the groom a gift. Both bride and groom give presents to their attendants. And the families usually give something rather special when they can afford to—a check, furniture, silver, even the wedding trip.

Very soon after the invitations go out, the wedding gifts will stream in from friends and relations, and part of your wedding plans should include a system of recording these so that you can acknowledge them without confusion. The safest thing is to write down in a special notebook the giver, the giver's address and an identifying description of each gift *as you open it*. The thank-yous must of course be by handwritten letter (see Chapter 23) and you'll eventually be very thankful if you write one or two each day rather then letting them accumulate.

You may display your gifts or not as you like. For obvious reasons, it's inconvenient to do so when the reception is not held in your home. (You could, if you liked, however, give a tea a few days before the wedding and display your gifts at that time.) At home you may set up tables, cover them with white cloths, and arrange the gifts on them the way they look best. While there's no rule against including the cards of the donors, it's in better taste not to, and many people think the same is true of displaying checks. (Checks can be recorded on cards which are propped up for display and read

"Check" or "Check $25." If you display the checks themselves, put them under glass with a strip of paper hiding the amount of the check but revealing the donor's name.)

The question of exchanging gifts is a delicate one. The main consideration, of course, is not to hurt the giver's feelings. Now and then you may exchange a gift without the donor's being any the wiser, if he lives at a distance or if the gift is something that would

not be on display if he did visit you. Or a close and understanding friend whose gift was something which is duplicated many times— it seems brides get either six salad bowls or none!—*probably* would not feel huffy if you explained the situation and asked if it could be exchanged for something you really need. One never knows, however—all you can be certain of is that in keeping the present you keep the friend.

When a gift arrives in a damaged condition, it's best to deal with it quietly on your own by taking it back to the store where it came from and explaining the situation. (In the case of an out-of-town store, write first, describing the gift and the damage, and await their instructions.) If the gift was packed and mailed by the donor *and was insured,* you may write and explain what happened. He'll undoubtedly ask you to mail it back—enclosing the original wrappings —and will replace it. If it wasn't insured, though, there's really nothing to do (except possibly in the case of an old friend to whom one tells all!) but to write your thank-you note just as if the gift had arrived intact.

Should your engagement unhappily be broken after wedding gifts have been received, the presents must go back, even if they're monogrammed. You or your mother should write brief notes thanking the givers for their kindness in sending such a lovely present. No explanation of the rupture is necessary—the simple statement that the marriage will not take place is sufficient.

THE REHEARSAL

This is held a few days before the ceremony, at the clergyman's convenience. For all but the smallest weddings it is essential and for even a small home wedding it will be helpful. All the attendants should be on hand, including the father of the bride, and of course the bride and groom. (The bride used to have a stand-in play her part; today's brides usually rehearse in person.) For a church wedding, the organist should also be there.

You will find the clergyman the greatest of help in explaining how things should go. His suggestions and rulings should be followed to the letter. He will decide whether the bride takes her father's left arm or his right, he will explain the tempo of the march and how far apart the groups should be, he and the organist will work with the wedding party so that the music brings bride and groom to the chancel precisely when the music ends. He'll know how and when the canvas should be unrolled, if there's to be one, and how the ribbons, if any, should be handled. Because he's of course familiar not only with the ceremony but with the limitations of the church building, he knows just where everyone should stand during the ceremony, and just when each person plays his part.

The order and form of the recessional is usually the bride's choice (see Chapter 34) but the arrangement should be decided on, and practiced, at rehearsal time.

WHO PAYS FOR WHAT

Small or large, the expenses of the wedding are divided in a time-honored way.

The bride's family pays for the invitations, the envelopes, the reception cards, pew cards, and announcements. They also pay for the rental, if any, of the place where the ceremony is to be held and any incidental expenses such as chairs, flowers, rent of canvas, ribbons, and so on. They pay the fee for the organist and for choir and soloist, if any. They may pay a sexton's fee, and the clergyman will advise them about this. They pay for the transportation of the bridal party from house to church and church to reception. They are responsible also for the bridesmaids' bouquets (*and* for their headdresses if these are made of real flowers), for the bride's gifts to the bridesmaids, and for hotel bills for out-of-town bridesmaids if they can't be accommodated at the house or stay with relatives. Of course, they foot the bill for the wedding dress and trousseau, and naturally for their own wedding finery. They pay for *all* the expenses of the reception. They pay for a bridal consultant if one is hired, for any traffic policemen who may be needed for special duties, and for attendants who park cars at the reception. In addition is their gift to the bride and groom. They may also pay for the bride's bouquet, though more usually it is the gift of the groom.

The groom is accountable for the engagement and wedding rings, the marriage license with attendant fees, and the contribution to the clergyman. For a very large and elaborate wedding the clergyman's gratuity may range from one hundred to two hundred dollars or even more. For a smaller wedding, from forty to fifty dollars is usual, and for a very informal wedding without attendants or with perhaps only one, from ten to twenty-five dollars would be adequate. (When the clergyman is a friend or a relative, it might be preferable to give him a present instead of the money.)

The groom pays for the flowers for the bride's mother, his own mother, and any especially honored relatives such as grandmothers or favorite aunts. He is responsible for the boutonnières for the best man and the ushers, for the gloves and ties at a formal wedding. He buys a gift for the bride, and also gifts for the best man and the ushers. He pays for the bachelor dinner too. If hotel accommodations are needed for ushers coming from out of town, he foots that bill. He pays for the expenses of the honeymoon.

The groom's parents are expected to pay for their own traveling and hotel expenses, for a wedding present to the couple, and for any entertaining they may do for them.

The attendants likewise pay for their own transportation when they come from out of town, as well as for their wedding outfits, any parties they give and their wedding presents to the bride and groom.

Wedding guests pay for their own transportation to and from the church and the reception and their own hotel expenses.

33

Wedding Invitations and Announcements

WEDDING INVITATIONS MAY BE FORMAL OR INFORMAL, OR YOU MAY if you wish dispense with them altogether and invite your friends to your small wedding by telephone or in person. But if you do use invitations, they must adhere quite strictly to certain conventions. The paper must be of good quality, in white, cream, or ivory, and is customarily a double sheet, the front page of which contains the message. The size varies, but the invitation should fit its envelope either without a fold or with only a single fold.

Traditionally, invitations for a formal or large semiformal wedding are always engraved and engraving is certainly preferable for an elaborate wedding. Many brides, however, order invitations with thermograph printing. This looks much like engraving, but is less expensive. There are many lettering styles, about which your jeweler or stationer can advise you. Script is a perennial favorite, but there is a wide choice among less traditional styles too. The engraving or printing should be in black.

Each invitation requires two envelopes—one the outside mailing envelope, the other a protective envelope (which isn't gummed, as it shouldn't be sealed) bearing the name of the person or couple to whom the invitation is going. It's well to order some extra envelopes, for those inevitable slips of the pen.

The printer or engraver also supplies a tissue with each invitation. This protects the message from smudging and should be put into the envelope with the invitation.

As with other formal invitations, the spacing and the wording are governed by certain conventions. All numbers (except very long street addresses) are spelled out. The time is written out. No parts of place names are abbreviated. There is no punctuation at the ends of the lines. Initials are not used—either omit the middle name or spell it in full. The only abbreviations which are permissible are Mr., Mrs., Dr., Jr.

The expression "the honour of your presence" is used on the invitation to a church wedding. It is not used on the reception card. (The English spelling, with a "u," has become a convention.) The reception card, as well as the invitation to a wedding at home, club or hotel, would request "the pleasure of your company."

There is no request for a response on the wedding invitation proper. On the reception card you may use R.S.V.P. (or R.s.v.p.) or, if there's space enough, "The favour of a reply is requested." (Here again, note the "u.") When the address to which an acknowledgment is to be sent differs from the place indicated for the reception, you may put either "Kindly send response to . . . ," or R.s.v.p. followed by the proper address.

ADDRESSING AND FOLDING INVITATIONS

It goes without saying that all the addressing is done by hand, in black or blue-black ink. The inner envelope, which isn't gummed, is addressed to "Mr. and Mrs. John Clarke," without middle initial. (The middle name if used must be spelled out.)

The outside envelope reads:

> Mr. and Mrs. John Clarke
> 24 Westmoreland Drive
> Haversham, Maine

(The indented form of address is preferable in social correspondence.)

It isn't ever correct to use the phrase "and family"—the others should get separate invitations. And when they are children, they should receive an invitation with the outside envelope addressed to "The Misses Clarke" or "The Messrs. Clarke." If the children are both boys and girls, you may write:

> The Misses Clarke
> The Messrs. Clarke

On the inside envelope, put the first names of the children:

> Mary, Ellen and Thomas Clarke

Fold the large, formal, one-fold invitation in half, inserting the protective tissue between. Then fit it into its inner envelope with the folded part foremost and the flap turned toward you but un-sealed. Now slide it into the outside mailing envelope.

The smaller invitation, already folded once, is not folded again, but is inserted (with its tissue) into the inner envelope with the engraving facing the flap.

Reception cards, ceremony cards, pew cards, or at-home cards which may accompany the large invitation are inserted next to the engraving, facing the same way. They are put inside the fold of a smaller invitation.

INVITATIONS TO FORMAL WEDDINGS

Let's suppose first that you're having a good-sized church wedding with a home or club reception to follow that may not include all the wedding guests. Your invitation would read like this:

> Mr. and Mrs. William Gordon Paige
> request the honour of your presence
> at the marriage of their daughter
> Rosemary
> to
> Mr. John Bryant Kerr
> on Saturday, the tenth of June
> at four o'clock
> Christ Church
> Newton, New York

Note that in wedding invitations (though never in announcements) the year may be omitted. If it is used, however, it must be spelled out, in one of two forms: "one thousand nine hundred and sixty-nine" or "nineteen hundred and sixty-nine."

Each guest invited to the reception would also receive, in the same envelope, a reception card. This card is about half the size of the invitation, and should be printed or engraved on matching stock. It would read this way:

> Mr. and Mrs. William Gordon Paige
> request the pleasure of your company
> on Saturday, the tenth of June
> at half after four o'clock
> at
> Newton Country Club

> R.S.V.P.
> 11 Blackberry Lane
> Newton, New York

When the reception is to be at your home, you may want to use a simpler form on a smaller card:

Reception
immediately following the ceremony
11 Blackberry Lane

R.S.V.P.

(Note that if the reception is to be earlier than two o'clock, its customary to say "breakfast" instead of "reception.")

When you are asking *all* the wedding guests to come to the reception, you may if you wish, merge the reception with the wedding invitation like this:

Mr. and Mrs. William Gordon Paige
request the honour of your presence
at the marriage of their daughter
Rosemary
to
Mr. John Bryant Kerr
on Saturday, the tenth of June
at four o'clock
Christ Church
Newton, New York
and afterward at
11 Blackberry Lane

R.S.V.P.

The invitations are similarly combined when you're having your wedding at home or in a club or hotel, for it would be most inhospitable to ask some of the guests, as it were, to go away after the ceremony and others to stay. In such a case, the reception would almost always be at the same place as the wedding, and therefore, the time named would be the hour of the ceremony, which need be followed only by the place—the street address of the home or the name of the hotel or club, plus city and state for the benefit of out-of-town guests. You would, of course, have to note under the R.s.v.p., the address where acknowledgments are to be sent if this differs from the locale of the reception.

If you are planning, for reasons of space perhaps, a very small wedding with a large reception, the invitations change places in importance. The reception invitation would go on the big formal sheet and the wedding invitation proper would go on a small card enclosed with it. The latter would read:

Ceremony
at five o'clock
Christ Church

(Or the bride's mother could just write the above words on her own calling card. Or the few wedding guests could be invited in person or by telephone.)

Here is the wording for the reception invitation itself:

Mr. and Mrs. William Gordon Paige
request the pleasure of your company
at the wedding reception of their daughter
Rosemary
and
Mr. John Bryant Kerr
on Saturday, the tenth of June
at half after five o'clock
11 Blackberry Lane
Newton, New York

R.S.V.P.

The most formal invitations of all, not so much used now as in more leisurely days, are those engraved with a blank line left for the guest's name, which is written in by hand on each invitation. Like this:

Mr. and Mrs. William Gordon Paige
request the honour of

presence at the marriage of their daughter

and so on. When this is done—and it would be only for a very large and very formal wedding—the reception card follows the same style, with the guest's handwritten name following "request the pleasure of."

PEW CARDS AND CHURCH CARDS

It's generally understood, as it should be, that a wedding is a private affair. When, however, one or the other (or both) of the families is prominent and newsworthy, church admission cards enclosed with the invitations help to keep out strangers who might fill up the church and leave invited guests without seats. They should be used only in case of real necessity, and should simply say:

Please present this card
at Christ Church
Saturday, the tenth of June

Again, when a church wedding is a tight fit for the seating and kinfolk abound, the bride and her family may wish to be certain that no tardy Aunt Josie or Cousin Phil will feel slighted by being perforce seated in the rear. In this case pew cards are enclosed with certain invitations, and the guests who have them present them to the ushers when they enter the church. The bride's mother's calling card will suffice, with "Pew 3" written in the lower left-hand corner. Or there may be a special engraved card just like a church admission card except that "Pew Number 3" appears in the lower left-hand corner. For a very large and very formal wedding, a "write-in" pew card may be used—a combination of handwriting and engraving which reads:

will please present this card to an usher
at Christ Church
Pew Number 3

These days, instead of pew cards, a formal wedding may make use of the "within-the-ribbons" convention. It amounts to the same thing, really, except that no pew numbers are provided. Instead the first few pews on either side of the row are marked off by white ribbons, and the family members and certain guests are directed to these when they show the usher a card just like a pew card except that the phrase "Within the Ribbons" takes the place of the expression "Pew Number 3."

AT-HOME CARDS

You may want to include with your invitations (or with your wedding announcements if you send them) cards which tell your friends where your future home is to be and when you'll be there starting your domestic life. These should be engraved, and would read:

At home
after the twenty-fifth of June
44 Clinton Road
Montrose, New York

Although it's considered by most authorities to be an incorrect usage, the enclosure of a "response card" is not uncommon and has its merits. The response card in its stamped, addressed envelope should be inserted next to the engraved side of the invitation, facing the same way, or inside the fold of a smaller invitation. The recipient will fill in—Mr. and Mrs. So-and-so will (or will not) attend—and mail the card back to the sender.

INVITATIONS FOR A SMALL, INFORMAL WEDDING

Because engraved invitations seem over-elaborate, perhaps even pretentious, for an informal wedding, handwritten personal notes are used instead. The bride's' mother writes these, and she uses her best white or cream stationery. The wording is like that of any informal invitation, its tone depending on how well she knows the addressee. To close friends of the family she might write:

Dear Agnes,

Miriam and Herbert [Herbert's last name would be added here if Agnes doesn't know him] are to be married here at the house on Saturday, the tenth of June, at four o'clock—a very small wedding with a reception afterward. You know how much all of us want you and Bob to be with us.

Affectionately,
Marian

The bride's mother, of course, writes at the same time to the relatives and friends of the groom who are on the guest list. If there's been long acquaintance between the two families, her notes would read much like the one above. If, however, the bride and her family are mostly strangers to the groom's group, she would write more fully and a bit more formally:

Dear Mrs. Aitken:

Our daughter Miriam and your nephew Herbert are being married at four o'clock on Saturday the tenth of June. The wedding is to be a small one, at the Pines Country Club here. We do hope you and Mr. Aitken will be able to be with us, and to stay for the reception afterwards. We are looking forward so much to meeting you.

Cordially,
Marian Grimes

Mrs. Paul Grimes
25 Allen Street
Peckham, Pennsylvania

INVITATIONS FOR SPECIAL SITUATIONS

When the bride has only one living parent, the invitations are issued in the name of that parent: Mrs. John Summerfield (never

Mrs. Louise Summerfield) or Mr. John Summerfield. If, however, the bride's mother has remarried, the situation is made clear in the first few lines of the invitation, which would read:

> Mr. and Mrs. Henry Hicks Bolton
> request the honour of your presence
> at the marriage of Mrs. Bolton's daughter
> Anne Summerfield. . . .

Often the bride has lived for some time with her parent and stepparent and she and they feel as if she were truly the daughter of both of them. In that case, the couple send out the invitations in their married name as usual to the marriage of "their" daughter, the only difference being that the daughter's surname will differ from that of the parents.

If the bride's widower father has remarried quite recently, the invitations clarify the situation in this way:

> Mr. and Mrs. Paul Grimes
> request the honour of your presence
> at the marriage of Mr. Grimes's daughter
> Evelyn. . . .

Matters are a little different when the bride's parents are divorced. When the mother has not remarried, the invitation should go out in the name that combines her maiden surname and her divorced husband's last name—Mrs. Thompson Werner. No surname is required for the bride in such an invitation.

Should the mother have remarried, the invitation may, if she likes, go out solely in her new name—Mrs. Harold Green. It seems warmer, however, for Mr. *and* Mrs. Harold Green to invite their friends to the marriage of "her" daughter, Catherine Werner.

If the bride is living with her father rather than with her divorced mother, it is he who issues the invitation.

When the bride has no living parent, invitations are sent in the name of her nearest relative—a grandmother, an aunt, sister or brother, whoever it may be—and the wording of the invitation specifies the relationship, with the bride's last name appearing when it differs from the sponsoring name:

> Mrs. Alexander Masters
> requests the honour of your presence
> at the marriage of her niece
> Christine Armston. . . .

Should the bride have no kinfolk to sponsor her, close friends may do so—Mr. and Mrs. Henry Best requesting the honour of your presence at the marriage of *Miss* Christine Armston. (The "Miss" indicates that there's no blood relationship between her and the Bests.)

SECOND MARRIAGES

As a rule these are quiet and informal affairs. While it's not in the best of taste, it may happen that a very young widow (or *young* divorcée) may plan a formal wedding. In such a case, the invitations would read like any formal wedding invitation, except that the bride's full name, without Miss or Mrs., would be used: Mr. and Mrs. Walter Dixon would invite guests to the marriage of their daughter Mary Dixon Bond.

The quiet wedding of an older widow would call for informal invitations. If engraved invitations *are* used, they would read like this:

The honour of your presence is requested
at the marriage of
Mrs. Henry Hall Jones
to
Mr. Alexander Howard. . . .

An older divorcée remarrying and sending formal invitations follows the form just above, except that her name, of course, would not include her husband's first name, but would combine her surname and his.

When a second marriage is held at a home or a club rather than a church, "The pleasure of your company is requested" is preferable to "The honour of your presence. . . ."

Note that the fact of the groom's having been divorced makes no difference whatsoever in the wording of any invitation.

REPLYING TO WEDDING INVITATIONS

You need not reply to a formal wedding invitation unless it includes an invitation to the reception or a reception card. Then the R.s.v.p., as always, indicates that a reply is expected, or a response card may be enclosed. Usually, however, you get out your best white or cream notepaper and your black (or blue) ink and reply in kind—a third-person answer, spaced and worded just like the invitation.

Mr. and Mrs. Morton Green
accept with pleasure
Mr. and Mrs. Paige's
kind invitation for
Saturday, the tenth of June
at half after four o'clock

On the envelope you would use the Paiges' full names just as they appear on the invitation. Note that in an acceptance you need repeat only the date and hour, although if you like you can follow the wording of the invitation right down the line. When you can't come, you write that Mr. and Mrs. Morton Green "regret that they are unable to accept" and repeat only the date.

Informal invitations are replied to informally. See Chapter 26 for details.

RECALLING INVITATIONS

Almost always this is done by telegram or telephone calls or handwritten notes, simply because there isn't time for anything else. When there is time, however, it's perfectly proper to mail engraved cards:

Mr. and Mrs. John Weill
regret that
owing to illness in the family
the invitations to
their daughter's wedding
on Saturday, the tenth of June
must be recalled

Note that it is not *necessary* to give any reason for either postponement, as above, or cancellation. In the latter case, the announcement would read:

Mr. and Mrs. John Weill
announce that the marriage of
their daughter
Evelyn
to
Mr. Jonathan Snyder
will not take place

These forms may be followed for handwritten notes as well—inscribed, of course, in black or blue ink on folded white notepaper. Telegrams go out under the signature of the parents—both of them. Those to people they don't know, such as many on the groom's list, may be worded rather formally:

THE MARRIAGE OF OUR DAUGHTER EVELYN TO MR. JONATHAN SNYDER WILL NOT TAKE PLACE

or:

REGRET THAT INVITATIONS TO WEDDING OF MISS WEILL AND MR. SNYDER MUST BE RECALLED

Close friends and relatives may simply receive a wire that says:

HAVE HAD TO CANCEL PLANS FOR EVELYN'S WEDDING

When invitations are to be recalled by phone, it's often helpful for friends or relatives of the bride's mother to take over some of the calling. There's bound to be curiosity, of course, but there's still no need for explanation. When the caller knows just what she's going to say and is formal (though cordial) in her manner, the person at the other end usually just accepts the message without any questioning. The formula may be something like this: "This is Josephine Murdock, Mrs. Weill's sister. Mrs. Weill has asked me to tell you that Evelyn's wedding (or to semistrangers, 'her daughter's wedding,'), which was to have taken place on Saturday, has been cancelled."

ANNOUNCEMENTS

The announcements, which spread the news of the marriage to those who might otherwise not hear of it, go to people who did not receive invitations to either the wedding or the reception. Even though you might have chosen informal notes instead of engraved invitations to your wedding, it's perfectly proper, and in fact customary, to have the announcements engraved. They may go out the day of the wedding or a few days thereafter. They should be on good quality white or cream double-fold paper, the same stock and size as the invitations (if any):

Mr. and Mrs. William Gregory
announce the marriage of their daughter
Paula Lee
to
Mr. James Hay Scott
on Saturday, the tenth of June
one thousand nine hundred and sixty-eight

Note that the year *must* be given. Immediately following it, the church or place where the wedding took place may appear if you desire, followed by the city and then by the state if the city is not a large one. Instead of "announce the marriage of their daughter," you may prefer either "have the honour to announce" or "have the honour of announcing."

When the bride and groom are announcing the marriage themselves, this is the form:

Miss Janet Mary Dobbs
and
Mr. Robert Farmer
announce their marriage
on Saturday, the tenth of June. . . .

It is also permissible for the brother or sister of the bride to announce her marriage. If they are married themselves, they would announce the marriage of their sister in the same form as if she were their daughter: "Mr. and Mrs. Gaynor Snowden . . . announce the marriage of their sister. . . . "

34

The Wedding Day

AT LAST, YOUR WEDDING DAY! ALL OVER TOWN THE WEDDING GUESTS
are primping, the bridesmaids are scurrying about the house, your
mother is ready and is doing up all those back buttons on your
wedding gown, your father's dressing, perhaps with somewhat
shaky knees. Nervous groom and confident (we hope) best man are
about to leave for the church, the ushers are already there. In a
few minutes it will all begin!

To have everything go smoothly on this big day is your dream,
whether yours is a big church wedding or a small affair at home.
And so it will, if the timing is right. Timing, to be sure, is not
quite so rigid at most home weddings, but some sort of rough
schedule helps, and a real timetable is essential for a big formal
affair, no matter where it's held.

FORMAL WEDDINGS

Of your bridal party, the ushers should be ready first and asked
to be at the church an hour before the ceremony. The sexton will
give the ushers their boutonnières, already delivered to the church
by the florist. About thirty-five minutes before the ceremony, the
first guests will arrive and the ushers will start seating them. If
there is to be music, it will be playing while the guests are being
seated.

Next to arrive are the bridesmaids, who have usually dressed at
the bride's house. They're taken to a room near the church entrance
and given their bouquets. Groom and best man arrive and retire to

the vestry, where they get their boutonnières. (At this time the best man may present the fee to the clergyman.)

About five minutes before the ceremony the groom's parents arrive and are led down the aisle by one of the ushers. After them comes the bride's mother—and now the susurrus of well-bred excitement begin. For she is always the very last to be seated (any later-comers creep up to the gallery or miss the ceremony) and everybody now turns heads to lose no glimpse of the wedding processional.

The bride and her father have arrived in their special car at the church (ideally at the exact hour) and have joined the waiting bridesmaids. It's now that the ushers unroll and fasten the pew ribbons, if any, in the way the clergyman or sexton has shown them, and unroll the white aisle canvas, if there is one. Then the ushers group for the procession.

Meanwhile the bride's mother and the guests have risen, the wedding march has begun, and the groom and best man are led into the church by the clergyman, to take their places as he directed at rehearsal time.

THE PROTESTANT CEREMONY

For the Protestant processional there is a more or less standard order. The ushers come first, in pairs, the shortest leading, and the bridesmaids next, in pairs or one by one. After them comes the maid (or matron) of honor. Flower girl, page or ring bearer, either one or two or all three, follow her, ring bearer last or paired off with the flower girl. At a somewhat greater interval than that between the others comes the bride on her father's left arm. And if there is a train bearer, he is of course last of all, holding up the train.

The grouping for the ceremony, at the chancel or altar, will have been decided by the clergyman and rehearsed by the wedding party. Most usually the ushers and bridesmaids separate as they come to the end of the aisle, dividing to left or right according to which side they're on. Best man and maid of honor go to either side aisle. A flower girl would stand with one set of the bridesmaids, other children beside her. Through the space opened up by these groupings walk the bride and her father. As they reach the place where the groom is standing, the bride lets go of her father's arm, moves toward the groom and side by side they step forward to stand together at the altar. (She usually changes her bouquet from her right to her left arm now.) The bride's father stands where she left him.

The illustration above shows the wedding party in the processional (left) and the recessional (right) as they would be seen from a pew at the back of the church.

Now the bride hands her bouquet to her maid of honor, and the ceremony proper is about to begin. Here again the exact procedure will have been demonstrated by the clergyman at the rehearsal. In general, after the responses of the bride and groom, the minister asks, "Who giveth this woman to be married to this man?" The father of the bride steps forward, usually on the bride's left, to put his daughter's right hand into that of either the clergyman or the groom, depending on the ritual that is being followed, and says, "I do." The father then turns and goes back to join his wife in their pew.

Now the clergyman asks for the ring, and the best man gives it to

the groom, who slips it on the fourth finger of his bride's left hand when he is so directed.

At the end of the ceremony the traditional kissing of the bride by the groom may take place if it has been agreed upon. (Many feel it to be a little out of place immediately following a very formal ceremony.) If he is to kiss her, the maid of honor lifts the bride's veil so that he may do so.

In preparation for the recessional, the maid of honor returns the bride's bouquet as the recessional music begins. The bride (on her husband's right arm) and groom lead off, followed by the flower girl if any, then by the bridesmaids and then the ushers, walking either as they did in the procession or paired off. The recessional is an essentially joyful rather than a solemn interlude, and consequently, though dignity is maintained, the outgoing pace is a bit faster than the more sedate incoming one. The guests, who have been standing while the party goes down the aisle, sit down again to wait while the ushers escort out of the church first the bride's mother and then the groom's mother and any other close female relatives. After that the guests may begin to leave.

The bride and groom and the other members of the wedding may either get in to their waiting cars to be taken to the place of the reception, or they may gather in the church vestibule or on the steps or lawn to greet friends. This is very often done when not all the guests are invited to the reception, and in such cases the bride's mother and her bridesmaids may receive, too. It is courteous to include the groom's mother as well. The fathers may mill about close by. This needn't be too formal an affair, but the bride and groom should be together so that their friends may greet them and wish them happiness.

When the bride and groom leave the church immediately instead of receiving, it behooves the truly considerate guest not to follow hot upon their trail and arrive at the reception before the bridal party has a chance to catch its collective breath and get ready to greet them! On the other hand, don't delay *too* long, for they are anxious to see their friends and get the merrymaking under way!

THE ROMAN CATHOLIC CEREMONY

As far as the processional is concerned, the Roman Catholic ceremony is much the same as the Protestant, except that at some large weddings the procession may be headed by choristers. One point of procedure is different, however. The bride's father does not accompany her to the altar in order to give her away there. Instead, bride and father pause at the top of the aisle and are met there by the groom, whereupon the father lifts the veil from her face and kisses her, then presents her to the groom, who escorts her the rest of the way while the father takes his place in his pew beside the bride's mother. (The veil remains lifted for the duration of the ceremony.)

The marriage ceremony proper is the same in all Catholic churches and is contained within the framework of the various Nuptial Masses which usually accompany it. There are Low and High Masses as well as the Solemn Nuptial Mass. Procedures vary somewhat with the type of Mass, and the priest will give thorough instruction to all of the bridal party about their places and roles. The bride and groom, maid of honor, and best man (perhaps also the rest of the bridal party and/or the parents at the taking of communion) at a Nuptial Mass stand within the sanctuary for a large part of the ceremony, sometimes kneeling on prie-dieux or sometimes, at the long Solemn Nuptial Mass, sitting on chairs provided for the purpose.

Nuptial Masses are permitted only in the hours before noon, and no Nuptial Mass may be said at any marriage between a Catholic and a non-Catholic. (Therefore the partaking of communion is not a part of the ceremony at such a wedding.) Catholics marrying outside the faith may nowadays be married, in most cases, in the church, but at the altar rail rather than within the sanctuary. The ceremony must be in the afternoon, before six o'clock.

At the wedding of two Catholics, the ring is always blessed, the best man at the proper time handing it to the server, who gives it to the priest to be blessed before the groom receives it to place it on the bride's finger. The ring is not blessed at the marriage of a Catholic to a non-Catholic.

Catholics may not have home weddings except for rare and special reasons. They may be married in church at any time of the year. During Lent and Advent, however, while church ceremonies may take place, they may not be solemnized—that is, only the simplest of ceremonies is permitted, without flowers and without music, and of course without Masses of any kind.

The recessional proceeds like that of the Protestant recessional described above.

THE JEWISH WEDDING

The Jewish Orthodox, Conservative, and Reform ceremonies differ a little from each other just as do some of the beliefs to which each group subscribes.

Immediately before the ceremony, the Jewish bride often receives guests in the anteroom of the synagogue or temple. (The synagogue is the name for the place of worship of Orthodox and Conservative Jews, the temple for that of the Reform Jews.) As a rule, the bride does not, however, receive the groom except at some Reform weddings.

Men are required to wear hats in a synagogue. *Yarmulkas*—the traditional skullcaps—are always provided, however, for those who forget their headgear. Among Reform congregations this usage is not adhered to.

Reform temples set aside the left-hand side for the bride's guests and the right-hand side for the groom's as Protestants do. The order may be reversed in a synagogue—there is no special rule.

Whether in a synagogue, temple, hotel, or home, a Jewish wedding is nearly always performed under a canopy of cloth or flowers placed before the altar and suspended from four standards.

THE PROCESSIONAL

At an Orthodox or Conservative wedding, first come the ushers in pairs, next the bridesmaids. After them walks the best man, by himself, followed by the groom walking between his mother (on his right) and father. This group is followed by the maid of honor and after her, the flower girl if there is one. Last of all comes the bride with her mother and father, the latter on her left. (If she's Orthodox, she wears a face veil.) When the wedding takes place in a temple or synagogue, the rabbi awaits the bride and groom at the altar. He may otherwise lead the processional. The father does not give his daughter away.

Bride and groom, together with best man and maid of honor, stand beneath the canopy, and if there is room, the two sets of parents stand under it also. If not, they stand just outside it. (In Orthodox and Conservative synagogues the bride is always on the groom's right.) Next to the rabbi stands a small table on which are two cups (or glasses or goblets) of ritual wine. First of all, a blessing is pronounced over the wine, and then the rabbi gives a glass to the groom, who sips from it and gives it to the bride for her to sip. At the proper time for the ring, the best man hands it to the rabbi, who a bit later in the service gives it to the groom. At a Reform ceremony, he will put it on the left-hand ring finger; at Orthodox and some Conservative ceremonies, on the index finger of the bride's right hand. The service which accompanies the wine sipping and the gift of the ring is always in Hebrew, the marriage covenant in Aramaic, which may be repeated in English translation. At Reform weddings, the greater part of the service is in English. As a part of both services the rabbi speaks earnestly to the bride and groom about the meaning of marriage and their responsibilities. After this, in Conservative and Orthodox ceremonies, a second glass of wine is sipped by the bride and groom, and then the groom steps on a glass which is placed at his feet by the rabbi or sexton, and crushes it.

At a Conservative or Orthodox wedding, the recessional is led off by the bride and groom, followed by the bride's parents, then the groom's parents, flower girl, if any, maid of honor paired off with the best man, and last of all the ushers and bridesmaids, paired off.

The recessional at a Reform wedding would be just like that for Catholic or Protestant weddings, and the procedure on leaving the church the same, since the parents would not be part of the procession.

SEMIFORMAL WEDDINGS

Since semiformal weddings are like formal weddings in so many respects, the time schedule, seating, processional, and recessional are the same, except that because the ushers do not have to attend to any aisle canvas or pew ribbons, and because there are fewer attendants, the elapsed time would be a bit shorter. The positions of the bride and her father, the groom and the attendants are like those at a formal wedding.

INFORMAL WEDDINGS

These are much less "staged," as it were, than their formal counterparts. Usually the members of the wedding all arrive at the church together, about fifteen minutes before the ceremony, and enter together. There is no seating of guests. The bride and groom stand before the clergyman, the maid of honor and best man stand to the left and right, respectively, behind them. At an informal ceremony such as this, just as there is no processional, there's no recessional. The bride and groom greet their friends in the church itself, in its vestibule, or on the steps.

HOME WEDDINGS

You may prefer a house to a church wedding if that house has been your home always. Or you may decide on it if your wedding is to be a small one and your church is so large it might seem to overwhelm the assembled party. Or if you and your husband-to-be are of different faiths, a home wedding may be essential.

Home weddings may be as formal or informal as you choose. Your only limitation is that you mustn't invite more people than the place will comfortably hold, not just for the ceremony but also for the reception, for of course everyone who witnesses the ceremony will attend the reception.

Formal or informal, you'll want to do some clearing out and rearranging of furniture to get space enough for the guests and the food servers to move easily from room to room. Even if there is to be only punch or champagne, you'll need to provide room for the party to circulate, but you mustn't forget to leave *some* places to sit, especially for the older guests.

Of course you consult the clergyman about the placing of the altar and other details of the ceremony. The best place for the ceremony is the largest room, usually the living room, away from the doors so that there's room to walk in toward the clergyman. The house may be decorated with flowers as simply or lavishly as you like. Most brides like to have flowers or greens arranged as a background for the wedding ceremony.

At most house weddings the guests stand, but you may rent chairs and set them up on either side of your "aisle," with a few in front especially for the families. You may, if you like, use white ribbons to mark these latter and to further define the aisle.

For a Protestant wedding a long, rather narrow table may be needed to serve as an altar, and for Episcopal and Roman Catholic weddings two prie-dieux for the bride and groom to kneel on. When these are used, an altar rail, often decorated with greens, may be called for. Your clergyman will advise you about this, and also about what covering may be needed for the altar table.

For a Jewish wedding, you'll probably want a canopy, and also the white-covered table for the ritual wine and glasses, as at a temple or synagogue wedding.

The bride's family greets the guests as they arrive, and the guests usually seat themselves informally. The ushers, if any, do not seat the guests formally (except an elderly or infirm one); they simply indicate which is the proper side of the aisle.

When everyone has arrived, the groom's parents take their seats in front on the right, then the bride's mother (a male relative or an usher may escort her) takes her place. If there's music it begins now, and next the groom and best man take their places.

Whether you have only one or two attendants or as many as four ushers and four bridesmaids, the processional order is just as it would be in your church, temple, or synagogue. The grouping at the altar would be the same as the proper church grouping, and the ceremony too.

At an informal home wedding, the bride and groom, who are already in the room, simply step before the clergyman, the bride on the groom's left, for the ceremony. If the bride's father is to give her away, he stands a little behind her to the left.

After the ceremony, the groom is the first to kiss the bride, of course—and at a house wedding he always does kiss her! As at informal church weddings, there is no recessional. Usually the guests come up right away to greet the bridal couple and their attendants on the spot. If, however, the couple wishes to receive in another room, they simply lead the way together, followed by the attendants.

SECOND MARRIAGES

Except in the case of a very young bride who has been widowed in her late teens or early twenties, the second wedding is usually a quiet affair. It may be semiformal or informal, and may be in church, but the bride doesn't wear white, doesn't plan on a veil (or a train), and usually limits the bridal party to one attendant, not counting the best man and one or two ushers if they're needed. Her reception is informal in its arrangements, and her cake is usually iced in a pastel color rather than white.

The bride who is a divorcée usually has a quiet home wedding or is married in a civil ceremony, not only as a matter of taste but also because the rules of her religion may not allow her to be married in church. Even though the guests at such a ceremony may be limited to the two witnesses, there's nothing to prevent an informal reception afterwards, at home or hotel or club.

When the groom has been married before, this doesn't usually affect the wedding plans unless it be for religious restrictions.

It used to be felt that children of former marriages should not attend the celebration of the remarriage. Nowadays we feel that what matters most is to buttress a child's security and welcome his participation from the outset in the new way of living which he faces; so if the child is old enough to understand what is taking place, if he wishes to attend and is wanted, so much the better.

OTHER SPECIAL SITUATIONS

Sometimes puzzlements and problems arise, particularly for the bride of divorced parents, because of family tempests and turmoils. For example, a bride may be devoted to her natural father more than to his successor, and wish *him* to give her away—or vice versa. Or a widowed bride may wonder whether it would be cruel to invite her first husband's parents to the wedding. There just aren't any etiquette rules in any of these situations; the heartfelt ones of kindness and tact are the only ones that apply. Let your feelings be your guide.

In the case of the bereaved parents of your first husband, it might be wise and tender to say in your note, telling them of the approaching wedding, that you want to send them an invitation and will, because you love them, but that you'll understand if they'd rather not come.

(The one etiquette rule that does apply is that the wedding invitation is *not* extended in the name of any man other than he who is to give away the bride. When Mr. and Mrs. Johnson invite guests to the wedding of Mrs. Johnson's daughter Charity Blake, Charity, of course, wouldn't ask her father, Thomas Blake, to give her away.)

When the bride's father is dead, she usually (unless she is an older bride planning on an informal ceremony) asks an older male relative or older friend of the family to give her away. When the bride's mother is dead, she almost always asks an older woman relative to stand in her mother's stead for the wedding formalities, although she need not, of course, especially if she decides to have an informal wedding.

35

The Reception

YOU WILL ALREADY HAVE DECIDED IN MAKING YOUR WEDDING PLANS what kind of reception yours is going to be. (Refer to Chapter 32.) The only *essentials* for a wedding reception are the cake and something with which to toast the bride. You can have these informally at home if the guest group is small—and nothing can be more charming —or you can go to the other extreme and have a big catered affair with a sit-down meal and dancing. And there are in-betweens, too!

All of them take some organizing. A small home reception doesn't involve any more than would be normal for a cocktail party or tea— arranging for the cake, homemade or bought, for the flowers (which could well be lilacs or gladiola or other blooms from the home garden), and for enough glassware, silver, and china to take care of the expected number. *And* the liquid refreshments! Champagne is always more than acceptable, of course, to toast the bride in. It may be a vintage wine, or a fine domestic if you like; just be sure you have enough of the appropriate stemmed glasses, and enough champagne or punch to go around generously.

One bottle (4/5 of a quart) of champagne will yield 7 to 8 servings in 3-ounce champagne glasses. Two and one-half gallons of punch will serve fifty people with about six ounces apiece.

However simple the party, it's as well for the mother of the bride to have some assistance. This is an occasion where she will be greeting people almost all the time and should be enjoying herself as well. So even if she is a wizard at giving parties without seeming to do any work, some kind friend or relative should be at hand to direct and someone in the kitchen to do the cleaning up.

A long table, prettily decorated and set like a buffet table, may hold the punch and the cake. When there is to be no receiving line and the affair is a stand-up one, or when the bridal party has already received before leaving the church, the toast may be proposed as soon as all the guests have arrived. The only toast that's essential is that given by the best man, though often his is followed by others.

The cake cutting is an age-old and beloved ceremonial which you will want to observe no matter how simple the reception. You take a silver knife in your right hand—the knife is often tied with white ribbon and sometimes with a knot of white flowers, too—and while your new husband places his right hand over yours you cut the first slice. This you and he share from the same plate. Then someone other than the bride cuts slices for all the guests.

While the cake's being eaten, you and your groom circulate among all the guests, together or singly, and speak to all of them. Then everyone is eager to see who'll catch your bouquet and so be the next to be wed. All the bridesmaids and the unmarried feminine guests

gather at the foot of the stairs (or the front door, if you and your groom are leaving immediately) and you toss the bouquet amidst the upraised hands. Of course you don't play obvious favorites, but there are not very many unmarried sisters who didn't have it pitched in their general direction!

If you and your husband are not leaving in the costumes you were married in, your maid of honor and no doubt some of the bridesmaids will scurry to your bedroom with you to help you change and do last-minute packing. It's very easy at this peak of excitement and flurry to skimp your attentions to the two sets of parents—but don't! When you're dressed, ask the maid of honor or a bridesmaid to fetch your new in-laws, say a little goodby to them, and then dispatch them to their son for their private farewells with him, which you'll be sure to give them enough time for. Then you'll ask *your* parents to come in for goodbys and for your thank-yous for this wonderful day. Your groom, of course, won't forget his thank-yous to them as you both leave.

So much for the basic pattern of all receptions—the toast, the cake, the bouquet tossing, all intermingled with joy and well-wishing. More formal receptions may include as well a receiving line, a bridal and parents' table with perhaps tables for guests as well, a more formal menu, and music and dancing. A formal reception may be held at home, particularly if home is capacious, but is more often given at a club or a hotel, and is usually catered.

Drinks may be cocktails and long drinks such as would be served at a large cocktail party, plus champagne for toasting, or may consist of champagne only.

After a formal morning wedding, what is called a "wedding breakfast" is served. This is actually a luncheon; a formal afternoon or evening wedding is often followed by a dinner. The food at a wedding reception can range all the way from sandwiches, little cakes, and ices to whole elaborate meals, but of course the wedding cake is the most important feature.

You may serve your guests buffet style if the guest list is not too unwieldy and if you plan a meal that's easy to handle standing or lap style. In this case, a big buffet table is arranged as you would any other, except that the wedding cake is the centerpiece and star player. Often even when the guests help themselves and stand to eat or take their plates to small tables, there's a bridal table and sometimes a parents' table served by waiters.

THE RECEIVING LINE

At a formal reception, you'll want first to receive your guests. There's a more or less standardized order for the receiving line, although this may vary in different communities and with different family situations. From left to right as the guests go through the receiving line, they will meet first the bride's mother, then the groom's father, the groom's mother, the bride's father, the bride, the groom, the maid of honor, and last the bridesmaids all in a row. The bride's father often does not receive and the groom's father need not either, particularly when the families are both long-time residents of the neighborhood. When the groom's parents come from another community, it's courteous to include them both so that they may meet the many guests they may not know.

When the clergyman is included, he stands between the bride and her father. The best man, the ushers, and the child attendants don't stand in the receiving line.

When the bride's mother is not living, the woman relative who represents her stands not first in line, but next in line after the bride's father. Or the bride's father alone may head the line. If one of the groom's parents is not living, the other may receive alone.

Should the bride's parents be divorced, her mother stands in the receiving line either alone or with her new husband, while the first husband takes no place in it but instead ranks as an important guest. If the bride's father is the host, perhaps with his second wife as hostess, it is the bride's mother who assumes the status of guest and does not stand on line with the others.

When everybody has been received, the line breaks up (at the bride's mother's signal) and goes to the room where the refreshments are.

As guests arrive, they make straight for the receiving line (after having left their wraps, if any) and greet each person in turn, beginning with the bride's mother. It's appropriate to tell the bride's parents what a lovely wedding it was, to congratulate the groom, to wish the bride happiness and tell her how charming she looks. And don't forget to pay compliments to the bridesmaids!

THE BRIDAL AND THE PARENTS' TABLES

The bridal table includes all of the wedding party proper. More often than not it is a long table at which they all sit along one side facing the room, although it may also be a large round or oval table. In any case, it is the bride and groom who are the central figures. She is seated on his right and the maid of honor on his left, while the best man is toward her right with a bridesmaid in between, the other bridesmaids and the ushers paired off symmetrically both left and right.

The bridal table is of course decorated with flowers, and place cards are both elegant and helpful.

The parents' table includes not only both sets of parents, but also the clergyman (with his wife, if any) and relatives and other guests of special importance. This table is not usually especially decorated, though it's often of necessity larger than the tables for other guests. Place cards—for all but the bride's parents—are helpful here, too.

The bride's mother and father sit across from each other as they would at a dinner at home. On her right is the groom's father, on his the groom's mother. The clergyman sits on the mother's left, and his wife, if he has one, sits on the left of the bride's father. (If the clergyman has no wife, some important woman guest takes her place.) Once these places of honor are taken care of, the seating alternates men and women around the table as usual.

If yours is a small wedding and you haven't many attendants, you may want to combine the bridal and parents' table. You and your new husband sit together, of course, at the center of one side, you on his right, the best man on your right and the maid of honor on his. Your father is at one table-end, your mother at the other, with the groom's father in the place of honor at her right, the groom's mother on your father's right. The clergyman sits on your mother's left, with either the clergyman's wife or another woman guest on your father's right. The other seats alternate men and women around the table.

As at less formal affairs, the best man is the one to propose the toast, and he does so when everyone in the room has been served the champagne or punch in which to drink it.

The cake-cutting is, of course, a star turn at the formal reception as at any other, and at the end of the meal proper, the orchestra signals with a fanfare that the time has come. If there's room, the cutting may be done at the bridal table; more often, a separate table is wheeled up for the ceremony.

THE ORDER OF THE DANCE

Another old and favorite wedding tradition is that it is always the bride and groom who dance together first. The music usually begins after the first course (though sometimes after the dessert) and at the first strains you and he leave the table and dance at least once around the dance floor—which for once is empty of everyone but you! Your husband then brings you back to the table, where your father claims you for *his* dance while your husband dances with your mother. Next the groom's father whirls you about, and the groom does the same with your mother. That's the end of the solo turns. Now the best man with the maid of honor and ushers with bridesmaids join in, and presently the dancing is general.

36

Anniversary and Shower Parties

ALL YOUR ANNIVERSARIES ARE FUN, OF COURSE, FROM THE VERY FIRST gay dinner for two through the more sedate middle years (when perhaps the budget won't stretch to a baby sitter and you dine festively alone or have friends in), all the way to the momentous twenty-fifth and fiftieth and seventy-fifth!

Those last-mentioned major anniversaries are especially meaningful and joyous landmarks and worthy of a celebration that almost parallels the wedding in formality. You'll invite the wedding party, all or many of the wedding guests, and no doubt newer friends as well. Perhaps your children want to give the party for you—in either case, the invitations may be engraved or handwritten, or they may be telephoned. (See Chapter 26 for invitation forms.)

Usually such an affair is a buffet or sit-down dinner. It's nice to have the table decorations and the cake (wedding cake, of course!) keyed to the kind of anniversary it is—silver for the twenty-fifth and golden for the fiftieth. (Just for the record, the seventy-fifth is diamond, at first glance a difficult assignment, but silver gauze and sequins will lend the requisite sparkle!)

It also adds to the festivity to have music at such an affair, if you can, and punch or champagne for the toasting is essential. One of the children may propose the toast, or if there are no children, the best man or a close friend may do it.

If it's a surprise party, play the wedding march as the couple enters. Later you can play a selection of popular songs of the wedding-day period. Be sure to have the wedding photograph on display, and the wedding album, if there was one, ready to pass around.

You might even have some candid shots of the couple taken now and then during the evening.

By all means have a wedding cake, readymade or homemade, iced in white, and have the "bride and groom" cut it together.

For the less formal anniversaries, informal gatherings are in order. It's still fun, though, to key the party to the theme—a barn or square dance, an outdoor barbecue, or a housewarming could appropriately celebrate the paper, cotton, wood, or pottery anniversaries.

Presents at anniversaries are often, of course, exchanged between you and your husband. They are not obligatory from friends, but practically everybody does enjoy selecting and bringing gifts for these occasions. You may omit naming the occasion on your invitations if you prefer not to seem to be asking for presents. For the really important anniversaries, however, the invitation itself gives the whole thing away and the affair is often like a shower of gifts.

As at weddings, money presents in the form of cash or checks are proper, and can be particularly appropriate in certain cases, as for example when the couple is planning to go on a second honeymoon. How nice to have some spending money for an extra treat or a special souvenir, rather than to add to the accumulation of twenty-five years still more silver trays, candy dishes, and teapots!

Here is today's list of anniversaries complete with the twentieth-century additions:

First	paper
Second	cotton
Third	leather
Fourth	fruits and flowers
Fifth	wood
Sixth	sugar and candy
Seventh	wool or copper
Eighth	bronze or pottery
Ninth	pottery or willow
Tenth	tin
Eleventh	steel
Twelfth	silk and linen
Thirteenth	lace
Fourteenth	ivory
Fifteenth	crystal
Twentieth	china
Twenty-fifth	silver
Thirtieth	pearls
Thirty-fifth	coral

Fortieth	ruby
Forty-fifth	sapphire
Fiftieth	gold
Fifty-fifth	emerald
Seventy-fifth	diamond

SHOWERS

Most women just love showers—giving them, buying for them, going to them. And a shower *is* a delightful kind of party which can serve to celebrate so many different occasions! For the bride-to-be, there can be kitchen showers, linen showers, stocking and glove showers. For the expectant mother there are baby or stork showers (see "Baby showers" below). For the dear friend about to set out on a cruise, a "traveling shower" is fun.

You can find gay shower invitations in the stationery stores, dozens of pretty designs in wrapping paper, and thoroughly festive table decorations—colorful paper cloths and napkins too, if you wish.

The invitation should include not only the where, when, and for whom, but should be as specific as possible about the kind of shower it's to be. The hostess must do some investigating first, in most cases, to find out sizes, color schemes, and so on, so that the stockings and gloves will fit, or the dish towels and condiment sets will be in the colors the bride plans for her kitchen! It's thoughtful, too, to consult the guest of honor's mother about convenient dates and about the guest list. Guests at a bridal shower should include all the women of the bridal party and of the bride's family, unless the shower is given by her office friends or by a sorority or similar group. (Now and then showers are given, usually in the evening, for both bride *and* groom, and then, of course, the ushers and best man and other males would be included.)

It's not proper for the mother, sister, grandmother, or close relatives of the to-be-showered girl to give the party. The groom's relatives may do so if they wish. This is the *strictest* etiquette, which is sometimes altered by community custom.

Any time of day is a proper shower time—breakfast, brunch, lunch, tea, dinner, or evening refreshments. When the men are to be included, however, it's usually an evening affair.

The considerate hostess, especially if there are to be several showers, as for a bride, keeps the shower-gift category on the inexpensive side so as not to work hardship on the guests, who must, as a rule, give wedding presents as well. Sometimes, especially at office showers, the guests chip in and give one major gift, like an electrical appliance. In the case of a mixed shower, the gifts should be tagged with the names of both bride and groom, and should not be either exclusively masculine or exclusively feminine.

OPENING THE GIFTS

There's nothing wrong with piling the gifts on a table near the guest of honor and having her open them as everybody looks on. (And certainly at a baby shower when the baby is expected quite soon, this would be the considerate way.) But it's also fun to make a game of it. You could hide the gifts in several different rooms and put an alarm clock in each place. Set them all so that they'll go off at fifteen-minute intervals. The idea is for the honored guest to locate the gift pile before the alarm stops ringing. Or you can attach a ribbon to the chair of honor; then she can follow the ribbon trail which will lead to various places in the house where gifts are hidden.

If you decide to have the gifts presented all at once, it adds to the festivity to select some special container for them—a wire shopping cart for a kitchen shower, say; a wicker bassinet or old-fashioned laundry basket for a baby shower; or a large carton wrapped in brown paper and addressed (as if for mailing) to the guest of honor. (See under "Baby Showers" on page 392 for a pretty ring-and-ribbon idea which can dramatize the gift giving for everyone.)

Assign a guest to collect the opened gifts and make sure that the right cards are put with the presents. She, or another guest, can also take care of the discarded wrappings and put them in the big wastebasket you will have provided. Have good-sized shopping bags available to put the opened presents in; and if your guest of honor has walked to the party, be sure to arrange transportation home for her and her new acquisitions.

MONEY GIFTS

Often the shower hostess knows that the couple needs and wants money more than fancy canisters and crystal ashtrays. In this case she may indicate this on the invitations—"Money-gift shower" or "Money-tree shower." You may buy a ready-made money tree at some party supply stores, or you may paint a tree branch white (or gold or silver or shocking pink!) and anchor it firmly in a pretty pot. Or, as a variation, you might suspend the branch from a doorway and call it a "money mobile." But the money tree is the most practical since it is stationary and it is easy to tie the little envelopes on the branches. Be sure to provide enough ribbons on the branches.

To achieve a unified look on the money tree, buy small envelopes in pastel colors and enclose one with each invitation. The guest puts the money inside and writes a message and her name on the outside: "With love and best wishes from Jane." Because it takes time to tie on those envelopes, set the guests' arrival time a bit before that of the guest of honor and let them help you with the task.

BABY SHOWERS

Baby showers are usually given just for the mother's first or second child. As a rule, they're held about a month before the baby is due, sometimes five or six weeks after the baby is born. Money gifts are acceptable, of course, in cash or checks enclosed in an envelope or small gift-wrapped box with a gift card. When it's a postnatal shower, United States Savings Bonds can be given as well. The bond is made out to the child with its mother as co-owner: "Alan Joseph Hart or Ellen Field Hart."

Other gifts can be sweaters and socks, blankets and booties, carry-alls, bath accessories, and so on. (It's a good idea for guests at baby showers not to limit the gifts solely to new-baby items—the one-year and year-and-a-half sizes will be needed in the twinkling of an eye!)

A traditional but charming and ever-fresh gift presentation to the expectant mother involves the use of the ribbons with which the gifts are tied. The ribbon from the first gift to be unwrapped is attached to the honor guest's wedding ring, which she temporarily donates. As the unwrapping proceeds, ribbon is tied on and wound around the ring. Then the guests stand in a circle, hands outstretched behind them. The guest of honor unwinds the ribbon as she passes from guest to guest. Anyone who gets a knot in her left hand will someday have a baby girl; in her right hand, a baby boy. Whoever gets the ring will be the next bride.

The ribbon idea can also be used at a bridal shower, with the engagement ring substituted for the wedding ring.

Expectant mothers appreciate "lady in waiting" showers, too, with gifts of cosmetics, spray colognes, dusting powders, bed jackets, slippers, paperback novels, and so on.

37

Christening and Brit Milah

THE BABY'S NAME GIVING AND HIS INITIATION INTO THE FAITH OF HIS
parents constitute one of our most joyous and significant ceremonies.
It is meaningful most of all, however, to the parents and other relatives and to close friends, and so the guest list is usually not a large
one. The ceremony itself is performed by a clergyman and a small
reception may follow.

The where and when of the christening—and to some extent, the
how—is determined by the faith of the parents. In any case, your
clergyman is the first person to consult, for the setting of the date
and for permission to have a home ceremony performed if that is
wanted and if it is permitted by the church in question.

INVITATIONS TO THE CHRISTENING

Because a christening is most often small and informal, most people
invite the guests by telephone or with informal notes. You may write:

Dear Jenny,
    The baby is to be christened at St. Luke's next Sunday after the
eleven o'clock service. We do hope that you and Tom can be there
and can come home with us afterward for luncheon.

Fondly,
Ruth

THE PROTESTANT CEREMONY

Protestant babies are usually christened at three to six months.
The parents ask several friends to be godparents—as a rule they
call on two godmothers and one godfather for a girl, two godfathers

and one godmother for a boy. This isn't a hard and fixed allocation, however, and you may have more or fewer godparents for your baby if you like. But they should be chosen with some care—they should be no older than the parents, and they should be *close* friends (in some cases, relatives), as they promise to be responsible for the child's spiritual welfare and even morally responsible for the child himself should the parents die. The fact that careful parents will have made legal guardian arrangements makes such a contingency unlikely; nevertheless godparenthood is a serious relationship which no one should assume, or be asked to assume, lightly. And it is practically impossible for a person to say no when he's asked to be a godparent! So for all these reasons, choose your baby's sponsors with a great deal of thought.

The godparents are often asked shortly after the baby's birth. They need not be physically present at the ceremony itself. They, or you, with their permission, can choose a proxy to act in their stead.

The godparents are usually and preferably of the same religion as the parents. (In fact, a non-Catholic may not be a godparent to a Catholic child, and Catholics are not allowed to sponsor non-Catholic children.)

Godparents maintain a close relationship with their godchildren especially in childhood, and remember them on birthdays and at Christmas. They also give a christening present, usually of silver, like a porringer, a cup, a spoon and fork.

IN THE CHURCH

More often than not, christenings take place immediately after the principal church service on Sunday, and there may be more than one baby to be christened. If you prefer a more formal affair, with a fair number of guests, your clergyman may find it possible to have the ceremony on a weekday instead. In that case you probably may, if you wish, decorate the church—but very, very simply, with a few greens or palms and some white flowers near the font.

Don't overlook the donation to the church which is given to the clergyman instead of a fee. Immediately after the ceremony, the father of the baby usually hands the clergyman a sealed envelope containing the contribution, which may range anywhere from five to fifty dollars or more, depending on the size and formality of the christening.

The guests and parents wear just what they would wear to church, including hats for the women. The baby may wear the long family christening robe or just a simple short white dress, with white bootees and a white afghan if the church is chilly, for his outdoor coat and cap will come off when he's brought inside. It's as well for the baby to be brought just on time so he won't get fretful while waiting. The guests as they arrive seat themselves in the front pews. The parents and godparents advance to the font and stand. When the clergyman comes, the mother hands the baby to the godmother, who moves directly in front of the clergyman while the guests all stand.

The clergyman often takes the child in his own arms for the actual baptism. When the clergyman asks for the child's name, the godmother must be sure to pronounce the names clearly and slowly: "Mary Ann." If she mumbles, the clergyman may pronounce the child's name to be "Marian"—and that, in effect, is that. (If the name is at all difficult, it's best for the parents to print it on a slip of paper and give it to the clergyman before the ceremony.)

At the end of the ceremony the godmother hands the baby over to his father. The clergyman signs the baptismal certificate and gives it to the parents, and then the group leaves the church for home. If the clergyman is to attend the reception (and he should always be invited), he will follow after changing out of his vestments.

AT HOME

The ceremonial part of a home christening is like that in a church. It's usually held in the living room which may have flowers here and there. You'll need a small white-covered table to hold the font, and a silver or china bowl to serve as the font. If there is room, you may like to put a couple of candles on the table.

Don't forget to have a room set aside in which the minister can change into his vestments (if he plans to wear them for the service) and afterwards change back to his street clothes for the reception.

At home christenings, the women wear afternoon clothes, and may dispense with hats if they like. The godmothers may be a shade dressier, as may the mother. The men would wear business suits.

Naturally the clergyman would be given a contribution just as he would for a church christening.

THE ROMAN CATHOLIC CEREMONY

Catholic babies are always christened in the church. (The only exceptions are babies who are so ill that they must be baptized in the hospital because of the danger of death.) Catholics and many Protestants use the term "baptism" rather than "christening," although they may use the latter term in speaking informally. This is because christening may indicate only a name-giving ceremony, whereas baptism signifies the sacrament that imparts grace to the soul. Catholic infants are always assigned, in addition to the given name, a patron saint whose name he will carry throughout his life.

Among Catholics, the ceremony should take place within the first month. The mother is encouraged to accompany the child to church, and the godmother holds the baby throughout the service.

The baptismal certificate is not necessarily signed on the spot, because it is always kept at the church to be available when needed for later sacraments in the baby's religious life.

THE RECEPTION AFTER THE CHRISTENING

The reception following may be a luncheon or tea. On the whole it is an informal gathering, but a happy one. Two features are traditional: an all-white christening cake (that is, white cake with white icing), which may or may not be decorated with the baby's initials and the date; and what used to be called the "caudle"—the hot eggnog in which is was customary to toast the baby. Nowadays the caudle cup is replaced by champagne or punch, and in this the baby's godfather proposes the little one's health and prosperity.

THE BRIT MILAH

The Brit Milah is an extremely important ceremony of the Jewish faith and is common to all three denominations of Jews. It involves the circumcision and at the same time the naming of boy babies. The operation is usually performed in a hospital when the baby is eight days old with the godfather holding the child during the process. When the operation is completed, there are benedictions and thanks said by the *Mohel,* the religious functionary trained to perform circumcisions. In the Jewish faith, the name is almost always that of a grandfather or uncle or other near relative who has died.

A festive reception usually follows.

The Jewish girl baby's naming also has its ceremony. On the Sabbath after the baby is born, the father goes to the synagogue or the temple, where her name is mentioned in a special prayer recited in her honor. The whole congregation is often invited to attend the celebration gathering, with refreshments, in the vestry room.

38

Confirmation and Bar Mitzvah

AMONG CATHOLICS AND PROTESTANTS, THE CONFIRMATION OF SONS and daughters, while it is a happy occasion as well as a deeply significant sacrament, is not celebrated in the social way christenings and weddings are. At the church ceremony the children and the parents will look forward to seeing grandparents and aunts and uncles among the congregation, and many close friends, too. Afterward there may be a family gathering at home, perhaps a picture taking and some gifts for the newly confirmed child—but not a party.

The confirmation ceremony is of course preceded by a period of special instruction extending over a considerable length of time,

and when confirmation day comes, the presiding church authority will satisfy himself as to the preparedness of the candidates.

The children dress as the clergyman directs—most often, for Protestants, dark blue suits for the boys and white dresses for the girls. Most Catholic and some Episcopalian girls also wear short white veils and carry flowers at their confirmation.

THE BAR MITZVAH

Bar Mitzvah, which means "Son of Duty" or "Son of the Commandment," is the name for the confirmation of a Jewish boy. Among Orthodox and Conservative Jews, this comes about after a period

of special study, on the first Sabbath after the boy's thirteenth birthday, and it signifies that he has completed his elementary course of religious study, that he is now sufficiently mature to be responsible for his own actions, and that from now on he is prepared to take his place with the other males of the congregation in the rituals of the synagogue.

Not only does becoming Bar Mitzvah have very deep religious significance, but also it is customarily celebrated as an important social event.

The name for the confirmation of Jewish girls is "Bas Mitzvah." Because in the Jewish religion women do not take active part in the ritual of worship, Orthodox Jews do not consider Bas Mitzvah to be an exact parallel to Bar Mitzah and rarely, if ever, celebrate it. It is occasionally observed among Conservative and some Reform Jews.

In some Reform temples a group ceremony called "confirmation" is substituted for both Bas and Bar Mitzvah. It is a group ceremony for boys and girls, possibly older than thirteen, who have completed a certain course of study. Each is blessed by the rabbi and given a diploma. Some Conservative Jewish congregations who observe the traditional Bar Mitzvah for the boys, hold this confirmation ceremony for the girls.

No matter to what branch of the Jewish religion his parents belong, it is a very great day for them and their boy, and is celebrated not only with the confirmation ceremonies proper, on Saturday morning, but also with post-ceremony refreshments served in the vestry room or social room of the synagogue or temple and, later on, a luncheon or dinner in honor of the boy. At the first gathering everyone of the congregation is welcome and in fact is expected to join in. The second affair may be quite large and is by invitation only. It may be held at home or in a hotel.

INVITATIONS

Usage as to invitations varies widely among communities and congregations. Depending on the size and elaborateness of the luncheon or evening banquet that crowns the occasion, invitations may be formal or informal, handwritten or thermographed or engraved. They must state not only the place, date, and time of the ceremony, but also the time and place of the party and the address to which a reply should be sent. Your local stationer can give you helpful advice on the forms.

Bar Mitzvah invitations are answered, like other invitations, in the form in which they are sent: a formal third-person reply to a formal invitation, a note in response to a note.

WHAT TO WEAR

For the morning ceremony, the guests wear whatever they ordinarily would to a main service at their church, temple, or synagogue. At an Orthodox or Conservative Jewish ceremony, men may wear their own skullcaps or may select one from the supply always ready in the vestibule. Skullcaps are always available, too, at Conservative and Orthodox celebrations, at the party, and are often laid on the tables, one at each man's place.

If the party is a luncheon held shortly after the ceremony, the guests will go on to the reception in their street clothes, but if the party is an evening affair, they will go home and change into formal clothes.

GIFTS

Everyone attending a Bar Mitzvah will naturally want to give the Bar Mitzvah boy a gift of lasting value to mark his very special day—perhaps gold cuff links or pen and pencil set, or a ring. A bond or check is a very welcome gift. The guests send their gifts ahead of time just as they would a wedding gift.

39

Funerals and Mourning

WHENEVER AND HOWEVER DEATH COMES TO A FAMILY, THE ACTUALITY is cataclysmic. It may have been foreseen, may perhaps even been awaited as a release from unbearable pain—still, it puts a shocking period to a time of anguish. Even when the end of a long and happy life slows to a peaceful stop, the loss is keen and immediate.

Whatever the death has been like, to whomever it has happened, the bitter fact is that at almost the peak of emotional fatigue and sometimes of physical exhaustion as well, the survivors must make plans for the burial ceremony—just when they are least prepared to do so. They are in no condition to act with cool judgment even if there were plenty of time to mull over and consider—and there never is.

It is to be hoped that a relative or close friend may be blessedly at hand, or may be summoned, to relieve the immediate family by taking much of this burden on his own shoulders. He should know or be informed of the wishes of the deceased, if they are known, and the wishes of the mourners about the kind of funeral they want. He should know at least approximately the family's financial circumstances. And he must be given the appropriate documents. With this information, he can proceed to make arrangements that will be both satisfying to the bereaved family and practical in terms of expense.

From time to time in recent years, clouds of controversy have risen about American funeral practices. There is little doubt that there have been and may continue to be abuses by some of those connected with the business of burying. And it is undeniable that when these abuses do take place, they are encouraged by the highly emotional state of most bereaved people. This is one of the strongest reasons why it is more practical, as well as less harrowing, to have someone act for the family.

At the same time, such a person should not override any of the family's very strong wishes, except perhaps to gently dissuade when these run counter to financial common sense. This is the family's last, their very last opportunity to serve and honor their dead—and who among mourners has not had the pain of this loss, the wish to pay this tribute, colored at least a little by remorse for unintended slights, unmeant withdrawals, failures to appreciate? For these reasons, there is in every culture, primitive or civilized, a *feeling* for the ceremonies for those who have died. The carrying out of these ceremonies marks a definite and proper end to a life, and is important for the emotional well-being of those who are left behind. They may prefer a simple memorial service or they may feel more comforted by an elaborate funeral. It is not important which they choose; the acceptance of and the affirmation of death is what matters.

WHAT TO DO FIRST

Do call immediately upon a close strong friend or kinsman to act for you in arranging the funeral. Be as direct with him as you can about the kind of service you want, and if economy must be a factor, make sure he knows that.

While you're waiting for him you can select the clothing that will be needed for the burial (see below), and get together the necessary papers.

The necessary documents for the burial include the death certificate, signed by the attending doctor, the coroner, or medical examiner, and the cemetery deed if there is one. These papers, as well as any written wishes of the deceased, such as that for cremation, should be kept, together with a copy of the will, in some safe but accessible place at home or office—*not* in the safety deposit box, which by law is sealed immediately upon its owner's death and can't be opened until after a lapse of time and considerable red tape.

When your helper comes, he will, unless you have already done so, notify the funeral director so that the body can be moved from the house or the hospital to the funeral home. He will also get in touch with your clergyman and tell him of the time and place of the services and burial. (If the family has no religious affiliation, a clergyman of any faith may be asked to take the service.)

AT THE FUNERAL HOME

The family representative discusses various details with the funeral director—whether to have a church or home service or one in the funeral-home chapel, whether to have visiting hours, what is to be the place of burial, how many cars may be needed, and so on. The family representative also selects the casket that he feels appropriate in appearance and in price. In many establishments the casket price determines the cost of the entire funeral—hearse, cars, drivers, use of a receiving room and the chapel, and cemetery fees. (Music may be extra.) It is, of course, up to the family representative to be sure exactly what the family is to receive for the money they are paying.

The funeral director must have the cemetery deed (or the information in it) in order to make the burial arrangements. (If the family has no burial place set aside, the funeral director can help arrange for the purchase of one. This will, of course, be an additional expense, as would any tombstone or marker placed over the grave afterwards.)

CLOTHING FOR THE BURIAL

Orthodox, Conservative, and some Reform Jews, whether men or women, are traditionally buried in a white shroud supplied by the funeral director. Others are dressed in a costume such as they might wear to church. A dark blue or dark gray suit (or possibly a cutaway) with white shirt and conservative tie is suitable for men. Women are usually dressed in some dignified gown of subdued color (rarely black), preferably not décolleté or short sleeved. Young children are dressed as if for Sunday school.

OBITUARIES AND PAID DEATH NOTICES

In the case of the death of someone of prominence in the community, the local papers, having learned of the death through the paid notice, will write an obituary which sums up the dead person's career. The paper may call upon the family for additional data or for a photograph.

The paid notice is a brief form sent to the papers by the family or by the funeral director. Here is a typical one:

JOHNSON—Henry Paine, on January 16, husband (or "beloved husband) of Jane Hart Johnson and father of Irene and Celia Johnson. Funeral at Morningside Funeral Home, 1220 Chelton Road, Thursday, January 28 at 10 A.M. Burial (or "Interment") at Shady Oaks Cemetery.

Notice that of the deceased's children, daughters are listed first, and that a married woman's maiden name is always given whether it is she or her husband who has died. You may always include the words "funeral private" if that's the way you want it. And you may also properly include "please omit flowers," or "in lieu of flowers, donations to the Heart Fund (or other charity) would be appreciated." When the deceased has many friends in another city, you may arrange for papers there to run the notice also, by including the direction, for example, "Philadelphia papers please copy."

The notice may also state the hours when friends may visit the funeral home: "Friends may call at (name and address of home) Thursday 2 P.M. to 4 P.M. and 7 P.M. to 9 P.M." It's understood that while friends may also call at other hours, these are the times when the immediate family (or a representative) will be there.

Parents' names are not included in a death announcement unless the deceased was unmarried.

The age of the deceased is not mentioned in the paid notice, although the obituaries usually carry it.

When the person who has died was not very old and illness has not preceded the death, the word "suddenly" is often inserted just before the death date.

The death notice sometimes includes the words "Interment private," which means that attendance at the graveside ceremony is to include just the family with possibly a few close friends, and is by invitation only. Invitations may be handwritten or extended by telephone. While people may properly limit the attendance at the burial for any reason, a private interment proves more practicable in those cases where the body is to be cremated, as there is often a day's delay or more between the services and the interment of the cremated remains.

The death announcements are scheduled to run in every edition of the paper up to and including the morning of the funeral. The first announcement must sometimes go to press before the funeral plans are completed, and in that case this announcement would contain "notice of funeral later," and subsequent notices would carry the date, the time and the place.

FUNERAL CALLS

Arrangements should always be made for receiving friends who wish to pay their formal calls of condolence. If the body is to lie at home, some family representative should be at hand to receive, as a succession of visitors can be emotionally exhausting to the immediately bereaved, who may, however, want to see one or two very close friends. When the body is to lie in a room at the funeral home, a family representative should be at hand during the late afternoon and early evening hours to receive callers there. The bereaved are not required to make an appearance, but many do, if only briefly.

PROTESTANT FUNERALS

The services may be held at home, in the chapel of the funeral home or in the church. In a church, the front right pew is usually reserved for the immediate family, and pallbearers, if there are any, are seated in the left front pew. Occasionally there may be ushers to seat the people; if there are, they walk alongside, but do not take the ladies' arms as they would at a wedding.

Pallbearers are often asked to serve at large funerals of important men. They are always men and are called "honorary" pallbearers because they do not, as in the old days, actually carry the casket. From four to ten men may be asked to serve as pallbearers, and a male member of the family should be among their number.

As a rule the casket is placed before the altar about half an hour before the service starts. The pallbearers, having gathered in the vestibule, go two by two down the aisle to their seats—the last to do so before the family, who come in from the vestry. At the end of the service, the pallbearers precede the casket out of the church, or go back into the vestry and meet their friends briefly and then get in their cars. Everyone else remains seated until the pallbearers and the family have left their pews.

At a service in a funeral-home chapel, there are no ushers, and seldom any pallbearers unless the chapel is quite large and the funeral an important one. The seating may otherwise be like that at a church funeral, or the immediate family may sit in an adjoining room where they can hear but not be seen.

When the services are to be held at home, the furniture in a large room, usually the living room, is either moved out or set against the walls. The funeral director supplies a stand to hold the coffin and chairs for people to sit on. Flowers may be set around the casket and often a blanket of flowers from the family rests upon it. Guests may be greeted at the door by some relative or close friends of the family. The immediately bereaved come in to sit in the front row just when the service is ready to begin.

CATHOLIC FUNERALS

A Catholic funeral never takes place anywhere but in church. The casket is not set in place before the ceremony. Instead there is a processional, often with choristers, the priest coming next, then the pallbearers if any, and then the casket. The immediate family follows, walks behind the casket to their seats at the right-hand front. When the service ends, the priest and the pallbearers precede the casket (the choristers do not take part in the recessional) and the family follows it.

JEWISH FUNERALS

Orthodox Jews bury their dead within twenty-four or thirty-six hours. Most Conservative and Reform Jews may allow a day or two to elapse to allow time for sons and daughters from distant places to attend. Jewish funerals never take place on Saturday or a festival day; cemeteries observe a Sabbath closing.

As we have said, Orthodox and strict Conservative Jews clothe the body in a shroud. They also traditionally use a plain wooden coffin.

Orthodox and Conservative Jewish funerals always take place either at home or the funeral home, for funerals may not be held in the synagogue unless the deceased is a rabbi or some extremely important dignitary.

THE INTERMENT

The minister, priest, or rabbi accompanies the family to the cemetery and conducts the graveside ceremony. If there are pallbearers, they come too, and transportation should be provided for them. The funeral director should have been asked to supply cars for the immediate family and for close relatives. Other kinfolk and friends often drive themselves to the cemetery.

FEES

The presiding minister usually receives a fee for his services. (In cases where the minister was not previously known to the family, the undertaker may include this charge among the others.) The amount depends first of all upon the family's circumstances, and is also governed by the size and cost of the funeral. A contribution of from seventy-five to one hundred dollars would be proper for a large funeral—ten, twenty-five, or fifty dollars for a simpler one. It isn't given to the minister at the time of the services, but may be sent to him shortly afterward with a cordial note of appreciation.

At church funerals there may also be fees to the sexton, and if there's music, to the organist. About $25 each is the average.

WHAT FRIENDS DO

Friends, of course, want to do everything possible to show their sympathy and their own sense of loss without in any way making things more difficult for the mourners. They write letters of condolence (see Chapter 23), they send flowers to the house or to the funeral home or both, unless for any reason flowers are not wanted, and they pay condolence calls. (See below.) They also attend the funeral, unless, of course, the notice says "Funeral private."

Close friends telephone immediately or go to the house and offer to help. There is nearly always something you can do—take small children for an afternoon, be on hand to answer the numerous telephone and doorbell ringings, even cooking or tidying-up.

FLOWERS

When the death notice says "Please omit flowers," you shouldn't send them. Nor should you send flowers to the funeral or home of any deceased person of the Orthodox Jewish faith, because even though no reference to flowers may be made in the death notice, they are considered symbols of joy and therefore would be altogether out of place. It is probably better not to send flowers to a Conservative or Reform Jewish funeral, either—certainly not without checking with some relative beforehand.

In the Catholic church, only the family's spray is allowed in the church. You send flowers to the funeral home, however, if you like.

In any case where you are certain that flowers would not be unacceptable, it is always a thoughtful gesture to send an arrangement or plant to the family later.

The community florists almost always know where the flowers for a specific funeral should go; nevertheless, it's a good idea to address the envelope enclosing your card:

The Funeral of Mr. Henry Paine Johnson
Morningside Funeral Home
Kingsfield, Vermont

(Note that the city is not necessary unless the flowers are to be wired from another out-of-town florist, and the street address of the funeral home does not need to be included.)

Flowers may also be sent to the church.

Inside this envelope goes a plain white card (your own or one supplied by the florist) with a simple message such as "Deepest sympathy from Marian and Bob," written, of course, in ink. You may also use a husband-and-wife visiting card to carry this message, drawing a line through the engraved names. (If it is an acquaintance who has died rather than one with whom you're on first name terms, you may prefer to leave the formal engraved names and just write below them, "Deepest sympathy.")

IN LIEU OF FLOWERS

When the funeral notice says no flowers and goes on to say that contributions to a certain hospital, medical center, or charity will be appreciated, you send a check, either immediately or shortly after the funeral, to the organization named, with a card saying "In Memory of Henry Paine Johnson from Mr. and Mrs. Robert Pelham." The organization will send a card to Mrs. Johnson to let her know of this contribution (the amount is seldom stated) and Mrs. Johnson will thank the Pelhams for it just as she would for flowers. (For letters of acknowledgment, see Chapter 23.)

CONDOLENCE CALLS

These may be made at the house or at the funeral home if the body is lying there. Or you may call at both places. Those who call at the funeral home should not overlook signing the memorial register, which will later be given to the family.

When you are paying a condolence call or are attending the service for someone of a different faith than your own, you behave as you would in any situation where the procedure is unfamiliar to you. Follow the majority's lead in such matters as rising and sitting. In matters of ritual, you need perform only those which do not conflict with your beliefs. All Catholics, for example, kneel and say a prayer at the casket of the Catholic departed; a non-Catholic may do this or not as he pleases.

To convey sympathy and consideration for the feelings of the bereaved is the purpose in paying a funeral call, no matter what the faith of the departed and his family. There is no need of elaborate speeches—a simple "I'm so sorry" is enough, with perhaps some mention of how much the dead person will be missed by everyone.

It is, of course, cruel and in the worst of taste to criticize by word or manner any of the arrangements that have been made.

WHAT FRIENDS WEAR TO THE FUNERAL

Both men and women wear for condolence calls and to the funeral simple street clothes, which should be on the dark rather than on the bright side, though they needn't be black. Women wear hats for a home or chapel service just as they would for a church or synagogue service. Non-Jewish men, of course, wear hats to the latter.

MASS CARDS

Among Catholics, Mass cards are considered just as much a token of respect and sympathy as flowers and often more so. Such a card means that a special Mass will be said for the soul of the departed. Many non-Catholics send these to the family of a deceased Catholic friend. If you want to do this, you may approach any priest and ask him to arrange for a Mass, High or Low, to be said in your name. You make a donation for the Mass and the priest gives you a Mass card, which you send to the family. This is most often done before the funeral, but it also may be done afterwards.

MOURNING

Our customs in the wearing of mourning and half-mourning have changed from those of the olden days. Most bereaved women do wear black at the funeral, often with a black chiffon veil, while men appear in navy or dark gray suits and ties, with white shirts and black shoes—unless the funeral is very large and elaborate, in which case they might wear cutaways.

After the funeral, it comforts many women, particularly older widows, to stay in mourning for six months to a year or more. Others may decide to keep right on wearing their regular wardrobes; women in business practically always do.

BUSINESS ETIQUETTE

40

Manners for Women in Business

GOOD MANNERS ARE JUST AS IMPORTANT IN BUSINESS AS THEY ARE anywhere. They've never been known, either, to harm a business relationship or to delay an advancement. Nine-to-five manners do, however, omit some of the niceties of social etiquette, particularly in the man-woman reference. You as a businesswoman will realize that you are a worker before you are a woman, and that you have superiors. Whether these are men or women, it is you who will defer to them, not they to you—and don't expect from the men the small punctilios you're accustomed to in the social world.

At the same time you don't want to be and shouldn't try to be like "one of the boys." Don't toss your femininity overboard—but don't make capital of it, either.

Perhaps the most important single attitude for the woman worker to maintain always is that of impersonality. This is hard for most women to achieve. Women are often inclined to take direction and criticism personally, a trait which is thoroughly trying to employers (and especially to men employers) and has no place in a business office. Remember always that in the office you are first and foremost a part of a machine. (Your bosses are machine parts, too—but much bigger ones!) When through haste or carelessness or ignorance you've slipped a cog, take the consequences gracefully. Apologize, correct the mistake, and go on from there. Make it a practice to leave your blue moods, your irritations, your wounded feelings, your personal worries at home where they belong.

Shun office politics and office gossip. Don't be a washroom wagtongue. Don't ask personal questions—and never, never ask anyone his or her salary! Don't be late and then spend ten more minutes doing your face over before getting down to work, and don't put the brakes on half an hour before quitting time. Honor the coffee break but abuse it not. Remember that you're getting paid for a full working day—don't fritter away your employer's time.

In most offices you are allowed a personal call from time to time, but try not to wear out the privilege. Don't write personal letters in the office unless you do it within your lunch hour, or when you have finished every piece of business that possibly can be attended to. It's best to discourage friends and relatives from dropping in at the office, although it's perfectly all right to have someone meet you there for a lunch or dinner date, provided you're ready when he comes.

Some offices allow smoking, others don't. Observe the rules of yours. If you smoke at your desk, have an ashtray at hand (a functional one, not a flat dinky one that will let your burning cigarette roll off), and use it. Empty it often.

Gum chewing, if done at all, should be carried on only in absolute privacy.

Always respect the ever-important office hierarchy. Go to your superior's office for any business discussion; he shouldn't be asked to come to yours. Of course you may call a subordinate to your desk. And for a talk between coworkers of equal rank, do whatever seems to be most convenient for you both. You will not use any superior's first name unless he asks you to. Don't go over your superior's head. And don't pass the buck.

Office parties, particularly Christmas parties, are not held so much as formerly. If your office does have them, of course enjoy yourself, but go very easy on any alcoholic drinks that may be served, or shame may be your diet for the following week at least.

Eating at the desk can be done when necessary (preferably not during working hours), but it should be done inconspicuously and the cleaning up attended to promptly.

APPEARANCE

Whether you're a neophyte or an experienced secretary or a young executive, you'll always remember that your appearance is of prime importance. That you must be clean and well-groomed goes without saying, or it ought to. Appropriateness should be the key to your business wardrobe, your jewelry, and your make-up. The office is no place for way-out hair-dos, jewelry that clanks, Mandarin finger-nails, bizarre make-up, teetery-heeled sandals. This doesn't mean style is out—certainly not. But do stay away from extremes. (Exception: if you're an executive in the world of high fashion, you already know these rules may be broken and you know just how to break them. If you're an apprentice in these fields, devote special care to your appearance, keep it stylish; but on the conservative side.)

IF YOU ARE A RECEPTIONIST

In this as in other jobs where you meet the public, do be warm and helpful. You are really the first link between the organization and the outside world. The fact that some callers may turn out to be nuisances doesn't relieve you of the necessity of being polite to every-one. Above all, don't treat any arrival by word, look, or manner in a way that implies he's quite fortunate to be allowed to approach! Your job is in its way a public relations job—make those relations pleasant.

IF YOU ARE A SECRETARY

Your first duty is, of course, to carry out your boss's orders in the way he likes them carried out. You take dictation capably and tran-scribe quickly and accurately, and you have learned as much about his end of the business as you need to know to be a capable assistant. You never comment on or question any aspect of his social life unless he invites you to, although you may be called upon to do some of his Christmas shopping, remind him of his wife's birthdays and their anniversaries, and to make the arrangements for his vacation cruise. Of course you never open any letter marked "personal," or one that even *looks* personal. You respect his privacy, too, by with-drawing from his office if you're there when a personal call comes in for him.

You may often be in touch with his wife, but it is she who makes the advances, if any. And never risk making her feel belittled by as-suming an attitude of superior knowledge about his affairs!

When your employer and his wife ask you to their home for dinner (or perhaps ask you to dine with them at a restaurant) that's a social occasion. When in the course of business he occasionally takes you to lunch or a dinner after working late, that isn't. Nor is it a date. (No need to be a Miss Prim about it, just matter-of-fact. He will pay the check, and you thank him politely as you would any host.)

Your boss may call you Dorothy after a while, or may do so from the very beginning if he has known you before. But you call *him* Mr. Ames, unless he insists that you do otherwise. And even then you should say "Mr. Ames" when outsiders are present.

When you are handling telephone calls for your employer, remember that the man who is doing the calling should be on the phone when the other picks it up. To call Mr. Burger for Mr. Ames and insist to Mr. Burger's secretary that Mr. Burger be on the wire before Mr. Ames gets on is extremely rude and will not bring your Mr. Ames bountiful harvests of good will.

When you're on the receiving end of a call for your boss, do try to avoid asking, "What do you want to see him *about?*" Naturally, you want to protect your boss from cranks, time-wasters, and salesmen in whose products you *know* he wouldn't be interested, but this may be a perfectly legitimate caller who doesn't want to and doesn't need to tell *you* "what it's about." Mr. Ames would probably rather pick up the phone himself than risk offending someone whose opinion he values. After all, he can brush off the others himself. If, however, he takes the position that you must do all the screening, do it—but do it tactfully. You can always say, "I'm afraid I can't reach him just now [or he's busy, or he's in a conference]—he'll be so sorry to have missed your call. May he call you back? Or is there any way that *I* could help you?"

When a caller comes to the boss's office, you are his official hostess. You greet him, usher him in (or find him a seat if he must wait) and say goodby when he leaves.

At the summons for dictation, you go into the office, take a chair, and put it where you can see and hear your boss best. He is not expected to get the chair for you or to rise when you come in.

Be conscientious about the time you put in. Don't start winding things up at twenty to five or come back late from lunch. Of course, he shouldn't make a practice of asking you to work overtime frequently, especially without warning. When he does have a late batch of letters, do them if you can. If you have a date, say so and ask if you may do them the next day.

When, as his secretary, you travel with your employer, always make the reservations in the firm name, asking for two single rooms "for Mr. Roger Ames and secretary." Rooms on the different floors will be assigned you if space is not at a premium. You may sign the register for both: "Roger Ames, Downing Brothers, 1150 Broad Street, New York" and "Miss Anne Craddock, secretary, same address." (If your employer arrives first and does the signing, he does it in the same way.)

While it would be improper ordinarily for a woman to go to a man's hotel room, it's perfectly all right for a secretary to do this for typing or dictation or note-taking. (He should not come to hers, however.) The door need not be open, but shouldn't be latched.

IF YOU ARE AN EXECUTIVE

By the time you've reached this rung on the ladder, you've learned long ago the bylaws of office etiquette. You've probably realized too that it takes both conscious purpose and self-discipline to avoid let-

ting your femininity sink out of sight in your career. You've learned to keep a constant watch lest any tendency toward bossiness or arrogance antagonize coworkers both men and women. Tact is the ticket.

You're learning, too, at this stage how to handle the sometimes difficult problem of "taking" a man to lunch—paying the check, that is to say, when it's an expense of your firm. Most businessmen are quite accustomed to this, but some need all the tact you can muster not to be made uncomfortable. If you're lunching with one of these, the best plan is to take him to a restaurant where your firm has an account, having made arrangements beforehand to sign the bill with the tip included. (If he's really old-fashioned, you can arrange beforehand to do this on the way out instead of having the bill brought to the table.) Or you may use your personal account and sign for the whole thing, putting it on your expense account afterwards. If both he and you are used to this sort of thing, you may give him a bill and ask him to settle the check for you—"It's on my expense account, of course."

WORKING WIVES AND MOTHERS

As a working wife, you won't want to be considered any different from your unmarried coworkers when it comes to juggling home and office responsibilities. You'll have to organize your marketing, meal-planning, cleaning, and laundry, and you'll do it so that your working hours remain intact. The working mother's task is more difficult because no matter how efficient the plan she has set up for her children's care, there are bound to be emergencies. While bosses can hardly be said to welcome these, no realistic employer hires a working mother without being resigned to the occasional inevitability of crises which require her presence at home. You just have to do the best you can and make up for lost time later if you're able.

Your employers will be able to accept those occasional absences with more equanimity, too, when they know you don't routinely bring in your domestic and maternal worries. You took the job because you felt you could handle both sets of responsibilities—so handle them. Keep to yourself your worries about the baby's tonsils or your adolescent's rebellion.

WHEN YOU WORK IN A STORE

Basic rules for the office are applicable in a store too. You should be clean and neat always, and dressed in accordance with the store's regulations. Clean and well-groomed hands are especially important for anyone who is caring for and displaying merchandise.

The ideal manner for a saleswoman is neither sugary nor pushy, but warm and helpful. When you can't materialize what the customer had in her mind's eye, it's sensible to suggest substitutes. But it's always a mistake to bully her into buying something she doesn't really want. (It will either be returned, or kept and resented. In the long run, that's not good for the store or for you.) Women appreciate constructive help and particularly like to be informed about fabrics, washability, and so on. Active assistance in ready-to-wear is another matter—some women need help in choosing among several garments, some want to make up their own minds. Be ready to offer advice, in a friendly way, if it's wanted, but be both tactful and sincere about it. Avoid calling the customer "honey," "dear," or other terms of endearment or familiarity.

Remember not to spoil the good impression you've made by losing all interest as soon as the sale is completed. Bring package and change back cheerfully, congratulate the customer on her choice, and say you hope to see her soon again. It will give you both a warm glow to call her by her name if the sales slip shows it.

Disagreeable customers are not so infrequent as they should be, and to soothe some of them is all but impossible unless you're a walking saint. But summon up all the tact you can command—and try, try, try!

It always seems to happen that there are no customers or three at once, and all of them impatient for your attention. Tell the two who are waiting, with a smile, that you'll be with them in just a moment. Sometimes you can get out some merchandise to let Customer Two examine while Customer One is deciding between the Wheat Beige and the Piccadilly Taupe.

41

Manners for Men in Business

BECAUSE OFFICE ETIQUETTE SOMETIMES HAS TO DO MORE WITH STATUS relationships than the social amenities, a businessman, particularly one with women subordinates, changes some of the conventions. Far from discarding the politenesses, however, he finds it as true in the office as it is in the world outside that courtesy is appreciated everywhere and is a smoother of many paths.

The young man beginning his business career will make it a point to be well groomed always and to dress as well and as conservatively as he can. He'll be prompt, and he'll be punctilious about not filching time on the coffee break or lunch hour. He'll keep personal calls to a minimum. He won't gossip or backbite. He won't blame his mistakes on someone else. He won't get involved in office politics. He won't go over his superior's head. And he will keep his subordinate position in mind—rising when his superior approaches, letting him go ahead through doors and into elevators, being prompt to reply to a summons. This isn't apple polishing—it's business common sense and good manners as well.

When he acquires a secretary, although he is naturally pleasant and courteous to her, he need not rise when she comes in for dictation. He may even precede her through doors with perfect propriety, though most men don't. And he lets her bring up her own chair for dictation.

While he does not rise for his secretary, he does for callers in his office—perhaps not for a coworker of equal status, but certainly for men visitors, for his superiors, and for women (except job applicants and juniors).

He may call his secretary by her first name, if he pleases, but always addresses her and refers to her as Miss So-and-So when outsiders are present. He never, of course, uses a superior's first name unless he has been invited to do so.

He doesn't take off his suit jacket in the office unless it is an office custom, and if he does he always puts it back on when he goes to his superior's office.

When he asks his secretary to do shopping or other personal errands for him, he doesn't make her subtract the time from her lunch hour. He tries to keep overtime work at a minimum and is appreciative of the real favor she renders him when she puts off an engagement to get out those urgent specifications. He needn't brace every

direction with a "please" and "thank you" fore and aft, but he knows that now and then those friendly words will be appreciated, and remembers too that praise for a job well and quickly done is never amiss.

When his secretary has gotten Alvin Werks on the phone for him, he doesn't embarrass her or anger Mr. Werks by having to be fetched while the latter hangs on—he's ready to pick up immediately on her signal. When he leaves his desk for any length of time, he tells her where he's going and approximately how long he'll be gone, and whether he can be interrupted there.

There's nothing wrong with a man's taking his secretary to lunch to discuss business or to dinner after working into the evening, and they both realize that. He should always be conscious, however, that to do it frequently is both indiscreet and an unfair drain on her free time.

Businessmen, like businesswomen, enjoy office parties, and so they should—but never to the point where superiors may be embarrassed or employees encouraged to be over-familiar.

A man is especially considerate of his secretary's reputation (and of his own) when they are traveling together. If he calls her to his room for dictation, he should be fully dressed and the room should have been made up, or at least the bed pulled together. He will not ask her to share drinks in his room. Meals are another matter—it may save time to have sandwiches sent up instead of going down to the crowded restaurant. They may have dinner in the room if time is of the essence, but going downstairs for it would be preferable. It certainly is not necessary for them to take every meal together just because they are traveling together.

When it is the man who arrives first at the hotel where they are to stay he signs the register for both of them, giving his name, firm name and business address, and following that with "Miss Anne Craddock, secretary, same address."

HELPFUL HOW-TO'S

Some Common French Menu Terms

AGNEAU—lamb
AILERONS—chicken wings
ANANAS—pineapple
ANCHOIS—anchovy
ANGUILLE—eel
ASPERGE—asparagus
AUBERGINE—eggplant
AU GRATIN—with cheese; usually covered with crumbs and browned
AU JUS—with natural (meat juice) gravy
AU MAIGRE—Lenten or fast dish, having no meat or meat stock
AU NATUREL—plain; sometimes uncooked
AU VIN BLANC—with white wine
AU VIN ROUGE—with red wine
BÉARNAISE—a variation of Hollandaise
BÉCHAMEL—a well-seasoned white sauce
BERCY—a cream sauce with fish or chicken stock
BEURRE—butter
BEURRE NOIR—browned butter
BIFTECK—steak
BIGARADE—brown sauce with orange peel
BOEUF—beef
BORDELAISE—a thin brown sauce
BOUILLABAISSE—rich fish stew
BOUILLÉ—boiled
CANARD—duck
CANETON—duckling

427

CASSOULET—hearty casserole, often of white beans and sausage
CERF—venison
CERISES—cherries
CERVELLES—brains
CHAMPIGNONS—mushrooms
CHARCUTERIE—cold cuts
CHATEAUBRIAND—filet mignon, large
CHOUCROUTE—sauerkraut
CHAUD-FROID—fowl or game in aspic, sliced
CITRON—lemon
COCOTTE—casserole
COMPOTE—stewed fruit
CONFITURE—jam or preserve
COQ AU VIN—chicken cooked in wine
COQUILLES—shell (en coquille: in its shell)
CÔTE—chop (as in côte d'agneau, lamb chop)
CÔTELETTE—chop or cutlet
CRÊPES—delicate pancakes
CRESSONS—cress
CREVETTES—shrimp
DINDE—turkey (hen)
DINDON—turkey (cock)
DINDONNEAU FARCI—stuffed young turkey
ÉCHALOTE—shallot
EN BROCHETTE—grilled on a skewer
ENTRECÔTE—rib steak
ENTREMETS—dishes served as sweets or after the main dish
ÉPINARDS—spinach
ESCALOPE—very thin slice, usually of veal as escalope de veau
ESCARGOTS—snails
FARCI—stuffed
FINES HERBES—various herbs finely chopped
FOIE DE VEAU—calf's liver
FOIE GRAS—very finely chopped goose liver, used often as a spread
              with appetizers
FLAN—usually a baked custard mixture; sometimes an open tart
FLORENTINE—with spinach
FRAISES—strawberries
FRAMBOISES—raspberries
FROMAGE—cheese
GÂTEAU—cake

GIGOT—(de mouton)—leg of mutton
GLACE—ice cream
GRENOUILLE—frog
HARICOTS VERTS—string beans
HOMARD—lobster
HUÎTRES—oysters
JAMBON—ham
JARDINIÈRE—with vegetables, especially carrots
JUS—juice
JULIENNE—cut into strips
LAITUE—lettuce
LANGOUSTE—crayfish
LAPIN—rabbit
LÉGUMES—vegetables
LENTILLES—lentils
MACÉDOINE—cut-up fruits, usually in gelatin
MADÈRE—sauce with Madeira wine
MADRILÈNE—clear soup like consommé, tomato juice added
MAQUEREAU—mackerel
MEUNIÈRE—sauce of browned butter and lemon juice
MOULES—mussels
MOUTON—mutton
NAVETS—turnips
OEUF—egg
   oeuf à la coque: soft-boiled egg
   oeufs brouillés: scrambled eggs
   oeuf dur: hard-boiled egg
   oeuf frit: fried egg
   oeuf poché: poached egg
OIE—goose
OIGNON—onion
PAMPLEMOUSSE—grapefruit
PÂTISSERIE—pastry
PAYSANNE—peasant style
PERSIL—parsley
PETIT PAIN—a roll
PETITS POIS—green peas, usually cooked in lettuce with cream
POISSONS—fish and fish dishes
POMMES DE TERRE—potatoes
   pommes de terre frites: fried
   pommes de terre à l'eau: boiled

pommes de terre rissolées: browned
purée de pommes de terre: mashed
POT AU FEU—meat stew
POTAGE—soup
potage St. Germain: pea soup
potage Volaille: chicken broth
potage portugais: a tomato soup
POULET—chicken
POUSSIN—squab chicken
PROVENÇALE—with garlic
RADIS—radish
RAISINS—grapes
RAGOÛT—a stew
RIS DE VEAU—calf sweetbread
ROGNON—kidney
ROGNON DE VEAU—veal kidney
RIS—rice
RÔTI—roast
SAUCISSE—sausage
SAUMON—salmon
TOURNEDOS—slices of beef filet
TRUITE—trout
VELOUTÉ—a white sauce with cream and chicken stock

How to Eat Difficult Foods

PEOPLE OFTEN DENY THEMSELVES THE PLEASURES OF SOME OF THE most delectable foods because they are not sure they know how to eat them. As previously mentioned, it is perfectly correct to glance at your hostess to see how she does it. However, the following list will provide some pointers.

ALLIGATOR PEARS: See "Avocados."

APPLES: Quarter and then peel them and cut out the core with your fruit knife.

APRICOTS: You don't need a knife for these. Raw ones you eat as they are, in several bites, taking the pits from your mouth with your fingers and transferring them to the side of the plate. Since stewed apricots are eaten with a spoon, your pits would go into the spoon rather than the fingers before being discarded.

ARTICHOKES: These are usually served with a butter or other sauce into which you dip the bottom end of each leaf after you have pulled it off the body of the plant. The edible part of the leaf is the lower third. You put this in your mouth, scrape off the meaty part of the leaf with your teeth, and discard the leaf either on one side of your plate or in a receptacle provided. When the big leaves are gone, the choke becomes visible; it is a pyramid of thin little leaves that are very prickly at the bottom. Under this is the base of the artichoke. Cutting away the spiny section carefully with a knife exposes the base of the artichoke, a delicacy you cut into pieces and eat with your fork, dipping bits into the sauce.

ASPARAGUS: Cut this with your fork, beginning with the tip. On quite informal occasions the end may be picked up in the fingers after the tip is eaten and a few more bites taken that way. If your host has grown the asparagus, you know not only that the stalks will be tender all the way down, but also that no gesture will please him more. Be careful, though, for the juice is inclined to run down your wrist.

AVOCADOS: These are the same as alligator pears. There is no problem when they are served cut up in a salad. However, when they are served in halves with a filling or sauce in the cavity, where the pit was, just steady the fruit with your left hand and use your spoon to scoop out the meat; it is all good right up to the outer skin.

BACON: Technically bacon is eaten with a fork. If it's been fried very crisp, however, it's better to pick it up and eat it with your fingers than to spray bacon bits all around by using your fork.

BANANAS: If these are served whole, it is more polite (except, of course, at a picnic) to remove the whole skin at once and then cut the fruit into pieces, eating it with fork or fingers.

BERRIES: These usually present no problem because you eat them with a spoon. If, however, strawberries are served whole with the hulls on, you are supposed to pick up one at a time and, holding it by the hull, dip it into the accompanying sugar, letting the hulls accumulate at the side of your plate.

BIRDS: Squab, Cornish hen, quail, partridge and so on are delicious but a little difficult to eat. Be sure when you carve into the bird that you have him very firmly anchored with your fork lest he skid off the plate and across the table. With a half of broiled chicken it is not good manners, except informally, to pick up the bones and eat from them, because the meat is comparatively easy to get at with a knife and fork. Fortunately, with tiny-boned birds such as squab it is perfectly all right after cutting off all the meat you can, to pick up the bone delicately and, with lips closed, chew the meat off and put the bone back on your plate.

BREAD AND BUTTER: It's best to break your bread or rolls into small pieces and butter these as you eat them. It is quite proper, however, to butter split-open popovers or small hot biscuits all at once because they are at their best when the heat of the bread melts the butter. If you are about to crack open a big hard roll, remember that special care is needed to avoid showering bits and crumbs over everything.

Spread the butter with your butter knife, or if you have been given none, with your dinner knife. If you are putting butter on something on your dinner plate such as an opened baked potato, do it with a fork.

Never lay a slice of bread on your palm and butter it as if the knife were a trowel.

CAKE: If this is sticky or has thick icing or soft filling, it is eaten with a fork, which should be served with it. Fruit cake, pound cake, tea cakes and small cupcakes are first broken and then eaten with the fingers.

CANDY: If you take a piece of candy from a box, take the little paper frill with it.

CELERY: You pick up a piece of celery when it is passed and lay it on your butter plate. You may either sprinkle salt on it or put a tiny pile of salt on the plate in which to dip it.

CHEESE: This you may spread or cut with either knife or fork. If it is soft, runny cheese like Camembert or Liederkranz, the knife is best.

CLAMS: When these are served on the half shell, you steady the shell with your left hand and use the oyster fork in your right to spear the clam. Dip the clam into the sauce, usually served in the center of the dish, and eat it whole.

Steamed clams are not served formally because though they're delicious, they're messy. You may encounter them, however, at an informal meal or a sea food restaurant. They are served with the shells opened, accompanied by a bowl of broth and another of melted butter. Take the clam out of its shell by the neck, pull the body out of the neck and discard the neck sheath. Holding the clam by the neck, dip it into broth and butter and put it in your mouth whole. (If large napkins or bibs, plates for the empty shells, and finger bowls with hot soapy water are not provided, they should have been.)

Fried clams are cut in pieces with a fork and eaten from the fork.

CORN ON THE COB: This is a food that is never served at a formal dinner party because it cannot be eaten with elegance. You can minimize the messiness without decreasing your enjoyment, however, if you butter and season only a couple of rows at a time, half the length of the cob. Hold the cob by the ends as you eat it. It is perfectly all right to break a very long cob in two.

CRAB: Crabmeat cocktail is simple enough, as it comes with the crab-meat shredded up in a bowl with sauce already on it or served separately. Simply take small amounts on your oyster fork with a little of the sauce. It is difficult in preparing it to keep every single shred of crab membrane out of the meat; if you happen to strike one of these, just take it out of your mouth with your fingers.

HARD-SHELLED CRABS: These, like lobster, take a little work but are worth it. The little claws are taken off the body with the fingers. The claws should already have been cracked, but a nutcracker is usually provided with which to crush them further if they need it. Eat the claws with your fingers, sucking the meat out as inaudibly as possible. Then you lift out the body meat and eat it piece by piece with your fork, dipping it into the butter or sauce as you go.

FISH: A small whole fish is quite easy to eat if it has been boned in the kitchen. If it hasn't, and you are dining in a restaurant, you can always ask the waiter to take it back and get it boned. If you should be served a small brook or rainbow trout whole, cut off the head while holding the body down with your fork; then run the knife down the underside to split the fish open lengthwise. Gently flop the top side over to expose the backbone, slide your knife under the neck edge of the backbone and carefully lift out the spine, laying it on the side of the plate. In most cases the backbone will come out whole, small bones and all. If not or if the backbone should break, you must, of course, be careful of tiny bones. If you get some, take them out of your mouth with your fingers (having first cleaned them as nearly dry as you can) and lay them aside with the backbone.

FROGS' LEGS: These, like small birds, have little slender bones which may be picked up in the fingers after you have taken most of the meat off with your knife and fork.

GRAPEFRUIT: This has usually been sectioned in the kitchen and so is comparatively easy to eat. Don't pick up the hull and squeeze it to get all the juice.

GRAPES: First rule about these is not to ruin your hostess' carefully arranged centerpiece by idly nipping off a few between courses. When they're served as a course or part of a course, that's different.

Seedless grapes are easy—you simply pull off a little group and eat them as they are, discarding the stem bits on your plate. Grapes with seeds in them are eaten whole, skins, and all, one at a time, the seeds bunched in the mouth and transferred in your fingers from there to the plate. Sometimes the skins are edible and enjoyable; if they are thick or tough or you distrust grape skins, separate the skins from the pulp in the mouth and dispose of them as you do the seeds.

GRAVY: As we said before, put gravy mostly on the meat, or put part of a helping on your mashed potatoes as you are served. Once the gravy is on your plate you may dip pieces of baked potato, for example, or bits of bread, into the gravy with your fork.

KUMQUATS: Eat these as you eat apricots—with the fingers—small ones in a bite, large ones in two or three bites.

LOBSTER: To the uninitiated, a lobster looks frighteningly difficult to eat. If you know how, though, it can be done efficiently and easily, and to most people the taste is well worth the effort of learning.

A lobster is usually split lengthwise when it is served. If it isn't, ask that it be cut from head to tail and spread open for you. Remove the dark vein and sac if it has not already been taken out. Then hold the tail section with your fingers and use an oyster fork to pry up one large chunk of meat from each half of this section.

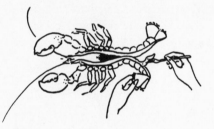

Remove the meat to your plate and with knife and fork cut it into bite-sized pieces which you dip into melted butter (with the fork) as you eat them.

Next, break off the flippers from the tail and suck or bite out the meat.

The green liver found in the body cavity is called tomalley and can be eaten—to many it is the best part of the lobster. Eat it plain or spread it on crackers. The coral-colored roe, found in females, is edible, too.

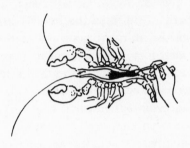

Use your fingers to break off, at each joint, the eight small claws on either side of the body section. Suck or bite out the meat and juices. Break apart the small joints at the base of the claws. Take them up in your fingers to chew off the meat.

Now for the claws. With a nutcracker, open the claws and knuckles at the thickest part. Pull the small part of each claw off where it is hinged and remove the shell from around the meat with your fingers. Watch out for the cartilage that runs through the claw meat, and for a little wooden peg that the fishermen sometimes put in the claw.

MANGOES: Be careful when you eat these as the juice makes stains that are very hard to get out. Mangoes are eaten in the same way as alligator pears, provided you find them halved and pitted on your plate. They are occasionally served whole as part of a collection of fruit. In this case, run a knife down and around the fruit lengthwise to cut it in half (you can feel the pit, which is quite large) and then once again to cut it in quarters. You may use the knife to free the fruit from the stone, which often sticks to the pulp. Then hold a quarter, skin up, on your plate with your fork and gently pull the skin away. Cut the meat in pieces and eat it with your fork, or leave the skin on and eat the meat with a spoon as you would an avocado.

MELONS: A cantaloupe is eaten with a spoon. Larger melons like honeydews and casabas may be eaten with a spoon or a fork. A watermelon is eaten with a fork. Use the edge of the fork to brush off as many seeds as you can. The seeds you are unable to avoid can be taken out of your mouth with your fingers and laid on the plate.

MUSSELS: Mussels are usually served in the shells with a bowl of good buttery sauce. You may use your fork to pick the meat from the shells or, just as properly and with much less trouble, pick up the shell in your fingers and quietly suck the meat and sauce from it, discarding the shells on your plate or on the plate provided for them. Then you may eat the rest of the sauce with your spoon and may put pieces of bread in it to soak up the juices and be picked up with your fork.

OLIVES: When these are pitted or stuffed, no problem—although it isn't the best of manners to put one of the super-colossal ones into your mouth whole; make two bites of it. When there is a pit, hold the olive in your fingers and eat the meat from around the pit. Don't try to clean the pit completely of the meat.

ORANGES: When oranges are served halved like grapefruit they are eaten with a spoon. Peel a whole orange with a knife—or informally, with knife and fingers. Separate the segments and eat them as they are if they're small; otherwise cut them in half. The seeds go from mouth to hand to plate.

OYSTERS: Raw on the half shell they are eaten like raw clams. Cooked oysters, prepared in such ways as deviled, à la Rockefeller, fried, and so on, are eaten with the fork. Sometimes they have been put back into the shells after cooking just for looks or to hold them while they're browning.

PEACHES: Cut into quarters with a sharp fruit knife, pull the skin off if it's loose, peel it if it's tight, and then cut up the peach and eat it with a fork, or with a spoon if no fork is provided. It's mannerly enough to eat a peach with the fingers unless it's dead-ripe, for then the juice usually runs down the chin.

PEARS: Treat them like apples. If they are very, very juicy it is safer not to eat them with the fingers.

PERSIMMONS: These are often served whole in their skins, but with the top cut off, and often replaced like a little lid. You eat them with a spoon.

PICKLES: Eat them with the fingers if they're small. If they're large, cut them first. When slices of pickles are served as an accompaniment to the meat course, the slices are eaten with your fork.

PINEAPPLE: If it's cut up in a bowl, eat it with a spoon as you would any other fruit so served. If you get whole rings, use knife and fork to cut them, fork to eat them. Pineapple sticks may be eaten with the fingers.

PLUMS: Eat them like apricots.

RADISHES: These are eaten whole in one or two bites. Should they be served with a bit of the green stem still on, use that as a handle and discard it after eating the radish itself.

RELISHES: These you may put on your dinner plate near the food they're intended to go with—a pickle relish near the meat, for instance—and eat them with your fork as you eat the meat. Cottage cheese is aften served as a relish and this may be put either on your dinner plate or your butter plate.

SALADS: Usually salads can be eaten with your fork with no trouble. If the lettuce is in long shreds or big pieces, by all means cut it with knife as well as fork, rather than saw away ineffectually while spraying dressing about.

SALT: It's considered rather impolite to salt the entire plateful of food before tasting it, and sometimes the salter is sorry after he does so. Put a little pile of salt on the side of your plate if you need it for celery or radish-dipping, and you may salt with a pinch of this any food on your plate that needs it. If there are salt shakers, shake out what you need. If there are open dishes, use the little salt spoon provided or the tip of a clean knife. If there are individual salt dishes without spoons, help yourself by taking a pinch in your fingers.

SANDWICHES: Tea sandwiches and thin regular ones like ham or cream cheese are eaten with the fingers. Big double or triple-deckers like club sandwiches you have to cut up first with knife and fork; eat the pieces with your fingers if they're not too thick or juicy, otherwise with your fork. A hot sandwich like roast beef with gravy will need knife and fork.

SAUCES: When you help yourself, put them on top of the food they go with. Cranberry sauce or cranberry jelly is more in the relish class and may go on the side of your dinner plate or on your butter plate.

SHRIMP: Eat shrimp cocktail like crabmeat cocktail. (When small shrimp are served with a dip as an hors d'oeuvre, use your fingers or a toothpick.) Fried shrimp are eaten with a fork, whole if tiny, cut up if big. Fried fantail shrimp have the shell still on the tail; use this as a handle with which to dip the shrimp body into the sauce and eat it, discarding the shell on the side of your plate. If you are served unshelled shrimp, you are expected to shell them yourself and eat them whole.

SNAILS: These are usually served very hot and so a little holder is often provided. With the holder in your left hand, clamp the shell in it and with your oyster fork (or pick) in the other hand, you coax out the snail and eat it whole. Once the juice has cooled, it is both polite and rewarding to tip the shell to your mouth and drink the juice from it.

SPAGHETTI: Some authorities recommend and some deplore the method of using a tablespoon in the left hand, upright on the plate, against which you twirl the spaghetti around the fork. Those who do not countenance this suggest just cutting the spaghetti into manageable pieces with your fork. Do whichever is the least awkward for you; the important thing is to find a way that avoids the ugliness of having to slurp in the dangling ends.

Tipping

No longer is tipping a reward, and not always is it an incentive. It's well known that the word "tip" derives from an eighteenth-century usage and stands for the words *"To Insure Promptness."* It doesn't always insure any such thing, as we all know. What a tip usually does insure, we trust, is a living wage for the tippee, and it has become obligatory.

For especially skilled and cheerful service, you may be moved to add to the basic tip—that *is* a reward and, let's hope, an incentive as well.

It must be remembered that a chart like this one can be only a guide, for tipping practices vary widely in different communities. In large cities and their suburbs, especially in the East, 15 per cent would be minimal and 20 per cent quite common. In other parts of the country 15 per cent is customary.

Many times tipping is done on a "now and then" basis—a quarter occasionally to the boy who delivers groceries, the same to the man from the liquor store (perhaps more if he's carried a rather heavy load), twenty-five cents to the boy at the filling station (even though you contribute to the Christmas kitty) if he's cleaned the wipers and checked the tires as well as made a good job of the standard chores.

There are some people whom Americans never tip. You would not tip any airline personnel, either office staff or aboard the plane. (You do, however, tip sky caps.) You shouldn't tip in most private clubs, as a member or as a guest—but the local country club and other informal clubs are often exceptions to this rule.

This table does not include amounts for tips aboard in the various foreign currencies. Many suggestions for whom to tip, and when, and about how much in American money, will be found in the chapter on traveling, Chapter 29.

This table does not include amounts for tips abroad in the various joys and worries and thoughts of their own. So when you tip, give something besides money—a smile and "Thank You!" makes the money more meaningful. And if the service has been very good indeed, a compliment should accompany your bonus tip.

Comments

Category	Whom To Tip	How Much	Comments
Airplane travel	Skycaps only	25¢ per bag average; if many bags, 15¢ per bag; one oversize bag, 40¢.	
Apartment houses	Elevator men Doormen Superintendents Janitors	See next column	This tipping is usually done at Christmas time, with the money often presented in new bills in gift envelopes. Amounts depend largely on the amount of your rent, and the total should come to from 2% to 2½% of the year's outlay. In inexpensive apartments where there are no elevators and where one or two men do all the work in the building, the annual tip should be 3% to 5% of the rental. In any building any special service should be rewarded specially. Visitors to apartment houses need only tip the doorman for calling a cab. 25¢ is customary.
Automobiles	Chauffeurs Parking attendants Garage workers	See next column	To the chauffeur of a rented car, you'd give, for an evening, 20% of the bill. To parking lot attendants, 25¢—if you're a steady customer, $1 now and again. You would contribute to the Christmas kitty of the garage where you're a steady patron; you might also tip 25¢ now and then for good or special service. For car delivery, 25¢ to 50¢.
Barber shops	Barber Manicurist	50¢ for each service, on the average.	In expensive barber shops you might tip 50¢ to $1.00 according to the extent of that service. In a very small town 15¢ might be the average tip.
Bars	Bartender	From 15% to 20% of the bill or a minimum of 15¢ per person.	15¢ is the minimum tip for one drink for one person. For several drinks for several people, 15% of the total check is a minimum.
Beauty parlors	Hairdresser Shampooer Manicurist Others	See next column	Beauty parlor tips show a wide variation. Much depends on locality, on the kind of establishment and its prices. In a big city, the hairdresser who cuts your hair gets $1, the manicurist 50¢, the shampoo operator 25¢. Other services such as tinting or dyeing require tips of an additional 50¢ to $1. In modest establishments you can cut these amounts almost in half (with the exception of the 25¢ tip). In a fashionable salon it is not customary to tip the owner, even though he cuts or sets your hair; in smaller shops in small communities you tip Mr. Perry just as you tip his wife, who may be the tint specialist. For a permanent, the standard tip is 10% of the cost or $1, whichever is greater.
Deliveries	Delivery boys	25¢ on occasion	A grocery boy may be tipped now and again. Department store deliveries require no tip. Delivery

442

Category	Whom To Tip	How Much	Comments
Deliveries (continued)			boys from florist, druggist and so on may be tipped if you like, particularly if the weather is bad. Western Union boys need not be tipped but often are. You should give 15¢ to the supermarket boy who carries your marketing to your car—25¢ for a long walk or in bad weather.
Hotels (Also see resorts, below.)	Bellboys	25¢ per bag; 25¢ for delivering packages, telegrams; 25¢ to 50¢ for errands or other special services.	On a stay of a week or more, many people prefer to tip once a week, especially if they use his services often. $1 a week and up is customary.
	Chambermaids	$1 to $2 a week, 50¢ for one or two days; in an expensive hotel, 10% of the cost of the room.	On a long stay, $2 to $3 per week.
	Doormen	25¢ for getting a cab; perhaps 50¢ if the weather is very bad. If he just helps you into a waiting cab, no tip is necessary.	On a long stay, a weekly tip of $1, depending on how often his services have been used.
	Dining room waiters	Table waiters, as in a restaurant. (See below).	On a long stay, you may want to tip the headwaiter $3 or more every other week.
	Room service waiters	25¢ minimum, depending on the hotel, for a small check. Over $2, 15% to 20% of the check.	
	Elevator men and starters	Nothing unless some special service has been rendered.	
	Porters and bell captains	50¢ to $1 for any special service such as getting reservations.	

443

Category	Whom To Tip	How Much	Comments
Lunch Counters	Waiter, waitress, or counterman	15¢ to 20¢ for a snack and beverage, 25¢ if the check is over $1.	
Motels	See right-hand column	See next column	In many motels and roadside cabins, no tipping is expected. In motel with staff, you give 25¢ or 50¢ to the boy who takes in the luggage, to the chambermaid nothing for a single night, $1 to $2 for a weekend.
Moving	Moving men Elevator men Superintendent	Tip moving men generously—$5 to $10 for two men, $12 to $15 or more for four men with over-size van. $1 or $2 each to others.	Elevator men and superintendents are listed here because in moving into apartment houses their help is invaluable.
Resorts	Various staff members who may double in brass for some jobs. Sports personnel may be included.	In general, a scale similar to that for a hotel.	Resort lodgings vary from camps to expensive heavily staffed hotels. In the latter, follow suggestions for tipping as in hotels above. In most others, a large tip is given (for pooling) to the manager at checkout time, and covers meal tips, maid, and routine services. Instructors in sports are not tipped. Helpers like boathouse boys, grooms, and others may be tipped 25¢ or 50¢ a time or a lump sum on leaving. Ask the manager for tipping guidance.
Restaurants and Night Clubs	Headwaiter Captain Waiter Busboy Wine steward	See next column	In the average restaurant you need be concerned only with your table waiter. In an expensive place, you give the headwaiter nothing, or $2 to $5 for special table or service. If the captain does something special for you, 25% to 35% of the total tip, otherwise nothing. Your table waiter gets the remainder of the tip, or gets the whole if he's done all the work. (Tip on 15% to 25% basis.) Busboy nothing. Wine steward 10% of the wine bill or $1, whichever is larger.
On Shipboard	Barroom steward Bath steward Cabin steward	See next column	On short voyages tips are given at trip's end. Barroom steward gets 15% to 20% of the bar bill; bath steward, if used, $2 to $3. The cabin steward and dining room steward get about $1.50 a day; the stewardess $2 or $3 or more if she's given you special service; $2 to the deck steward if used.

444

Category	Whom To Tip	How Much	Comments
On Shipboard (continued)	Deck steward Dining-room steward		Dining room steward $2 to $5 for special service. Round tips off to nearest top dollar. If you're a first-class passenger on a deluxe ship you increase these amounts by a dollar or so. On voyages of 2 weeks or more distribute half of tip money halfway through the voyage; on long cruises tip every other week. These tips are on the low side—adequate but many people prefer to tip more lavishly. You never tip a ship's officer.
On trains	Dining car waiters	As you would in a restaurant: 15% to 20% of each check.	When you require special services, as when traveling with small children, tip the head dining steward, and give an extra tip to the porter who brought bottles, etc.
	Pullman porters	25¢ to 50¢ for a day trip; 50¢ to $1 for one-night berth, $1 to $1.50 in roomette; $2 drawing room. For several nights, reduce the rate per night, for example $5 for three nights in drawing room.)	
Taxis	Driver	10% to 15% of the meter for a ride. 15¢ to 20¢ for a ride well under $1.	This figure should be raised to reward any special service, such as a long haul late at night or helping with luggage. In small communities the regular commuters seldom tip the station (unmetered) taximan, and the visitor need not unless he wishes.
Visiting	Servant or servants	See next column	On an overnight visit, you need not tip any servant unless some special service has been rendered. On a weekend, $1 or $2, more for special service, would be all right in the one-servant household. In others, give a waitress the same as the maid. Give the chauffeur about $1, more for special or frequent trips. Give tips just before leaving, as inconspicuously as possible. In a house with a large staff you do not tip those you have not seen, such as the cook.

FORMS OF ADDRESS

Forms of Address

ALTHOUGH WE MAY NOT OFTEN HAVE THE OPPORTUNITY TO WRITE TO or to introduce personages of special distinction such as churchmen of high degree, high-ranking government officials, or military men, we need to know how to do it properly when the occasion does arise—hence the following chart. (For other helpful correspondence guides, see Chapters 23 through 25.)

SOME SPECIAL NOTES

"Sir" and "Dear Sir" are both acceptable openings for formal letters; "Dear Mr. Green" and "My Dear Mr. Green" for informal letters. (Take note here, however, of one important exception: in Great Britain "My dear . . ." is never used for strangers or acquaintances but is reserved for close friends.) The closing of letters is also fairly flexible. In this chart you will find "Very truly yours" as the preferred formal closing; but "Sincerely yours, "Respectfully yours," and "Faithfully yours" (or "Yours respectfully" and "Yours faithfully") are acceptable substitutions, and the latter four are often used in writing to the clergy.

In most of the places on the chart the salutation is followed by a colon, rather than the comma used in other nonbusiness correspondence. It is not wrong to use a comma. But in addressing prominent churchmen, diplomats, government officials, and military leaders the colon seems to add a stronger note of dignity and ceremony than does the comma, especially when the letter is of an official nature.

In the United States, women who hold public office are addressed by the masculine form of their title—"Mayor" rather than "Mayoress." With her title the woman uses her given name: The Honorable Marian Oakes. If she is married, a social invitation which includes her husband would be addressed to their home and would be sent to "Mr. and Mrs. Marvin Oakes."

Women ambassadors are referred to and introduced as "Madam Ambassador;" women ministers as "Madam Minister." They may be addressed in writing as "The American Ambassador [or Minister], Mrs. Lowery."

The wife of any official, no matter how elevated his position, is addressed simply as "Mrs.," just as any other married woman would be. The wife of an American ambassador also, though she may as a social courtesy be referred to as "Ambassadress," is properly called "Mrs." Note, however, that with the exception of representatives from countries where English is the principal language, the wives of foreign diplomats are addressed and referred to as "Madame"—that is, Madame Torres rather than Mrs. Torres or Señora Torres.

It is the custom in the United States to give the title of "The Honorable" to many high state and federal officials. There are three important things to bear in mind about this designation. First, it is always used with "The," with the full name and *without* any other title—i.e., "The Honorable James Carter Ridges," not "The Honorable Captain Ridges" even if he *is* a captain. This applies to women also: "The Honorable Mary Wilson Saxe." Second, the person never uses this appellation in speaking of himself; it is altogether for the use of others. And third, once a person has been an "Honorable," he is thus spoken of for the rest of his life, even after he retires from office.

THE CLERGY

Personage	The Envelope:	A formal letter begins and ends:	An informal letter begins and ends:	Speaking to:	Introducing
Roman Catholic cardinal	His Eminence Joseph Cardinal Ryan Archbishop of Detroit Detroit, Michigan	Your Eminence: Respectfully yours,	Your Eminence: Sincerely yours,	Your Eminence	One is presented to His Eminence, Cardinal
Roman Catholic archbishop and bishop	The Most Reverend Michael Grey (Arch)Bishop of Chicago Chicago, Illinois	Your Excellency: Respectfully yours,	Your Excellency: Sincerely yours,	Your Excellency	The Most Reverend Michael Grey or His Excellency, Michael Grey
Roman Catholic monsignor	The Right Reverend Monsignor Dale Cincinnati, Ohio NOTE: There are two classes of monsignori: "Right Reverend" and "Very Reverend." The former takes precedence.	Right Reverend and dear Monsignor Dale: Respectfully yours,	Dear Monsignor Dale: Sincerely yours,	Monsignor Dale	Monsignor Dale
Roman Catholic Priest	The Reverend William Lovejoy St. Francis Church St. Louis, Missouri	Reverend and dear Father: Very truly yours,	Dear Father Lovejoy: Faithfully yours,	Father or Father Lovejoy	The Reverend Father Lovejoy
Abbot	The Right Reverend Paul Murphy The Abbot of Wellsley Roanoke, Virginia	Right Reverend Abbot: Faithfully yours,	My dear Father Abbot: Sincerely yours,	Father Abbot	The Reverend Father Abbot Murphy
Mother Superior	Reverend Mother Mary (and the initials of her order) The Convent of St. Agnes Jackson, Mississippi	Reverend Mother: Very truly yours,	Dear Reverend Mother Mary: Sincerely yours,	Reverend Mother	Reverend Mother
Member of religious order	Sister Anne, O.S.D. (initials of order) Brother Jonathan, O.B.M. Sacred Heart College Denver, Colorado	My dear Sister: My dear Brother: Yours respectfully,	Dear Sister Anne: Dear Brother Jonathan: Sincerely yours,	Sister Anne Brother Jonathan or Brother	Sister Anne Brother Jonathan

The Clergy (cont.)

Personage	The Envelope:	A formal letter begins and ends:	An informal letter begins and ends:	Speaking to:	Introducing:
Rabbi with scholastic degree	Rabbi Milton Fried Temple Israel San Francisco, California	Sir: Very truly yours,	My dear Dr. Fried: Sincerely yours,	Rabbi Fried *or* Dr. Fried	Rabbi Fried *or* Dr. Fried
Rabbi without scholastic degree	Rabbi Milton Steinberg Temple Beth David New York, New York	Sir: Very truly yours,	My dear Rabbi Steinberg: Sincerely yours,	Rabbi Steinberg *or* Rabbi	Rabbi Steinberg
Cantor	Cantor Jacob Gold Temple Emanu-El Trenton, New Jersey	Sir: Very truly yours,	My dear Cantor Gold: Sincerely yours,	Cantor Gold	Cantor Gold
Protestant bishop	The Right Reverend Francis Mann Bishop of Texas Houston, Texas	Right Reverend Sir: Respectfully yours,	My dear Bishop Mann: Sincerely yours,	Bishop Mann	Bishop Mann
Archdeacon	The Venerable Phillip Craig The Archdeacon of Boston Boston, Mass.	Venerable Sir: Very truly yours,	My dear Archdeacon: Sincerely yours,	Archdeacon Craig	Archdeacon Craig
Protestant clergyman with doctor's degree	The Reverend Timothy Cox, D.D. Watertown, Connecticut	Reverend Sir: Very truly yours,	My dear Dr. Cox: Sincerely yours,	Dr. Cox	The Reverend Dr. Cox
Protestant clergyman without doctor's degree	The Reverend Samuel Franklin Tallahassee, Florida	Reverend Sir: Very truly yours,	My dear Mr. Franklin: Sincerely yours,	Mr. Franklin	The Reverend Samuel Franklin
Canon	The Reverend Frank White Williamsburg, Virginia	Reverend Sir: Very truly yours,	My dear Canon White: Sincerely yours,	Canon White	Canon White

DIPLOMATS

Personage	The Envelope:	A formal letter begins and ends:	An informal letter begins and ends:	Speaking to:	Introducing:
American ambassador	The Honorable Mark Logan American Ambassador	Sir: Respectfully yours,	My dear Mr. Ambassador: Sincerely yours,	Excellency *or* Mr. Ambassador *or* Sir	The American Ambassador*
Foreign ambassador	His Excellency Jacques Robert The Ambassador of Belgium				His Excellency, the Ambassador of Belgium
American minister	The Honorable John Brown American Minister* Rome, Italy	Sir: Very truly yours,	My dear Mr. Minister: Sincerely yours,	Mr. Minister *or* Mr. Brown	The American Minister *or* Mr. Brown
Foreign minister plenipotentiary	The Honorable Ludwig Schultz The Minister of Austria			Mr. Minister	The Minister of Austria
Consul Consul general Vice consul Chargé d'Affaires	Frederick Brenner, Esquire American Consul Madrid, Spain	Sir: Very truly yours,	My dear Mr. Brenner: Sincerely yours,	Mr. Brenner	Mr. Brenner

* In any Latin American country, or on any occasion when Latin Americans are among those present, our own ambassadors, ministers, embassies and legations should be designated by the full title: ". . . of the United States of America."

NOTE: In addressing the foreign diplomat who has a royal title such as His Highness, Prince, etc., the title "His Excellency" for an ambassador or "The Honorable" for a minister is omitted and only the royal title precedes the name.

453

GOVERNMENT OFFICIALS

Personage	The Envelope:	A formal letter begins and ends:	An informal letter begins and ends:	Speaking to:	Introducing:
The President	The President The White House Washington, D.C.	Mr. President: Respectfully,	My dear Mr. President: Sincerely yours,	Mr. President	The President
The President's wife	Mrs. Jones The White House Washington, D.C.	Dear Mrs. Jones: Very truly yours,	My dear Mrs. Jones: Sincerely yours,	Mrs. Jones	Mrs. Jones
The Vice President	The Vice President United States Senate Washington, D.C.	Sir: Very truly yours,	My dear Mr. Vice President: Sincerely yours,	Mr. Vice President	The Vice President
The Chief Justice	The Chief Justice The Supreme Court Washington, D.C.	Sir: Very truly yours,	My dear Mr. Chief Justice: Sincerely yours,	Mr. Chief Justice	Mr. Chief Justice
Associate Justice	Mr. Justice Martin The Supreme Court Washington, D.C.	Sir: Very truly yours,	My dear Mr. Justice: Sincerely yours,	Mr. Justice *or* Mr. Justice Martin	Mr. Justice Martin
Member of the President's Cabinet except Attorney General and Postmaster General	The Honorable Sam Green The Secretary of Labor Washington, D.C.	Sir: Very truly yours,	My dear Mr. Secretary: Sincerely yours,	Mr. Secretary *or* Sir	The Secretary of Labor
The Attorney General	The Honorable Frank Gibbs The Attorney General Washington, D.C.	Sir: Very truly yours,	My dear Mr. Attorney General: Sincerely yours,	Mr. Attorney General	The Attorney General
The Postmaster General	The Honorable Edward Hindes The Postmaster General Washington, D.C.	Sir: Very truly yours,	My dear Mr. Postmaster General: Sincerely yours,	Mr. Postmaster General	The Postmaster General

Personage	The Envelope:	A formal letter begins and ends:	An informal letter begins and ends:	Speaking to:	Introducing:
United States *or* state senator	The Honorable Lyle Cox United States Senate Washington, D.C. (appropriate address for state office)	Sir: Very truly yours,	My dear Senator Cox: Sincerely yours,	Senator Cox *or* Senator	Senator Cox
Member of Congress *or* state legislature	The Honorable Len Parker U.S. House of Representatives Washington, D.C. (appropriate address for state office)	Sir: Very truly yours,	My dear Mr. Parker: Sincerely yours,	Mr. Parker	Representative (or Congressman Parker from (name of state)
Governor	The Honorable George Dunham Governor of Michigan Lansing, Michigan	Sir: Very truly yours,	My dear Governor: Sincerely yours,	Governor Dunham *or* Governor	Governor Dunham *or* The Governor
Mayor	The Honorable Stanley White Mayor of New York New York, N.Y.	Sir: Very truly yours,	My dear Mayor White: Sincerely yours,	Mayor White *or* Mr. Mayor	Mayor White *or* the Mayor
Judge	The Honorable John Castle Judge of Whatever Court Chicago, Illinois*	Sir:* Very truly yours,	My dear Judge Castle:* Sincerely yours,	Judge Castle	Judge Castle

* NOTE: The one exception to the above form is for the presiding justice of an Appellate Division He is addressed "Presiding Justice, Appellate Division, Supreme Court"; and a letter to him would begin "My dear Mr. Justice."

455

MILITARY MEN

Personage	The Envelope:	A formal letter begins and ends:	An informal letter begins and ends:	Speaking to:	Introducing:
Officers of the Army, Air Force, and Marine Corps with grade of captain or higher (men and women) Officers of the Navy with grade of commander or higher (men and women)	Rank or rating is used in all grades in all the services when addressing an envelope	Dear Sir: Very truly yours,	My dear General Black: My dear Admiral Fenster: Sincerely yours,	Higher officers are always verbally addressed by their rank as title. All grades of General (e.g. Major General, Brigadier General) are called General. Similarly, all grades of Admiral (Vice, Rear, etc.) are called Admiral. Always include the surname: "General Black," *not* just "General." This is true of lower ranks also.	General Black Admiral Fenster When introducing a captain of the Navy, it is imperative to add "of the Navy" because his rank equals that of a Colonel in the Army.
Junior Officers in the Navy, Army, Air Force, and Marine Corps	2nd Lieutenant Harvey Smith Ensign Chester Jones	Dear Sir: Very truly yours,	My dear Mr. Smith: My dear Mr. Jones: Sincerely yours,	Mr. Smith Mr. Jones	Lieutenant Smith Ensign Jones
National Guard and reserve officers	Rank and titles are used only when on active duty. The name must be followed by proper initials: NG—National Guard USAR—United States Army Reserve USNR—United States Naval Reserve USMCR—United States Marine Corps Reserve				

Note: Cadets of the United States Military Academy and Midshipmen of the United States Naval Academy are addressed socially as "Mister," officially as "Cadet" or "Midshipman." Noncommissioned officers and enlisted men of all services are addressed by rank, with the exception of Warrant Officer, who is called "Mister." Doctors are called by rank; occasionally those in junior grades are called "Doctor." Chaplains are addressed as "Chaplain," though often Catholic chaplains are called "Father."

456

VARIOUS INDIVIDUALS

Personage	The Envelope:	A formal letter begins and ends:	An informal letter begins and ends:	Speaking to:	Introducing:
University professor	Professor or Assoc. Professor or Ass't Professor Richard Hopkins or Dr. Richard Hopkins (if he holds a doctor's degree) or Richard Hopkins, Ph.D.	Dear Sir, Very truly yours,	Dear Professor or Dr. Hopkins, Sincerely yours,	Mr. Hopkins or Dr. Hopkins	Professor Hopkins or Dr. Hopkins
Widow	Mrs. Homer Brown (exactly as when her husband was alive)	Dear Mrs. Brown, Very truly yours,	Dear Mrs. Brown, Sincerely yours,	Mrs. Brown	Mrs. Brown
Divorcée	Mrs. Randall Jones (her maiden surname followed by her ex-husband's last name.)	Dear Mrs. Jones, Very truly yours,	Dear Mrs. Jones, Sincerely yours,	Mrs. Jones	Mrs. Jones

Index

Abbreviations, 223-224, 226
Abroad, tipping, 321-323
    traveling, 321-325
Acceptance, *see* Invitations, accepting
Address, on calling cards, 251, 253
    to employer, 417-418, 423
    forms of, 222-224, 447-455
    and servants, 209
    wedding invitations, 223-224, 359-360
Adolescents, manners of, 54-58
Adoption announcements, 263-264
Allergies, 86, 104
Alligator pears, how to eat, 431, 432
Allowances, children's, 56
Anecdotes and spouses, 39-40
Anniversary parties, 271-273, 388-390
Announcements, adoption, 263-264
    birth, 263-264
    death, 405-406
    engagement, 336-338, 339
    wedding, 368-369
Apartment, and woman alone, 28-29
Appearance, businesswoman's, 13, 416-417
Apples, how to eat, 431
Apricots, how to eat, 431
Aprons, maid's, 207
Arguments, and guests, 130, 137
    and spouses, 39
Artichokes, how to eat, 431
Ashtrays, 185, 187, 416
Asparagus, how to eat, 431
Attendants, bridal, 346-347
    groom's, 348-350
Attitude, women in business, 415-416
Automobile, travel by, 312-314
Avocadoes, how to eat, 432

Baby showers, 391-393
Baby sitting, 64
Bacon, how to eat, 432
Balls, debutante, 329-330, 331-333
Bananas, how to eat, 432
Baptism, 397
Barbecue party, 121-122, 192
Bar Mitzvah, 400-402

Bartender, hired, 194
Bas Mitzvah, 400-402
Bed linens, 160-161
Beer glasses, 173
Behavior, children's, 45-53
    See also Children
Berries, how to eat, 432
Berths, train, 309-310
Best man, attire, 351
    choosing, 346-347
    duties, 348-349
    toast, 383, 386
Birds, how to eat, 432
Birth announcements, 263-264, 266
Birthday cards, 42, 256
"Black Tie," 13, 26-27, 258
Blind, behavior with, 295-296
Boss, and secretary, 417-419, 421-424
Bouquet, bride's, 347, 350, 352, 357
    tossing, 383-384
Boutonnières, wedding, 349, 351, 352, 357, 370, 371
Bread and butter, how to eat, 432
Bread-and-butter letter, 42, 139, 155, 229
Breakfast, china, 170, 183
    table settings, 182-183
    tray, 146, 150, 182
    wedding, 361
Bride, attire, 350, 351, 379
    cake-cutting, 383, 386-387
    dancing at wedding, 387
    initials of, 163
    invitation list, 345-346
    monogram of, 163, 165, 173
    showers for, 390-391, 392, 393
    in special situations, 364-366, 380-381
    table at reception, 386
    tossing bouquet, 383-384
    trousseau, 346
    and wedding expenses, 356-357
Bridal consultants, 343
Bridesmaids, 346, 347
    attire, 350-351
Brit Malah, 398
Brunch, 124

Buffet, card table, 191-192
  for cocktail party, 129
  maid's duties, 120, 194-195
  manners for guests, 84-85
  supper, 118-121, 189-190
  table setting, 190-191
  for wedding reception, 385
Business cards, 252-253
Business letters, 239-248
  closing, 221, 241
  of complaint, 242-243
  of condolence, 235
  form, 239-241
  making reservations, 242
  ordering from a store, 241
  of recommendation, 243-246
  of reference, 246-248
  see also Forms of address,
Businessmen, dress, 25, 27
  manners for, 422-424
Businesswoman, dress, 13, 416-417
  and mourning, 411
  personal affairs, 415-416, 420
  receptionist, 417
  secretary, 417-419, 421-424
Butter, 155, 189
  plates, 181, 185, 188

Cake, how to eat, 433
  cutting wedding, 383, 386-387
Calls, on bereaved, 407
  on fiancé's parents, 334
Calling cards, 215, 249-253, 260
  business, 252-253
  children's, 252
  men's, 251-252
  women's, 251
Cancellation, of dates, 31
  of invitations, 258, 265-266
  of wedding, 367-368
Candles, 177, 192
  hurricane, 192
  lighting, 120
Candy, 188
  how to eat, 433
Canopy, 376, 379
Canvas, at wedding, 356, 371, 377
Card games, 131
Card table buffet, 191-192
Cards, at-home, 360, 363-364
  birthday, 42, 256
  calling, 215, 249-253, 260, 263
  Christmas, 253-256
  church, 362-363
  greetings by, 249-256
  pew, 350, 360, 362-363
  reception, 356, 359, 360, 361, 362
  "response," 363, 364

Cars, getting out of, 15
  teen-agers' use, 57-58, 62-63, 64
  travel by, 312-314
Carving set, on table, 112, 185
Caterers, 195
Catholics, baptism, 397
  church decorum, 283
  confirmation, 399
  fast days, 106
  funerals, 408, 409, 410, 411
  godparents, 395
  wedding, 374-375
Cats and house guests, 147
Celebrities, manners with, 296-297
Celery, how to eat, 433
Centerpiece, buffet, 119-120, 177, 190, 192
  for dinner table, 107, 149, 176-177
  for formal tea, 193
Ceremony cards, 362
Champagne, 382, 388
  serving, 116
Chaperones, 32, 134
Charm, 6-7
  and clothes, 10-14
  and conversation, 17-18
  and grace, 14-15
  and men, 16-17
  and older women, 18-19
  and smoking, 15-17
Checks, for anniversary gifts, 389
  in lieu of flowers, 410
  paying, 94, 99, 419-420
  wedding, 353, 354-355
Cheese, how to eat, 433
Children, Bar Mitzvah, 400-402
  Bas Mitzvah, 400-401
  and books, 46
  calling cards, 252
  and ceremonies, 53
  christening, 394-398
  confirmation, 399-401
  and dinner party, 109, 115
  of former marriages, 380
  godparents, 394-398
  as guests, 50-51, 152-153
  as hospital visitors, 290
  as hosts, 50-51
  of house guests, 147, 149
  and introductions, 49-50, 73
  and invitations, 51
  manners in public, 50-52
  and parents' manners, 38, 45
  on planes, 317
  and privacy, 46
  and property, 46
  in restaurant, 48-49
  and servants, 52, 201-206, 209, 246-248
  on shipboard, 317, 320-321
  and speech, 53

Children (*Continued*)
stationery for, 218
in stores, 293, 294
table manners, 46, 47-48
and telephone, 52-53
thank-you notes, 51-52
on trains, 311
travel by car, 314
wedding invitations, 223-224, 359
See also Teen-agers
China, breakfast, 170, 183
buying, 168-169
defined, 168
"open stock," 169
traditional, 166-167
Christening, home, 394, 397
Protestant ceremony, 394-397
See also Baptism
Christmas cards, 42, 253-256
Church, funerals, 407-408, 409
manners in, 282-283
weddings, 341, 342, 344, 348-351, 354,
356, 360-363, 370-377
Cigarettes, and consideration, 137
formal dinner, 187
and women, 15-16, 17
See also Smoking
Clams, how to eat, 433
Cleaning woman, 200, 208-209
Clergyman, christening, 394, 395, 396, 397
confirmation, 400
funeral, 408-409
gratuities, 349, 357, 395, 397, 409
and wedding, 342-343, 356, 385, 386
Clothes, 10-14
for bridal party, 350, 351, 359
for businesswoman, 13, 416-417
for car trips, 312, 314
for clubwoman, 306
for debut, 333
in hotel, 287
on plane, 315
for shipboard, 318-320
for sports, 12
suitability of, 7-9
for travel, 13-14
on train, 310
for wedding guests, 10, 351-352
Club car, 311-312
Club, joining, 300-302
Clubwoman, clothes, 306
entertaining speaker, 304-307
manners of, 300-307
Cocktail glasses, 171-172
Cocktail parties, 126-129, 136
maid's duties, 117, 127, 194
Cocktails, for brunch, 124
at dinner party, 109, 115, 117, 118
in restaurant, 91, 97, 98

Coffee, abroad, 324
after-dinner, 113, 114, 118
demitasse, 113, 169, 185, 189
serving, 197
Color, and linens, 143, 159, 161-162
and menus, 178
of stationery, 213, 215, 216-217, 218
Commencement invitations, 260
Complaint, letters of, 242-243
Condolence, letters of, 232-236
Confirmation, 399-401
Congratulation, letters of, 231-232
Consideration and servants, 52, 209
Convention and living alone, 32
Conversation, at after-dinner parties, 130
and charm, 17-18
cocktail party, 137
at dinner table, 48, 87, 114
for hospital visitor, 290
after introduction, 72, 75
Cook-out, *see* Barbecue
Corn on the cob, how to eat, 433
Correspondence, business, 239-248
formal, 215, 216, 449-455
social, 220-238, 359, 449-455
see also Forms of Address, Invitations,
Letters, Notes, Telegrams
Courtesy, and charm, 16
and dating, 30-32
and marriage, 38-44
and popularity, 60
Crab, how to eat, 433-434
Crystal, 171, 172, 173

Dances, for debutantes, 331, 332
invitations, 270
for teen-agers, 134
Dancing, at night club party, 100
at home, 132-134
at wedding reception, 387
Dating, 28-29, 30-33
and teen-agers, 64-65, 66-67
Deaf, behavior with, 296
Death notices, 405-406
Debut, invitations, 275-278
mass, 329-330, 331, 333
Debutantes, 329-333
Declining, *see* Invitations, declining
Demitasse, 113, 169, 185, 189
Dessert and coffee, 129
Dessert silver, 87-88, 197
for lunch, 183-184
maidless dinner, 113
placement, 180-181
Dieting, 86, 87, 113
Diner, train, 310
Dinner, for debutante, 330-331, 332
dress, 13

Dinner (*Continued*)
  formal, 185-187
    maid's uniform, 207
    table setting, 187-189
  hour, abroad, 323
  jacket, 26-27, 319
  parties, informal, 102-122
    coffee, 113, 116
    drinks, 109, 114, 115, 116
    flowers, 107, 108
    host, 115-116, 118
    lists, 107-108
    invitations, 103
    maidless, 103, 109, 112-116
    menus, 103-107
    punctuality, 21, 323
    seating, 109-112
    serving, 112-113
    table setting, 184-185
    wine, 116
  partners, 74
Dishes, *see* China
Divorced parents, and engagement announcement, 337
  at wedding, 385
  and wedding invitations, 365, 366
Divorcée, 380
  changing name, 35
  manners for, 33-35
  remarriage, 365, 366, 369, 380
  rings, 35
  wedding announcement, 369
    invitations, 366
Doctors, manners with, 297-299
Dogs, and house guests, 147, 151
  of bridal party, 350, 351, 359
Dress
  for car travel, 312
  for christenings, 395-396, 397, 401
  for dates, 30-31
  at debut, 333
  at funeral, 411
  formal, 13, 26-27, 258, 319, 333, 350-351
  at hotels, 287
  for men, 25-28, 319
  at office, 13, 416-417
  for plane, 13, 315
  for shipboard, 318-320
  for sports, 12
  suitability of, 7-9
  and teen-agers, 66-67
  on train, 310
  for travel, 13-14, 310-320
  of wedding guests, 10, 351-352
Drinks, for after dinner, 129-130
  for brunch, 124
  for cocktail party, 127-128
  for dinner party, 109, 115
  and guests, 138
  and teen-agers, 68

Eating gracefully, 85-86, 88
  see also How to Eat Difficult Foods, 431-439
  when to start, 83
  which silver to use, 83
Elevator manners, 23
Employer, and secretary, 415-419, 422
Engagement, 334-340
  announcement, 336-338
  behavior during, 340
  broken, 339, 355
  and parents, 334-335, 336-338
  party, 338-339
  ring, 35, 37, 335-336, 339
Entertaining, and divorcée, 34-35
  celebrities, 296-297
  at home, 102-134
    after-dinner coffee, 113, 114, 118
    after-dinner parties, 129-130
    barbecues, 121-122
    brunch, 124
    buffet supper, 118-121
    cards, 131
    cocktail parties, 126-129
    cocktails, 109
    dances, 132-134
    dessert and coffee, 129
    dinner parties, 102-122
    games, 131
    goodbys, 114-115, 116
    invitations, 103
    kinds of parties, 102
    lists, 108
    lunch, 122-123
    with maid, 116-118
    maidless dinner, 109, 112-116
    menus, 103-107
    preparations for, 103, 107-108
    seating at dinner, 109-112
    television party, 131-132
    wine at table, 116
  for house guests, 145-147
  at night club, 99-100
  in restaurant, 96-99
  on shipboard, 320
  and widow, 36
  and woman alone, 32
Envelopes, addressing, 226-227, 449-455
Europe, manners in, 322-324
Evening dress, for men, 25-28, 319
  on shipboard, 14, 319-320
  for women, 10, 13, 319-320
Expenses of wedding, 356-357

Father, and debutante, 329-330, 332, 333
  wedding attire, 351
Favors, for wedding guests, 352-353
Fees, for christenings, 395, 397

Fees (*Continued*)
  for funerals, 408-409
  for weddings, 356-357
Fingerbowls, 87-88, 172, 188, 197
Fingers, and eating, 85, 87
  See also How to Eat Difficult Foods, 431-439
Fish, how to eat, 434
Flower arrangements, for buffet, 119-120, 177, 190, 192
  artificial, 176
  breakfast tray, 182
  centerpiece, 107, 149, 176-177
Flower girl, 347, 371
Flowers, for bride, 350, 352
  for debutante, 332
  for funerals, 408, 409-410
  and hospitals, 289
  and house guests, 143, 149
  for weddings, 352, 356, 357
Forms of address, 222-224, 447-455
Food, for after-dinner party, 130
  for buffet, 119, 190-191
  menu planning, 103-107
  ordering in restaurant, 91-92, 98-99
  and religious rules, 105-107
  for servants, 206, 208
Food, how to eat difficult, 431-439
Forks, setting table, 120, 179-182
  use of, 83
Frogs' legs, how to eat, 434
French menu terms, 427-430
Friends, and divorce, 34
  and funeral, 409
  and widow, 36
Funerals, 403-411
  condolence calls, 407, 410-411
  casket, 405
  Catholic, 408, 409, 410
  clothing for burial, 405
  documents for burial, 404, 405
  dress for, 411
  flowers, 408, 409-410
  funeral home, 404-405, 407, 408
  interment, 408
  Jewish, 405, 408, 409
  obituaries, 405-406
  Protestant services, 407-408
  what to do first, 404-405

Games, 131, 138
Gifts, accepting man's, 33
  Bar Mitzvah, 402
  of bride, 354, 356
  christening, 395
  of groom, 354, 357
  for hospital patient, 289
  hostess, 154
  thank-you notes, 229-230

Gifts (*Continued*)
  wedding, 354-355
Glassware, 171-173
  for beer, 173
  buying, 171-172
  for cocktails, 127
  for formal dinner, 187
  for informal dinner, 185
  iced tea, 184
  renting, 127, 133, 172
Gloves, 10-11
  and bride, 350
  and hand shaking, 18
  removing, 11, 24
  and ushers, 349
  and wedding guests, 351
Godparents, 394-395, 396, 397, 398
Goodbys, 50, 76, 384
Grace, 81-82
Grapefruit, how to eat, 434
Grapes, how to eat, 435
Gravy, how to eat, 435
Greetings, 18
  by card, 249-256
Groom, attire of, 351
  invitation list, 345-346
  and wedding expenses, 357
Grooming, 8
Guest, bathroom for, 143-144
  of honor, 97, 98, 109-112, 136, 271
  room, 141-143
Guests, at buffet, 84-85
  children as, 50-51
  helpful, 34, 113, 137, 146-150, 152, 154
  house, 140-155
  how to be, 135-139
  at night club, 99-100
  out-of-town, 138-139
  at restaurant, 91, 92, 96-99, 138
  seating, 97-98, 109-112
  and telephone, 78, 79, 153
  at theater, 100-101
  unexpected, 43
  wedding, 10, 357, 371, 374
    dress, 10, 351-352, 345-346
    and ushers, 349-350
Guides, tipping, 322
Gum chewing, 16, 202, 282, 314, 416

Hairdresser, 293-294
Handicapped, behavior with, 294-295
Hand shaking, 18
  and children, 50
  and introductions, 75
  and men, 23-24
  and teen-agers, 64-65
Hats, for men, 23, 26, 376
  for women, 10, 285, 307, 351, 396, 397
Hiring a maid, 199-204

Hobbies, 29-30
Home, manners at, 38-39
  entertaining at, 102-134
  See Entertaining
Honeymoon, 357
Hors d'oeuvres, at cocktail party, 128
  hot, 117, 194, 195
  preparing, 107
Hospital manners, for patients, 290-292
  for visitors, 288-290
Host, at buffet, 121
  child as, 50-51
  at cocktail party, 127-128
  at dances, 133, 134
  dinner with maid, 118
  at maidless dinner, 112, 115-116
  at night club party, 99-100
  in restaurant, 96-99
  of theater party, 100-101
Hostess, of club guest, 304-307
  at cocktail party, 126-127
  at dance, 132-134
  dinner with maid, 116-118
  gift, 154
  and house guests, 140-147, 149, 150, 152-
    154
  at maidless dinner, 103, 109, 112-115
  secretary as, 418
  at table, 87
  welcoming guests, 75
  wife only, 266
Hotels, manners at, 285-287
  registering, 285, 418-419, 424
  reservations, 242, 285
  resort, 287-288
  traveling with boss, 418-419, 423-424
  wedding guests, 356, 357
  wedding reception, 344-345
House guest, and breakfast, 146, 150
  bringing to party, 259
  entertaining, 140-157
  how to be, 148-155
Husband, introducing, 72
  manners for, 38-43

Informals, 215-216, 249, 260-262
  for invitations, 260-263
  in wedding ring, 348
Initials, bride's, 163, 165
In-laws, and engagement, 334-335
  introducing, 74
  manners with, 40, 43, 44
  after wedding, 384
Interviews with maid, 201-202
Introduction, letters of, 236-238
Introductions, 71-76
  acknowledging, 75
  and children, 73
  and first names, 72

Introductions (Continued)
  group, 72-73
  husband and wife, 42, 72
  of in-laws, 74
  introducing oneself, 74
  and parents, 73-74
  at parties, 75, 127
  and servants, 75
  shaking hands, 18
  and "sir," 24
  of women to men, 74
Invitation list, wedding, 345-346
Invitations, accepting, 257-258, 259-260,
    262, 269, 270, 271, 272, 274, 277,
    278, 366-367
  to barbecue, 121
  to Bar Mitzvah, 401
  canceling, 258, 265-266
  and children, 51
  to cocktail party, 126
  to dance, 133
  and dating, 30, 31
  to debut, 331
  declining telephone, 80
    written, 257, 258, 259, 260, 269, 271,
      272, 274, 277, 278, 367
  form of, 260
  formal, 266-268
  group, 260, 267, 271-272, 274-275
  to house guests, 144-145
  joint, 223-224, 359
  partially engraved, 266-267
  recalling, 365-366
  replying, 136
  stationery for, 266, 267
  See also Informals
  "store-bought," 260
  telephoned, 79-80
  wedding, 356, 358-368
  wording of, 360-362, 364-366
  and widow, 36
  and wives, 42

Jewelry, bridesmaids', 351
  and evening dress, 13
  and gloves, 11
  in office, 416-417
Jews, Bar Mitzvah, 400-402
  Bas Mitzvah, 400-402
  Brit Malah, 398
  and Christmas cards, 254
  in church, 283
  dietary laws, 106-107
  funerals, 405, 408, 409
  grace, 81-82
  weddings, 376-377

Knives, setting table, 179-182
  use of, 83, 84

Kumquats, how to eat, 435

Ladies' room, 9
  abroad, 324
Language, foreign, 324
  See also French menu terms
Latin America, 322, 323
Lawyers, manners with, 297
Letters, abbreviations, 222-224, 226
  bread-and-butter, 42, 139, 155, 229
  business, 239-248
  closings, 221, 447, 449-455
  of condolence, 232-236
  of congratulation, 231-232
  forms of address, 222-224, 447-455
  good, 227-229
  of introduction, 236-238
  numbering pages, 224
  signatures, 221-222
  social, 220-238, 449-455
  titles, 222-224, 447-448
License, marriage, 342, 357
Line, receiving, 331-332, 385
Linens, basic, 160
  extras, 160-162
  how to buy, 162-163
  initialing, 163
Liqueurs, 116, 197
Lobster, how to eat, 435-436
Luggage, on car trips, 312, 313
  on planes, 315-316
  on shipboard, 317, 319
  on trains, 310
Lunch, 122-123
  invitations, 122
  menu, 123
  table setting, 123, 183-184
  women executive, 419-420
"Luncheon," 123

Maid, at buffet supper, 120, 121
  at cocktail party, 127
  for dinner party at home, 116-118
  at formal dinner, 189
  full-time, 204-207
    and children, 204, 205, 206
    room, 204-205
    time off, 205-206
    uniforms, 206-207
    wages, 206
  health, 203-204
  part-time, 208-209
  rehearsing, 117, 198-199
  serving at table, 87-88, 117-118, 120, 127, 194-199
Maid of honor, 346-347, 371, 373, 376
Make-up, 8, 9
  in office, 416
  and teen-agers, 66

Mangoes, how to eat, 436-437
Manners, abroad, 323-324
  of children, 45-53
    See also Children
  driving car, 63, 65
  while engaged, 340
  married, 38-44
  for men, 20-25, 72, 75, 422-424
  teen-agers in public, 63-64
  for women, 16-19, 30-31, 38-44, 75
    in business, 415-421
    See also Guest *and* Hostess
Marriage, manners and, 38-44
  second, 366, 379-380
Matches for table, 187
  at wedding, 352-353
Matron of honor, 346, 347
  See also Maid of honor
Mats, table, 174-175
Meat, carving, 112, 185
  cutting, at table, 83, 84
Melon, how to eat, 437
Men, calling cards, 251-252
  introducing women to, 74
  manners for, 21-25, 38-44, 72, 75, 422-424
  See also Guest, Host, Father, Groom
Menu, for buffet party, 119
  for brunch, 124
  for lunch, 123
  planning, 103-107
  for tea, 125-126
  terms, French, 427-430
Minister, *see* Clergyman
Money bag, 353
  presents, 352, 354-355, 389, 392
Monograms, on clothes, 26, 27
  for glassware, 173
  and linens, 163
  for silver, 165
  on stationery, 213, 214, 215-216, 218
Moslems, 105-106
Motels, 313
Mothers, at debut, 331, 333
  wedding attire, 351
  working, 420
Mourning, clothes for, 37, 41
  stationery, 37, 219
Movies, 283-284
Music, for dancing, 132-133
  for wedding, 342
Mussels, how to eat, 437

Name, on calling cards, 251, 252, 253
  on Christmas cards, 255
  crossing out on cards, 250, 263
  divorcée changing, 35
  of widow, 37

Name-giving, 396, 397, 398
Napkins, 160-162
  for buffet, 120, 191
  cocktail, 125, 128, 161
  dinner, 82, 162, 175-176, 188
  folding, 176
  informal dinner, 185
  with mats, 161, 175
  paper, 122, 125, 178
  placing, 120, 178
Neatness and marriage, 41
Newspaper announcement, adoption, 263
  engagement, 336-338, 339
Night club entertaining, 99-100
Notepaper, formal, 215
  informal, 216-217
    See also Informals
  for mourning, 37
Notes, thank-you, 229-231
  See also Correspondence and Letters
Nurse, treatment of, 291-292
Nuts, 188

Obituaries, 405-406
Office, clothes for, 13, 25, 27
Office, manners, 23, 415-424
  parties, 416, 423
Olives, how to eat, 437
Oranges, how to eat, 437
Ordering, for restaurant party, 98-99
  with escort, 31, 91-92
Organist, 342, 356, 409
Outdoor entertaining, 192
Oysters, how to eat, 437

Pallbearers, 407, 408
Paper cups and plates, 122, 191
  napkins, 191, 192
Parents, and children, see Children
  and debut, 329-333
  divorced, 365
  and engagement, 334-335, 336, 339
  introductions, 73-74
  and teen-agers, 48-58, 60-63
  and wedding, 351, 353, 356-357, 367-368,
    371, 376, 379, 380, 384, 386, 387
Parlor games, 131
Parties, after-dinner, 129-130
  barbecue, 121-122
  brunch, 124
  buffet, 118-121
  cocktail, 126-129
  dinner, 102-118
  lunch, 122-123
  night club, 99-100
  prewedding, 347
  restaurant, 96-99

Parties (Continued)
  saying goodby, 76
  tea, 124-126
  types of, 102
Party line, telephone, 80
Patients, hospital, 290-292
  visiting, 288-290
Peaches, how to eat, 437-438
Pears, how to eat, 438
Perfume, 8-9, 66
Persimmons, how to eat, 438
Personages, see Forms of address
"Personal," 227
Pets, and house guests, 147, 151, 153
Pew cards, 362-363
Photographs, bridal, 343-353
  engagement, 338
Physicians, manners with, 297-299
Pickles, how to eat, 438
Pineapple, how to eat, 438
Place cards, 112, 188
Place setting, china, 169
  silver, 165-166
Plates, butter, 184, 185, 188
  heating, 191, 196-197, 199
  service, 169-170, 181-182, 185, 196
Plums, how to eat, 438
Poise, elements of, 6
  and teen-ager, 68
Postponement of invitation, 265-266
  of wedding, 367-368
Posture, 14
  at table, 82
Pourers at formal tea, 193
Processional, wedding, 371, 374-375, 376
Professionals, manners with, 296-297
Presents, wedding, 354-355
Priest, see Clergyman
Privacy, and house guests, 141, 150, 151
  respecting, 46
  of teen-ager, 61
Protestants, chirstening, 394-397
  confirmation, 399-401
  funeral, 407-408
  wedding, 371-374
Public, behavior in, 281-282
Punch at dance, 133
Punctuality, 21, 135-136, 323
  in business, 416, 422
  at ceremonies, 282-283
  and dates, 30

R.s.v.p., 257-258, 260, 261, 265
  wedding reception card, 359, 361
Rabbi, see Clergyman
Radio and teen-agers, 62
Radishes, how to eat, 438
Receiving line, 136, 331-332, 385

Reception, Bar Mitzvas, 401-402
  cards for wedding, 356, 361, 362
  after christening, 397-398
  for debutants, 331
  wedding, 343-345, 350, 374, 382-387
    at church, 374
    formal, 384, 385-387
    at home, 382-383, 384
Reception line, 136, 31-332, 385
Receptionist, 417
Recessional, wedding, 373-374, 377
Recommendation, letters of, 243-246
References, checking maid's, 202-203
  writing letters of, 246-248
Refreshments, for dance, 133
Register, hotel, 285, 418-419, 424
Regrets, 267-278
  wedding invitations, 267-268
Rehearsal, wedding, 347, 349, 356
Relatives, criticizing, 40, 43
Relishes, how to eat, 438
Replies, to invitations, 267-278, 359, 366-367
Reservations, making, 242
  night club, 99-100
  resorts, 242, 285
  restaurant, 90
Resorts, manners at, 287-288
  reservations, 242, 285
Responsibilities, and teen-agers, 60
Restaurant, 89-95
  checkroom, 89, 95
  children in, 48-49
  and dates, 31
  entertaining guests, 96-99, 138
  finding table, 89-90
  menu, 90-91, 427-430
  ordering, 31, 91-92, 98-99
  paying check, 93-95, 419-420
  reservations, 90, 96
  service, 93
  tipping, 94
  wedding reception, 344-345
  wine, 92
Ribbons, shower game, 392-393
  "within the," 350, 363
Ring, and divorcée, 35
  engagement, 335-336, 339, 357
  and shower, 392-393
  wedding, 335, 348, 349, 357, 373, 375, 377
  of widow, 37
Rising, in restaurant, 24
  and secretary, 418, 422
Road, courtesies of, 312-313
Rolls, at formal dinner, 188

Salad, course, 197
  how to eat, 438

Salespeople, 294
  manners of, 420-421
Salt, how to eat, 438
Salt and peppers, 185, 187
Sandwiches, how to eat, 438-439
Sauces, how to eat, 439
Seating, bridal table, 386
  at-home dinner, 109-112
  at night club, 100
  parents' table, 386
  of restaurant party, 97-98
  at theater, 101
Secretary, 417-419, 421-424
Servants, and children, 52, 201-206, 209, 246-248
  hiring, 200-204
  and house guests, 153, 154-155, 322-323
  managing, 200-209
  references, 203, 246-248
Service plates, 169-170, 185, 196
  table settings, 181-182
Serving, details of, 198-199
  hostess first, 82
  with maid, 117-118, 120, 127, 194-199
  without maid, 112-115, 120-121
  order of, 198
Serving pieces, china, 170
  setting table, 120, 181
  silver, 120, 166, 170, 181, 185, 189
Shaving, 20
Shoes, for sports, 12
  for travel, 14
  suitability, 11-12, 26, 27
Shorts, 12, 27
Showers, baby, 391-393
  bridal, 390-391
Shrimp, how to eat, 439
Signatures, 221-222
  on Christmas cards, 255
  of divorcée, 35
  of widow, 37
Silence cloth, 162, 175
Silver, breakfast tray, 183
  buffet, 118, 119, 120, 191
  card table buffet, 192
  dessert, 87-88, 113, 180, 184, 197
  lunch, 183-184
  formal dinner, 186
  informal dinner, 185
  lunch, 183-184
  monogram for, 165
  place setting, 165-166, 178
  plated, 164, 166
  selecting, 163-166
  setting table, 179-182
  use of table, 83-84
"Sir," 24
Sitting, gracefully, 15
Skullcaps, 376, 401

Sleepers, plane, 316
    train, 309-311
Smoking, 15-16
    abroad, 324
    in cars, 313
    in hospital, 289, 291
    and men, 17
    at movies, 283
    in office, 416
    on planes, 316
    on shipboard, 318
    on street, 15
    at table, 21, 324
    and teen-agers, 68
Snails, how to eat, 439
Soup, and spoons, 83, 85-86
Spaghetti, how to eat, 439
Speaker, dress of, 307
    entertaining club, 304-307
Spoons, serving, 185
    setting table, 179-182
    use of, 83-84
Sports clothes, 12, 309
Stationery, Bar Mitzvah invitations, 401
    calling cards, 250-251
    children's, 218
    color of, 213, 215, 216-217, 218
    correspondence cards, 213, 214
    for country house, 218-219
    informal wedding invitations, 364
    for invitations, 260-262, 266-267
    men's, 217-218
    monogram, 213, 215-216, 218
    mourning, 219
    printed, 213-219
    women's, 213-217
Steel, stainless, 164
Stores, manners in, 293-294
    saleswoman, 420-421
Street, behavior on, 281-282
Summer, office clothes for, 13
Supper, buffet, 118-119, 130
Sympathy, letters of, 233-236
Synagogue, hat in, 23, 376, 401
    manners in, 283
    wedding, 376

Table, bridal, 386
    card, 161-162, 191
    clearing, 113, 114, 197, 198
    parents', at wedding, 386
Tablecloths, for barbecue, 122
    for card tables, 191-192
    damask, 161, 162, 175, 186
    lace, 161, 175, 186
    paper, 192
Table linens, 160-162
Table manners, 9, 11, 21, 81-88
    at buffet, 84-85

Table manners (Continued)
    children's, 46, 47-48
    conversation, 87
    and dieting, 86-87
    fingerbowls, 87-88
    grace, 81
    how to eat, 85-86, 88, 431-439
    mishaps at table, 86
    napkins, 82
    passing condiments, 83
    posture, 82
    use of silver, 83, 87-88
    when a maid serves, 87-88
    when to start eating, 83
Table pads, 162, 175
Table settings, 174-193
    breakfast, 182-183
    buffet, 120, 189-190
    candles, 177
    card table buffets, 191-192
    centerpiece, 176-177
    color and menus, 177-178
    dinner, formal, 185-188
        informal, 184-185
    for formal tea, 193
    lunch, 123, 183-184
    mats, 175
    napkins, 161-162, 175-176, 178
    outdoors, 192
    service plates, 181-182
    silver, 179
    tablecloths, 161-162, 175, 186, 192
Taxis, getting out of, 15, 22-23
Tea dance, 331
Tea tray, 125, 193
Teas, 124-126
    club, 307
    for debutants, 331
    formal, 192
    maid's duties, 194
Teen-agers, advice to, 59-68
    allowances, 56
    and car, 57-58, 62-63, 64
    consideration for family, 62
    dances, 133, 134
    and dress, 66-67
    drinking, 68
    manners, 54-58, 63-64
    and parents, 54-58, 60-63
    smoking, 68
    table manners, 49
    telephone, 56-57
Telegrams, 232, 242
    cancelling wedding, 367-368
    informal invitation, 259-260
Telephone, answering, 77-78
    and businessman, 423
    cancelling invitations, 265, 367-368
    children and, 52-53, 56-57

Telephone (Continued)
  checking references, 203
  and hospital, 289
  and house guests, 79, 153
  invitations by, 79-80, 259
  making calls, 78-79
  number on stationery, 217
  at office, 416, 418
  party line, 80
  teen-agers and, 56-57
  toll calls, 79
Television party, 131-132
Thank-you notes, children's, 51-52
  dinner guest, 139, 324
  house guest, 155
  for gifts, 42, 229-231
Theater, dress at, 285
  entertaining at, 100-101
  manners at, 23, 284-285
  tipping, abroad, 322
Thoughtfulness, at funerals, 409
  and men, 21-23, 24-25, 423-424
  and women, 15-19
Tipping, 440-445
  abroad, 321-323
  at hotel, 286, 288
  as house guest, 154-155, 322-323
  and nurses, 291
  on planes, 316
  in restaurant, 94
  on shipboard, 320, 321
  on trains, 310
Titles, 222-224, 447-448
Toasts, best man's, 349, 383, 386
  at christening party, 397-398
  engagement party, 339
Trains, travel on, 309-312
Transportation, of wedding party, 353,
  356
Traveling, 308-321
  by car, 312-314
  with children, 311, 314, 317, 320-321
  with secretary, 418-419, 423-424
  with tours, 322
  on trains, 309-312
Trousseau, 346, 356
Typewriter, and business letters, 241
  and social correspondence, 213, 221, 225-
  226

Umbrellas, 25, 281-282
Uniforms, maid's, 206-207
Ushers, 349-350, 357, 370, 371-372, 376

Vegetarians, 105-106
Visiting cards, see Calling cards
Visitors, in hospital, 288-290
Voice, attractive, 6

Wages, of maids, 206, 208, 209
Waiter, 90-95, 98-99
Waitress, in restaurant, 93
  at home, 195, 207
Walking, 281-282
Wedding announcements, 368-369
  attire for bridal party, 350-352
  attire of guests, 351, 352
  best man's duties, 348-349
  breakfast, 384
  cake, 341, 352
  ceremony, home, 378-379, 380
    Jewish, 376-377
    Protestant, 371-374
    Roman Catholic, 374-375
  counselors, 343
  day, 370-381
  expenses of, 356-357
  formal, 342, 350-351, 360, 370-371
  gifts, 165, 347, 349
    displaying, 354-355
    exchanging, 355
    returning, 355
    thank-you notes, 230-231
  guests, 345-346, 357, 371, 374
    dress, 10, 351-352
    and ushers, 349-350
  home, 364, 375, 376, 378-379, 380
  informal, 342, 364, 377
  invitation list, 345-346
  invitations, 223-224, 358-368
    recalling, 367-368
    replying to, 366-367
    wording, 359, 364-366
  maid of honor's duties, 347
  matron of honor, 347
  party, attire, 350
    entrance of, 350, 370-371
  photographs, 353-354
  planning for, 341-357
  reception, 343-345, 382-387
  recessional, 373-374, 377
  rehearsal, 347, 349, 356
  ring, 335, 348, 373, 375, 377
    of divorcée, 35
    of widow, 37
  semiformal, 342, 351-352, 377
  transportation, 353, 356
  See also Bride; Groom
"White tie," 13, 26, 258
Widows, manners for, 35-37
  mourning, 41
  stationery, 37, 219
Wife, employer's 417
  introducing, 72
  manners for, 38-43
  working, 420
Wine, and maid, 195
  in restaurant, 92, 98-99

Wine (*Continued*)
  ritual, 376-377
  serving, 116
Wine glasses, buying, 172-173
  table setting, 185, 187, 188
Woman alone, 28-37
  cocktail party, 127
  in hotel, 286-287

Women, in business, 253, 415-421
  calling cards, 251, 252, 253, 263
  preceding men, 22-23, 310
  who pays for what, 32-33, 348, 356-357

YWCA, 28, 29-30